An Introduction to

Early
Childhood

Education at SAGE

SAGE is a leading international publisher of journals, books, and electronic media for academic, educational, and professional markets.

Our education publishing includes:

- accessible and comprehensive texts for aspiring education professionals and practitioners looking to further their careers through continuing professional development

- inspirational advice and guidance for the classroom

- authoritative state of the art reference from the leading authors in the field

Find out more at: **www.sagepub.co.uk/education**

An Introduction to

Early
Childhood

third edition

LRC Stoke Park
GUILDFORD COLLEGE

Edited by

Tim Waller and
Geraldine Davis

Los Angeles | London | New Delhi
Singapore | Washington DC

Los Angeles | London | New Delhi
Singapore | Washington DC

SAGE Publications Ltd
1 Oliver's Yard
55 City Road
London EC1Y 1SP

SAGE Publications Inc.
2455 Teller Road
Thousand Oaks, California 91320

SAGE Publications India Pvt Ltd
B 1/I 1 Mohan Cooperative Industrial Area
Mathura Road
New Delhi 110 044

SAGE Publications Asia-Pacific Pte Ltd
3 Church Street
#10-04 Samsung Hub
Singapore 049483

Editor: Jude Bowen/Amy Jarrold
Development editor: Robin Lupton
Associate editor: Miriam Davey
Production editor: Nicola Marshall
Copyeditor: Elaine Leek
Proofreader: Sharon Cawood
Indexer: Silvia Benvenuto
Marketing executive: Dilhara Attygalle
Cover design: Wendy Scott
Typeset by: C&M Digitals (P) Ltd, Chennai, India
Printed and bound in Great Britain by Ashford
Colour Press Ltd

First edition published 2005
Second edition published 2009
Reprinted 2009, 2010, 2011 and 2012
Editorial arrangement and Introduction © Tim Waller and Geraldine
Davis 2014
Chapter 1 © Michael Wyness 2014
Chapter 2 © Tim Waller 2014
Chapter 3 © Libby Lee-Hammond with Tim Waller
Chapter 4 © Gill Handley
Chapter 5 © Prospera Tedam
Chapter 6 © Christine Hickman and Kyffin Jones
Chapter 7 © Paulette Luff
Chapter 8 © Helen Tovey and Tim Waller
Chapter 9 © Jane O'Connor
Chapter 10 © Sharon Smith and Tania Hart
Chapter 11 © Jane Waters
Chapter 12 © Celia Doyle
Chapter 13 © Eunice Lumsden and Celia Doyle
Chapter 14 © Denise Hevey
Chapter 15 © Eunice Lumsden
Chapter 16 © Geraldine Davis
Chapter 17 © Jane Murray
Chapter 18 © Caroline Jones

Library of Congress Control Number: 2013945236

British Library Cataloguing in Publication data

A catalogue record for this book is available from
the British Library

ISBN 978-1-4462-5484-4
ISBN 978-1-4462-5485-1 (P)

Contents

Praise for the book

'This revised edition introduces readers to a wide range of contemporary issues in early childhood, issues that are fundamental for working respectfully with young children. Each chapter has been skilfully constructed with the professional in mind, as accessible and current information is provided, overviews of research studies, useful web-links, podcast options, and thought-provoking case studies all assist with demystifying each topic. What I really like about this book is how it challenges us to think differently about children in an adult-centred society, and it equips readers with ways to better understand children's lifeworlds.'

Anna Kilderry, Senior Lecturer Early Childhood Education, Victoria University Australia

'This book provides a rich introduction to key issues that concern early childhood. It makes us think about what matters to young children and what professionals can do to protect their well-being. The broad coverage and the reflective nature of the book make it an invaluable resource for those who are new to early childhood studies, for practitioners and researchers, and also for anyone who cares about the quality of early childhood practice.'

Hiroko Fumoto, Programme Manager and Senior Lecturer, Early Childhood Education Programme

'This book has to be one of the most refreshing and realistic books on early years holistic care and education on the market. There is a wide range of highly relevant issues included, all presented in a way that provokes the reader to reflect and analysis their developing knowledge and understanding. It is an excellent resource for students studying early years care and education. It provides a stimulating and thought provoking insight into the field of early childhood.'

Ally Dunhill, Director of Learning and Teaching, University of Hull

Praise for the 2nd Edition

'This is an interesting, comprehensive and up-to-date book, which will be useful not just for students, but for experienced practitioners who want to gain a broader, more strategic understanding of the development of early childhood services.'

Early Years Update

'This is a stimulating, well-structured book with excellent references to further relevant research. I am confident students will find this a meaningful key text in their study of early childhood, early years leadership and every aspect of early years education and practice.'

Denise Corfield, Edge Hill University

'Excellent book that gives a wide range of contemporary issues relating to ECE. Useful reflection points for discussion in class.'

Jackie Musgrave, Early Years Department, Solihull College

'A variety of chapters that fits directly with the course modules. The chapters are easy to read and clearly guided with subheadings. The case studies and reflective questions help students develop a deeper understanding of the topic material.'

Alyson Lewis, Dept of Care & Continuing Education, Ystrad Mynach College

'A clear and well structured publication that covers a wide range of topics in good detail and with associated case study information.'

Mark Tymms, Division of Youth & Community, De Montfort University

Acknowledgements

The authors and SAGE would like to thank all the reviewers for their time, help and feedback which supported the creation of the new edition of this book:

Ally Dunhill, Lecturer in Children's Services and Integrated Working, University of Hull
Dr Caroline Bath, Programme Leader for Early Childhood Education and Research Development, Liverpool John Moores University
Mandy Lee, Programme Manager, Early Childhood, University of the West of England
Hiroko Fumoto, Programme Manager, Senior Lecturer, Yew Chung Community College, Hong Kong
Babs Anderson, Lecturer in Childhood Studies, Liverpool Hope University
Louise Dryden, Freelance consultant in early years education
Dr Anna Kilderry, Senior Lecturer Early Childhood Education, Victoria University Australia
Lee Hurrell, Associate Lecturer, Plymouth University
Linda Tyler, Senior Lecturer and Course Leader BA(Hons) Early Childhood with Practitioner Options, University of Worcester
Helen Bradford, Lecturer, University of Cambridge

SAGE and the authors would also like to thank the following for their individual contributions to the book and its online resources:

Tracy Hutchinson and Nicola Wallace from Beach Babies Nursery in Cambridge for allowing us to visit their wonderful setting and record child observational videos in support of this book.
Kay Fisher, Sheila Homer and Lynsey Thomas for providing the case studies in Chapter 7.
Sandra Davison for providing the case study for Chapter 16.

About the Editors

Tim Waller is Professor of Child and Family Studies in the Faculty of Health, Social Care and Education at Anglia Ruskin University. Tim is a Convener of the Outdoor Learning SIG in the European Early Childhood Education Research Association (EECERA). He has worked in higher education for over twenty years. Previously he taught in nursery, infant and primary schools in London and has also worked in the USA. His research interests include wellbeing, outdoor learning, pedagogy and social justice in early childhood. Tim is leading the UK research contributing to the SUPREME project (Suicide Prevention by Internet and Media Based Mental Health Promotion), aimed at developing an internet-based mental health promotion and suicide prevention programme, targeting young people aged 14–24. Anglia Ruskin has joined academic institutions in Sweden, Estonia, Hungary, Italy, Lithuania and Spain to carry out the study. Tim was Co-Director of the Longitudinal Evaluation of the Role and Impact of Early Years Professionals (in England) – commissioned by the Children's Workforce Development Council (2009–12). Since September 2003 he has been coordinating an ongoing research project designed to investigate children's perspectives on their outdoor play. This project has involved developing and using a range of 'participatory' methods for research with young children. Recently, he has edited a Special Edition of the *European Early Childhood Education Association Journal* on Outdoor Play and Learning and, with Deborah Harcourt and Bob Perry, *Researching Young Children's Perspectives: Debating the Ethics and Dilemmas of Educational Research with Children* (published by Routledge in March 2011).

Geraldine Davis is Principal Lecturer and Director of the Doctorate in Education at Anglia Ruskin University. She has worked in higher education for 12 years, with a particular focus on professional learning and how theory is translated into effective practice. Prior to her work in universities, Geraldine worked in the health service and then taught in further education and in the health service both in the UK and in Australia. Geraldine's research interests lie in the field of professional learning across the education and health sectors and she has investigated uses of knowledge in nursing practice, midwives use of knowledge in health education of women, and Early Years graduate leaders use of their knowledge to impact on their leadership practice, a three-year funded study into the impact of graduate leader status on outcomes for children. Her work successfully integrates teaching and research. She leads the Masters degree in Early Years Professional Practice, with students who are graduate leaders in their work settings. This has been an exciting venture demonstrating the continued value of professional development for the early childhood workforce beyond graduate status. Research based on this work has led to an emerging theory of leadership in early childhood settings. She teaches human development, leadership and professional issues, and research methodology and supervises students undertaking Masters and Doctoral research studies.

About the Contributors

Celia Doyle is a Research Associate with the University of Northampton. Formerly, as Senior Lecturer at the University she taught child development, welfare and protection in the Schools of Health and Education. Earlier in her career she specialised in child-care and protection, initially as a local authority social worker then as an NSPCC team member. She has published extensively on childcare and protection and has recently published the fourth edition of *Working with Abused Children*. With co-author Charles Timms, she has written a forthcoming book on child neglect and emotional abuse. A key theme of her current research is how children, especially those experiencing emotional distress, can be helped to communicate their experiences, emotions, opinions and wishes.

Libby Lee-Hammond is Associate Professor of Early Childhood Education at Murdoch University in Perth, Western Australia. Areas of special interest include social justice, Aboriginal education, bush schools (outdoor learning) and the use of technologies to support teaching and learning. Her current research focuses on partnerships between Aboriginal communities and schools, in particular the transition to school, school engagement and retention of young Aboriginal children.

Gill Handley is a Senior Lecturer in the School of Education at the University of Northampton, teaching on the BA (Hons) Early Childhood Studies, Sure Start Foundation degree and Early Years Professional programmes. Her background is in social work, having over twenty years' experience working in a variety of adoption and child protection roles, most recently as a manager in the Children and Family Court Advisory and Support Service, representing the interests of children in court proceedings. She has also taught on the Open University social work programmes and acted as a mentor and supervisor for post-qualifying awards in social work.

Tania Hart is a Senior Lecturer in Mental Health in the School of Health at the University of Northampton. Tania's background is in mental health nursing whereby, as a Clinical Nurse Specialist, Tania worked in the field of child and adolescent mental health and, more specifically, children's eating disorders. Tania is particularly interested in how children's mental health can be better supported by non-health professionals, such as teachers and nursery care workers, and at present Tania is undertaking a PhD study that looks to explore how children with identified mental health difficulties can be better supported in mainstream education.

Denise Hevey is Professor of Early Years and Head of the Division of Early Years in the School of Education, University of Northampton. Her background includes the production of distance-learning materials in areas such as child abuse and neglect, and in working with children and young people. She also has particular knowledge of relevant legal and regulatory frameworks, and government policy relating to children's services from experience at a senior level in Ofsted and the (former) Department for Education and Skills.

Christine Hickman has taught in secondary, primary and special schools in Leicestershire. She moved into being a Learning and Support Advisor for Leicester City LEA, having autism as her specialism. She has worked in higher education since 2000, having been at the University of Northampton before moving to Liverpool John Moores University. Her academic background is in both art and special educational needs. At Northampton, Christine was School of Education Art coordinator and taught on all Initial Teacher Training courses. Christine has an interest in creative and therapeutic approaches, especially in the fields of art and music. She is involved in various international link programmes, especially in Sweden. She is Programme Leader for the PGCE Early Years programme at LJMU. In addition, Christine teaches across several programmes, including the MA programme and both postgraduate and undergraduate ITT courses.

Caroline Jones is Course Director for the Sector-Endorsed Foundation Degree in Early Years (SEFDEY) at the University of Warwick. She started her career as a teacher in mainstream primary and special education, working across the Midlands area for fifteen years. Caroline first joined the University of Warwick in 1994 as a part-time associate tutor on the undergraduate teacher-training programme (BA QTS). She taught on a variety of programmes and assumed responsibility for the Early Years Foundation Degree when it was introduced in 2001. She is a founder member of the National SEFDEY Network and Chair of the Midlands Region.

Kyffin Jones is a Senior Lecturer in Education at the University of Northampton. Prior to joining the university, Kyffin worked as an advisory teacher for SEN and has taught in both special and mainstream schools in the UK and the USA. Currently he has responsibility for the Erasmus programme at the School of Education and facilitates study visits to Sweden and The Netherlands with groups of students. Current research is focused on the nature of 'fitting in' at school and the implications of this for inclusive practice.

Paulette Luff joined Anglia Ruskin University in 2003 and is currently a Senior Lecturer in the Department of Education. She currently leads the MA course in Early Childhood Professional Practice and is also convenor of the Early Childhood Research

Group. Paulette has worked in the field of early childhood throughout her career as a teacher, foster carer, school–home liaison worker, nursery practitioner and advisor, and as a lecturer in further education.

Eunice Lumsden is Head of Early Years at the University of Northampton. Prior to joining the university she was a social work practitioner. She has contributed to a number of research projects and her doctoral research was into the development of the Early Years Professional.

Jane Murray is currently a Senior Lecturer at the University of Northampton where she has led on the MA Education (Early Years) and the early years undergraduate teacher training programme. Jane currently works as a researcher within the Centre for Education and Research at The University of Northampton; she has a varied port-folio which includes project work for the EU Commission and the Norwegian and Georgian governments as well as small-scale neighbourhood projects. Jane's specialist research interests include early childhood pedagogies, epistemology and young chil-dren's agency and participation; she has numerous publications in these areas. Jane supervises PhD students and continues to do some teaching on undergraduate and postgraduate programmes. Before moving to work in higher education, Jane was an early years and primary teacher and she is a qualified headteacher.

Jane O'Connor is a Senior Researcher in Early Years at Birmingham City University. Her background is in education and she worked as a primary school teacher before entering academia. Her thesis on child stardom formed the basis of her first book, which was published by Routledge in 2008. Her research interests lie with representa-tions of children in the media, especially 'exceptional' children and child stars. Jane is currently working on a project investigating parental attitudes towards 0–3-year-olds' use of touch screen technology. She is also co-authoring a paper on the child stars of the 2012 London Olympics.

Sharon Smith is a Senior Lecturer in Early Years and Child Health at the University of Northampton. Sharon has a varied background in child health, trained as a chil-dren's nurse and is an experienced health visitor. Sharon led the Health Visiting course at the University and is now course leader for the Foundation Degree in Early Years. Her teaching focus is predominantly child and family health promotion. She is cur-rently a doctoral student; her research interests include infant nutrition, maternal mental health and the role of non-health professionals in supporting health outcomes.

Prospera Tedam is a Senior Lecturer in Social Work at the University of Northampton, where she has worked since 2006. A qualified and registered social worker by training, Prospera has worked in the statutory and voluntary sectors since qualifying in 1996, specialising in Children and Family Social Work. Prospera is currently undertaking a professional doctorate and has research interests in equality and diversity, cultural competence and social justice and is a member of the Independent Family Returns Panel at the Home Office.

Helen Tovey is Principal Lecturer in Early Childhood Studies at the University of Roehampton, London, where she teaches on BA and MA and professional development courses. Her main research interests are outdoor play and young children's risk-taking outdoors. Helen is a Froebel-trained teacher and a former nursery school headteacher. She is author of numerous texts, including *Playing Outdoors, Spaces and Places, Risk and Challenge,* published by Open University Press (2007), and *Bringing the Froebel Approach to your Early Years Practice*, published by Routledge (2013).

Jane Waters is the Director of Primary Initial Teacher Education and Training in the South West Wales Centre of Teacher Education at University of Wales Trinity Saint David: Swansea Metropolitan. Jane lectures in outdoor play and learning, adult–child interaction, early years education and the ethics of research with young children. Current research projects include working with international colleagues to consider pedagogical intersubjectivity in early education contexts in different countries.

Michael Wyness is an Associate Professor in Childhood Studies in the Institute of Education. His research interests are in the sociologies of childhood and education. His book *Childhood and Society* (2006, Palgrave) has just gone into a second edition (2012). His previous books were *Contesting Childhood* (1999) and *Schooling Welfare and Parental Responsibility* (1995), both published by RoutledgeFalmer. His research interests are in children's participation, childhood and theory, children's transitions and home–school relations.

How to Use the Book and its Online Resources

How to use the book

The new edition of *An Introduction to Early Childhood* is filled with useful learning resources to help guide your study including:

Key chapter objectives identify the topics you will understand at the end of the chapter.

Case studies show how early years theory works in practice.

Reflective questions linked to each case study at the end of each chapter help with reflective practice and encourage you to start thinking like a practitioner.

Research in context boxes unpick recent research and show how it impacts on early years education.

Chapter summaries aid revision by recapping key concepts covered in each chapter.

Further reading and **recommended websites** direct you to additional resources to deepen your understanding. They are a great starting point for assignments and literature reviews.

How to use the companion website

An Introduction to Early Childhood is also supported by a wealth of online resources which you can access at www.sagepub.co.uk/walleranddavis3e.
  Visit the website to:

Listen to podcasts from chapter authors giving a deeper insight into the issues discussed in each chapter and their implications for early childhood.

Check out employability and placement resources discussing how to get the most out of your early years placement and what prospective employers are looking for in staff.

View and discuss child observation videos showing child behaviour in settings to give you a deeper understanding of what to expect in practice.

Access a selection of free SAGE journal articles supplementing each chapter. Ideal for your literature review!

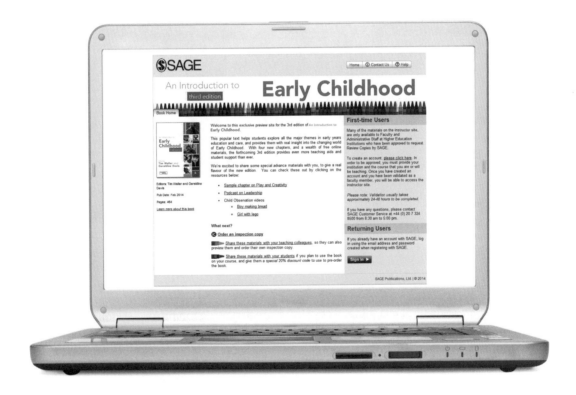

Introduction

Tim Waller and Geraldine Davis

Welcome to the third edition of *An Introduction to Early Childhood*. This new edition has been significantly expanded and updated to include five new chapters from a range of well-known authors, in addition to a variety of supporting online resources, such as podcasts and video material specifically developed for the book. For this edition Tim Waller is joined by colleague Gerry Davis as co-editor and Tim is very grateful for her significant contribution.

The original version of this book was conceived by the Early Childhood Studies (ECS) degree team of tutors at the University of Northampton in 2004, in response to a perceived gap in the specific literature for ECS identified by students, practitioners and tutors. It is very pleasing to note that all of the original contributors have written again for this edition and that many of the original ECS students who inspired this book have become successful professional practitioners.

The advantage of taking a multi-disciplinary approach to studying early childhood is that it can help us to understand the wide range of cultural, social, economic, political, structural and historical contexts of modern childhoods, at the level of children and their families, the wider community and society (Rogoff, 2003) and the tensions and relationships between the various layers (Corsaro, 2011; Moss, 2012).

The chapters included in this book represent a growing body of work concerning early childhood reflecting a challenge to traditional 'deficit' models of children and childhood and recognising the need to seek and consider children's perspectives. Also, there is an acknowledgement that we know far more about children's lives in Western industrialised countries than in other parts of the world. Much further published research is needed to better understand children's lives across the world.

Since the second edition was published in 2009 there have been significant changes to the wider social and economic context impacting on young children and their families on a global scale, particularly in relation to 'austerity cuts' and reductions to the public funding of early childhood education and care (ECEC). Even in Nordic countries long established traditions of high quality ECEC are being threatened by politically motivated drives to cut public spending, despite increased evidence of the benefits of good quality ECEC (see Peeters and Urban, 2011 and Sylva et al., 2010, for example).

In England a clear strategy that aimed to raise the quality and develop a graduate workforce was put in place by the Children's Workforce Development Council (CWDC) from 2007 to 2011. There is a growing body of evidence that this graduate workforce (Early Years Professionals) is making an impact on ECEC in England (Davis and Capes, 2013; Hadfield et al., 2012; Lumsden, 2012). However, following the election of a new right-wing government in 2010, ECEC provision has been seriously threatened by a 'market-driven' approach and the CWDC has been shut down. Despite the Nutbrown Review (2012b) of the qualifications for ECEC there is still concern that the current arrangements for training and accrediting the professional workforce in England are not 'fit for purpose' and maintain previous inequalities between the various professionals working with young children. As Lloyd and Hallet (2010) contend: is this a missed opportunity?

Ominously, it seems that 'austerity cuts' in public funding have a far greater impact on less wealthy children and families generally throughout the world. There is currently particular concern about the lives of many children in Southern Europe, in countries such as Greece, Italy, Spain and Portugal, as well as Ireland, due to the economic conditions. However, there is no clear geographical division in wealth. For example, in the UK the Marmot Review (2010) has demonstrated clear links between inequality and health. According to Marmot, women and children in the UK would have longer and healthier lives if they lived in Cyprus, Italy or Spain. Death rates among the under-5s are worse in the UK, where there is also more child poverty. Marmot reports that in the UK one in four children live in poverty – more than in many other European countries. Iceland has the fewest in poverty (one in ten) – closely followed by Norway, Denmark, Slovenia, Cyprus, Finland, Sweden and the Czech Republic. Only half the children living in poverty reach what the report defines as 'a good level of development' by the time they are 5, compared with two-thirds of the others. Marmot argues that whilst good quality early-years provision can help improve outcomes, especially for the most disadvantaged, childcare is expensive in the UK, and many people cannot afford to utilise it or go back to work after having children.

The *Good Childhood Report* (The Children's Society, 2013: 6) also reports a clear link between inequality, poverty and wellbeing. 'Children who lack five or more items on our deprivation index are 13 times less likely to feel safe at home and six times less likely to feel positive about the future.' Whilst children in the UK generally experienced a rise in wellbeing between 1994 and 2008, the *Good Childhood Report* argues that this trend has been reversed in recent years, identifying a significant decline in some children's wellbeing. Worryingly, the Report shows that children with low well-being are over 20 times less likely than other children to 'feel safe at home' and five times more likely to report having recently been bullied.

In 2011 UNICEF conducted a survey on what children needed to be happy. For children, the three most important aspects were:

1. Time (especially with families)
2. Friendships
3. Being outdoors.

However, there is growing statistical evidence that opportunities for outdoor play have become much more restricted over the last three generations due to the rise in traffic, greater institutionalisation of childhood (organised clubs, etc.) and parents' safety concerns (Tovey, 2007). At the same time, access to the outdoors for children has become limited, with far greater use now of adult-controlled and structured space. The net effect on children's lives is that it minimises both their world outside home and school and their confidence to operate in this world. There is, however, also an increasing group of adults who are now concerned to give children regular opportunities for play in outdoor environments and in the UK, for example, Project Wild Thing (projectwildthing.com/film) is a film-led movement to get more children (and their parents) outside and reconnecting with nature.

One aspect of many children's lives is their engagement with digital technologies for communication, play and gaming, etc. There is an argument that these activities are replacing outdoor play, but there is no reason why children cannot enjoy *both* experiences. Thanks to the work of Marsh (2007) and Yelland (2011), for example, we know that young children are just as engaged in current digital communicative and social practices as the older members of their families and communities. Many children have become experts in using technology and are able to access and use information in different ways as a result (Facer, 2011, 2012). There is, however, more research to be undertaken in relation to how using digital technologies leads children to participate in the same consumerism and commodity fetishism as many adults!

In contrast, over the past twenty years or so there has also been an increasing trend in both public policy and practice in early years education towards fostering children's participation and voice. The introduction of the United Nations Convention on the Rights of the Child (UNCRC) in 1989 helped change the dominant image of childhood and bring about a new culture in relation to children's rights and interests in many parts of the world (Smith, 2011). This has shifted the debate from deficit models to children's wellbeing and children's interests in the *here and now* (Urban, 2010), to strengths-based perceptions of children, where children are regarded as competent social actors who are experts on their own lives (James and Prout, 1997; Mayall, 2002; Rinaldi, 2006). The study of early childhood is certainly compatible with a rights-based approach, especially towards ethical and methodological issues in research with children (Smith, 2011). It is engaged in producing new knowledge of children's experience, grounded in children's perspectives, and it has been productive in extending our understanding of childhood.

The aim of the book

The purpose of the book is to provide a contemporary, holistic and multidisciplinary early years reader that covers the theoretical background relating to significant aspects of current international debate regarding early childhood. The book is based partly on the popular curriculum for the Early Childhood Studies degree at the University of Northampton and similar courses at other universities in the UK. While the aim is to introduce students to some of the key areas, it is also hoped that the ideas presented will challenge students' thinking and encourage reflection, further reading and study. Through a consideration of multi-disciplinary perspectives the book is intended as a complement to other recent texts in the field – although, inevitably, it has not been possible to give attention to all aspects of modern childhoods and the chapters in this book refer to a selection of possible topics, drawing on the strengths and interests of the authors.

Content

The content is designed for a broad range of readers, in particular those with little previous opportunity to study early childhood. The introductory coverage and emphasis on core ideas make it an appropriate text for students who are new to the field and also students wishing to develop their understanding of contemporary issues in the early years.

The following themes underpin and frame discussion in each of the chapters:

- respecting and protecting children's rights and individuality
- equality of opportunity
- family and community experience and support
- multi-professional and multi-disciplinary collaboration
- opportunities for reflection on the reader's own experience and learning.

This third edition of *An Introduction to Early Childhood* has been expanded to include five new chapters – A History of Childhood, Play and Creativity, Children and Media, Leadership and Change Management in Early Childhood, and Reflective Practice. Each new chapter concerns an aspect of childhood that reflects recent developments or was identified as a perceived gap in the original edition. We are grateful for student feedback and the comments of reviewers in this respect.

As the number of chapters has increased from fourteen to eighteen, the book has been re-organised into six sections comprising: Histories and Theories of Childhood, Inclusion and Diversity, Learning and Play, Health, Wellbeing and Protection, Professional Working, and Research and Reflection. Each of the original chapters has been revised to discuss recent and current research, literature, policy and legislation, as appropriate. Many of the authors have also been able to draw on their own research in the field.

The first three chapters in Part One provide a contextual and theoretical foundation for the book. In a new Chapter 1 Michael Wyness explores the historical nature of contemporary childhood with reference to the theory of social constructionism, research on schooling and the significance of key concepts within the social sciences relating to child development. Secondly, he examines the role that children themselves played in the history of childhood to provide an informed and broad-based overview of how childhood has developed historically. In Chapter 2, on modern childhoods, Tim Waller has revised and updated the original chapter to develop and discuss five key tenets of modern theory about early childhoods. This chapter is viewed as complementary to Chapter 1 and has been kept as a whole from the version published in the previous edition of this book. Libby Lee-Hammond (with Tim Waller) critically discusses international perspectives in Chapter 3. In particular, Libby has considerably revised the chapter to discuss findings from recent international comparisons of early childhood education and care, provide an overview of issues related to early years policy and provision in OECD countries, reflect on diverse curricula and the notions of 'quality' and 'equity' and examine examples of early years education and care in various countries. Importantly, this chapter introduces students to the insights that can be developed through comparison.

Part Two includes three chapters focusing on inclusion and diversity, all of which have been revised and updated since the second edition. In Chapter 4 Gill Handley discusses children's rights to participation. The chapter explores the difficulties of identifying what participation means in practice and identifies the conflicts between children's participation and protection rights. The chapter also gives detailed consideration to the dilemmas and difficulties of judging children's competence in relation to participation and introduces some of the complexities of upholding very young children's rights to participation. The following chapter is written by Prospera Tedam and focuses on understanding diversity. Prospera explores the concept of 'diversity' within the context of early years care and education and aims to identify the role of practitioners, parents and the wider community in supporting young children to gain an understanding of difference. In addition, the chapter highlights relevant national and international legislative and policy frameworks that underpin diversity and supports students' development of understanding of the barriers to equal opportunities and explores strategies for removing the barriers. In Chapter 6 on inclusive practice for children with special educational needs (SEN) Christine Hickman and Kyffin Jones consider the historical and legislative profile of special educational needs provision. In the context of a multi-agency approach they discuss the concept of inclusion in relation to young children with SEN. The chapter discusses how the individual needs of pupils with SEN may be met, acknowledging advocacy and the voice of the child.

Part Three concerns learning and play. Chapter 7 is a new chapter written by Paulette Luff. She explores definitions of play and creativity, in the context of early childhood education. In particular, Paulette identifies features of environments that stimulate and enable creativity and discusses adults' roles within children's play and creativity. This chapter also debates the use of pedagogical documentation to record and reflect on play and creativity. Chapter 8, on outdoor play and learning, has been significantly revised and strengthened by Helen Tovey to provide an overview of recent literature on outdoor play and learning and discuss the reasons why opportunities for outdoor play have become restricted. The chapter also considers the growing international research on the benefits of outdoor play and learning. Tim Waller has updated his report on findings from the ongoing Outdoor Learning Project (now in its eleventh year!). Jane O'Connor has kindly written Chapter 9 on children and media. Jane outlines the polarised debate around children using media technology and reflects on issues around children's 'consumption' of media, focusing on television. In this new chapter Jane investigates children's use and production of media products, including computer games, and the learning opportunities this may bring. She also considers the impact of media on children's wellbeing and development.

Part Four of this book includes four chapters on health, wellbeing and protection. In Chapter 10, on child health, Sharon Smith and Tania Hart have revised their original work to emphasise the importance of early years settings in promoting, protecting and supporting children's physical and emotional health. They focus on the significance of supporting the child's family in order that they are better equipped to meet the needs of their child. In particular, the chapter highlights the importance of strong multi-agency partnership working in order to promote good child health and better support the child with complex health needs. Jane Waters has revised and updated her original chapter on wellbeing for Chapter 11. Jane critically considers the concept of wellbeing as complex rather than simplistic. In this comprehensive chapter Jane also exemplifies aspects of wellbeing within UK policy and practice contexts and considers elements of self-esteem in relation to wellbeing. For practitioners the chapter examines the implications of a focus on children's wellbeing and critically considers measures of wellbeing, international comparative literature and national survey data concerning the wellbeing of children in the UK. In Chapter 12 the focus is on protecting and safeguarding children. Here author Celia Doyle has also revised the original chapter in order to help the reader understand the nature of safeguarding and protection, including the role of power in definitions of abuse. The chapter seeks to enhance the reader's awareness of the contexts in which abuse can occur and help the reader recognise key features of the different forms of abuses, including the targeting and grooming of young children by sex offenders. In addition the chapter aims to help the reader appreciate how child victims might respond to abuse and why they do so, and to provide pointers to aspects of intervention, including responding to disclosures and recording concerns. The final chapter in Part Four of the book is Chapter 13 on working with families by Eunice Lumsden and Celia Doyle. Once again this chapter has been updated to explore what is meant by 'family' within a diverse society and why family is important for children. The chapter considers the implications of what it means for children when they do not have an identifiable 'family' and discusses early years policy initiatives in relation to children and their families. Importantly, this chapter seeks to acknowledge the relationship between the statutory and the private, voluntary and independent sectors in work with families.

Part Five of the book has three chapters on professional working in ECEC. Chapter 14 by Denise Hevey on professional work in early childhood is updated to explain the historical context of training and qualifications in childcare and to identify and debate the characteristics of professionalism. In particular, the chapter distinguishes between mothering/informal caring and professional roles with young children and provides an understanding of the difference between teachers with QTS, social pedagogues and Early Years Professionals/new Early Years Teachers. In Chapter 15 Eunice Lumsden has revised 'Joined-up thinking in practice: an exploration of professional collaboration'. This chapter discusses policy drivers for integrated practice in children's services and the development of interagency collaboration. It examines the language of collaboration, and considers the characteristics of effective communication and the barriers to integrated working. The chapter ends with a discussion of the place of training and the inclusion of service users. Geraldine Davis has also contributed a new chapter on leadership and management in early childhood. In Chapter 16, Geraldine reviews the different aspects of leadership that are evident in the literature and in practice in early childhood settings. It includes examples taken directly from practice and Geraldine has also drawn on her research involving Early Years Professionals to consider the leadership impacts on many aspects of early childhood including: improving outcomes for children and families; developing a community of practice; developing staff and oneself; working with parents and carers; and developing the quality of education and care in early childhood education settings.

The book is completed by Part Six, with two chapters focusing on research and reflection. Firstly, Jane Murray has updated Chapter 17, 'Researching young children's worlds'. This chapter explores issues concerning young children and research, to identify conflicts between children's participation and protection rights and to consider the dilemmas and difficulties of judging children's competence in relation to participation. In the chapter Jane explores the proposition that one of the key challenges for adults in recognising children as researchers is that adults often struggle to understand children's behaviours. Within the chapter there is consideration of how these issues were encountered and addressed as part of the Young Children As Researchers (YCAR) project. Chapter 18 on reflective practice by Caroline Jones concludes the book. In this chapter Caroline conceptualises reflective practice from a sociocultural historical perspective and highlights case studies and research relating to reflective practice. In particular, the chapter identifies the key features of reflection and reflective practices and considers the factors influencing the process of reflective practice. Caroline also explores the links between reflective practices and professionalism in early childhood education and care.

Once more – welcome to the study of early childhood!

Part One
Histories and Theories of Childhood

1

A History of Childhood: Adult Constructs and Children's Agency

Michael Wyness

 Key chapter objectives

- To explore the historical nature of contemporary childhood
- To discuss a history of childhood in two ways: as the historical development of childhood as a set of powerful ideas about how to think about, relate to and treat children, and as an examination of the historical impact of children

Introduction

This chapter explores two interrelated themes within the history of childhood: the historical development of childhood and work that focuses on the historical impact of children within local, national and global contexts. While there is clearly a relationship between the idea of childhood, and the embodied 'real' child and his or her social environments, there remains a question mark over the extent to which children themselves play any part in the historical development of their childhoods. The distinction between 'childhood' and 'children' is thus important: the former emphasises the development of adult thinking on the 'physiologically immature', or what we commonly refer to as children. The issue here is how childhood was shaped as a powerful set of ideas about the treatment and expectations of children and the nature of adult–child relations. Much has been written about how the modern idea of childhood developed through the intersection of ideas and sentiments at political, social, economic and moral levels (Ariès, 1962). The latter, on the other hand, emphasises embodied versions of childhood – children as flesh-and-blood social actors. Much less has been written historically about the roles that children themselves played in their social environments.

This chapter will explore these two approaches to the history of childhood. I will first discuss the historical development of childhood with reference to the theory of social constructionism and a number of historical conceptions of childhood that reflect growing concerns over and interest in the nature of childhood. Secondly, I move on to examine the role that children themselves played in the history of childhood. In the final section I bring these two themes together and argue that the inclusion of work on the history of children provides a more informed and broad-based overview of how childhood has developed historically.

Constructing childhood historically

Recent innovations in the study of children and childhood owe a considerable debt to the work of social historians, such as Edward Shorter's (1976) *The Making of the Modern Family* and his argument that motherhood is a product of modernity; Lloyd DeMause's (1976) thesis on the changing nature of parent–child relations; and Neil Postman's (1982) 'rise and fall' of a technologically driven American childhood. But it is the work of social historian Phillipe Ariès (1962) that is most influential in challenging the biological basis to childhood, in arguing childhood is a product of modernity. Modern childhood is often taken for granted as a universal feature of societies largely because processes of growing up and development are assumed to be predominantly based on the biological unfolding of the child as a future adult. Children's emotional, social and moral wellbeing are inferred from this process of 'growing up', with childhood an all-encompassing and ever-present feature of societies and historical periods that incorporates these processes. Ariès (1962) challenges this powerful conception of childhood through a historical analysis of the rise of powerful adult ideas and sentiments, ways of expressing adults' feelings and emotions towards children. According to Ariès, in medieval times childhood did not exist:

> The idea of childhood ... corresponds with an awareness of a particular nature of childhood, that particular nature which distinguishes the child from the adult, even the young adult. In medieval society this awareness was lacking. That is why as soon as the child could live without the constant solicitude of his [*sic*] mother, his nanny or his cradle rocker he belonged to adult society. (1962: 125)

Ideas and sentiments that eventually separated children from adult society developed slowly over time, but from the 16th to the 19th century Ariès charts the way that these adult conceptions of the 'physiologically immature' converged on the idea of childhood. Moreover, these ideas started to affect the way that children were treated and heavily influenced the nature of relations between adults and children inside and outside the home. In effect, Ariès argues that by the 19th century children were necessarily segregated from the adult population in order that they go through an extended period of nurturing and development before being 'released' into the wider society as adults.

Ariès based his argument on an inferential approach to his data: the development of childhood is drawn from a range of literary and visual representations of family life, schooling and child's play. Ariès inferred from a range of artistic representations the meaning of childhood and, by tracing the historical changes in these representations over several centuries, was able to discern how those meanings changed over time. To take one example, Ariès documents trends in family portraits from the 12th to the 19th century. The child in the earlier period was depicted as 'a man on a smaller scale', with a similar-shaped body and clothing because children were not perceived as being anything other than miniature adults (Ariès, 1962: 10). This is compared with the later period where family portraits denoted a much stronger conception of the child as physically distinct from adults, with 'child-like' features within the family, with the adult parental gaze downwards on the child, suggesting a powerful protective circle within which the small, vulnerable child is able to develop. The child became literally and metaphorically central here: '[it] was in the 17th century ... that the family portrait ... tended to plan itself around the child' (Ariès, 1962: 44). Ariès' work is significant because he provides us with the idea that modern societies were characterised by the development of adult sentiments towards children. Rather than adults being indifferent to children, children became the focal point in both families and schools, and in time they also became a critical feature of policy making.

If we explore this concept of adult sentiment and interest in children, it becomes clear that there were considerable differences in how adults actually perceived children and thus major differences in how childhood was conceptualised. In effect we can distinguish between 'adult' and 'child' in terms of the way that adults started to view children differently from themselves – what we might call a concept of childhood. At the same time, children can be viewed separately from adults in different kinds of ways; in other words a number of different generational distinctions can be made – what Archard (2004) refers to as different conceptions of childhood. Archard (2004) revises Ariès' argument in that he emphasises the different adult rationales for the segregation of children from the adult world. I want to go on and discuss these differences with respect to four dominant conceptions of childhood: the innocent child; the troublesome child; the child as an investment in the future; and the developmental child.

The innocent child

The concept of innocence came to be associated with children's lives and their essential being through the work of French philosopher Emile Rousseau in the 18th century and in England in the latter part of the 18th and early 19th centuries through the work of the romantic poets such as Wordsworth and Blake. Rousseau counterposed the child as a 'noble savage' with the negative and pernicious influence of society. In his famous text *Emile* (1762), Rousseau writes that childhood was the quintessential embodiment of nature that was irrevocably lost as children grew up. In particular this essential goodness was compromised as children were influenced by schooling: education taught children to conform to the rules and structures of society. Rousseau argues that in order to retain this innocence, within broad protective constraints children should be allowed to express themselves and thus draw out their creative instincts.

This comparison between the essence of nature and the artifice of society was later reaffirmed through the Romantics' focus on innocence and purity set against an equally powerful image of the exploitable child labourer in the early part of 19th century industrial Britain. Wordsworth associates childhood in a spiritual sense with nature; Blake evokes darker images of this 'nature' having a fleeting presence in our lives as children are confronted by the material realities of poverty and hardship. Both symbolically equate childhood with all that is good and unsullied (Hendrick, 1997).

Rousseau and the Romantics emphasised the importance of innocence, with adults playing the role of protecting and nurturing this innocence within the child. The concept of innocence is in some respects synonymous with a modern concept of childhood. Adult perceptions of childhood generate the impulse to protect and care for children. Within a professional context this has been translated into child-centredness. Educational philosophy in the early part of the 20th century and its professional and practical counterpart later in that century has focused on the need to centre the curriculum and teaching approaches around the child. European and North American practice in early years and primary schooling during this period emphasised schools and teachers fitting in with the interests of the child. Thus, rather than children's educational experiences being driven by the demands of an adult-structured curriculum, professionals were to try to work around the interests of children. Among other things, teachers were to nurture children's creative capacities with a loosely structured curriculum having to work its way through the initiatives, interests and needs of children.

The troublesome child

It is not always clear that the need to regulate children, particularly those in adolescence, is a relatively recent concern. Shakespeare reminds us of the difficulties adults have in regulating the behaviour of teenagers:

> I would there no age between sixteen and three and twenty, or that youth would sleep out the rest; for there is nothing in the between but getting wenches with child, wronging the ancientry, stealing, fighting. (*The Winter's Tale*, Act III, Scene iii)

Moreover, Hobbes' (1651) famous work *Leviathan* in the 17th century emphasised the importance of constraining the wills and appetites of individuals and set down a framework of thinking that emphasised the importance of institutions and authority figures in disciplining the less 'civilised' instincts of children. However, it was in the 18th and 19th centuries that these more puritanical conceptions of childhood became prominent, offering a clear contrast with the ideas of the Romantics. The influence of John Wesley's Methodism and the later Evangelical movement of Hannah More were evident in the way that discipline rather than nurture became a dominant theme in the ways of relating to children. In the former case, the will of the child was to be broken, control and physical punishment characterising parental approaches to their children rather than opening up of spaces for their expression (Hendrick, 1997). This emphasis on control as well as protection became a dominant motif throughout the 19th century in England. Jenks (1996) talks about the powerful image of the Dionysian child, from the Greek god Dionysus who symbolises chaos and unpredictability. The child here is inherently evil and wayward rather than innately good.

One powerful idea about children here is that they are social incompetents, incapable of making the right moral choices and therefore in a position to be easily led by more charismatic and powerful friends and peers. Dickens picks up on this theme in *Oliver Twist*, his fictional characterisation of street life in London in the mid-19th century. But there was a more general public concern in England during this period. Hendrick (1997) refers to the concept of the 'delinquent child': children, particularly urban working-class children, were perceived to constitute a public order problem. Various campaigns were started and reports published to try to strengthen legislation to curb a perceived increase in the incidence of crime committed by children on the street. Juvenile delinquency became a separate category of crime and social policy at this time was concerned with getting 'vagrants' off the streets and back into the home. Working-class children were to be domesticated and brought in line with growing middle-class norms of childhood dependence.

 Research in context

Pearson, G. (1983) *Hooligan: A History of Respectable Fears.* Basingstoke: Macmillan.

The need to discipline and regulate children, particularly 'children of the dangerous classes', was a critical feature of public policy in Britain in the mid- to late 19th century onwards (Pearson, 1983: 159). The concept of socialisation was significant here, with delinquency attributed to inadequate parental socialisation and control, particularly in relation to working-class parents. This is a theme that continued throughout the 19th and 20th centuries, with periodic public anxieties in England

(Continued)

(Continued)

centring on the behaviour and disposition of children and young people. Pearson (1983) in his classic study refers to these as recurring public fears that punctuate British history during this period. The late Victorian period was particularly important, with the focal points here being mainly working-class boys and men. Thus 'Hooligan' gangs were targeted for apparently running amok through the streets of London in the 1890s; and the 'Scuttlers' and the 'Peaky Blinders' were the focal points in Manchester and Birmingham respectively during this period. Pearson also looks at earlier 'troublesome' youth groups, such as the London Garroters of the 1860s and later groups such as the Teddy Boys, who were perceived to be the personification of all that was wrong in British society during the coronation year of Elizabeth II in 1953. Each problem was accompanied by widespread public and political concern articulated through the national press and debated in parliament. The same recurring themes were debated: the lack of respect for adult authority, the decline of traditional family values and the rise of new forms of media that acted as countervailing frames of reference for the young.

The child as an investment

One powerful historical development throughout the 19th and 20th centuries across Europe and North America was the role of the school in children's lives. This in turn has been seminal in shaping modern Western conceptions of childhood. Until the early part of the 19th century schooling was the preserve of the middle classes, with few working class parents able to pay for their children's schooling over a prolonged period of their childhoods. Gradually greater importance was attached to mass compulsory schooling among children, their families and communities. But it was not until the early part of the 20th century that schooling was a taken-for-granted feature of children's lives. Moreover, it was only in this later period that schooling helped to define a more universalised conception of childhood.

Until the early 19th century there was little evidence of systems of education in either Europe or North America. Ariès (1962: 317) argues that the early medieval school was 'not intended for children: it was a sort of technical school for the instruction of clerics, young and old ... Thus it welcomed equally and indifferently, children, youths and adults, the precocious and the backward'. Schools during this period in France were disorganised, lacking any structured curriculum and any sense that children needed to be segregated in terms of age. This is neatly contrasted with developments in the 18th century; the new colleges segregated children from adults and over time became more focused on the social and moral development of children (Ariès, 1962: 62). There was a strong sentiment towards children as a separate sector of the population that had to be physically and morally segregated from the adult population. Children here were to be protected, nurtured and schooled according to age-related criteria. Thus childhood as a period of growing up towards adulthood started to be more clearly measured and assessed in terms of age-related criteria.

The introduction of mass compulsory schooling did not come into being in Europe until the early 19th century in Germany, a generation or so later in the USA, and it was not fully developed until the end of the 19th century in England and Wales (Cunningham, 1995). Lee (2001: 27) analyses the concept of childhood in terms of the role of politics, in particular the rise of the 'developmental state'. Children in the modern era became a form of investment, 'embodiments in the future', with the state expecting a return for its initial investment in children. Thus a range of educationalists and experts developed from the late 19th century until the mid-20th century to help support children within their families and their schools. In effect the multiplication of adults with a professional interest in children helped to reinforce the view that children had to be separated from the adult world and prepared as a future adult generation.

This 'economic' theme of childhood was further developed by Bowles and Gintis (1976) in their historical analysis of mass compulsory schooling in the USA during this formative period. They argued that a fully formed education system, in the USA followed from the development of a capitalist economic system, with children being subject to 'bureaucratisation, tracking and test orientation', with children viewed as a future disciplined workforce (Bowles and Gintis, 1976: 2). A curriculum was created to provide a developing population of working-class children with a basic education and at the same time schools were designed to resemble the way that working-class American men were supposed to behave on the factory production line. Thus children's moral, social and cognitive development in school was primarily about the shaping of the adult American character: children were segregated, controlled and moulded to meet the demands of an expanding system of economic production.

In England the concerns were moral as well as economic. In some respects the problems of delinquency and vagrancy generated much stronger arguments for compulsory schooling. Delinquency was associated with precocity and there was a demand to render children dependent and malleable. Children also had to be rendered ignorant, that is, they had to start from the beginning in terms of the acquisition of legitimate knowledge, with this knowledge, or what came to be known as a curriculum, eventually being distributed to children incrementally as they got older. Continuous and regular schooling was one of the means to these moral ends and helped to reinforce more modernist notions that all children require to be protected, controlled and educated.

The developmental child

The standard position within psychology is that childhood is based on 'immutable facts' of biology: children are dependent and immature beings and need to follow a developmental path that clearly tracks their growth and movement away from this initial state of immaturity. Moreover 'childhood' naturally triggers emotional responses from parents to bond with, and more generally protect, children (Shahar, cited in Oswell, 2013: 18). Thus as children grow biologically so they develop internally according to theories of psychological growth. This growth at least in the early years needs to be constantly monitored by adults. Historians have been able to support the biological premise of these contentions. Pollock's (1983) critique of Ariès and Shorter, for example, is that in the medieval period adults were indeed aware of a concept of childhood in the way that adults wrote about their children during their lives and when children died early they expressed considerable emotion. According to Pollock there was during this early period no absence of adult sentiment, and no sense that children were simply scaled-down adults. Although children were separated from adults through childhood, given the different economic and cultural conditions, childhood in medieval times was quite different from the modern form. Thus Pollock is saying that parents are biologically programmed to love and care for their children.

Stainton Rogers and Stainton Rogers (1992) challenge this view through a radical reading of developmental psychology. They locate childhood as a compelling modernist story based on the historical development of the social sciences in the latter half of the 19th century. In their book *Stories of Childhood* (1992) they refer to one powerful compelling narrative of childhood that shapes the way that adults view, relate to and treat children. The rise of developmental psychology throughout the first half of the 20th century defines childhood as a series of facts about biological and psychological growth. Stainton Rogers and Stainton Rogers (1992), on the other hand, 'deconstruct' or critically analyse these facts as plausible stories about human development. The general trend towards researching children in laboratory conditions, to monitor, observe and discreetly regulate children's behaviour within what were seen as 'controlled environments', was perceived to be a means of discerning scientific truths about childhood development. The Stainton-Rogers (1992) argue that these 'truths' were stories that had significant political and moral implications. Thus, while developmental psychology was in the business of discerning the scientific facts about a pre-existing essential feature of modern childhood, social constructionists like the Stainton-Rogers were arguing that these scientific procedures helped to bring 'childhood' into being. In effect 'childhood' became a powerful focal point within the social sciences throughout the 20th century. Notions of child development and 'attachment' helped to shape childhood, particularly early childhood, providing more nuanced and more scientific support for those working with children (Bowlby, 1953; Turmel, 2008).

Children as historical subjects

Recent historians have emphasised childhood as a product of modernity. In effect they have focused on its socially constructed nature. Rather than being a biological feature of all societies and historical periods, childhood is viewed as the historical convergence of political, economic and moral forces. This approach to the study of childhood might provide a framework for exploring the roles that children themselves played in the construction of childhood. However, there is some ambiguity here. On the one hand, the focus on historical social forces gives us more opportunity to identify the different ways that children exercise what we might call historical agency. For the purposes of this chapter I define agency as children 'acting purposively' and making a difference within their social environments (Valentine, 2011: 351). The idea of childhood as an outcome of historical forces opens up the possibility for identifying a diversity of distinctive forms of childhood. Just as societies take different forms over and across time, so the contours of childhood adapt to the structures of society. While there is no clear functional fit between micro-social phenomena such as childhood and family and broader cultural and social systems, we can at the very least say that different systems are likely to generate different ways of understanding childhood.

Moreover, with the exception of the more radical constructionism of the Stainton-Rogers, the biological basis to childhood has never been completely rejected. What we have seen in recent years is a reappraisal of the relationship between the biological and the cultural and social aspects of childhood. In effect, they have been prised apart from their causal universalised relationship: recent research within childhood studies has questioned the inferences made from children's biological inferiority by developmental psychologists. Most research would argue that children are indeed limited by their biology but nevertheless children's social and political capacities often belie their age and inexperience. Thus, in moving beyond psychological developmental conventions that stress an inevitable link between biology and culture, we can start to think of ways in which children are able to exercise a degree of agency. The emphasis on childhood as a social and cultural phenomenon also offers us space within which to explore the role that children themselves play historically in the construction of childhood.

At the same time, social constructionist theory has been more interested in the convergence of historical, political and social influences on the child, a focus on the role that institutions and structures organised by adults play in shaping what are referred to as discourses on childhood. Ariès' (1962) historical analysis is seminal in providing a modern conception of childhood but the roles of children themselves are notably absent in this historical construction. Various others have followed suit in providing historical constructions of childhood (Rose, 1992; Turmel, 2008). Far fewer have provided a social history of children and examined the contributions children have made in a number of spheres over time.

One obstacle to a fuller history of children's agency is the difficulty in accessing children's voices on their historical involvement. There has been a lack of interest in and awareness of children's historical involvement, which means relevant data, particularly data that capture children's accounts of their lives and contributions, are thin on the ground. As Hendrick (2008: 45) states: 'while a history of childhood as a changing form is possible, that of children, by virtue of their apparent "silence" as subjects can never be satisfactorily written'. There are obvious parallels here with the history of women throughout the first half of the 20th century (Oakley, 1994). As women were not considered to be prominent social actors, so the history of women's lives taken from women's perspectives was largely neglected during this period. Thus if sectors of the population are not treated as having any historical interest by historians, then these sectors of the population are written out of history. In some respects the problem goes deeper: historians may simply reflect broader values about childhood. Children are neglected due to their relative powerlessness. And the problem for historians of children or at least those with a commitment to writing about the past from children's perspectives, is that this lowly social status is reflected in the absence of public records that report their voices. In effect, children's lowly status makes it difficult for historians to write a history of children's lives from children's perspectives. Jordanova (1989: 5) provides a bleak assessment here: '(t)here can be no authentic voice of childhood speaking to us from the past because the adult world dominates the child'.

Despite these limitations, three approaches have prevailed here with respect to the quality and quantity of evidence on children's historical perspectives in the past. Firstly, we can distil from the public and private records the limited level of children's testimonies available to us. Secondly, the oral historical approach allows us to go back as far as the first half of the twentieth century in listening to narratives from adults about their childhoods. Despite demographic trends towards people living much longer in the West, this is clearly limiting in chronological terms with a history of children's lives unlikely to go back much further than the 1930s. However, this oral history is often seen as a history from the bottom up, with historians committed to listening to the voices of the poor – localised histories of those actors hidden from the more conventional historical narratives (Thompson, 1978). Thirdly, we can rely on sympathetic reports of how adults think children felt and experienced life in the past. In most instances it is the third approach that prevails, with historians narrating the accounts of children and childhood given by adults.

In the following I discuss the role that children themselves play both in the development of 'childhood' and more generally within their communities and nations. I will also introduce the notion of children's agency here and explore three areas where children have exercised their agency and made contributions. First of all I discuss the child's involvement in political struggles and changes. Second, I assess the historical involvement of children as economic actors. Third, I explore children's historical roles in military conflict.

The political child

As Hannah Arendt, a famous critic of children's involvement in politics, argued, children are to be hidden within the private sphere of 'natality, love and intimacy' where they are protected from the pressures of the public realm (Bethke Elshtain, 1996: 14). Arendt was highly critical of the 'racial' desegregation that took place in Little Rock schools in the United States in the 1950s as it exposed children to the politics of race before they were developmentally ready. In some instances children's exposure to the 'external' world of politics is seen as a form of political indoctrination, with vulnerable children being exploited by adults in the interests of political ideology. Conventional historical narratives have thus tended to exclude the political or historical role of children. However, a more constructionist approach allows us to challenge this conventional viewpoint. Bethke Elshtain (1996), for example, argues that the absence of children within these narratives is at variance with a range of historical events and situations where children have been highly political.

In the more recent historical past of 1960s and 1970s apartheid South Africa, black South African children and young people were arguably at the forefront of the anti-apartheid movement. There was a rapid expansion of education in the 1960s, and young blacks were able to take advantage of this in becoming much more politically conscious of their situation. This consciousness took the form of a mass street protest in Soweto in 1976, with between 15,000 and 20,000 children and young people involved. Up to 200 school children were gunned down by government forces (Bundy, 1987). The impetus here was the introduction to the curriculum of Afrikaans, the language of the white minority rulers, as a compulsory language. While there was some criticism of the role of adult leaders from the youthful political leaders, many children were highly politicised and engaged with the struggle to end apartheid, working alongside their parents (Ndebele, 1995).

Children as economic actors

Despite the continuing coverage of child labour in less affluent regions of the world, children's paid employment in the Western countries has largely disappeared as a political issue after the introduction of mass compulsory schooling (ILO, 2011). However, this was not always the case and it was not until the very end of the 19th century that children's more routine economic activities declined. The 19th century was a crucial period in English history for the shaping of a modern conception of childhood. Prior to this children were heavily involved in economic activity: they were often intrinsic features of the domestic economy, with parents relying heavily on their income. We can go much further back, to medieval times when children were often sent out to the households of the local elite and the clergy from a very early age to work as servants. Children from the more affluent peasantry were often expected to learn a trade (Heywood, 2001). Hendrick (1997) refers to the problem of the child labourer in 19th century England, which manifested itself politically through the passing of the Factory Acts in 1802, 1819 and 1833. The Factory Acts gradually restricted the hours that children could work and the type of work that they could do. They were also importantly a precursor to a prolonged period of public debate over the merit and implications of the state providing free education to children. Throughout this period public commentary helped to shape modern childhood in the way that the discourse shifted from viewing children as being easily exploitable by adults in terms of their wages and conditions of employment, to viewing work as an activity that compromised what were starting to be seen as 'innate' characteristics of childhood – children's dependence and innocence. It was not until the 1930s that legislation was passed in the UK that effectively defined children's employment as a peripheral secondary activity for 'pocket money' (Wyness, 2012). Similar legislation was passed in the United States in 1938 – the Fair Labour Standards Act – that reflected public attitudes to children's economic activities. Children by then had emotional and social meaning for adults rather than economic value (Zelizer, 1985).

Children and military conflict

Children have tended to be viewed as relatively passive victims of military conflict rather than military protagonists. But just as the political child has little cultural purchase in modern Western societies, so the idea of children as military protagonists similarly has counterintuitive appeal. In part there is a sense that contemporary 'child soldiers' evoke a sense of unease in that children are perceived to be biologically and developmentally incapable of taking part in military conflict, with military service being seen as an exclusively adult activity. Despite these reservations there is some historical evidence to suggest that children were more integral features of armies and military campaigns in the past. David Rosen (2005) examines the central role of children in military conflict in a number of historical settings. Boys were regularly signed up by the English army during the medieval period, particularly during the Crusades. In the 1770s the English army regularly recruited 12- and 13-year-old boys to suppress the insurgent American rebellion in the American War of Independence. Dann (1980) has written about Henry Yeager, who signed up as a 13-year-old to fight for the rebel army. He became a drummer boy for George Washington and for a while was arrested and sentenced to death by the British army for espionage. The sentence was later commuted after the boy had spent some weeks in prison. He was eventually captured on board a rebel boat and spent a further two years in prison.

The American Civil War in the 1860s was seen as 'a war of boy soldiers' (Rosen, 2005: 5), with historians estimating that between 10% and 20% of combatants were children. In the 20th century children also played significant roles in military campaigns in Palestine and in Central and Eastern Europe. The latter was notable on two counts: many children, despite the age restriction imposed by the British government, routinely signed up to fight during the First World War. In the Second World War children played formative roles in Jewish resistance movements, challenging Nazi occupation in Eastern Europe. While figures are estimates, around a third of all Jewish resistance fighters were aged between 15 and 20 (Rosen, 2005: 21).

For some, the difficulty with children's agency is associating any form of choice with children's actions (Kimmel and Roby, 2007). Arendt (1959) saw children's involvement at

Little Rock as a form of political indoctrination, with vulnerable children being exploited by adults in the interests of political ideology. And it is clear that the Holocaust made it almost impossible for children to make an informed choice about whether to participate. Thus we may be struggling to discern any conception of agency here. Moreover, Denov (2012) cautions us against constructing the child soldier as either a victim, an offender or a superhero. Notions of agency here are complex: on the one hand, the recruitment of child soldiers through coercion accentuates children's victim status; on the other, the various high-profile cases of war crimes committed by children reinforce their culpability and in one sense their agentic status (McAdam-Crisp [2006], in her analysis of children's roles in the Rwandan Genocide in 1994, notes that almost 3,000 children were imprisoned for their involvement in the genocide). Nevertheless, Rosen (2005) refers to the way that children and their families during the Holocaust saw the passive acceptance of death at the hands of the Nazis as a form of 'dishonour'. In many of these historical cases children were encouraged by parents and schools to take up arms with their involvement seen as a moral duty. Referring to the work of Primo Levi, a holocaust survivor, Rosen states that for Levi, as for other child partisans involved in the resistance movement, 'there is no doubt that even a child has moral agency' (Rosen, 2005: 24).

CASE STUDY ONE

Children's collective industrial struggles

We have a very limited history of the different ways that children in the past made a difference collectively as economic actors. However, there are two notable examples, from Marson in the United Kingdom and Woodhouse in the United States. Marson (1973) focuses on children's political 'industrial' potential in his account of the children's strikes of 1911. Working-class children from across more than sixty towns and cities in Great Britain left their classrooms and schools and marched on the street. Within a broader political context of industrial unrest, children demanded the ending of corporal punishment and a shorter school day. While the authority's responses were predictably punitive, with strikers being labelled the 'truant class' and the 'ragged edge' of the school population, the children did exercise agency in terms of their independence and their ability to organise and coordinate their movements across a number of local schools.

   This level of collective agency was also evident in the USA at the turn of the 20th century, with children aged between 8 and 14 demonstrating entrepreneurial skills and some industrial muscle in their roles as newspaper sellers on the streets of New York. The 'Newsies' became a regular feature on the streets of New York,

(Continued)

(Continued)

selling newspapers (Woodhouse, 2009). They had to buy the newspapers from the publishers and so they were under pressure to sell all their stock to ensure they made a profit on the street. Despite their popularity, their position on the street was tenuous. But they were a well-organised group who eventually formed their own union to protect their collective interests. In 1899 their union demonstrated its strength in a dispute with the powerful Hearst and Pulitzer publishing empires, who were attempting to pay the boys a lower rate for distributing their newspapers. Their collective strength enabled them to strike, forcing the newspaper owners to climb down and maintain their rate of pay.

 Reflection for case study

- To what extent do striking children challenge children's more contemporary status as dependents?

In affluent countries like the UK and the USA, 21st century childhoods emphasise the child as having rights to schooling and protection, and having the ability to immerse themselves in new technologies, often at a much faster pace than adults. Nevertheless, children are still viewed as the responsibility of adult carers and educators and there is still an expectation that children's growing up is carefully regulated and controlled by adults. Thus while some children in affluent countries like the USA a century ago were earning an income and confronting their employers, American children today are expected to be found engaging with their school work safely either offline or online with their peers and teachers within the classroom.

Chapter summary

This chapter has outlined two general approaches to researching the history of childhood. First, there is an emphasis on broad historical forces that converge and generate 'childhood' as a powerful bundle of sentiments and ideas about the treatment and expectations of children. I discussed these ideas in terms of four historical conceptions of childhood. While some of the sets of ideas were developed at different times during the 19th and 20th centuries, there are important links between them which underpin a more complex 21st century model of childhood, particularly in the more affluent regions of the world. First of all we can see the troublesome delinquent child arising out of the innocent child in terms of notions of vulnerability. Thus a failure to protect this innocence leaves vulnerable children exposed to the more brutal public world of criminality. Contemporary analyses of childhood bring both sets of ideas together through the notion of the neglected child. Second, 'innocence' and 'trouble' form a historical rationale for the rise of compulsory schooling in Britain from the mid-19th century onwards. Initially the regulation of working-class childhood through the incremental development of compulsory schooling was about physical control and moral influence. Mass compulsory schooling was a means through which children would become dependent and ignorant and thus in need of adult guidance and protection. Gradually throughout the 20th century this regulation was seen to be articulated as a necessary investment in the future, with social and education policy emphasising the need to tap into the potential of working-class children for social, political and economic ends. Third, while the developmental child had an important scientific basis, education throughout the 20th century drew on this relatively new science of childhood in helping to categorise, select and remedy difficulties within childhood. Rose (1992) talks about a developing welfare network of support for children involving families, professionals and academics, which incorporates all four historical models of childhood. Moreover, this conception of childhood can be viewed in terms of the incremental involvement of the state. The more recent Every Child Matters initiative in the UK (DfES, 2004c) is illustrative of this trend, with statutory responsibilities for childhood incorporating the need to protect, nurture, control and educate children.

These historical constructions of childhood have been understood to develop out of a complex interplay of the political, economic and social interests of adults. In turning to the second major theme of this chapter, there is more attention placed on the possible historical roles that children themselves play. While the evidence is limited in terms of the extent to which children were able to play a prominent part in the construction of childhood, it is pretty clear that the inclusion of children as historical agents provides a more nuanced and informed history of childhood.

Questions for reflection and discussion

1. Do the historical constructions of childhood discussed in the first part of the chapter have any relevance to contemporary society?
2. Given the changes that have taken place in children's lives over the past twenty years, will there be more opportunities to write a history of childhood drawing on accounts from children themselves at the end of the 21st century?
3. Can you think of other examples where children are exercising agency?
4. While the chapter has focused on the variety of understandings of childhood over time, is there anything common that links these different conceptions of childhood?

Recommended reading

Ariès, P. (1962) *Centuries of Childhood*. Harmondsworth: Penguin.
This book pioneered the idea that far from being universal, childhood is a product of social, cultural and political factors.

Hendrick, H. (1997) 'Constructions and re-constructions of British childhood: an interpretive survey, 1800 to the present', in A. James and A. Prout (eds), *Constructing and Reconstructing Childhood*, 2nd edn. London: Falmer. pp. 33–60.
This chapter explores the way that the balance of political, economic and social forces converge and generate historically specific understandings of childhood.

Pearson, G. (1983) *Hooligan: A History of Respectable Fears*. Basingstoke: Macmillan.
This book offers an analysis of the 'youth as problem' theme as a recurring historical fear in English society.

Rosen, D. (2005) *Armies of the Young: Child Soldiers in War and Terrorism*. New Brunswick, NJ: Rutgers University Press.
This book offers an historical and contemporary examination of the role that children play in military conflict.

Childhood: A Journal of Global Child Research
An international peer-reviewed journal and a forum for research relating to children in global society.

Recommended websites

http://childrensparticipation.blogspot.co.uk/
A blog collecting information and resources on children's agency and participation.

www.childhistory.org/
The History of Children website offers links to primary and secondary sources for historical research on children and childhood

Want to learn more about this chapter? Visit the companion website at **www.sagepub.co.uk/walleranddavis3e** to access podcasts from the author and child observation videos.

2

Modern Childhoods: Contemporary Theories and Children's Lives

Tim Waller

 Key chapter objectives

- To review recent literature and research underpinning the study of early childhood

- To outline the main features of contemporary childhoods and children's lives identified by the literature

- To critically examine the role of child development in our understanding of children's lives

- To consider a range of perspectives on early childhoods

- To develop and discuss five key tenets of modern theory about early childhoods

---

This chapter is viewed as complementary to Chapter 1 and has been kept as a whole from the version published in the previous (2009) edition of this book, but updated where appropriate. As well as including new theories, this chapter includes further discussion of some of the concepts that are evident in Chapter 1. However, whereas Chapter 1 has a focus on the historical views of childhood, how these views have developed over time and their impact on contemporary childhood, this chapter has its focus on modern childhoods.

The chapter provides an overview of current international literature and research that underpins the study of early childhood. Much of the recent literature has been critical of the central role of 'child development' in theory concerning young children. In order to provide a contemporary account of the young child, the chapter identifies and critically discusses the following five key tenets of modern theory:

1. There are multiple and diverse childhoods.
2. There are multiple perspectives on childhood.
3. Children are involved in co-constructing their own childhoods.
4. Children's participation in family, community and culture makes a particular contribution to their lives.
5. We are still learning about childhood.

Childhood may be defined as the life period during which a human being is regarded as a child, and the cultural, social and economic characteristics of that period (Frones, 1994: 148).

Drawing from a range of sources (for example, Corsaro, 2011; Dahlberg et al., 2007; Kehily, 2009; MacNaughton, 2003; Maynard and Thomas, 2009; Penn, 2008), this chapter identifies five features of contemporary theories about children's 'development' and discusses their relevance to modern childhoods. The explicit purpose of the chapter is therefore to explore alternative, contemporary views and not to repeat traditional texts (of which there are many) that consider children and childhood mainly from a psychological point of view.

Brown (1998), MacNaughton (2003) and Robinson and Diaz (2006), for example, remind us of the importance of equity and the need to examine and question our own assumptions about children and childhood. It is common for adults to underestimate children. It is generally acknowledged that children are unique individuals, who live in a social world, and that there is no such thing as 'normal' development (Donaldson, 1978; Dunn, 1988; Rose, 1989).

Moving towards a contemporary view of the child, the terms 'child' and 'child development' and the whole concept of childhood have been questioned. Drawing on a range of perspectives, including the emerging sociology of childhood, the concept of childhood and the social history of children are examined and discussed and an holistic view is promoted. The chapter considers issues of equality and how they affect children and also focuses on children's participation in the family and community (equality and diversity are discussed in detail in Chapter 5). Insights offered by recent research into early brain development are also evaluated.

There are multiple and diverse childhoods

A contemporary view acknowledges that childhood is not fixed and is not universal, rather it is 'mobile and shifting' (Walkerdine, 2009). This means that children experience many different and varied childhoods. There are local variations and global forms, depending on class, 'race', gender, geography, time, etc. (see Penn, 2005, 2008, for a detailed discussion of alternative childhoods). Until recently, most of the published research and writing about children, childhood and child development have focused on individual development as a natural progress towards adulthood. This natural progress is conceived as the same for all children regardless of class, gender or 'race' (see MacNaughton, 2003: 73). Much of this considerable body of work, written from the perspective of psychology and developmental psychology, has promoted what Walkerdine (2004: 107) suggests is an 'essential childhood'. This is a traditional, Western, developmental view of the child, which is used to categorise all children throughout the world (Dahlberg, 1985; Walkerdine, 1993). Penn (2005) cites Rose (1989), who makes the point that a 'normal' child is a:

> curious mix of statistical averages and historically specific value judgements. The most striking aspect of the 'normal' child is how abnormal he or she is, since there is no such person in reality and never has been. The advantage of defining normality is that it is a device that enables those in control or in charge to define, classify and treat those who do not seem to fit in. (Penn, 2005: 7)

Over 95 per cent of this literature originates from the USA (Fawcett, 2000) and much of it has been written by men, or from a male perspective. Walkerdine (1993: 451) argues that so-called 'scientific' psychological 'truths' about child development 'have to be understood in terms of the historical circumstances in which the knowledge was generated'. For Walkerdine, therefore, this knowledge has been generated in a patriarchal society and the story of child development is one that has been dominated by a male view. She argues strongly that relying on psychology to explain child development 'universalizes the masculine and European' (1993: 452).

Recently, due to the growing influence of a new sociology of childhood, cultural and anthropological studies, an alternative view which argues that childhood is an adult construction that changes over time and place has been put forward (see, for example, Gittins, 2004; James et al., 1998; Mayall, 2002; Prout and James, 1997). For MacNaughton (2003), the development of the child is not a fact but a cultural construction. When we describe a child's development, we are describing our cultural understandings and biases, not what exists in fact (Dahlberg et al., 2007).

As Penn (2005: 97) reminds us, 'the situation of most of the world's children is very different from those we study in North America and Europe'. The circumstances of the 80 per cent of the children who live in other parts of the world are significantly different in terms of wealth, health and culture (see Penn, 2005: 98–108):

> 1 in 6 children is severely hungry
>
> 1 in 7 has no health care at all
>
> 1 in 5 has no safe water and 1 in 3 has no toilet or sanitation facilities at home
>
> Over 640 million children live in dwellings with mud floors or extreme overcrowding

Over 120 million children are shut out of primary schools, the majority of them girls

180 million children work in the worst forms of child labour

1.2 million children are trafficked each year

2 million children, mostly girls, are exploited in the sex industry

Nearly half the 3.6 million people killed in conflict during the 1990s (45%) were children

Of the 15 million children orphaned by AIDS, 80% are African.

(The State of the World's Children, UNICEF, 2004)

Further, the whole idea and usefulness of actually categorising and studying something called 'child development' has been questioned (see Fawcett, 2000 for a more detailed critique). Clearly, change and transformation happen throughout human life, but the argument is about how that change is understood and constituted. Dahlberg (1985) asserts that due to the central and dominant influence of developmental psychology, our view of the child has been constrained to a scientific model of natural growth. Typically, this model of the child defines development in terms of a relatively narrow range of psychological aspects such as social, emotional and cognitive or intellectual and physical development. However, as Riley (2007) points out, these interrelated aspects are complex and developmentalism does not fully account for the complexity nor explain how they operate together in an holistic way. Zuckerman (1993) also argues that theories which suggest regular and predictable patterns of development oversimplify the reality of children's lives and actually hinder our understanding of childhood.

Dahlberg et al. (2007) contend that development itself is a problematic term to apply to childhood because it produces oppressive practices. Walkerdine (1993) and Silin (1995) argue that our perspectives on the child have contributed to their oppression and exploitation in different ways because 'we are in a process of judging their differences to us as inadequacies or weaknesses rather than alternative ways of knowing' (Silin, 1995: 49). MacNaughton (2003: 75) discusses this point and cites Cannella (1997: 64), who asserts that 'child development is an imperialist notion that justifies categorising children and diverse cultures as backward and needing help from those who are more advanced'.

However, while there is an argument for the recognition of the social construction of childhood and the emerging sociology of childhood, as articulated above and in the section below, this is only one of multiple perspectives of childhood. Walkerdine (2004), for example, rightly questions the place of modern accounts of childhood that replace psychological understandings of individual development with sociological interpretations that focus on 'how child subjects are produced' (2004: 96). She argues that this 'dualism' replaces internal views of the child with external views and that child development has a place. Considering childhood as a simple progression through defined stages is, however, too simplistic. There are multiple and diverse childhoods and, in order to study childhood, one has to consider a range of perspectives.

There are multiple perspectives on childhood

A number of alternative and multiple perspectives can be drawn on to explain contemporary childhood (Walkerdine, 2009). These perspectives are culturally influenced and change over time. As Kehily (2004) points out, different disciplines have for a long time developed different ways of approaching the study of children. Recently, however, a growing body of international work – from the perspective of sociology (Mayall, 2002; Prout, 2005), early childhood education (MacNaughton, 2003), critical theory and feminism (Walkerdine, 1993) and cultural studies (Cole, 1996) – has been critical of the place of developmental psychology in producing explanations of children as potential subjects, whose presence is only understood in terms of their place on a path towards becoming an adult (Walkerdine, 2009). A current understanding of children's development is, therefore, that it can be approached from a variety of perspectives and that these perspectives are culturally influenced and change over time.

Prout and James (1997: 8) identified the following key features of the 'new sociology of childhood':

- childhood is understood as a social construction
- childhood is a variable of social analysis
- children's relationships and cultures are worthy of study in their own right
- children are active social agents
- studying childhood involves engagement with the process of reconstructing childhood in society.

They suggest that 'the immaturity of children is a biological fact of life but the ways in which this immaturity is understood and made meaningful is a fact of culture'. For Cunningham (1995: 3), 'childhood cannot be studied in isolation from society as a whole'. In contemporary culture, childhood has become a formal category with a social status, and is seen as an important stage in development. This status has been given boundaries by our society's institutions: families, clinics, early years settings and schools, etc. Jenks (1982) and Hoyles and Evans (1989) infer that this analysis places 'childhood' within a social construct, rather than it being a natural phenomenon.

The idea of childhood as a separate state to adulthood is a modern one. Ariès (1962: 152) argues that very little distinction between children and adults was made until sometime around the 15th century: 'in mediaeval society childhood did not exist'. From the 15th century onwards, children began to appear as children, reflecting their gradual removal from everyday adult society. Then, following the advent of compulsory schooling in the late 19th century (in Europe), the specific category of 'childhood' was produced, constructed (Ariès, 1962) and institutionalised (Walkerdine, 1993).

Alternatively, Pollock (1983) suggests that it is mistaken to believe that because a past society did not possess the contemporary Western view of childhood, that society had no such concept. Even if children were regarded differently in the past, this does not mean that they were not regarded as children. However, he does acknowledge that the particular form of modern childhood is historically specific. Historical studies of childhood suggest that, in the UK, childhood was re-conceptualised between the end of the 19th century and the start of the First World War (Gittins, 1998). These studies demonstrate a significant shift in the economic and sentimental value of children. Over a fairly short period, the position of working-class children changed from one of supplementing the family income to that of a relatively inactive member of the household in economic terms to be protected from the adult world of hardship (Cunningham, 1995). Zelizer (1985) argues that children's contributions to the family in Western contexts is 'economically worthless' but 'emotionally priceless'. Children's value lies in their ability to give meaning and fulfilment to their parents' lives.

Alwin (1990) points out that the distinct category of childhood arose out of attitudinal shifts that placed children in the centre of the family and encouraged an affectionate bond between parents and their children. Thus, for Alwin, childhood is defined by four criteria: protection, segregation, dependence and delayed responsibility. Further, Gittins (2004) argues that the development of childhood as a concept was class-specific, reflecting the values and practices of a rising European middle class that increasingly differentiated adults and children, girls and boys.

Views of childhood, therefore, *have changed* and *are changing*. The main factors impacting on childhood are: economic, demographic, cultural and political. Since 1945, as a result of economic conditions in the West and the increase of compulsory schooling to the age of 16, a 'teenage' culture involving clothes, music, media and films has been constructed. Teenagers are defined by their potential spending power and targeted by advertising in the same way as adults. More recently, a further group of 'tweenagers' or 'tweenies' have been distinguished (Guardian, 2001). These are defined as 7- to 12-year-olds who already show teenage tendencies – for example, 7- to 12-year-old girls who currently shop for 'designer' clothes, wear make-up and own mobile phones.

As soon as they are born, many children across the world are immersed in a way of life where digital technology is used for a range of complex social and communication practices. These practices, which are constantly changing, include using a range of handheld devices such as mobile phones, tablet computers, multimedia players (iPods) and games consoles, playing interactive games on digital and satellite television and accessing the internet to communicate images and text, hold telephone conversations and play games with participants across the world. Currently, social network websites (shared databases of photographs that facilitate group discussion), short text messages (tweets) and blogging (contributing to online web diaries) are very popular, but as the technology develops, new and different communicative possibilities and practices will evolve (see Waller, 2010b). Although there are concerns about children who are excluded from modern communicative practices and 'digital divides' (Waller, 2010b), there is a growing recognition of the impact of digital technology on many children's lives. For example, scholars in the USA (Labbo and Reinking, 2003), Australia (Knobel and Lankshear, 2007; Yelland, 2006) and the UK (Facer et al., 2003; Marsh et al., 2005) put forward the view that electronic media has a significant influence on childhood and suggest that children's early literacy and play experiences are shaped increasingly by electronic media. Marsh (2007) contends that young children are just as engaged in current digital communicative and social practices as the older members of their families and communities.

While Postman (1983) predicted that computer use would lead to greater divisions between children and adults, this has not appeared to be the case. Many children have become experts in using technology and are able to access and use information in different ways as a result (see Facer, 2011, 2012). Yelland (2006), significantly, also argues that we need to take account of the child's perspective of electronic media.

Children are involved in co-constructing their own childhoods

While a child is clearly biologically determined as a young person, a 'child' is also socially determined in time, place, economics and culture. There is debate about the role of adults in this social construction of childhood and the agency of children in their own lives. Mayall (1996: 1), for example, has argued that 'children's lives are lived through childhoods constructed for them by adults' understanding of childhood and what children are and should be'. Currently, there is an acknowledgement of the significance of the dimension of power in relations between children and adults, and the impact of this relationship on our concept, study and understanding of children and childhood (Riley, 2007). As Connell (1987) points out, power sometimes involves the direct use of force but it is always also accompanied by the development of ideas (ideologies) that justify the actions of the powerful. Cannella and Greishaber (2001) argue that adult/child categories create an ageism that privileges adults' meanings over those of children.

Alderson (2005) draws on gender studies to identify and emphasise the significance of these adult definitions and ideas in the lives of all children. The columns in Table 2.1 relate to what women and men were assumed to be like, and Column 1 can also be applied to how children are perceived and presented in traditional child development literature and adult constructs of the child.

Alderson (2005: 131) argues that:

- children often seem weak and ignorant because they are kept in helpless dependence
- children who try to move to Column 2 may be punished
- children are not allowed to gain knowledge and experience
- it suits adults to keep Column 2 for themselves.

Table 2.1   'Half people'

Column 1 – Women	Column 2 – Men
Ignorant	Knowing
Inexperienced	Experienced
Volatile	Stable
Foolish	Wise
Dependent	Protective
Unreliable	Reliable
Weak	Strong
Immature	Mature
Irrational	Rational
Incompetent	Competent

Source: Alderson (2005: 129). Reproduced with kind permission of the Open University Press

While there are many recent examples of literature that promote positive views of competent children, Alderson argues that there is a problem, especially with older approaches, that emphasise negative stereotypes of children (based on Column 1) because of their age.

A modern view of the child acknowledges agency, that is, children's capacity to understand and act upon their world. It acknowledges that children demonstrate extraordinary competence from birth. 'Agency' and 'participation' are two key features of the new sociology of childhood, which have influenced policy and practice in early childhood education and care, as well as contemporary understanding. These are now discussed in turn.

Agency

'Agency' involves children's capacity to understand and act upon their world, thus demonstrating competence from birth (e.g. James et al., 1998; Mayall, 2002; Wyness, 2000). In addition, children are perceived as actively involved in the co-construction of their own lives. From this perspective, children are viewed as active agents who construct their own cultures (Corsaro, 2011), and have their own activities, their own time and their own space (Qvortrup et al., 1994). It seeks to understand the definitions and meaning children give to their own lives and recognises children's competence and capacity to understand and act upon their world. This perspective, therefore, sees the child as actively participating in her own childhood in accordance with Malaguzzi's (1993) concept of the 'rich child' – the child who is 'rich in potential, strong, powerful and competent' (1993: 10). For example, a child who may start to walk unaided at 11 months old is seen as playing an important role in influencing the development of this skill in the particular context of experiences within her family and community from birth, as opposed to an alternative view which suggests that the new found skill is the result of 'normal maturation'. The new sociology of childhood has therefore been critical of the place of developmental psychology in producing explanations of children as potential subjects, which classify children and their abilities into boxes, according to their age (Corsaro, 2011), and where the child is studied and tested in an 'individual' way (Cannella, 1999: 37). Despite the fact that children's agency seems to be recognised broadly in the field, there is an ongoing debate about power and the role of adults in the social construction of childhood and the agency of children in their own lives. There is therefore a need for further discussion and illumination of the terms 'agent' and 'actor'.

The fact that children can express their feelings and emotions in their surroundings confirms their ability to act competently. Nevertheless, the term 'agency' embeds a more active role (Mayall, 2002). Children as agents can express not only their desires and wishes but they can also negotiate and interact within their environment causing change. However, Cannella and Greishaber (2001) argue that adult/child categories create an ageism that privileges adults' meanings over those of children. For example, Wyness (1999) states that in practice the school system has failed to recognise the child either as a competent actor or as an agent. Mayall (2002) contends that children are best regarded as a minority social group and she locates children's agency within the restriction of this minority status. However, Hendrick (1997) makes an important point about the agency of the child. He contends that changes in the conception of childhood did not just happen, they were contested, and not least important amongst the contestants were the children themselves, but in the context of joint interaction with peers and adults.

Participation

Following on from the acknowledgement of the significance of children's agency is the recognition that children have the right to participate in processes and decisions that affect their lives. Children's views of their own childhood are therefore particularly significant. In the UK, the Children Act 1989 and the Every Child Matters agenda (DfES, 2004c) established the right of the child to be listened to. An important aspect is children's own views of their daily experience (shared with peers and adults – Emilson and Folkesson, 2006). Qvortrup et al. (1994: 2) contend that 'children are often denied the right to speak for themselves either because they are held incompetent in making judgements or because they are thought of as unreliable witnesses about their own lives'. Thomas (2001) suggests that if there is presumption of competence, rather than incompetence, children often turn out to be more capable and sophisticated than they are given credit for. He argues that the advantages of working with a presumption of competence and respect for children and what they wish to communicate are apparent in both childcare work and social research.

Central to developments in policy and services for children is a growing acknowledgement of the legitimacy and value of children's participation in research and decision-making processes. Increasingly, however, there are reservations about whether children's participation actually results in worthwhile changes and benefits for the children involved (Badham, 2004; Tisdall et al., 2004). Hill (2006), for example, discusses the problematic nature of the 'participation agenda', identifying the multiple and sometimes conflicting views of the purposes of children's participation. As Sinclair (2004) asserts, while in principle children's views should always have an impact, it is questionable whether children's views have persistently been allowed to influence the direction of research, policy and services. Hill (2006) argues that adults' views, including the underestimation of children's capacities and a desire to protect their position of power over children, are significant barriers to participation. A critical factor, therefore, is the possibility that adults have used and 'institutionalised' the participation process to keep and exert control over children (Francis and Lorenzo, 2002; Moss and Petrie, 2002; Prout, 2003). As Clark and Statham (2005) point out, most 'participatory' research still has an adult agenda.

Notions of 'agency' are also contested by Jans (2004), Kjørholt (2002) and Vandenbroeck and Bouverne-De Bie (2006), for example. Vandenbroeck and Bouverne-De Bie (2006) analyse the construction of the participating child at both micro and macro levels. They argue that participatory research and practice may actually be exclusionary because, if children are constructed as a separate but homogeneous category, their age, gender, ethnic or cultural dimensions or inequalities are masked. Vandenbroeck and Bouverne-De Bie propose reconsidering children's agency with further emphasis on context (i.e. agency has differing forms in different contexts). A key challenge in promoting children's participation therefore is how to ensure children have the space to articulate their views and perspectives beyond the constraints of adult views, interpretation and agenda (see also Chapter 4).

MacNaughton (2004: 46) suggests that 'children make their own meanings, but not under conditions of their own choosing'. MacNaughton (p. 47) identifies four 'conditions of power' that impact on children:

1. The power of pre-existing cultural imagery and cultural meanings.
2. The power of expectations.
3. The power of positions.
4. The power of the marketplace.

MacNaughton argues that children enter a pre-existing world in which each of these conditions of power is already accomplished. As an example, she discusses the children's entertainment and toy industry to show how global capital produces the material culture through which children construct their meanings. However, as Riley (2007) points out, children are powerful consumers in the multi-million-dollar industry of childhood that is focused around clothes, toys, books, and electronic and digital media (see Marsh, 2005).

The Children's Society has published research on children and young people's well-being every year since 2006. A significant on-going concern was disclosed by the Society's Good Childhood Inquiry, which revealed a consensus among adults that increasing commercialisation is damaging children's wellbeing. Eighty-nine per cent of adults felt that children nowadays are more materialistic than in past generations. Also, evidence submitted to the inquiry from children themselves suggests that they do feel under pressure to keep up with the latest trends (The Children's Society, 2008).

Professor Philip Graham (Emeritus Professor of Child Psychiatry at the Institute of Child Health, London, and an inquiry panel member) believes that commercial pressures may have worrying psychological effects on children. Evidence both from the USA and from the UK (Schor, 2004) suggests that those most influenced by commercial pressures also show higher rates of mental health problems. Bob Reitemeier (chief executive of The Children's Society) said: 'A crucial question raised by the inquiry is whether childhood should be a space where developing minds are free from concentrated sales techniques. As adults we have to take responsibility for the current level of marketing to children. To accuse children of being materialistic in such a culture is a cop out. Unless we question our own behaviour as a society we risk creating a generation who are left unfulfilled through chasing unattainable lifestyles' (The Children's Society, 2008).

The most recent *Good Childhood Report* (The Children's Society, 2013) explores the connections between wellbeing and other issues in children's lives in the UK (see also Chapter 12). This report argues that children's levels of wellbeing can be changed and improved by external factors. In particular, the report shows that children in their early teenage years appear to 'fare worse than other age groups. In the eight to 17 age range, 14- and 15-year-olds have lower wellbeing than younger or older children for most aspects of their lives. In addition, whilst children in the UK experienced a rise in wellbeing between 1994 and 2008, this appears to have stalled and may have begun to reverse in the most recent years' (2013: 6).

Although the report acknowledges that 'around four-fifths of children are "flourishing", meaning that they are both satisfied with their lives and find their lives worthwhile', worryingly the report makes a clear link between poverty and low wellbeing and the subsequent impact on children's lives:

> Children with low wellbeing are over 20 times less likely than other children to feel safe at home, eight times more likely to say that their family does not get along well together and five times more likely to report having recently been bullied. Children who lack five or more items on our deprivation index are 13 times less likely to feel safe at home and six times less likely to feel positive about the future. (The Children's Society, 2013: 6)

However, whilst it is important to acknowledge the serious effect of external factors on children's lives, such as poverty, there is debate in contemporary literature about the influence of adult power on childhood – here, children are seen as actively involved in the co-construction of their own lives. A modern explanation of childhoods therefore seeks to understand the definitions and meaning children give to their own lives and recognises children's competence and capacity to understand and act upon their world.

Children's participation in family, community and culture makes a particular contribution to their own life

Much of the recent literature in the field of early childhood argues that there is a need to consider the wider political, social and cultural context of childhood. Bronfenbrenner (1977) acknowledged a range of contextual factors that impact directly and indirectly on the development of a child in his concept of ecological systems (see Berk, 2007 for a more detailed discussion). Ecological systems theory represents the child's development as multi-layered and the benefit of this model is that it places the child and the child's experience at the heart of the process of development. While it is a useful framework, it can be used to imply that context is something that impacts *on* the child, rather than *with* and *through* the child's participation. It does not fully articulate agency and co-construction.

The recent influential work of proponents of the sociocultural or 'situative perspective', such as Rogoff (1998, 2003), will now be briefly considered. The sociocultural perspective has adapted and enhanced the ideas of Vygotsky (1978, 1986) and provided valuable new insights into the collaborative nature of learning and the social construction of knowledge. It has been particularly influential in the field of early childhood. This perspective takes into account not just the child, but the social, historical, institutional and cultural factors in which the child participates and co-constructs. It recognises that human activity is heavily influenced by *context*, which includes artefacts and other people. The sociocultural approach also emphasises the shared construction and distribution of knowledge, leading to the development of shared understanding and common knowledge, (Edwards and Mercer, 1987; Greeno, 1997; Lave, 1988; Rogoff, 1990). As a result, the child is not seen as an individual learner but as a participant in a range of meaningful and instructional social practices. Learning and development are inseparable from the concerns of families and interpersonal and community processes. This is a dynamic and evolving cultural context, in which it is meaningless to study the child apart from other people. Participation, as contrasted with acquisition, is therefore a key concept here.

Jordan's (2004) model of co-construction, where there is equal partnership between the adult and child and the emphasis is on the child as a powerful player in his/her own learning, is particularly relevant here. Rogoff (2003) has argued that communities of learners involve complex group relationships among students who learn to take responsibility for contributing to their own learning and to the group's projects. In these communities of learners, meaning is only established when ideas are jointly understood and enacted within the particular community. For Lave and Wenger (1991), learning therefore involves a deepening process of participation in a community of practice. This process also involved the development of a range of resources such as tools, documents, routines, vocabulary and symbols that store the accumulated knowledge of the community (Wenger, 1998).

Rogoff (1990) proposed the concept of guided participation to explain the way that children learn as they participate in, and are guided by, the values and practices of their cultural communities. Guided participation involves two basic processes or shared endeavours supported by a mutual structuring of participation (each other's involvement to facilitate engagement in the shared activity), leading to the co-construction of knowledge (Rogoff, 2003: 283). Children experience competence and are recognised as competent (Wenger, 1998).

Theoretically, both Rogoff (2003) and Corsaro (2011) view children's transition into society through the lens of participation in collective mutual communities. What Corsaro et al. (2002) call 'priming events' is similar to Rogoff's notion of 'participatory appropriation' and 'guided participation', while both argue that the personal, interpersonal and institutional should be analysed together, not separately and in isolation. Additionally, they believe that in the process of interpretative reproduction, common and collective activities take place where children construct and produce culture with peers and adults. However, the difference between interpretive reproduction and Rogoff's theory is the fact that the latter does not fully consider 'the importance of socio-economic and power relations' (Corsaro et al., 2002: 323).

For this reason Corsaro et al. (2002), in their study about children's transition from the pre-school to the elementary school in the USA and Italy, focus on the interpersonal, community and individual analysis (as Rogoff, 2003), but they extend the process by also looking at peer culture and how the power of social policies in early years education and care has influenced values and activities. Corsaro (2011) also found that children's participation in adults' initiatives and activities often produces annoyance, confusion, fear and uncertainty due to the power imbalance between the child and the adult. Thus he states that often children's intentions arise as a result of their effort to make sense of the adult's world.

For Corsaro, children's participation in cultural routines is extremely valuable. Daily routines with their vibrancy, predictability, safekeeping and shared understanding provide the habits that make children and adults feel membership of a community, where they can deal with contentious or dubious issues. The process of participation in cultural routines begins from the time that a child is born. It starts as a limited participation based on the 'as-if assumption' (Corsaro, 2011: 19), where the infant is treated as if they are socially competent and goes forward to full participation, not due to the fact that the child learns the rules but due to the security that they feel and control of the activity or the discussion, which the infant then embellishes with new thoughts and activities.

The significant contribution of the sociology of childhood to contesting 'normative', singular and static notions of the child and childhood should be recognised. As James (2009) argues, what is most important is for adults to understand children's contribution to society and their right for agency, or, as Ratner (2000) asserts, the democratic circumstances under which the child can show the potentiality of agency. However, a number of conceptual tensions in these powerful ideas have recently been identified. Uprichard (2008), for example, suggests that the arguments around the child as 'being' and 'becoming' are problematic. She recommends an alternative concept of the child underpinned by the temporality of the two terms. Uprichard (2008) argues that the fact that children are not always children but are moving towards adulthood creates a temporality.

Further, as Bae (2009) and Ratner (2000) contend, there is an overemphasis on the notion of the autonomous child and the other aspect of 'the child in need' is underestimated. Thus Uprichard (2008) and Corsaro (2011) state that the new sociology of childhood, in an effort to define the child as socially constructed individually, neglects the great contribution of the development of the child through interaction in sociocultural processes. Here, as Smith (2007) states, is the contribution of sociocultural theory – discerning how children are supported in the co-construction of activities (Rogoff, 2003). The role of the adult is to sustain and encourage a child's interest to 'help focus on the goal, draw attention to critical features of the task, and reduce the complexity of the task. But there has to be social engagement before children can learn and gradually take on more responsibility' (Smith, 2007: 154).

As Waller and Bitou (2011) argue, a key challenge in promoting children's participation is how to ensure that children have the space to articulate their views and perspectives beyond the constraints of adult views, interpretations and agendas. There remain reservations about whether children's participation actually results in worthwhile changes and benefits for the children involved (Hill, 2006), the danger that participation has become institutionalised and also the possibility that participatory research and practice may actually be exclusionary (Vandenbroeck and Bouverne-De Bie, 2006).

We are still learning about children and childhood

If children are active participants in dynamic and evolving cultural contexts, as argued above, it follows that we will always be learning about children and childhood. In addition, changes in technology and new methods of investigation and research can also generate new areas of knowledge and understanding. One aspect of young children's progress that has received considerable attention over the past fifteen years is early brain development. Following recent advances in computer technology, leading to the development of brain imaging techniques, such as functional magnetic resonance imaging (fMRI) and positron emission tomography (PET) scans, neuroscientists have been able to measure activity in the brain and map the growth of the brain (Blakemore, 2000; Goswami, 2004).

However, there has been considerable debate surrounding the implications of this neuroscientific research for education and care in the early years (BERA SIG, 2003) which has led to a number of misconceptions and 'neuromyths' (CERI, 2007). Bruer (1997), for example, argued that making links between cognitive neuroscience and education is 'a bridge too far'. Alternatively, whilst Goswami (2004) views some of the popular beliefs about the potential of neuroscience for early education as 'unrealistic', she argues that new brain science technologies can complement rather than replace traditional methods of educational enquiry.

What the research has usefully shown is that there is a very rapid increase in the development of the brain for young children, especially those under 3 years of age (Riley, 2007). The brain appears as early as the third week after conception (27 days) and develops rapidly, so that by the end of the seventh month of pregnancy, the baby's brain has all the neurons of the adult brain and many to spare (Catherwood, 1999). Crucial are the synapses – the connections between cells (neurons) where information is exchanged. Most of the development of synapses occurs after birth, however, at birth, the neonate has approximately half the number of synapses of the adult brain. Very rapid growth then occurs from 2 to 4 months, so that by 6 months a baby has more synapses than an adult. Stimulation from the environment causes 'learning' either by stabilising existing networks in the brain or by forging new ones. The ability of the brain to develop connections (or synapses) is known as plasticity. Recent brain research summarised by the Royal Society (2011) shows that plasticity tends to decrease with age and Blakemore (2000) revealed that, after the age of 3, plasticity continues at a slower rate until the age of 10.

Bransford et al. (2000) review the work of sixteen leading researchers in cognitive science in the USA. Key conclusions from this evidence suggest, according to BERA SIG (2003), that learning changes the structure of the brain; learning organises and reorganises the brain, and different parts of the brain may be ready to learn at different times. Thus, although there are prime times for certain types of learning, the brain also has a remarkable capacity to change.

BERA SIG (2003: 19) also usefully summarises evidence from brain research that matches with psychological research, as follows:

1. Experience – everything that goes on around the young child changes the brain.
2. Everything the baby sees, hears, touches and smells influences the developing network of connections among the brain cells.
3. Other people play a critical role.
4. Babies and young children have powerful learning capacities.
5. Babies and young children actually participate in building their own brain.
6. Radically deprived environments may influence development.

The OECD Centre for Educational Research and Innovation (CERI, 2007) identified a number of 'neuromyths' where scientific findings are translated into misinformation about the benefits of neuroscience for education. In particular, the OECD report focused on myths around 'critical periods' for learning, when plasticity is greatest.

The argument is that if children do not have certain experiences during these critical periods, they will forever miss the opportunity to benefit from the experience, and that the most effective educational interventions need to be timed with these periods (Goswami, 2004). For this reason, some writers (such as Brierley, 1994; Sylwester, 1995) advocate 'hothousing' – for example, starting to teach music to children under 3, because the brain is so receptive to learning early on (see Blakemore, 2000).

It is now argued that while there are optimal 'windows of opportunity' for the development of synapses in the first three years, the brain is extremely flexible (CERI, 2007). An individual's capacities are therefore not fixed at birth, or in the first three years of life (Bransford et al., 2000). Blakemore and Frith (2005) assert that research on plasticity suggests that the brain is well equipped for lifelong learning and adaptation to the environment, and that there is no biological necessity to rush and start formal teaching earlier and earlier. As a result, OECD contends that there are no 'critical periods' when learning must take place, but there are 'sensitive periods' when an individual is particularly primed to engage in specific learning activities (CERI, 2007). Further, it is increasingly recognised that efficient learning does not take place when the learner is experiencing fear or inappropriate stress (Goswami, 2004), and the technology used in neuroscience has helped to demonstrate the effect that inappropriate stress has on both physiological and cognitive functioning. For Blakemore and Frith (2005), the main implication of the current research findings on sensitive periods is that it is important to identify and, if possible, treat children's sensory problems (such as visual and hearing difficulties), because the findings suggest that early sensory deprivation can have lasting consequences. However, they also suggest that even after sensory deprivation, it is possible for recovery and learning still to take place.

There is, therefore, much further research to be done in the field of neuroscience, and into how this research may support our understanding of young children's lives. There is some continued scepticism in early childhood about the limited currency of biomedical explanations of learning. Wilson (2002), for example, discusses how neuroscientific research has provided the impetus for the introduction of early intervention programmes targeting groups who are considered to be 'at risk'. She argues that 'the factors impacting on childhood outcomes are complex and cannot be reduced solely to biomedical explanations. A more effective way to tackle child health and welfare problems would involve a multi-dimensional approach and include the elimination of poverty and the scrutiny of all public policy' (2002: 191). In addition, the Teaching and Learning Research Project (TLRP) (2007: 10) also argue that 'contrary to much popular belief, there is no convincing neuroscientific case for starting formal education as early as possible'. The TLRP also contends that because research based on the fMRI (neuroimaging) is often not appropriate for studies of young children, the literature in this field tells us more about the adult brain than about that of a developing child.

Finally, both the TLRP and the recent Royal Society (2011) report on neuroscience and the implications for education, argue that there is a growing need for a multi-disciplinary approach that involves collaborations between neuroscience, psychology and education. This collaboration could involve the development of a common language, or grammar, in the field of neuroscience and education, but we are still at an early stage in our understanding of the brain.

We also have much to learn about children's lives and childhood across the world, although despite the continued paucity of published research about children from developing countries, we are now much better informed about their (often tragic) circumstances due to the series of detailed reports entitled *The State of the World's Children* published every year by the United Nations Children's Fund (UNICEF). *The State of the World's Children 2005* focused on children's rights and argued that the promise underpinning the United Nations Convention of the Rights of the Child (UNCRC) (United Nations, 1989) already appears broken, as poverty, armed conflict and HIV/AIDS threaten children's survival and development. The report calls on all stakeholders – governments, donors, international agencies, as well as communities, families, businesses and individuals – to reaffirm and recommit to their moral and legal responsibilities to children (UNICEF, 2005).

Since 2005, the reports have shifted focus to make recommendations for action to improve the lives of children that are related to the Millennium Development Goals (MDGs). The MDGs are eight targets to be achieved by 2015 that respond to the world's main development challenges:

Goal 1: Eradicate extreme poverty and hunger

Goal 2: Achieve universal primary education

Goal 3: Promote gender equality and empower women

Goal 4: Reduce child mortality

Goal 5: Improve maternal health

Goal 6: Combat HIV/AIDS, malaria and other diseases

Goal 7: Ensure environmental sustainability

Goal 8: Develop a Global Partnership for Development

The MDGs are drawn from the actions and targets contained in the Millennium Declaration that was adopted by 189 nations and signed by 147 heads of state and governments during the UN Millennium Summit in September 2000 (see www.un.org/millenniumgoals/).

The State of the World's Children 2006 (UNICEF, 2006) concerned excluded and invisible children, including those living in the poorest countries and most deprived communities; children facing discrimination on the basis of gender, ethnicity, disability or membership of an indigenous group; children caught up in armed conflict or affected by HIV/AIDS; and children who lack a formal identity, who suffer child protection abuses or who are not treated as children. The report focused on the actions that those responsible for their wellbeing must take to safeguard and include them. *The State of the World's Children 2007* (UNICEF, 2007a) investigated the discrimination and disempowerment women face throughout their lives – and outlined action that should be taken to eliminate gender discrimination and empower women and girls. *The State of the World's Children 2008: Child Survival* (UNICEF, 2008a) examined the global realities of maternal and child survival and the prospects for meeting the health-related Millennium Development Goals (MDGs) for children and mothers in each of the five main sub-regions of Africa. Consequently, in 2008 UNICEF was moved to publish the inaugural edition of *The State of Africa's Children* (UNICEF, 2008b), which identified the urgent need for large-scale investment in health care for Africa to help prevent the deaths of 5 million children every year. This was further emphasised in 2009, when *The State of the World's Children* (UNICEF, 2009a) focused on Africa and Asia, identifed the importance of maternal and newborn health in achieving the targets set, and the need for antenatal care and skilled attendants during birth and in the period after birth.

A Special Edition of *The State of the World's Children* was produced in 2010, with a focus on children's rights and providing updates across all eight of the targets set (UNICEF, 2010). Since that special edition, further reports have identified the need to ensure adolescents have access to opportunities to enable them to have fulfilling lives, without fear of abuse or exploitation, and the need to ensure urban children, who represent almost half of all children, have their needs identified and met. The 2013 report of *The State of the World's Children* identified the importance of recognising what disabled children can do, rather than what they cannot achieve (UNICEF, 2013).

UNICEF maintains that meeting the Millennium Development Goals (MDGs) and the broader aims of the Millennium Declaration would transform the lives of millions of children who would be spared illness and premature death, escape extreme poverty and malnutrition, gain access to safe water and decent sanitation facilities and complete primary schooling.

Chapter summary

This chapter has identified and discussed five key tenets of contemporary childhood. The tenets have articulated a complex model of childhood that is fundamentally different from a narrow 'developmental' approach. This model acknowledges that there are multiple and diverse childhoods. There are local variations and global forms, depending on class, 'race', gender, geography and time. This model also acknowledges that while there are multiple perspectives on childhood, it would be wrong to ignore or disregard developmental insights. Views of childhood have changed and are changing. Students of early childhood need to understand how and why child development theory is a product of certain historical, cultural and economic conditions. Some theoretical perspectives are particularly suited to explaining certain aspects of growth and change over time but the complex and interlinked nature of children's 'development' needs to be recognised. Developmental psychology should be studied alongside sociological, historical and anthropological accounts of childhood.

However, a critical difference between contemporary and traditional views of childhood is that the former recognises the differing contexts of children's lives, children's agency and the significance of children's involvement in co-constructing their own childhood through participation in family, community and culture.

After 150 years of recognised child study, we are still learning about children and childhood, the power of adults and the ability of children to determine their own future. Greater recognition of children's perspectives, the impact of new technology on children's lives and research methods will lead to further insights that will strengthen understanding and articulate new theories of early childhood.

Questions for reflection and discussion

1. How do children shape their own development?
2. How does change occur?
3. How do children become so different from each other?
4. How can you find out?
5. How should we deal with theories that do not recognise multiple and diverse childhoods and the power relationships between children and adults?

Recommended reading

Corsaro, W.A. (2011) *The Sociology of Childhood*, 3rd edn. London: Sage.

Dahlberg, G., Moss, P. and Pence, A. (2007) *Beyond Quality in Early Childhood Education and Care: Languages of Evaluation*, 2nd edn. London and New York: RoutledgeFalmer.

Harcourt, D., Perry, B. and Waller, T. (eds) (2011) *Researching Young Children's Perspectives: Debating the Ethics and Dilemmas of Educational Research with Children*. Abingdon: Routledge.

Penn, H. (2008) *Understanding Early Childhood: Issues and Controversies*, 2nd edn. Maidenhead: Open University Press/McGraw-Hill.

Prout, A. (2005) *The Future of Childhood: Towards the Interdisciplinary Study of Children*. London: Falmer Press.

Recommended websites

www.goodchildhood.org.uk
The reports of the *Good Childhood Inquiry* on The Children's Society website.

www.unicef.org/publications/index.html
For the UNICEF yearly reports on *The State of the World's Children*.

Want to learn more about this chapter? Visit the companion website at **www.sagepub.co.uk/walleranddavis3e** to access podcasts from the author and child observation videos.

3

International Perspectives

Libby Lee-Hammond with Tim Waller

 Key chapter objectives

- To discuss findings from recent international comparisons of early childhood education and care
- To provide an overview of issues related to early years policy and provision in OECD countries
- To consider diverse curricula and the notions of 'quality' and 'equity'
- To examine examples of early years education and care in various countries
- To introduce students to the insights that can be developed through comparison

Introduction

This chapter will discuss findings from recent international comparative studies of early childhood education and care, in particular the recent OECD (Organization for Economic Cooperation and Development) thematic review (2012) reported in *Starting Strong III* will be examined. A discussion of approaches to early childhood curricula from a range of countries will provide students with an overview of international trends and provision for early childhood education and care.

Within this discussion, important debates about what constitutes 'quality' and 'equity' in early childhood settings will be explored with regard to policy implications and provision of early years programmes with particular reference to First Nations (also known as Indigenous or Aboriginal) children.

Current issues and significant trends in early years care and education are identified and discussed in this chapter and a number of significant similarities and trends are identified, however it is recognised that wider evidence is needed to represent a global view of early childhood education and care (ECEC). It is not the intention to provide detailed statistics, although some are given, rather to enable students of early childhood to engage in critical reflection on the benefit of cross-national studies.

Increasingly, the UK is taking note of early years care and education policy and practice in other countries – notably those within Europe and the OECD. This chapter explores the principles and practices adopted by a selected group of countries using the OECD thematic review as a framework. It aims to give students the opportunity to compare a variety of practices and consider possible outcomes and implications for children related to a holistic perspective. The chapter discusses both curricular and policy issues and encourages readers to critically analyse current policy and practice in early years care and education.

It is important to note, as Clark and Waller (2007) demonstrate, that for ECEC, children's services and many of the policies that impact on young children and their families, there are growing differences between England, Northern Ireland, Scotland and Wales as a result of devolved government. Therefore, it is misleading to consider the UK as a whole in these matters.

Recently, the range of information and knowledge about international aspects of early years care has increased due to the availability of online data and publications (see, for example, online early years journals such as *Contemporary Issues in Early Childhood* [www.words.co.uk/ciec] and the *Journal of Early Childhood Research* [ecr.sagepub.com]). However, it should be acknowledged that most of the online material is available in English and to a large extent concerns English-speaking countries and Europe, so it does not represent a global perspective and a complete picture of early childhood education and care internationally (see Clark and Waller, 2007). As Moss et al. (2003) point out, one of the problems of limiting our attention to those countries to which we are similar is that we risk missing some of the most important reasons for doing cross-national study. There is a need for wider comparison through further data from a greater number of countries around the world.

Philosophical approaches informing early years provision

In their work comparing English, Italian and New Zealand early years provision, Soler and Miller (2003) note that 'Parents, teachers, researchers and politicians often have strong and conflicting views about what is right for young children in the years before school.

Curricula can become "sites of struggle" between ideas about what early childhood education is for, and what are appropriate content and contexts for learning and development in early childhood' (p. 57); in different contexts these views are expressed through the curriculum.

In making comparisons between the different curricula, Soler and Miller point out that there is considerable tension between an instrumental/vocational approach to education and a sociocultural/progressive approach to early years learning, noting that:

> a growing pressure from vocational and instrumental influences can impact on progressive and socioculturally inspired early childhood curricula and approaches. A comparison of these examples also reveals how early childhood curricula and educational systems are often forged amidst differing contexts in relation to national and local control of early childhood curricula and approaches. These differing contexts can also give rise to differing conceptualisations of knowledge, learning and pedagogy. (Soler and Miller, 2003: 57)

Little has changed since this paper was published in 2003 and in many countries this struggle continues. It is these philosophical positions of instrumental and sociocultural that we will now explore in more detail.

Philosophical positions regarding the goals of early education and care

Philosophical approaches to ECEC can be described in many ways; one simple way to think of these approaches is as existing on a continuum from *instrumental* to *progressive*. Those that are *instrumental* are primarily informed by economic arguments exemplified in the oft-quoted statement that for every pound spent on ECEC a nation can save up to seven times that amount on 'fixing problems' later in life. This rationale for ECEC is informed by the 'economic benefit' to the country. The progressive approach is focused more on the child in context and the importance of quality experiences to provide a foundation for individual and social wellbeing.

An argument for ECEC that aligns with an instrumental approach is that 'we need productive workers for a strong economy'. Instrumental approaches can have a detrimental impact on early years education and ultimately on our entire society. Let's explore why this is so. The economic instrumental argument for ECEC is flawed because the underlying rationale is economic benefit and is founded on the belief that humans must be trained to make a contribution as workers, above all else. We know that the *whole person* is part of this mechanism and it is their social, spiritual, cultural, emotional and relational wellbeing that actually contributes to a healthy and functioning society. If we value more highly someone's economic contribution above all else, we become enslaved to the notion that education is about preparation for work.

The end product of schooling then is primarily labour-driven. In many countries conservative governments systematically measure educational outcomes through standardised testing of literacy and numeracy as if these were the only benchmarks of a worthwhile education. Freire and others, such as Dewey and Rousseau, invite us to consider education as a process of social change. An instrumental approach promotes the status quo. An example of a schooling system adopting an instrumental approach can be found in Australia, where national testing, teacher competencies and standardised curricula have become mandated in all schools. Student results on national tests are now linked to teacher appraisal and salaries, and are published on the internet. This public identification of low-achieving schools, by implication, identifies 'low performing' teachers with no regard for the socioeconomic factors impacting on particular school cohorts and student performance. Such a system propagates a culture of market competition based on student performance and this is having an impact on the earliest years of school, where a more formal curriculum is taught earlier than in the past in the belief that this will result in higher test scores in later years. The resultant demise of creative play experiences in ECEC will have a large impact when this generation leaves the school system with skills to pass tests but with little or no critical or creative skills (Lee-Hammond, 2012a). Freire (1970) argued that this instrumental approach to education was detrimental to creativity. We will see later in this chapter how an instrumental approach to education has been particularly problematic for Indigenous populations.

Freire, a Brazilian philosopher and educator, argued in 1985 that education institutions are highly political places and are designed to transmit knowledge that is instrumental to the existing structures in society. Freire was particularly interested in the impact of mainstream education on the oppressed. His seminal work *Pedagogy of the Oppressed* made a major contribution to what is now known as *critical pedagogy*. Freire referred to schooling as a banking model whereby 'it transforms students into receiving objects. It attempts to control thinking and action, leads men and women to adjust to the world, and inhibits their creative power' (Freire, 1970: 77). Freire encouraged resistance to instrumental education and the liberation of the oppressed through educational reform.

Programmes that are *progressive* draw on the early work of Rousseau, Dewey, Froebel, Montessori and Malaguzzi, who see the child as a *protagonist*, or active participant, in their learning. These progressive approaches have been elaborated in sociocultural theory (Rogoff, 2003; Vygotsky, 1978) which acknowledges the social context of the learning environment as a fundamental ingredient in the learning process. Prior knowledge and experience play a vital role in a sociocultural learning environment; the educator determines the child's current level of knowledge and what he or she is capable of doing with some adult support through discussion. Interactions are very important in a sociocultural learning environment where the educator provides learning opportunities for young children in the immediate vicinity of their existing knowledge. Vygotsky named this space between the child's independent knowledge and skills and that which they might attain, but where they need support of a 'more expert other', as the Zone of Proximal Development (Vygotsky, 1978). The Reggio Emilia schools in Italy provide an excellent example of a sociocultural approach, using local, contextualised child-initiated approaches to curriculum (Edwards et al., 1998), rather than the centralised, vocation-oriented approaches used in countries like Australia, England and the USA.

Policy context

The OECD has conducted a series of analyses of early childhood policies from 1998 to 2012 (see www.oecd.org/education/preschoolandschool/). This series provides useful insights into the diverse approaches to early education and care across a number of countries. Comparative research in early childhood is still dominated by the OECD countries (Bennett, 2011), however some work from developing countries and the BRIC countries (Brazil, Russia, India and China) is emerging. National policies for care and education have been analysed in the OECD reports and what has been identified is a great variation in the organisation of early childhood systems across OECD countries.

Bennett (2011) provides an extremely useful insight into how this diversity came about through the historical development of provision for young children and their families. From the 18th century, charitable care institutions began to appear in large European cities; these were primarily for poor, abandoned or orphaned children. Subsequently, in the 19th century, more affluent children were afforded early education to teach national languages and culture. Hence, two separate systems evolved: one that came under the auspices of the health or social ministries of government and the other that became the responsibility of the education ministry. In many OECD countries this dichotomy of 'care' and 'education' has remained. In the 20th century, the rise of feminism and two world wars contributed to further changes in Nordic countries following the Second World War. With the increasing number of women in the workforce and an unprecedented demand for childcare, a decision was made in some Nordic countries to integrate the two jurisdictions for ease of administration and efficiency. This integration of care and education became the norm in Nordic and Soviet countries. Since that time, numerous other countries have followed suit, such as New Zealand, Australia, Iceland, Spain, England, Scotland, Slovenia and the Netherlands (Bennett, 2011), while, according to Corter et al. (2006), nine OECD countries have combined early education and care systems for children under 6 years of age.

Integrated children's services

There is a large body of literature considering the benefits and rationale of an integrated model for the ECEC needs of children, their families and carers (see, for example: Anning, 2005; Bennett, 2008; Corter et al., 2006; Davis, 2011; French, 2007; Hawker, 2006, 2010; Lepler et al., 2006; Percy-Smith, 2005; Siraj-Blatchford, 2007; Tunstill et al., 2006; Valentine et al., 2007).

It is clear that family life is more complex now than it has ever been (Hayes et al., 2010; Walsh, 2012). Provision for families and children must respond to the changing nature of family life in the 21st century. A trend away from 'service provision' to partnership is supported by Whalley (2006), who notes:

> the aim of Children's Centres is to develop the capacity of children and parents to be competent users of services – not just 'clients' passively receiving generous dollops of welfare state services but equal and active partners in developing and reviewing the effectiveness of what's on offer. (Whalley, 2006: 8)

Hence, *partnerships* and *relationships* will be essential to coherent and integrated provision for families and children in the new millennium (O'Donnell et al., 2010).

Snapshot from Canada

Canada has been at the forefront of offering a range of Indigenous-specific integrated early childhood programmes utilising community-oriented and holistic approaches with families and children (Sims et al., 2008). This is best exemplified in Toronto 'First Duty' (City of Toronto, 2011). This model incorporates professional teams of carers, health professionals and educators working in an integrated manner. An important feature of this model and a key to its success is the full participation in decision making of the community members themselves. Elders have had major input into developing programmes and curricula based around cultural knowledge and community-driven priorities. Later in this chapter we will examine a model in New Zealand with similar Indigenous self-determination as its basis. These are examples of Freire's (1985) argument that oppressed communities can only change from within by taking control of the systems that have oppressed them. Both Canada and New Zealand, then, are examples of systemic efforts to enable progressive or sociocultural approaches to be embedded in national provision for families and young children.

Snapshot from England

The Every Child Matters initiative (DfES, 2004c) became England's model of integrated services for children and families. Known as 'joined up' programmes, the integrated support for families and children was manifest in the Sure Start Centres that replaced previously isolated centres based around the division of care and education. The Sure Start Centres were designed to 'provide early education integrated with health and family support services, and childcare' (Sure Start, 2008). Although the service has now been reduced, these Sure Start Centres continue to provide an important base for integrated services. The Every Child Matters agenda has been superseded by a new policy document, *Supporting Families in the Foundation Years* (DfE, 2011a). The changes in policy direction within England, with the change of government in 2010, are discussed in Chapter 16.

Policy and provision

The OECD report *Starting Strong III: A Quality Toolbox for Early Childhood Education and Care* (2012) notes that the overall benefits of ECEC are well documented. However, the report does recognise that not all provision is 'equal' and that an emphasis on the *quality* of programmes offered to young children is essential. An understanding of what is regarded as high quality varies between countries and is highly contested in the literature (Dahlberg et al., 2007; Laevers, 1994; Raban et al., 2003; Tobin, 2005). In this section we will explore the notion of quality as it relates to curriculum and pedagogy, and parental and community engagement.

Starting Strong III examines *quality* in terms of both setting quality goals and setting minimum standards. *Starting Strong III* identifies that key expectations for ECEC are diverse and context-dependent. The priorities of diverse groups make a definition of quality as a singular concept very difficult. The key quality goals across countries in the OECD vary substantially. In some countries, where childcare and early childhood education remain separate, differences are identified in quality goals, funding arrangements and training. Bennett (2008) describes this as a 'patchwork of private providers and individual family day carers' (p. 3). The distinction between education and care can result in families having to navigate across different sectors with different goals, funding and regulations, and often it is the lower income families who miss out on costly care for children in an unregulated system. In addition, staff in these settings are often poorly paid, have low educational attainment and may not be protected by wage agreements and other benefits. Recently, Australia has adopted a National Quality Framework for Education and Care (Australian Government, 2013), bringing the care and education sectors into alignment for the first time and demanding that all childcare centres employ a qualified Early Childhood Educator. The nomenclature for qualified staff working with children has also changed from 'carer' or 'teacher' to *'educator'* regardless of the setting (i.e. childcare centres, family day care or kindergarten). The professionalisation of the childcare sector is a major shift in consciousness in Australia, affording more importance to the work of those educating the very young.

The Starting Strong III toolkit mentioned earlier notes that the philosophical orientation of ECEC in a country (instrumental through to progressive) has a major influence on the way in which it provides for young children and their families. If the country's broad view regarding the early years is instrumental, there tends to be little government involvement in the 0–3 age range as this childcare is seen as the parents' responsibility (Dearing et al., 2009; Rutanen, 2011). In countries where there is a more progressive or sociocultural view of early childhood, services tend to be more holistic and integrated across care and education and a shared understanding of the objectives of ECEC tends to exist between practitioners, parents and others (Bennett, 2008; OECD, 2006).

In the *Starting Strong III* report it is argued that shared quality goals are essential to provide purpose and orientation to programmes, coherence for families and clarity for practitioners. They also enable a shared dialogue with government around the allocation of resources and thus minimising overlap and gaps in provision for families. The Starting Strong III toolkit nominates a set of 'policy levers' to effectively ensure quality goals can be attained. They are designed to be used by policy makers to enable easy access to the research and strategies that will bring about high quality provision for young children and their families. The levers are:

1. Setting out quality goals and regulations
2. Designing and implementing curricula and standards
3. Improving qualifications, training and working conditions
4. Engaging families and communities
5. Advancing data collection, research and monitoring

These levers indicate a movement towards progressive approaches to early years education and care in OECD countries, particularly with the emphasis on engaging families and communities.

Investigating quality: the EPPE project

The Effective Provision of Pre-school Education (EPPE) project is a study of 3,000 English children. The EPPE study utilised the the Early Childhood Environment Rating Scale – Revised (ECERS) (Harms et al., 1998) to predict children's intellectual and language progress from age 3 (entry to school) to 5 years. The study sought to examine the relationship between the quality of the environment (using the ECERS) and the developmental progress of the 3,000 children (Sylva et al., 2004, 2006).

Major findings of the study (Sylva et al., 2004) include:

*   There is a significant link between high quality (as measured with the ECERS) and child outcomes.
*   Children in high quality pre-school settings were better prepared socially for transitioning to school.

- Quality is not dependent on the type of service although integrated services tended to have higher ratings while playgroups and private nurseries had lower scores.
- Staff qualifications are strongly related to quality; in particular, if a manager or director of a centre has ECEC qualifications, quality is higher.
- Qualified teachers working directly with children are associated with better outcomes for children in reading and social development.

In addition to using the rating scales in a range of settings, the EPPE study investigated a dozen centres identified as high quality, conducting case studies to further understand the elements that contribute to high quality ratings. The findings of the case studies are useful for practitioners wishing to ensure that the learning environments they prepare are optimal. The elements are (Sylva et al., 2004):

- quality of adult–child verbal interactions
- staff knowledge and understanding of the curriculum
- knowledge of how young children learn
- adults' skill in supporting children to resolve conflicts
- helping parents to support children's learning at home.

Investigating quality: the CLASS

Like the ECERS, the Classroom Assessment Scoring System (CLASS) (Pianta et al., 2008) draws on developmental theory to measure quality in learning environments. The instrument is based on the premise that interactions between adults and children are the most influential aspect of the learning environment on student learning. The instrument is devised in a way that utilises a series of observations of classroom environments in three domains: emotional support, classroom organisation and instructional support. The three domains are supported by ten dimensions (see below) and exemplars for each are provided. The dimensions are allocated scores on a continuum of low to high, based on their presence or absence during the six observation periods.

Emotional support consists of: positive climate, negative climate, teacher sensitivity, regard for student perspectives.

Classroom organisation consists of: behaviour management, productivity, instructional learning formats.

Instructional support consists of: concept development, quality of feedback and language modelling.

This instrument therefore enables observers to pinpoint quality aspects of the learning environment. For example, an environment might score very high on positive climate and very low on concept development. This enables educators, through reflective practice, to appreciate the strengths of the environment and address those areas of the learning environment that are less than optimal.

Equity measures

Equity is the most commonly cited policy priority for ECEC among OECD countries (OECD, 2012). The following section will outline policy and provision to promote equity in international contexts with particular reference to First Nations children in Australia, New Zealand, Canada, Norway and Finland. A case study of Aboriginal early years in Australia (Harrison, 2011; Lee-Hammond, 2012b) will be presented with sub-sequent discussion regarding Aboriginal children in Canada (Preston et al., 2012) and Sámi early years education in Norway and Finland (Keskitalo et al., 2011).

Provision for First Nations children is particularly important because of the globally documented disadvantage experienced by First Nations populations. It is clear that many funded ECEC programmes are founded on values of the dominant culture. In particular these values include: individual achievement, outcomes, competition, objectivity and judgement. These values are a poor fit with First Nations ways of knowing and being (Preston et al., 2012). Programmes for young Indigenous children that are specifically organised around a more culturally appropriate set of values are critical if the unacceptable inequalities in life expectancy, health and education are to be addressed. Examples in New Zealand, Australia, Canada and Finland all point to some common principles in appropriately catering for First Nations children, their families and communities.

Australia

In order to address the unacceptable social and economic disadvantage experienced throughout Aboriginal Australia, the Council of Australian Governments (COAG) set some national targets in 2008, which were:

- closing the life expectancy gap within a generation
- halving the gap in mortality rates for Indigenous children under 5 years within a decade
- ensuring that all Indigenous 4-year-olds in remote communities have access to early childhood education by 2013.

Changes in early childhood policy and provision have been a direct result of the setting of these targets. To date, eight Indigenous Integrated Children and Families Centres have been established throughout Australia in regions where the statistics informing the above targets are the most alarming. These centres are in their infancy and the impacts are yet to be measured.

Diversity in Aboriginal communities and languages in Australia necessitates a diversity of approaches to Aboriginal education and care. Empirical research with Aboriginal communities highlights features of care and education that are considered necessary for them to be culturally appropriate (Lee-Hammond, 2013). The national Early Years Learning Framework for Australia, the EYLF, pays particular attention to educators needing to be culturally competent with regard to Aboriginal ways of relating, knowing and being. To date, services for Aboriginal families have been segregated from mainstream provisions, for example the Multifunctional Aboriginal Children's Centres (MACS) throughout Australia have operated outside the previous national childcare regulations and have sought to provide culturally safe and appropriate environments for Aboriginal children and families. These centres provide excellent examples of joined up or integrated provision for families and children.

Aboriginal children and families living in remote areas are at the most risk of disadvantage and hence these communities are the recipients of substantial efforts to address the social and economic gap that exists between Indigenous and non-Indigenous Australians. Unlike their neighbour New Zealand, the Traditional Owners in Australia have no treaty and hence they do not have the same legal rights as the Māori to their own sovereignty and decision making regarding the care and education of young children and support for their families.

 ### Research in context

Lee-Hammond, L. and Jackson-Barrett, E. (2013) 'Aboriginal children's engagement in Bush School', in S. Knight (ed.), *International Perspectives on Forest School.* London: Sage.

In 2011 and 2012, Libby Lee-Hammond in collaboration with an Aboriginal colleague, Libby Jackson-Barrett, implemented an adaptation of the Forest School with specific reference to Aboriginal ways of knowing and being (Lee-Hammond and Jackson-Barrett, 2013). In this project, an Aboriginal Elder was invited to participate in a term-long project with young Aboriginal children in a local site of significance. He was invited to share the *boodja* (land) and the *dreaming* (creation stories) with the children in an outdoor learning project. The children were taught traditional methods for fishing and hunting as well as learning about the plants and animals that inhabited the area. Children's levels of wellbeing and involvement were measured using Laever's Involvement Scale (1994) during the sessions and these measures were also taken in the classroom environment. The levels of wellbeing and involvement in the outdoor setting were much higher. An unexpected outcome of the study was that children's overall school attendance increased.

New Zealand

Te Whāriki, the early childhood curriculum framework developed in New Zealand in 1996, has received a great deal of worldwide interest due to its innovative holistic and emergent approach to the curriculum. Whāriki (or woven mat) is used as a metaphor to signify the weaving together of the principles and strands, as well as the diverse peoples, philosophies and services that participate in early education (Anning et al., 2004).

Te Whāriki identifies learning outcomes for children as: working theories about the people, places and things in learners' lives and as learning dispositions (Ministry of Education, 1996). Te Whāriki invites practitioners to weave their own curriculum drawing on the framework of Principles, Strands and Goals. The focus is also on children's perspectives to define and evaluate (quality) practices in early childhood centres.

The goals within each strand highlight ways in which practitioners support children, rather than skills or content, promoting a project-based approach drawing from the children's interests. Thus, the content emerges from children's interests, which are tracked through the four principles. The guidelines apply to all children in all settings, including those with special educational needs who may be given an Individual Development Plan (IDP).

New Zealand provides an excellent model of the primacy of Māori culture, language and traditional knowledge in the care and education of young children; in addition, the school curriculum is informed by the well documented *Kaupapa Māori*, a Māori educational philosophy grounded in the principles set out in Table 3.2 (Rangahau, 2013).

New Zealand has been a role model for many nations with large Indigenous populations and the Waitangi Treaty has played a critical part in enabling this pedagogy to be widely adopted throughout New Zealand. Referring back to the beginning of this chapter, such a pedagogy represents a working example of Freire's view that the oppressed or colonised must reclaim the power to self-determine in order to be truly free. Education as a site of struggle for the colonised is reclaimed by the Māori through

Table 3.1   Principles and strands of Te Whāriki

Four central principles	Five strands
Empowerment	Wellbeing
Holistic development	Belonging
Family and community	Contribution
Relationships	Communication
	Exploration

Table 3.2   Principles of *Kaupapa Māori*

Kaupapa Māori principle	*Kaupapa Māori* implications
Self-determination	Allowing Māori to control their own culture, aspirations and destiny
Cultural aspiration	Māori ways of knowing, doing and understanding the world are considered valid in their own right
Culturally preferred pedagogy	Acknowledges teaching and learning practices that are inherent and unique to Māori, as well as practices that may not be traditionally derived but are preferred by Māori
Socioeconomic mediation	Asserts the need to mediate and assist in the alleviation of negative pressures and disadvantages experienced by Māori communities
Extended family structure	Acknowledges the relationships that Māori have to one another and to the world around them
Collective philosophy	The 'Kaupapa' refers to the collective vision, aspiration and purpose of Māori communities
Treaty of Waitangi	Te Tiriti Te Tiriti o Waitangi (1840) is a crucial document, which defines the relationship between Māori and the Crown in New Zealand
Growing respectful relationships	Relates specifically to the building and nurturing of relationships. It acts as a guide to the understanding of relationships and wellbeing when engaging with Māori

Source: Rangahau, 2013

the *Kaupapa Māori* and sets a framework for other colonised First Nations communities to take control of their future.

Canada

Aboriginal pedagogy in Canada shares similarities with other First Nations pedagogies regarding assessment and evaluation of learning. This differs dramatically from mainstream practices that focus on testing and written assessment. Aboriginal Peoples tend to see learning as a journey rather than a destination and its measurement cannot be done in isolation from other factors (Tunison, 2007) such as reflection and self-growth, which are extremely personal processes evident within the spiritual, emotional, intellectual and physical and cultural experiences of each child (Preston et al., 2012). For Canadian Aboriginal Peoples, learning is experiential and best facilitated through group activities such as storytelling, discussion, cooperative tasks, modelling and demonstration of skills and processes and hands-on experiences.

Despite diversity within Aboriginal communities throughout Canada, some principles appear to be universal. Preston et al. (2012) note that high quality Aboriginal early childhood education privileges Aboriginal pedagogy, promotes Indigenous languages and culture, is adequately staffed by qualified Aboriginal educators, empowers Aboriginal parents and communities and, in the case of kindergarten services, provides a full-day timetable (Preston et al., 2012: 7). Mainstream measures of quality such as the ECERS and the CLASS, discussed earlier, are formed around dominant discourses regarding quality and are not necessarily reflective of quality environments for Aboriginal children.

Norway and Finland

Following similar principles to those discussed for First Nations children and families in Australia, New Zealand and Canada, the high quality care education of Sámi children in Norway and Finland is considered by Keskitalo, Määttä and Uusiautti (2011: 89) to have the following four factors:

- creation of the Sámi curriculum based on Sámi values of time, place and knowledge and cultural knowledge systems
- strengthening the position of the Sámi language as a core aspect of curriculum as particular concepts can only be understood and transmitted in the mother tongue
- culturally sensitive teaching arrangements, particularly with regard to time, space and flexibility. The Sámi 's traditional life of reindeer herding revolves around eight seasons and following the sun; this flexibility is essential to traditional life, and the strict scheduling of lessons in indoor environments tends to alienate Sámi students and perpetuates the dominant cultural use of time and scheduling. In addition, a stronger connection to nature and the outdoors is seen as an essential component in Sámi learning and wellbeing
- community-centred school-work. Education and care experiences must link closely to the life worlds of the Sámi, embracing traditional knowledge through collaboration with Elders and a true co-operation between the school or centre and the community it serves.

To echo the earlier observation that sociocultural/progressive pedagogies are the pedagogies of the oppressed, Keskitalo et al. argue that 'When adapting the traditional Sámi upbringing and knowledge at the Sámi School, teaching should lean on the ideas of social constructivism and reform pedagogy more powerfully' (2011: 98).

Curriculum

Variation in what constitutes early childhood curricula internationally will be presented in this section, with the latest OECD data (2012). Figure 3.1 provides detailed information regarding the various types of provision and ages at which they are offered in the OECD's thirty-four member countries (see www.oecd.org/about/membersandpartners/).

	Standards/curriculum for Care
	Standards/curriculum for Early Education or Education and Care (ECEC)
	No standard curriculum is in place for the specified age group
	Compulsory schooling

Age	0	1	2	3	4	5	6	7
Australia	Belonging, Being, Becoming – Early Years Learning Framework for Australia							
Austria								
Belgium (Flemish Comm.)			2.5y	Ontwikkelingsdoelen				
Belgium (French Comm.)			2.5y					
Canada (British Columbia)	British Columbia Early Learning Framework for 0–5-year-olds					British Columbia Early Learning Framework for 5–6-year-olds		
Canada (Manitoba)			Early Returns Curriculum					
						Manitoba Kindergarten Curriculum		
Canada (Prince Edward Island)	Early Learning Framework							
Czech Republic				Framework Educational Programme for Pre-school Education				
Denmark	Preschool Curriculum Læreplaner							
Estonia		1.5y	Framework Curriculum of Preschool Education					
Finland	National curriculum guidelines on early childhood education						Core Curriculum for Pre-primary Education	
France			2.5y National curriculum for école maternelle					

(Continued)

Figure 3.1 *(Continued)*

Age	0	1	2	3	4	5	6	7
Germany (Baden-Württemberg)	Orientierungsplan für Bildung und Erziehung für die baden-württembergischen Kindergärten						up to 10	
Germany (Bavaria)	Bildung, Erziehung und Betreuung für Kinder in den ersten drei lebensjahren			Der Bayerische Bildungs- und Erziehungsplan für Kinder in Tageseinrichtungen bis zur Einschulung				
Germany (Berlin)	Berliner Bildungsprogramm für die Bildung, Erziehung und Betreuung für Kinder in Tageseinrichtungen bis zu ihrem Schuleintritt							
Germany (Brandenburg)	Grundsätze der Förderung elementarer Bildung in Einrichtungen der Kindertagesbetreuung in Brandenburg							
Germany (Bremen)	Rahmenplan für Bildung und Erziehung im Elementarbereich							
Germany (Hamburg)	Hamburger Bildungsempfehlungen für die Bildung und Erziehung von Kindern in Tageseinrichtungen						up to 15	
Germany (Hesse)	Bildung und Erziehungsplans für Kinder von bis 10 Jahren in Hessen						up to 10	
Germany (Mecklenburg-Western Pomerania)	Bildungskonzeption für 0- bis 10-jährige Kinder in Mecklenburg-Voropommern						up to 10	
Germany (Lower Saxony)	Orientierungsplan für Bildung und Erziehung im Elementarbereich niedersächssischer Tageseinrichtungen für Kinder							
Germany (North Rhine-Westphalia)	Mehr Chancen durch Bildung von Anfang an – Grundsätze zur Bildungsförderung für Kinder von 0 bis 10 Jahren in Kindertageserinrichtungen und Schulen in Primarbereich in Nordrhein-Westfalen						up to 10	
Germany (Rhineland-Palatinate)	Bildungs- und Erziehungsempfehlungen für Kindertagesstätten in Rhineland-Pfaiz						up to 15	
Germany (Saarland)	Bildungsprogramm für saariändische Kindergärten							
Germany (Saxony)	Sächsischer Bildungsplan – ein Leitfaden für pädagogische Fachkräfte in Krippen, Kindergärten und Horten sowie für Kinderttagespflege						up to 10	
Germany (Saxony-Anhalt)	Bildungsprogramm für Kindertageseinrichtungen in Sachsen-Anhalt							

Age	0	1	2	3	4	5	6	7
Germany (Schleswig-Holstein)	Erfolgreich starten: Leitllinien zum Bildungsauftrag in Kindertageseinrichtungen						up to 15	
Germany (Thuringia)	Thüringer Bildungsplan für Kinder bis 10 Jahre						up to 10	
Hungary			National Core Programme of Kindergarten					
Ireland	Early Childhood Curriculum Framework: Aistear							
Israel			Framework Programme for Preschool Education					
Italy		3 months	Guidelines for the curriculum					
Japan			Course of Study for Kindergarten					
	National curriculum of day care centres							
Korea			National curriculum for kindergarten	Nuri Curriculum				
	Standardised childcare curriculum							
Luxembourg		Le plan d'études						
Mexico	Childcare curriculum	Early childhood education curriculum						
Netherlands		2.5y	Development goals/competences					
New Zealand	Te Whäriki							
Norway	Framework Plan for the Content and Tasks of Kindergartens							
Poland*			Core Curriculum for Preschool Education					
Portugal			The Curriculum Guidelines for Pre-School Education					
Slovak Republic			The National Education Programme					
Slovenia		National Curriculum for Pre-school Institutions						
Spain	Early Childhood Curriculum							

(Continued)

Figure 3.1   *(Continued)*

Sweden		Läroplan for förskolan lpfö 98	Läroplan för grundskolan, Förskoleklassen och dritidshem-met Lgr 11
Turkey		Pre-school education programme	
United Kingdom (England)	Statutory Framework for the Early Years Foundation Stage		
United Kingdom (Scotland)	Pre-birth to three – staff guidelines	Curriculum for Excellence	up to 18
United States (Georgia)		Georgia's Pre-K content Standards	
United States (Massachusetts)		Guidelines for Preschool Learning Experiences	
United States (North Carolina)		Early Learning Standards for North Carolina Preschoolers and Strategies to Guide Their	
United States (Oklahoma)		Priority Academic Student Skills	

Figure 3.1   *Coverage of ECEC curriculum frameworks or guidelines by age group in thirty-four countries (from OECD, 'Encouraging Quality in Early Childhood Education and Care (ECEC)', www.oecd.org/edu/school/48623811.pdf, with permission)*

Note: For Poland, the compulsory school age was lowered from age 7 to 6 in 2009 with a transition period of three years (until 2012), during which time parents can choose if their child starts school at age 6 or 7. For Sweden, *Läroplan för förskplan* is the curriculum for the preschool; *Läroplan för grundskolan, förskoleklassen och fritidshement* regards the curriculum for the preschool class, compulsory school and out-of-school centres.

Source: OECD Network on Early Childhood Education and Care's Survey for the Quality Toolbox and ECEC Portal, June 2011.

As a result of previous Starting Strong reports (OECD, 2001, 2006), some countries (e.g. Australia) have made significant policy changes and the implementation of these is currently under way. A comparison of the revised English Early Years Foundation Stage (DfE, 2012d) and the Australian Early Years Learning Framework (Commonwealth of Australia, 2009) will highlight similarities and differences in emphasis and scope in two OECD countries.

Australian Early Years Learning Framework

In 2009, Australia introduced its first national Early Years Learning Framework (EYLF). Titled *Belonging, Being and Becoming* the document aims to assist educators working with the years birth to 5 (Commonwealth of Australia, 2009). The document recognises the centrality of the family and home as the child's first and most influential educators. The motifs of Belonging, Being and Becoming speak to each child's relationships, communities and identities and embrace the notion that early childhood is a unique stage of life with intrinsic value: 'the early childhood years are not solely preparation for the future but also about the present' (Commonwealth of Australia, 2009: 7). Despite a growing emphasis on National Testing incorporating literacy and numeracy performance and a subsequent emphasis on more formal learning earlier, the EYLF has a strong emphasis on play as the primary medium for learning in the early years and comprises five broad outcomes:

- Children have a strong sense of identity.
- Children are connected with and contribute to their world.
- Children have a strong sense of wellbeing.
- Children are confident and involved learners.
- Children are effective communicators.

The Commonwealth Government states that the framework 'guides educators in their curriculum decision making and assists in planning, implementing and evaluating quality in early childhood settings. It also underpins the implementation of more specific curriculum relevant to each local community and early childhood setting' (Commonwealth of Australia, 2009: 8).

The accompanying EYLF Educators Guide (Commonwealth of Australia, 2010) gives specific support to educators regarding implementation of the EYLF with a particular emphasis on cultural competence. This refers to the extensive cultural diversity in 21st-century Australia and makes particular reference to the Traditional Owners of Australia, the Aboriginal people, who, as a direct result of British colonisation, experienced a serious disadvantage 'gap' in health, education and life expectancy, noting:

> The Early Years Learning Framework is an important and timely resource for early childhood. It embraces a vision for a new Australia:
>
> - a future that embraces all Australians
> - a future based on mutual respect, mutual resolve and mutual responsibility
> - a future where all Australians, whatever their origins, are truly equal partners, with equal opportunities and with an equal stake in shaping the next chapter in the history of Australia. (Commonwealth of Australia, 2010: 3)

The EYLF is now interpreted by educators working in the early years of schooling alongside the new Australian National Curriculum (ANC) (ACARA, 2012). The national curriculum specifies particular content for children in the first years of compulsory schooling.

The overlap of the EYLF and the ANC for 5-year-old children is presently a space of navigation and negotiation for early years educators and policy makers in Australia (Australian Government, 2013).

England's Early Years Foundation Stage (EYFS)

The Practice Guide for the early years (EYFS) specifies goals for children based on their chronological age. This is based on developmental theory and adopts an ages and stages approach to children in the age ranges 0–11 months, 8–20 months, 16–26 months, 22–36 months, 30–50 months and 40–60+ months.

Originally, these goals were assigned in six categories:

1. Dispositions and attitudes
2. Self-confidence and self-esteem
3. Making relationships
4. Behaviour and self-control
5. Self-care
6. Sense of community

However, the Early Years Foundation Stage has been revised following a review, and areas of learning have been changed and the number of early learning goals has been reduced to better support the implementation. The new early learning goals are:

1. Communication and language
2. Physical development
3. Personal, social and emotional development

The new EYFS Framework makes a number of improvements on the previous iteration, namely:

- reducing bureaucracy for professionals, simplifying assessment of children's development at 5 years of age
- simplifying the learning and development requirements by reducing the number of early learning goals from 69 to 17
- stronger emphasis on the three prime areas, which are most essential for children's healthy development
- for parents, a new progress check at age 2 on their child's development so that children get any additional support they need before they start school
- strengthening partnerships between professionals and parents, ensuring that the new framework uses clear language.
  (DfE, 2012b)

Trends internationally to identify essential curriculum goals for children's care and education are emerging and will no doubt be the subject of subsequent OECD research.

Chapter summary

International comparisons of early childhood education and care are important in developing an understanding of the diversity of curricula and provision in the early years. This chapter has highlighted notions of quality and equity as contested and highly contextual and draws on examples from several countries to explore these notions further.

Questions for reflection and discussion

1. What can be learnt from the EPPE project with regard to the quality and effectiveness of early childhood provision? How are measures of 'quality' designed and used in practice?
2. To what extent do mainstream early childhood care and education centres provide for Indigenous children and their families?
3. What are the benefits of an integrated early years care and education centre for families?
4. What are some examples of Freire's 'banking' model of education that are evident in 21st century early years programmes? What is your opinion of this?
5. How does research contribute to our understanding of 'quality' in ECEC?
6. How does research contribute to our understanding of 'equity' in ECEC?

Recommended reading

Preston, J.P., Cottrell, M., Pelletier, T.R. and Pearce, J.V. (2012) 'Aboriginal early childhood education in Canada: issues of context', *Journal of Early Childhood Research*, 10 (1): 3–18. Available at: http://ecr.sagepub.com/content/10/1/3.full.pdf+html
This paper identifies key features of quality Aboriginal early childhood programmes in Canada. The authors make a very interesting case for incorporating Aboriginal pedagogy, language and culture.

Rutanen, N. (2011) 'Space for toddlers in the guidelines and curricula for early childhood education and care in Finland', *Childhood*, 18 (4): 526–39. Available at: http://chd.sagepub.com/content/18/4/526.full.pdf+html
This article explores the historical division in Finland between the care of babies and toddlers (0–3) and older children. The author deconstructs the conflicting policies and discourses regarding the very young.

Recommended websites

http://eppe.ioe.ac.uk/eppe/eppeintro.htm
The website of the Effective Provision of Pre-school Education project. This is a very useful resource for obtaining more detail on the longitudinal study of 3,000 British children known as

the EPPE project. The research available on this website is very valuable since it is considered a landmark study of quality and provision for young children.

www.oecd.org/edu/preschoolandschool/startingstrongiiiaqualitytoolboxforearly
   childhoodeducationandcare.htm

The Organisation for Economic Co-operation and Development (OECD) report *Starting Strong III: A Quality Toolbox for Early Childhood Education and Care* (2012) is accessible from this site. It focuses on quality issues in ECEC, defining 'quality' as it relates to children and families. It outlines five policy levers that can enhance quality in ECEC. This is the most recent in a series of Starting Strong reports that have been highly influential in early years policy in OECD countries.

www.toronto.ca/firstduty/

The Toronto First Duty website provides reports and information regarding a highly successful integrated services model in Canada.

> Want to learn more about this chapter? Visit the companion website at **www.sagepub.co.uk/walleranddavis3e** to access podcasts from the author and child observation videos.

Part Two
Inclusion and Diversity

4

Children's Rights to Participation

Gill Handley

 Key chapter objectives

- To discuss the difficulties of identifying what participation means in practice
- To identify the conflicts between children's participation and protection rights
- To consider the dilemmas and difficulties of judging children's competence in relation to participation
- To introduce some of the complexities of upholding very young children's rights to participation

This chapter begins by discussing the difficulties of defining children's rights. There is an analysis of the fundamental conflict between participation rights and protection rights, as advanced by the United Nations Convention on the Rights of the Child (UNCRC) (United Nations, 1989), with specific reference to the lives of working children across the world, and the lives of young children involved in divorce proceedings in England. The role of competence in the exercise of children's participation rights and the problems of judging competence and authenticity are discussed. Three case studies are included which address some of the complex issues involved in young children's active participation in decision making. Conclusions are drawn about the implications for early years work in relation to children's participation and how children's rights to participation might be advanced. Significant questions and suggested texts/websites for further study are given.

The main focus of this chapter will be on the participation rights of children and assessing how far legislation and practice uphold these rights, both in England and internationally. A major argument will be that the participation rights of children are among the most difficult and controversial children's rights to be understood, implemented and upheld because of the fundamental conflict between them and the competing rights to protection (Burr, 2004). It will be argued that despite increasing awareness of children's competence to make decisions that affect their lives, their need for protection continues to take precedence as this fits with the predominant discourses of childhood, which see children as in need of guidance, protection and adult control, rather than as young citizens who are entitled to respect as agents in their own lives and able to actively participate (James and Prout, 1997). A major challenge for all those who work with children and young people is how to redress this balance, particularly for very young children and those with special needs, so that their right to participate is upheld whilst recognising that they are at the same time vulnerable and dependent (Bae, 2010).

What are children's rights?

The language used in relation to children's rights, and rights in general, is confused and confusing. What is understood by the term 'rights' is not a given but reflects different and changing social and political ideologies and values (Roche, 2001). Take, for example, the current notions of individualistic human rights as defined in the European Convention on Human Rights (ECHRC, 1950) and the UNCRC (United Nations, 1989). These are rooted in liberal, democratic Western philosophy and thought, rather than Southern or Eastern philosophies, as the latter tend to place greater emphasis on family and community responsibilities than on individual interests (Burr, 2002; Millei and Imre, 2009). The term 'rights' is also used to refer to both moral and legal rights, as well as notions of what ought to happen in everyday life (Eekelaar, 1992; Fortin, 2003; Freeman, 1983; Macormick, 1982). Although the notion of rights generally involves some idea of an entitlement to something, what the entitlement is to, and who is entitled, again varies and changes with different historical, social and political contexts. For example, women in the UK were not seen as having a right to vote until the early 20th century, and children were not seen as being a group of people eligible to have rights independently from adults until the latter part of the 20th century; there is still debate as to whether or not children can be full holders of rights at all, if a precondition is seen as the capacity to be able to choose whether or not to exercise them (Fortin, 2003; Freeman, 1983).

There is also a continuing debate about the effectiveness of a rights-based focus per se, in empowering the disadvantaged and vulnerable, which includes children. It is argued that rights are abstract legal principles that cannot be exercised outside of human relation-ships and, as such, do not take into account power differences between individuals. As Rhedding-Jones et al. (2008: 54) caution:

> Giving children a voice, listening to their stories, watching their agentic actions and really seeing them has to be grounded in an awareness of the asymmetric power relations between children and adults. A focus on children's voices [should not be] just a conveni-ent way to legitimize postmodern knowledge.

The voice of the child needs to be 'authentic' but there can be problems ensuring authenticity (Spyrou, 2011) because the expression of a child's views is likely to be influenced by context and is open to different interpretation depending on the per-spective of the adult as well as the nature of the relationship between adult and child, and the power differences between them.

It is further argued, by opponents of children's rights, that 'needs' are a more impor-tant consideration than rights and that the latter are essentially 'ideological constructs of cultural imperialism serving the hegemonic agenda of the West … [and that] the language of rights is a cog in the machinery that restricts possibilities and draws actors into making certain choices' (Reynolds et al., 2006: 293) rather than meeting the varied needs of children in different contexts. An example of this is where rights are given a particular legal construction, which can be disempowering, such as in divorce cases where there is the issue of contact with the parent who does not have care of the child. James et al. point out, in discussing Dame Elizabeth Butler-Sloss's argument that 'the child [has] a right to a relationship with [his or her] father even if he [or she] did not want it', that: 'this particular construction of the concept of the child's right has the effect of transforming the child's right into a responsibility or even a duty to see his father, since such a conception of rights fails to endow the child with the equivalent right not to have such contact' (James et al., 2004: 201).

It can also be argued that a rights-based perspective is just another adult construc-tion of childhood (Gabriel, 2004), which again neglects the child's own view and perspective on their lives, and further, that consultation with children may mean that children are open to being more observed and controlled by adults as the latter then have greater knowledge of their interests and preferences (Clark et al., 2005).

In considering which children are afforded rights, there is also the complication of defining what is meant by both childhood and its corollary, 'a child'. Examination of the understanding of the terms in different contexts has led to a social constructivist per-spective of childhood which sees childhood itself as a social construct rather than as a biological given (Franklin, 2002; Jenks, 2004; Stainton Rogers, 1992). What is seen as childhood, at what age it starts and at what age it ends, varies and changes (Ariès, 1962; Fortin, 2003), and there may be different and competing constructions of childhood prevalent at the same time. For example, in England, children tend to be seen either as innocent angels in need of protection or as 'villains' in need of control (Franklin, 2002; Goldson, 2001). Burr (2002) argues that street children in Vietnam are similarly seen as either victims or villains. Legislation also constructs childhood and 'the child' in different ways (James and James, 1999). For example, the age of criminal responsibility varies across European legislation from 8 in Scotland and 10 in England to 18 in Belgium. In English law, a child is sometimes seen as being a person under 16 and sometimes under 18. For example, a 16-year-old can work full time but cannot hold a tenancy. Critics of a 'social constructivist perspective' argue that it tends to see children and childhood as a 'series of adult constructions ... forgetting real children' (Willan et al., 2004: 53) (see Chapters 1 and 2 for a more detailed discussion of childhood).

Protection rights versus participation rights

Notwithstanding these significant and important debates, over the past thirty years acceptance has grown, in social and political arenas, that children have their own individual rights separate from those of adults (Harcourt and Einarsdottir, 2011; Lansdown, 2001). Children are increasingly regarded as agents within their own lives. Rather than seeing children as passive recipients of adults' care and decision making, children are increasingly being seen as competent to make a range of decisions about themselves (Alderson, 2008; James and James, 1999; Millei and Imre, 2009). It becomes increasingly important to acknowledge this competence when the damaging effect of adults' decisions in the past is recognised. For example, children suffered emotional trauma when adults decided that they should be separated from their parents by evacuation during the Second World War, or when undergoing hospital treatment (Lansdown, 2001). Ideas of prescribed and incremental development, which medical and psychological theories have put forward, have been criticised for ignoring the complex and varied range of abilities children of similar ages may have, and for ignoring their individual capacities and competences (Alderson, 2008), and the different contexts in which they live (Walkerdine, 2004). Kaltenborn (2001) found that, in relation to custody and residence disputes, even very young infants could be regarded as having enough emotional intelligence to be able to express reasonable opinions. This is not to say that the overall framework of children developing increasing abilities with age should be dismissed, or that children should be able to do whatever they choose, any more than adults can, but rather that a more complex pattern of competences and abilities should be acknowledged, and meaningful and inclusive ways found of enabling children's perspectives to be considered.

However, there has continued to be debate and controversy about the extent to which children's rights to protection from various forms of harm and exploitation should take precedence over their rights to self-determination, and, how far, and in what contexts, children can make decisions about their own lives. Child liberationists, such as Holt (1974) and Farson (1974), have argued that children of any age are in need of liberation from the domination and control of adults. This view has been challenged by those who consider that children need shielding from the responsibility and burden of making decisions (King, 1987). They see children as fundamentally vulnerable and dependent and, therefore, in need of protection from various forms of harm, exploitation and responsibility (James et al., 2004). The extremes of both positions can be challenged, but the fundamental differences in the images of childhood, and related perspectives on children's rights that they are then aligned with, do help in understanding the complexity of: 'how to identify children's rights, how to balance one set of rights against another, in the event of conflict between them, and how to mediate between children's rights and those of adults' (Fortin, 2003: 3).

These ongoing debates are reflected throughout legislation and practice in many spheres of children's lives such as health, planning, research, social work, education and day care, within England, other UK countries and internationally. The next section will consider some examples of the complexities and conflicts in relation to the exercise of protection and participation rights of children in a number of different contexts.

The United Nations Convention On the Rights of the Child (UNCRC) 1989

The UNCRC was adopted by the United Nations in 1989. It identified children as having rights separate from adults and was an attempt to improve the living conditions and experiences of children throughout the world. Its aims were to prevent the extreme suffering and exploitation of children, as well as to improve more everyday aspects of children's lives (Alderson, 2008; Millei and Imre, 2009). The 54 Articles of the Convention set out a wide range of rights, which, it argues, all children of the world should enjoy. These rights range from the right to life through to the right to play. Although not incorporated into the law of UK countries, the latter have ratified the UNCRC, as have all other countries in the world except Somalia and the USA. So, potentially, the UNCRC has a worldwide influence on the advancement of children's rights (Burr, 2004; Millei and Imre, 2009).

The UNCRC identifies three broad types of rights: protection rights, provision rights and participation rights (Alderson, 2008; Burr, 2004; Franklin, 2002). The participation rights include the right of children to participate in decisions affecting them (Article 12), the right to freedom of expression (Article 13), the right to freedom of thought, conscience and religion (Article 14) and the right for young disabled people to participate in their community (Article 23). Although the UNCRC raises the awareness of children's right to participate in various aspects of their lives, the effectiveness and practice of upholding these rights raise a number of ethical, process and practical issues which include the conflict between children's need for participation and protection, and the different ways childhood is constructed in different social and political contexts (Penn, 2009).

First, there is no clear definition of what participation means, and how it differs from consultation, involvement or citizenship (Millei and Imre, 2009; Willow et al., 2004).

There have been various models and charts developed to help analyse the different extents to which children may be involved in decisions affecting them, and the processes that may be used (Crimmens and West, 2004; Hart, 1992). These range from Arnstein's (1969) original 'ladder of participation' which sees tokenism as the bottom rung and full control of the decision-making process as the top rung, to less hierarchical, more circular models, such as that of Treseder (1997) which gives equal importance to the different degrees of participation, as each is seen to have relevance in different contexts. All tend to include practices that range from asking children to make a choice between a limited number of alternatives, to children identifying the problem and alternative solutions themselves (Crimmens and West, 2004). They can be seen to reflect, in various ways, the fundamental difference between children merely being asked for their views about something and children actually devising decision-making systems themselves (Alderson, 2008; Willow et al., 2004). The various processes involved can also be seen as reflecting the difference between seeing children as 'objects' of processes rather than as 'subjects' (Bae, 2010; Willow et al., 2004), and between seeing children as in need of protection rather than as being agents in their own lives. Treseder (1997), however, argues that all these various forms of participation can be empowering for children and young people, even when they have relatively little control and influence, provided the extent of their influence is clear and that adults and children work in partnership, where 'participants interact in ways that respect each other's dignity, with the intention of achieving a shared goal' (Blanchet-Cohen and Rainbow, 2006: 114). In reality, this may pose difficulties because the partnership working that effective children's participation requires is 'not something that comes naturally, as is often assumed … it calls for an attitude change that is difficult in an adult-led and increasingly result-based world' (Blanchet-Cohen and Rainbow, 2006: 125). Even in early years care and education contexts, where there is more of an emphasis on using a variety of media and approaches to understanding children's experiences and views, including children with a range of needs and in different cultural contexts, it is a challenge to involve children when there is an emphasis on achieving targets and outcomes for children (Theobold and Kulti, 2012).

Second, the exercise of participation rights under the UNCRC is not absolute. In relation to Article 12, it is dependent on the 'age and maturity of the child', and in relation to Article 14, it has to be consistent with the 'evolving capacities of the child' (United Nations, 1989). Thus, the level of competence of a child is one of the factors that have to be considered in relation to the exercise of his or her right to participation. How the level of competence is to be judged, and who is to judge it, and in what context, is not clear, but, as later discussions suggest, in practice, it will be by various groups of adults, not children themselves, and will change over time.

Third, there is also evidence that the right to participation tends to be actively overruled when there is seen to be a competing right to protection, as understood under the UNCRC. The following is an example of children's right to protection being seen as taking precedence over their right to participation.

CASE STUDY ONE

In relation to street children in Vietnam, aged between 6 and 16, Burr (2002, 2004) found that the particular view of the rights to protection and education promoted by aid agencies, operating within the guidelines of the UNCRC, tended to conflict with what some children said they wanted, that is to work to earn money, and with what they themselves defined as their needs. Some of the children identified the need to work as significant, as it enabled them to earn money, and thus not be forced to return to rural lives of poverty. By working from a young age, they were also able to give financial support to their families, who could not support them. Some aid agencies sought to protect the children from what was considered exploitation, by returning them to more adult-led environments, and by requiring them to receive formal day-time education. By doing so, the agencies failed to listen to the children, understand the contexts of their lives and give credence to the children's own decision to work and be part of the urban communities they saw as their families (Burr, 2002, 2004).

In Guatemala, similarly, the rights as set out under the UNCRC were found to have little relevance to the everyday lives of children working on the streets (Snodgrass-Godoy, 1999). Burr (2004) argues that the UNCRC rights are based on a Western view of childhood, which sees childhood as idyllic. She argues that the assumption that Southern and Eastern children are seen as in need of rescuing by the more affluent Western countries fails to recognise the different needs of children in different social, political and economic contexts. Furthermore, where their needs, for example for income earned on the streets, conflict with the concept of rights to protection, education and family life as promoted by the UNCRC, the latter will predominate, even when children themselves express their own views to have the right to work. Ennew (1995, quoted in Snodgrass-Godoy, 1999: 437) points out that, in relation to Guatemalan street children, 'the UNCRC takes as its starting point western modern childhood, which has been globalised first through colonialism and then through the imperialism of aid'. This imperialism can affect both the effectiveness and the provision of services (UNESCO, 2006).

     ### Reflection for case study 1

Rather than the UNCRC upholding individual children's rights to participate in major decisions affecting them, these examples show that attempts to

(Continued)

(Continued)

impose the UNCRC rights can negate children's participation rights. They also highlight some of the complexities of balancing competing rights for protection and participation in circumstances of extreme poverty. For example, it could be argued that children do not have a real 'choice' when the alternatives are working or starvation. It could also be argued that respecting children's wish to work prolongs their exploitation and lack of real choice.

- Do you think children in these situations should be able to have their wishes acted upon?
- Does your view depend on the age of the child?

The Children Acts 1989 and 2004

The UNCRC provided the context for the enactment of the Children Act 1989 in England (HM Government, 1989), which saw a shift away from children being seen as passive recipients of adult care and control to them being seen as individuals to whom their parents had responsibilities. It recognised their right to be heard in relation to some significant decisions affecting them, by having their wishes and feelings taken into account (James and James, 1999).

However, it can be argued that the Children Act 1989 is limited in its support of children's participation rights, in terms of both its principles and its operation in practice (Fortin, 2003; Thomas, 2004). First, children's wishes and feelings are only likely to be considered once the courts become involved in decisions about their care (section 1 [3] [a]). Although there is some limited requirement on local authorities, outside of court proceedings, to consider children's wishes and feelings before making any decision affecting them (section 22), there is no general requirement for parents to 'have regard to a child's views when making any major decision affecting them' as there is in Scottish law under the Children (Scotland) Act 1995, section 6 [1] (HM Government, 1995a).

Second, although the child's welfare is paramount, welfare is seen in terms of protection and safeguarding, not in terms of rights or of promoting active participation (Lansdown, 2001). So, while a court has a duty under section 1 (3) (a) to 'have regard to … the ascertainable wishes and feelings of the child concerned', the court only has to have regard to them, rather than actively consider or act upon them. In contact and residence decisions, they do not have to be considered at all if the parents agree on arrangements for the child (James et al., 2004; Monk, 2004), the assumption being that children's views are irrelevant if parents agree. Furthermore, any weight given to a child's wishes or feelings will depend on their age and understanding – in other words, their level of competence (Monk, 2004). Local authorities, similarly, under section 22, have a duty to ascertain a child's wishes and feelings but only in so far as it is 'reasonably practicable' to do so.

The Children Act 2004 (HM Government, 2004) is concerned primarily with the protection of children and putting into place structures and procedures to help ensure that children are better safeguarded. Yet, despite this focus on improving the protection of children, section 58 of the Children Act 2004 failed to effectively 'ban smacking' for children in England and Wales. While it removed the defence of 'reasonable punishment' in cases where a parent, or those acting *in loco parentis*, were charged with assault occasioning actual bodily harm, inflicting grievous bodily harm, or causing cruelty to a child, the defence is still available, in effect, for those who smack or physically hurt their child in other ways, provided there are no visible injuries. In Scotland, section 51 of the Criminal Justice (Scotland) Act 2003 (HM Government, 2003) attempted to clarify the law, by allowing a defence of 'reasonable chastisement', while at the same time specifically prohibiting blows to the head, shaking and the use of an implement. This again, like the Children Act 2004, still allows smacking and other forms of physical punishment to be acceptable as they are seen as 'reasonable chastisement'. This is despite the views of children. In 2007, a review was undertaken to look at the effectiveness of section 58 in preventing the abuse of children. Children of the ages 4–16 were consulted and the report of their views (DCSF, 2007b: 15) concludes that 'overall, most children in this sample struggled to endorse smacking as an effective form of punishment'.

As well as continuing to uphold the rights of parents to smack their children, the Children Act 2004 does not appear to advance the participation rights of children, in so far as there continue to be limitations on the extent to which children's 'wishes and feelings' may influence decision making. For example, although the widening of the range of circumstances in which local authorities in England must include the wishes and feelings of children (section 53) could be seen as a positive step forward in relation to children's participation rights, any weight given to them will again depend on the child's age and understanding or competence (section 53 [1] [b] and [3] [b]). It could also be argued that the establishment of a Children's Commissioner in England (section 1), who has 'the function of promoting awareness of the views and interests of children' (section 2 [2]), could be seen as a step forward in the advancement of children's rights to participation. But, as Goldthorpe (2004) and Hunter (2004) point out, the abilities of the Commissioner to actively advance children's rights were limited, as the role was stripped of its powers to promote and safeguard individual children's rights and had a weaker role in promoting rights than its equivalent in Wales, Scotland, Northern Ireland and other European countries. The Dunford Review of the role of the Children's Commissioner (2010) has recommended changes to improve the independence of the Commissioner and reinstate the power to promote and protect the rights of children (CRAE, 2012). However, as the recent Children's Rights Alliance for England's report (CRAE, 2012) into the implementation of the UNCRC in UK countries highlights, while these changes are commendable, they may not go far enough in promoting the independence of the Commissioner. The report further points out that there is continuing inconsistency in the current government approach to supporting children's rights generally. For example, while in some areas there is evidence of an increasing emphasis in policy and practice for consultation with children and young people in the development of services and policy, such as in the requirement under the Childcare Act 2006 for local authorities to 'have regard' to children's views in planning early childhood services [section 3(5)], local authorities need only do so where it 'appears to them to be relevant' (HM Government, 2006). Furthermore, some recommendations have not been brought into force at all, such as the part of the Education and Skills Act 2008 that supports children's rights to be heard and taken seriously in education contexts (CRAE, 2012), and further that its draft legislation for 'reforming provision for children and young people with special educational needs' contains little detail about how children and young people will be able to express their views on matters that affect them, with many of the clauses stating that the detail will be set out in regulations. In addition, where opportunities for participating in decision making are specified, they apply to parents and to young people above the age of 16 – excluding the majority of children from the opportunity to make decisions about their own lives (CRAE, 2012: 27).

Competence

There is much confusion within the law, both in UK countries and internationally, as to how the level of competence of a child is to be judged. In legal terms, competence is not necessarily linked to age. For example, in England, children aged between 16 and 18 are at present deemed to be sufficiently competent to make decisions in relation to sex and leaving school, but are not considered competent to vote or to marry without their parents' consent. Children aged 10 and over are held to be criminally responsible in English law, and can be made the subject of antisocial behaviour orders under the Criminal Justice Act 1998, but are not deemed to be responsible enough to buy a pet until they are 12 (Fortin, 2003).

The case of *Gillick* v *West Norfolk and Wisbech Area Health Authority* [1985] was seen as a landmark case in terms of young people's rights and in establishing that competence is not necessarily linked to age. It established the principle that a young person under the age of 16 could consent to medical treatment without their parents' consent or knowledge, if they were deemed to be competent enough (BMA, 2001: 34). However, it did not clarify how to assess competence, and again the decision about competence lay in the hands of adults, this time in the hands of a medical practitioner. Moreover, a few years later, the Court of Appeal confused matters by deciding in two cases (*Re: R* and *Re: W*, cited in BMA, 2001: 35) that the courts could overrule a teenager's decision to refuse life-saving treatment even when they had been considered 'Gillick competent'. It seemed that the competence of a child could be overruled depending on the seriousness of the decision involved.

Over the past ten years there has been some evidence that there is a more consistent approach to upholding children and young people's views, particularly in relation to medical decisions. For example, in July 2004, the government introduced new guidance for medical practitioners in relation to young people's right to confidentiality about sexual matters and for the first time enabled competent young people to consent to abortion without their parents' knowledge (DH, 2004a). There was much media-reported criticism of the guidance, particularly in relation to abortion. Mrs Axon, a mother of two teenage girls, applied for judicial review of the guidance as she disagreed with parents not being routinely consulted in relation to abortion (Powell, 2004). However, the courts ruled against her and considered the guidance lawful [*The Queen on the Application of Sue Axon* v *The Secretary of State for Health (The Family Planning Association: intervening)* [2006] EWCA 37 (Admin.)]. In this situation, the Court again significantly upheld a young person's right to make their own decision about a major issue, abortion, and allowed doctors to support young people's right to make their own decisions.

CASE STUDY TWO

In 2008, a 13-year-old girl's right to refuse life-saving medical treatment was upheld by a local authority, her parents and doctors. Her decision was likely to significantly limit her life. Read more and consider the implications by following the links below. You may find the case a distressing and upsetting one.

   http://news.bbc.co.uk/1/hi/england/hereford/worcs/7721231.stm

   http://link.brightcove.com/services/player/bcpid1529573111?bclid=1915439238&bctid=1915448858

Reflection for case study 2

- The decisions in cases like this are difficult and distressing for all involved. Even though you may have found the case upsetting, do you agree that Hannah was entitled to have her views acted on? Or, do you think her views should have been overruled? Would your view be different if Hannah was only 9 years old or if she were 18 years old? If so, why? Are you arguing from a protectionist or children's rights perspective?

It is interesting to note the support of the government for children's right to make at least some decisions in relation to their health and bodies, in comparison to the lack of support for them to be more involved in decisions about their education. As Fortin (2003: 161) states: 'the principles of education law currently show little appreciation for the maturing child's capacity for taking responsibility for his or her school life or for reaching important decisions over his or her education'. For example, the CRAE (2012) report highlights the continuing breach of UNCRC Article 12 participation rights which was revealed in the Inquiry by the Children's Commissioner into the school exclusion system (Office of the Children's Commissioner, 2012). While the revised (non-statutory) exclusions guidance of 2007 encourages pupils under the age of 18 to attend the appeals hearing, the parent has to agree to the pupil's attendance and furthermore pupils under 18 have no right to appeal against exclusion from school themselves; it is only their parents who can do that. The Inquiry found that children and young people's views were neither sought nor taken into account on a consistent basis in the exclusion process.

This confusion about required levels of competence for participation in decisions can also be seen in relation to contact or residence matters within the courts. In cases where contact is being considered with a parent about whom there have been allegations of domestic violence, the courts have sought the advice of two eminent psychiatrists about the age at which children's views should be taken into account. Sturge and Glaser's (2000: 620) advice is that:

> the older the child the more seriously [their views] should be viewed and the more insulting and discrediting to the child to have them ignored. As a rough rule we would see these as needing to be taken into account at any age; above 10 we see these as carrying considerable weight with 6–10 as an intermediate stage and at under 6 as often indistinguishable in many ways from the wishes of the main carer (assuming normal development).

While this advice may not be entirely clear, it does emphasise the importance of taking into account children's views, whatever their age. Despite this, it appears from the following studies that children's views are not routinely sought by the courts or professionals involved, and that when they are sought, they may still not be actively heard by the courts.

May and Smart (2004) looked at three County Courts' practices in relation to seeking children's views about contact and residence disputes. In half of the cases they looked at, a CAFCASS (Children and Family Court Advisory and Support Service) officer or a social worker had been asked to prepare a welfare report, which is expected to include the wishes and feelings of the child as well as advice about the effects of various decisions on the welfare of the child. May and Smart (2004) found that in only half of these cases – thus only a quarter of their total sample – had the children actually been consulted. They found that, of those consulted, children over the age of 7 tended to have their views taken seriously, particularly if they could 'vote with their feet' and where there was conflict between the parents. May and Smart were left particularly concerned about the young children involved in disputes, as they appeared to have clear views which were more often overlooked, particularly if they did not accord with the recommendations of the CAFCASS officer, and thus were effectively denied a voice in the proceedings.

James et al. (2004) considered how child welfare professionals from CAFCASS represent a child's views to the courts in family proceedings. They included both private law cases, such as contact and residence matters, and public law cases where local authorities had sought court orders to protect children from harm. They found that the professional's own understanding and construction of childhood influenced how they balanced the tensions inherent in wishing to protect the children from the responsibility of making a choice about their future care, while also ensuring their wishes were made known to the court. Generally, a more protectionist and welfare perspective dominated and children's voices were filtered out and effectively silenced if they did not fit in with the perspective of the professional involved (James et al., 2004).

A further factor influencing both whether or not children are actually consulted, and the ways in which they are consulted in legal proceedings, is the lack of social workers' training and confidence in communicating with young children (Handley and Doyle, 2012; Vis et al., 2012). Handley and Doyle (2012) found that social workers considered they had inadequate training to prepare them for communicating with young children in legal contexts, and this may have influence on their decision to involve and consult, particularly with the very youngest children.

It appears from the above studies that, as long as a more protectionist view prevails, alongside lack of training in ways to communicate with young children, family proceedings under the Children Act 1989 are 'more likely to remain a site for upholding contingent and highly romanticized ideas of family life rather than a space for listening and responding to the voices of real children' (Monk, 2004: 166). Hopefully, this will change with the recent emphasis by Munro (2011) and the Social Work Reform Board (2012) on the need for child development theory and skills in communicating with children to be included in both qualifying and post-qualifying training and development.

CASE STUDY THREE

The parents of a 3-year-old girl and 6-year-old boy are divorcing and each has applied to the Court for the care of the children. The social worker from CAFCASS has spent time with both children and, using a variety of techniques, such as drawings, observations, photographs and discussions, considers that she has found out the reasonably authentic views of the children; the 3-year-old wishes to live with

(Continued)

(Continued)

her mother and the 6-year-old with his father. The CAFCASS officer recommends the 3-year-old live with her mother and the 6-year-old with his father, but spend weekends together at alternate parental homes. Both parents are equally able to care for the children and have a good relationship with the children but consider that the children should grow up together. They consider that to separate them would be to deprive the children, and themselves, of their right to family life (Article 8 of the European Convention on Human Rights). They decide that they will agree for the children to stay together but share their time between each parent. On the advice of their solicitors, and in line with the recommendations of the Norgrove (2011) review of the Family Justice System, the parents draw up a parental agreement detailing the time each child will spend with each parent. In view of the parents' agreement, the court decides to give shared care to the parents so that the children stay together and spend equal time with each parent.

Reflection for case study

This example illustrates how rights do not exist in a vacuum, and how different rights can compete and conflict, making the decision-making processes difficult.

- In this case, do you consider that the children were able to participate effectively in the Court's decision?
- Do you think that, in view of their ages, it was right to overrule their wishes? Or do you think that the decision provides a balance between their right to family life and right to participate?

Participation of young children

While the above issues are relevant to the participation of children of all ages in decision making, 'much of the practice-based literature on children's participation and specific guidance about children's involvement in decision making tends to relate to children older than eight, particularly teenagers. Young children are almost invisible and babies appear not to exist at all' (Kirby and Marchant, 2004: 93). Where they are consulted, this can sometimes be at worst damaging, and at best ineffective, if the media used are designed for older children, or if they are one-off events unconnected with children's lives, and where 'adult "consultation" has dangerously come to mean an expert adult intervention done to children, with or without their genuine consent, often by adults who do not know them and have no other involvement in their lives' (Kirby and Marchant, 2004: 93) or where they do not have the training or skills to effectively communicate with young children (Handley and Doyle, 2012).

As discussed above, Blanchet-Cohen and Rainbow (2006) argue that many of the difficulties in achieving meaningful and effective participation could be avoided by systems and processes involving children as active participants in everyday life. If social and educational systems encouraged children to participate in such decision making from an early age, active 'citizenship' would be more of a reality for them, and further:

> such a shift would reduce the need for one-off, distant consultations because genuinely participative cultures would provide contexts in which young children could easily be consulted about a range of issues. For example, in community regeneration initiatives, local parent and toddler groups in the area would already be routinely ascertaining young children's views. In the development of health services, children who are spending time in hospital would be used to 'having a real say' in how things are for them. Curriculum development would be a regular focus for young children in school. (Kirby and Marchant, 2004: 95)

But how can young children be empowered to participate in decisions affecting their lives? The United Nations Committee on the Rights of the Child (2009) General Comment 12 advises that 'full implementation of Article 12 requires recognition of, and respect for, non-verbal forms of communication including play, body language, facial expressions, and drawing and painting, through which very young children demonstrate understanding, choices and preferences' (p. 9). The following research illustrates how the use of such a range of approaches can effectively enable children to express their views.

 ## Research in context

Harcourt, D. (2011) 'An encounter with children: seeking meaning and understanding about childhood', *European Early Childhood Education Research Journal*, 19 (3): 331–43.

Harcourt (2011) sought the views and opinions of fifteen children aged 3 to 6 years 'on their understandings of childhood and adulthood. The children were invited to theorize differences in perspectives and propose reasons why this may be so' (p. 331). The children discussed with the researcher, 'what might be expected within

(Continued)

(Continued)

the partnership' (p. 336) and agreed how they would express consent to participate at various stages of the research process. In order to empower the children to give their views, an adaptation of the Mosaic approach (Clark and Moss, 2011) was used, where children chose a preferred medium such as conversations, drawings, text and photographs. To minimise interpreter bias, and help ensure authenticity of the children's voices, the children and the researcher together interpreted the data and agreed how it should be presented.

Findings indicated that this method did enable children's perspectives to be explored. Children were able to explain the different ways they saw childhood and adulthood, including recognition of some of the limitations of being a child as well as the complexities and responsibilities of adulthood and the expectations they had of adults. It was also clear that adults were often wrong in their assumptions about children's views and experiences.

 Reflection

Read more about the Mosaic approach to help you decide if this provides an effective and meaningful way for children to actively participate in decisions in their lives.

- Is it effective for all children including those with special needs, English as an additional language or pre-verbal children?
- Or is it, as discussed at the beginning of this chapter, a way of adults having more knowledge and thereby more control over children's lives?

This philosophy and practice of active participation from an early age was advocated by the OECD's *Starting Strong II* report (2006: 219), which reviewed the OECD countries' policies in relation to early childhood care and education. This report recommended that governments recognise the important and influential voice of young children. It gives section 3 of Norway's Kindergarten Act 2006 as an example of legislation that explicitly supports the UNCRC participation rights of very young children in all aspects of life in the kindergarten, as it states that:

- Children in kindergartens shall have the right to express their views on the day-to-day activities of the kindergarten.

- Children shall regularly be given the opportunity to take an active part in planning and assessing the activities of the kindergarten.
- The children's views shall be given due weight according to their age and maturity.

While highlighting the importance of individual children's voices being heard, *Starting Strong II* also points out that encouraging young children's participation in early years settings should not mean that 'individual choice is put forward as a supreme value' (OECD, 2006: 219), but that awareness of the democratic values of social and community responsibilities is also encouraged. It argues that 'children should be encouraged to participate and share with others, and ... learning [should be] seen as primarily interactive, experiential and social. *Learning to be, learning to do, learning to learn and learning to live together* are each important goals for young children' (p. 219, emphasis as original). However, Bae (2010), in a study looking at how practitioners in Norwegian kindergartens actually interpret the Norwegian framework, found that practitioners tended to emphasise self-determination and individual choice rather than community-based and shared participation.

Balancing children's individual rights and those of the group within a childcare setting is a complex task (Bae, 2010). How, for example, should an early years practitioner manage a situation where an individual child wishes to pursue a task they are engaged in when a group activity is planned, if both individual agency and sharing experiences are important values? Furthermore, as Cameron (2007) argues, how do practitioners manage to balance children's agency 'in an advanced liberal state such as England [where] there is a paradox between valorizing independence as an expression of individual autonomy and the highly governed practice, through regulation, of early childhood services'? (2007: 467–8). Dictates of curriculum or the pressure to demonstrate outcomes may make the encouragement of participation and agency far less of a priority, either in an individualised or community sense.

Chapter summary

The notion of children having participation rights, what these are and how they can, or should, be exercised is of current and continuing significance for all those who work with children and are concerned about their wellbeing. In practice, balancing a child's right to protection with their right to participate is difficult for all involved with children. Promoting children's rights to participate does not mean advocating that children should make all decisions themselves, whatever their age or level of competence. However, it is clear that children are not able to participate effectively in many decisions affecting their lives. The influence of dominant constructions of childhood, as well as of prevalent incremental theories of development, and lack of adult skills in communicating with children, particularly where the child is non-verbal, has special educational needs or has English as an additional language, can prevent a child's individual needs and levels of competence being recognised, and can lead to him or her being seen as one of a uniform group of people rather than a separate and unique person. As discussed above, this can be seen within the courts making contact and residence decisions in England and within the work of aid agencies working under the auspices of the UNCRC.

It is a difficult challenge for all of us, as adults used to having various amounts of power and control over children, to acknowledge and promote the participation rights of children (Lansdown, 2001). Those working in early years contexts face particular difficulties, as the younger the child, the more incompetent he or she tends to be viewed and the less likely he or she is to have their right to participation addressed. However, various methods of facilitating young children's participation are being used in settings as diverse as nurseries and local council planning departments, with encouraging results and significant implications for future practice (see Willow et al., 2004 for a helpful review of various initiatives).

It is incumbent on all of us to recognise the importance of children's active participation in all areas of their lives, not only because it is their right, but also because it may lead to better decisions as well as improving a child's self-esteem and confidence (Thomas, 2001). Children's effective participation will not become a reality unless we are able to actively challenge our own values and beliefs about children, as well as those of the many institutions, agencies and organisations that influence children's lives.

Questions for reflection and discussion

1. Why is it difficult to define children's rights?
2. Are children's rights, as set out under the UNCRC, universally applicable?
3. Is a rights-based approach helpful in improving the lives of children?
4. How can competence in young children be assessed?
5. How can young children be actively involved in research and decisions?

Recommended reading

Alderson, P. (2008) *Young Children's Rights: Exploring Beliefs, Principles and Practice*. London: Jessica Kingsley.
A comprehensive look at competing children's rights and the importance of communicating with even the youngest children to understand their perspectives.

Children's Rights Alliance for England (2012) *The State of Children's Rights in England*. London: CRAE.
A detailed and comprehensive report covering all aspects of children's lives in England in 2012.

Clark, A. and Moss, P. (2011) *Listening to Young Children: The Mosaic Approach*, 2nd edn. London: National Children's Bureau Enterprises.
Explains this very important and useful approach to gaining children's (and adults') perspectives.

James, A. and James, A. (2004) *Constructing Childhood: Theory, Policy and Social Practice.* Basingstoke: Palgrave.
Good background reading looking at the impact our perspectives on childhood have on our understanding of children's experiences.

OECD (2006) *Starting Strong II: Early Childhood Education and Care.* Paris: OECD.
Looks at the importance of early childhood care and education in relation to children's development and has links to useful and important research.

A reading list for further articles and resources relating to working with very young children can be found at: www.ncb.org.uk/media/59372/consulting_children_reading_list.pdf.

Recommended websites

www.childrenscommissioner.gov.uk/
This is the web page of the Children's Commissioner for England. As well as explaining the role of the Commissioner, it has links to a useful range of significant publications and enquiries relating to children's rights and experiences in England.

www.crae.org.uk
This is the website of the Children's Rights Alliance for England (CRAE). It provides advice for children and young people and organisations that seek to support children's rights. CRAE publishes an annual report about the state of children's rights in England. The website has useful guidance and information and links to annual reports.

www.edcm.org.uk/resources.aspx
This is the website of 'Every Disabled Child Matters' (EDCM), a campaigning group run by Contact a Family, the Council for Disabled Children, Mencap and the Special Educational Consortium. It has links to other organisations and resources relating to involving disabled children in decision making.

www.ncb.org.uk/what-we-do/involving-young-people
This is the National Children's Bureau web page relating to the involvement of children and young people in a range of aspects of their lives. It has links to other organisations and campaigns to improve involvement, including the young children's voices network which works to improve the involvement of very young children.

Want to learn more about this chapter? Visit the companion website at **www.sagepub.co.uk/walleranddavis3e** to access podcasts from the author and child observation videos.

5

Understanding Diversity

Prospera Tedam

 Key chapter objectives

- To explore the concept of 'diversity' within the context of early years care and education
- To identify the role of practitioners, parents and the wider community in supporting young children to gain an understanding of difference
- To highlight relevant national and international legislative and policy frameworks that underpin diversity
- To develop students' understanding of the barriers to equal opportunities and to explore strategies for removing the barriers

The purpose of this chapter is to provide students with an understanding of contemporary research concerning diversity and inclusive practice in the early years. This chapter will explore the concept of diversity and the idea of valuing individuals and their differences as a means to further enriching society and achieving social justice. The chapter will also argue that understanding diversity will add value to the professional's approach to working with young children, who all have individual characteristics that make them unique and form part of their identity. The role that professionals, parents and the wider community have in encouraging and supporting young children in understanding issues of diversity in contemporary society will be explored in detail. An overview of current national and international legislation and policy frameworks that underpin diversity will be given and the implications for early years practice will be outlined.

The chapter will also consider the barriers to equal opportunities for children, families and early years practitioners, and explore ways of removing barriers to offer equality of service, regardless of individual differences such as special needs, abilities, 'race', gender or socioeconomic status. Two case studies will be used to enhance the reader's understanding of the value of diversity and the nature and meaning of inclusion within society. The breadth, depth and scope of diversity make it impossible to attempt to address all aspects within a single defined chapter such as this. Texts such as that by Devarakonda (2013) provide such depth and breadth. Consequently, this chapter will examine diversity in line with the stated objectives highlighted above.

Nelson Mandela, in 1994, during his inauguration as President of South Africa, stated: 'no one is born hating another person because of the colour of his skin, or his background or his religion. People must learn to hate, and if they can learn to hate, they can be taught to love, for love comes more naturally to the human heart than its opposite' (cited in Brown, 2001: xii). It is argued here that this statement forms the foundation on which issues of diversity should be developed and understood, especially in relation to children who should be taught, at an early age, to appreciate and respect difference and to value their uniqueness as human beings.

This view is supported by the Department for Education and Skills (DfES, 2007f: 9), where it is suggested that in terms of early years provision, 'providers have a responsibility to ensure positive attitudes to diversity and difference – not only so that every child is included and not disadvantaged, but also so that they learn from the earliest age to value diversity in others and grow up making a positive contribution to society'. More recently the Department for Education stipulated as one of its standards the 'equality of opportunity and anti-discriminatory practice, ensuring that every child is included and supported' (DfE, 2012d: 2). This further emphasises the importance of equality of opportunity for children, recognised at local and national levels.

People who work with children will be striving to support the development of children into adulthoods that are positive, productive and respectful. Our values would be in question if, during the early years, children were not taught to love and respect each other and were instead taught to hate, disrespect and discriminate against other children who are different from themselves.

Diversity language and terminology

According to Thompson (2006), societies are characterised by differentiation. This means that societies are made up of a diverse range of people whose social divisions such as gender, socioeconomic status, age, race, etc. play a central role in determining the opportunities available and the power distribution and status of individuals, groups and communities. We cannot ignore the fact that contemporary British society is becoming increasingly diverse, due primarily to immigration and the resettlement of people from around the globe. According to Haynes (cited in Coombe and Little, 1986), the end of the Second World War saw Britain turning to her colonies for semi-skilled and unskilled labour; this resulted in the migration of people from the Caribbean and South Asia to work in the UK. The end of the economic boom in the final quarter of the 20th century saw a rise in poverty and disadvantage for many black people in the UK, which was characterised by low income, poor housing and social exclusion (Cohen et al., 2001). More recently, the free movement of members of the European Union has further contributed to the diversity in Britain.

In 1996, NCH Action for Children conducted a study which revealed that about 3.2 million people, or 6% of the population, were from minority ethnic groups with around 36% of this figure being children under 16 (NCH Action for Children, 1996: 24–5). The national census of 2011 revealed that 14% of the UK population come from black and minority ethnic groups (Office for National Statistics, 2012a). This challenges professionals in the early years education and childcare sector not only to become aware of the benefits this diversity brings to our society, but also to consider the tensions that may arise due to insensitivity, misunderstanding or intolerance to difference. Diversity enriches society through the different ideas, knowledge and experiences that people hold.

There are many aspects of difference between and among people, including gender, age, religion and faith, ethnicity, race, economic status, health, sexuality, family structure and disabilities, yet this list is not exhaustive. There also exist additional characteristics that further differentiate people. For example, a child of Somali origin may also be Muslim, female, disabled, born in Britain or may be a refugee or 'asylum seeker'. For the purposes of this chapter, the focus will be on age, gender and sexuality, race and economic status. While the author understands the importance of all forms of difference, there is little opportunity to explore these areas in detail. Where this is the case, the reader will be signposted to additional relevant texts that discuss these themes in greater depth.

Race and ethnicity

This section will begin with conceptualising 'race' and 'ethnicity' in relation to how these concepts are used within this chapter. The concept of 'race' can be understood as a social construct as: 'a vast group of people loosely bound together by a historically contingent, socially significant element of their ancestry' (Haney-Lopez, 2000: 165).

Ethnicity, according to Storkey (1991: 109–10, cited in Thompson, 2006: 72), can be defined as: 'All the characteristics which go to make up cultural identity: origins, physical appearance, language, family structure, religious beliefs, politics, food, art, music, literature, attitudes towards the body, gender roles, clothing, education.'

From a very early age, children will notice difference in skin colour but are unlikely to make sense of this until they are a little older. The views of their family, friends and the media all contribute towards their understanding of race and will also influence their views of people who are different from them. Very young children do not have the capacity to be racist, however once they begin to question the difference within their school or provision, it is the role of professionals to help them make sense of race and to understand the need to treat all people in a fair manner. According to Husband (2012), what is required in early childhood training and education is the teaching of anti-racist practice that can in turn benefit children in early childhood settings. Children for whom English is an additional language should not be viewed by early years practitioners through a deficit lens; they should rather consider their bi- and multi-lingual skills as enhancing and celebrating what Robinson and Diaz (2006: 172) refer to as 'bilingual identities'.

The role of the media is a powerful vehicle for fuelling racialised and discriminatory behaviour and attitudes. Siraj-Blatchford (1994) suggests that the media portrayal of black people as inferior or problematic, and the stereotyping of minority ethnic communities, misinform people and can negatively shape the opinions and conceptions of young children.

Early years practitioners will need to be aware of racism and its longer-term effects on children's self-esteem and identity. Incidents of racism that are not properly dealt with will send the message that practitioners or early years provisions condone racist and discriminatory behaviour and attitudes. Victims of racism, no matter how young, have to be supported and reassured that the incidents will be dealt with in an appropriate way. Perpetrators of racial abuse should be cautioned in an age-appropriate manner and the parents or carers duly informed that such behaviour is unacceptable and advised accordingly. The Swann Report (DES, 1985) highlighted that a small minority of teachers were consciously racist and a good number were 'unintentionally racist', and as a result made children from black and minority ethnic groups feel inferior by the use of certain books and other educational material.

A child's early years are important because it is the period during which children develop self-awareness and begin to form their racial and personal identity, and practitioners should be skilled enough to support children through this period.

Early years practitioners should understand the implications of discrimination legislation in general, and the Equality Act 2010 (HM Government, 2010) in particular, for their work:

Early years practitioners should examine teaching resources such as books, toys and artefacts to see if they positively represent all sectors of society.

Practitioners should receive training on race equality issues and be required to attend refresher courses on similar topics. (QCA, 2007)

CASE STUDY ONE

Suzie is a 5-year-old Chinese girl who has recently started the Foundation Stage at her local school. Prior to this, Suzie attended a local authority-run day nursery. Suzie had been at the new school for nearly five weeks and seemed to be enjoying school until one day when she returned from school sullen and upset. She told her parents about her day at school. Suzie started off by saying that she no longer liked her hair and wanted to have blonde hair. When asked by her parents why she felt this way, Suzie explained that she was upset because during the school break she had made a 'den' with her friends but then was not allowed into the 'den' because the criterion for going into the den was that one had to have 'blonde hair'. Suzie's parents explained that Suzie had nice hair and that her hair is and would remain as it is. Suzie's parents decided to talk to her about difference, explaining that everyone is different and special, adding that her different hair colour and texture should be a source of pride. Suzie appeared to understand the discussion, however getting her to school the following day was difficult as she was concerned that she would still not be allowed to play in the 'den' because her hair was not blonde. Suzie's parents arranged a meeting with the class teacher to discuss their concerns.

 ### Reflection for case study 1

- What issues are raised for you in this case study?
- How could the class teacher support Suzie to feel accepted and not excluded?
- Is there a need to speak to the children concerned?
- What could happen if this issue is not addressed?

Inclusion

For the purposes of this chapter, this section will focus on inclusion in the wider context of early years, as the next chapter will explore inclusion in terms of special educational needs (SEN).

Inclusion is a term that often generates debate and discussion, and there is no fixed definition for inclusion. There is a school of thought that defines inclusion as 'a process of identifying, understanding and breaking down the barriers to participation and belonging' (Early Childhood Forum, 2003). There is another school of thought which suggests that 'inclusion' is a universal human right with the aim of embracing all people, irrespective of race, disability, gender, sexuality, and medical or other need.

Inclusion has been described as a process and not a static state and it cannot be said to be universal in its application. The process of inclusion creates a supportive and nurturing environment for young children and early years practitioners should strive towards making their settings inclusive and nurturing. For this author, talking about 'inclusion' means that, invariably, some people or groups will be 'excluded' and so it is important to identify the meaning of inclusion within specific contexts. Young children need to be included and need to feel that they are not different. Ensuring the inclusion of all children in early years will stem from the provision of equal opportunities for children to participate in school and learn with their peers, irrespective of their gender, socioeconomic background and race.

CASE STUDY TWO

The following discussion took place between a 6-year-old child with additional needs and a member of staff at the local after-school provision:

Staff: Children, would you all please line up behind the table.
Ben: [*stands in the line but keeps moving about*]
Staff: Ben, the instruction was to line up and stand still.
Ben: [*still talking to a friend and moving about*]
Staff: Ben, do you understand English?
Ben: Yes, I do.
Staff: Then, what part of 'line up behind the table' was said in Greek?

★ Reflection for case study 2

- What questions are raised for you by the above?
- How could the member of staff express themselves more appropriately?
- Are there grounds for a complaint against this member of staff?
- What future training needs (if any) would you recommend for this member of staff?

Children need a range of educational opportunities to assist them in achieving their full potential. They need to develop the skills, attitudes and knowledge which will enable them to interact positively with people from diverse backgrounds and groups.

According to Bondy et al. (1995), the concept of inclusion is not restricted to children with disabilities but also children living in poverty, children for whom English is an additional language, homeless children and so on. Children from Traveller communities, refugee and asylum seeking children as well as children who have been trafficked will need to be actively included in early years provision. Asylum seekers in the UK face stigma and discrimination on many levels. Adapting to new environments, a new way of life, culture and language is difficult for many adults and particularly for young children (Whitmarsh, 2011). Attitudes to education and to teachers may also present challenges for children and their families seeking asylum. An early childhood environment should be welcoming of groups like this and children and practitioners are particularly encouraged to 'recognise and respect the difference of immigrant mothers explicitly' (Vandenbroeck et al., 2009: 212) as a means to engaging effectively with them.

In the past twenty years obesity in children has been on the increase in the UK and elsewhere, and according to the World Health Organisation (2012) there are over 42 million children aged 0–5 years worldwide who are classed as obese or overweight. The presence of this public health concern in the UK also requires some consideration within the context of respecting diversity in early childhood. Stigmatisation, ridicule and name calling can have serious emotional and mental health implications for children. Cale and Harris (2011) propose attitudinal changes to body weight and obesity in children, which include: being more aware of the messages practitioners give to children about their weight, examining personal beliefs, values, prejudices and attitudes about obesity, promoting the celebration of being unique and special, and finally, avoiding practices that further disadvantage and discriminate against obese children, for example games in which children have to pass through narrow frames.

The role of parents, professionals and the wider community is central in ensuring that children have an understanding of and respect for diversity. Children and young people are influenced by the society in which they live and belong, therefore professionals will need to begin from the point of building good working relationships with parents by understanding the difficulties they face, their strengths, skills and expertise (Brown, 2001).

It is useful to note the reasons why it is important for children to understand difference and diversity. According to Brown (1998), there are three main reasons:

Legal considerations – understanding diversity on the part of early years practitioners will assist in challenging any personal prejudices or stereotypes they might have and will enable them to work in compliance with the law. There are a number of key policy and legislative frameworks that promote inclusion and make discrimination unlawful. Whilst children are not subject to these legal repercussions in their early childhood, they will be when they grow older and hence they should be encouraged to understand that discrimination in all its forms is unwelcome in contemporary society and that there is a need to embrace and respect diversity.

Ethical considerations – to some people, it may seem moral and ethical to provide fair treatment and equality of opportunities to all people, regardless of individual differences. There is also the recognition of social justice and its centrality in discussions of diversity and equal opportunities. Miller and Pedro (2006: 293) emphasise the importance of creating 'respectful classroom environments' and assert that teachers have a duty to ensure and promote positive interactions and relationships among their pupils and also between teachers and their pupils. Where there may be difficulties achieving this, early childhood practitioners are encouraged to intervene by not tolerating discrimination and exclusion of children in their settings.

Social considerations – children will learn from what they have observed of inclusive and non-discriminatory practices and are likely to grow into adults who will respect diversity and who can make positive contributions to their communities and the nation as a whole. In this respect, Graham (2007: 65) asserts that as a strategy for equality, 'diversity recognizes that everyone has a contribution to make' and children, as much as adults, are central to the understanding and respect of diversity.

Gender equity

Gender debates in relation to biological and social differences between the genders are important in early years professional training and work and have been seen by some as being socially constructed, and children tend to be socialised into either the male or female role (Woodhead and Montgomery, 2003). It is further suggested by Woodhead and Montgomery (2003: 181) that it may be difficult to understand the nature of childhood without taking into account the differences in 'girls' worlds and boys' worlds' and that children learn gender-appropriate behaviour by observation.

The area of play is an important one in early years settings as children begin to identify with aspects of play that are likely to reflect their gender. The type of play children engage in, for example dolls for girls, as suggested by Haralambos and Holborn (2004), serves to reinforce the stereotype of women as carers, while boys are often given toys that are designed to develop their scientific and constructional skills. Practitioners are encouraged to support children's play and experiment with toys, games and activities that transcend gender.

It is difficult to imagine how young children will perceive gender equity if in practice there are far more females than males in the early years profession.

This chapter does not seek to explain why the early years profession is as gendered as it is, as this is an extensive area worthy of a much fuller debate. Instead, this section aims to highlight the need for a balanced gender mix in practitioners, in order that children learn from and understand diversity from a gender perspective.

Owen (2003) asserts that in 1991 out of a total of 57,000 nursery nurses there were only 600 men, which is a little over 1%. The report continues to state that by 2001/2002 this picture had not changed significantly. The Nutbrown Review (2012b) highlights that between 98 and 99% of the early years workforce is female and acknowledges the importance of increasing male representation through targeted recruitment efforts. There is therefore the need for children to see both females and males in the caring profession as this is likely to challenge their stereotypes about gender and gender-related roles in early years provision. Cameron (2006) confirms that this trend is similar in other European countries, with Denmark having the highest employment rates for males in the early childhood workforce, primarily due to the effective marketing and recruitment strategies adopted.

Socioeconomic status

Vast differences exist between children in the early years in terms of their parents' or families' socioeconomic status. With parental unemployment, low-income families and widespread childhood poverty, early years settings are certain to have children whose socioeconomic background means that they are 'different' and possibly excluded by other children. The media plays a significant role in making young children aware of the 'must-have' toys, games and gadgets and, in some settings, children are allowed to take these into school to 'show and tell' at various points in the term, thereby placing pressure on the other children to own such toys and games.

Poverty in the 21st century is widespread and is usually understood in terms of material, social and emotional shortages. There are currently around 3.5 million children living in poverty in the UK (DWP, 2013) – this equates to 1 in 3 children, which is a significant increase from the 1970s when the figure was 1 in 10 (Wyse, 2004).

The impact of poverty on children is devastating, and as research by the End Child Poverty Campaign indicates, poverty shapes children's development and can shorten lives (End Child Poverty Campaign, 2008). It is useful, therefore, for early years practitioners to understand the nature and impact of poverty on children's learning, achievement and social presentation and to ensure that children in their care are treated equally and fairly, irrespective of their family's socioeconomic background.

In order to ensure equity when working with young children, it is essential that practitioners do not encourage the excessive display of wealth by some children, as this greatly disadvantages and disempowers children from other socioeconomic backgrounds. Professionals will also need to ensure that their requests of parents and carers to provide, for example, costumes for various activities are reasonable and do not in any way undermine the position and financial capabilities of parents and carers. Children from lower socioeconomic backgrounds may also be black, disabled, have gay, lesbian or single and/or asylum seeking parents, which places them in a situation of multiple disadvantage. This needs to be carefully considered by practitioners to promote equality of opportunity for children they work with.

The UK government's target to halve child poverty by 2010 has not come to fruition and strategies to eliminate it by 2020 are ongoing, albeit with little prospect of becoming reality. This target is enshrined in the Child Poverty Act 2010 and should hold the government to account if progress is not made in this area. Given this backdrop of ongoing socioeconomic hardship for many families, early years settings and staff are entreated to work in a manner that does not highlight the financial and income disparities between and among children as this could perpetuate inequality and oppression towards specific children.

Social justice

Social justice and equality are closely linked, and, as Kobayashi and Ray (2000) assert, educational institutions contribute to the defining of which social inequality issues will be tolerated by the public. Vincent (2003: 18) argues that social justice can be understood within a framework and has a number of facets. These are associational, distributive and cultural justice. Associational justice is the absence of the 'patterns of association amongst individuals and amongst groups which prevent people from participating fully in decisions which affect the conditions within which they live and act' (Gewirtz, 2001: 41, cited in Vincent, 2003). This understanding of associational justice is one which has the closest links to the theme of this chapter. One could argue that children are unable to participate fully in matters that affect them and that any treatment meted out to children as a result of their age, gender, race and socioeconomic status is one that infringes on social justice. Vincent (2003) goes on to perceive distributive justice as the process through which goods and services are shared in society. This form of social justice relates to the socioeconomic status of children, groups and communities. The final framework for understanding social justice is the cultural perspective, which implies disrespect and non-recognition of cultures that are different from our own. Social justice and anti-discriminatory practice go together and can be used as a vehicle of empowerment and celebration of diversity and difference. Early years practitioners will need to understand the value of advancing the notion of social justice, in order to effectively challenge discrimination and promote equality of opportunity for all children.

A professional approach to working with diversity and difference

Early years practitioners provide the preparation of children for the future, support the elimination of the disadvantages faced by some groups of children and also strive to provide an environment free from discrimination (Willan et al., 2004). In order to achieve this effectively, they are required to first and foremost understand difference and diversity, the impact on various groups of children and the exclusion faced by some of such children. Robinson (2005) suggests that early years practitioners should feel able to take risks in challenging inequality and discrimination and that practitioners should make this a priority area. All early years settings have to ensure that their staff (permanent and temporary) understand the legislative and policy framework governing their service area and are aware of the implications of non-adherence to the law.

A professional approach for practitioners involved in early years settings takes account of practitioners' understanding of the importance of respecting difference and acknowledging the benefits of difference. It is also important to mention that within staff teams there will be diversity in personality, attitudes, backgrounds, gender, faith and religious beliefs, culture, language and abilities. The starting point, therefore, for professionals will be to acknowledge the differences that exist among colleagues and to treat everyone with respect. It is only by working in this inclusive way as practitioners that young children will be able to learn inclusive and non-discriminatory behaviour and attitudes.

Policy frameworks

A range of legislation exists, both nationally and internationally, that provides a framework for anti-discriminatory practice generally and more specific legislation affecting children. The success or failure of these pieces of legislation will rest on practitioners' ability to translate them into practice within their early years provision for children. In addition to specific pieces of legislation, government guidance on various topics has been written and should be read and applied alongside relevant legislation. For example, the 2008 publication by the Department for Children, Schools and Families entitled 'The Inclusion of Gypsy, Roma and Traveller Children and Young People' (DCSF, 2008b) highlighted children in this category as being the group that is most 'at risk' in education, due primarily to low achievement exacerbated by factors such as racism, discrimination and stereotyping. Lord Adonis, the Parliamentary Under-Secretary of State for Schools, stated in his foreword that 'we need to create an inclusive learning environment for all children' and that raising the achievement of Gypsy and Roma children is 'the responsibility of everyone within the education system' (DCSF, 2008b: 5).

The national picture

The rights of children in Britain are enshrined in a number of specific pieces of legislation. In England and Wales, the Children Act 1989 and the Education Act 1944 emphasise children's right to be protected from unfair discrimination. The Race Relations (Amendment) Act 2000 was introduced following an enquiry into the murder of a black teenager, Stephen Lawrence, in 1993 and placed statutory duties on local authorities, including local education authorities, to promote race equality and equal opportunities and to ensure positive relationships among people of different races (Maynard and Thomas, 2004). The Macpherson Report in 1999 found that 'institutional racism' was the reason for the flawed and poorly handled investigation into the black teenager's death. The Report defined institutional racism as:

> The collective failure of an organisation to provide an appropriate and professional ser-
> vice to people because of their colour, culture, or ethnic origin. It can be seen or detected
> in processes, attitudes and behaviour which amount to discrimination through unwitting
> prejudice, ignorance, thoughtlessness and racist stereotyping which disadvantage minor-
> ity ethnic people. (Macpherson, 1999: paragraph 6.34)

What this means for schools and early years provision is that policies, procedures, rules, practice and guidelines should seek to include all children. A report by the DfES in 2006 concerning a pattern of high numbers of exclusions of African-Caribbean boys in comparison with their white peers was highlighted and echoed previous studies that suggested schools' policies were discriminatory towards African-Caribbean boys (DfES, 2006a: 10). It is important to note that a number of separate pieces of legislation have been brought together to form the Equality Act 2010 (HM Government, 2010). This legislation includes: the Race Relations (Amendment) Act 2000, the Disability Discrimination Act 1995 and the Sex Discrimination Act 1975, among others.

The Children Act 2004 (HM Government, 2004), which came into force as a direct result of the death of Victoria Climbié and the subsequent inquiry by Lord Laming into the 8-year-old girl's death, highlighted the government's vision for all children in England and Wales to: stay safe, be healthy, enjoy and achieve, make a positive contribution and achieve economic wellbeing. These targets, known as the five outcomes, demonstrate a commitment on the part of the government and public authorities to ensure that all children in England and Wales achieve a good standard of life and maximise their potential.

In addition to the above, in the Childcare Act of 2006, which was seen as a pioneering piece of legislation due to its focus on early years and childcare provision in England and Wales, sections 1–5 emphasise the need for local authorities and NHS trusts to work together towards the reduction of inequalities between and among children and to support the achievement of the five outcomes as stated above. The Act further places a duty on local authorities to assess childcare provision in their areas and to ensure that children with disabilities and children from low-income families are provided with services to meet their needs (HM Government, 2006). Also, the Education and Inspections Act 2006 introduced a duty on all maintained schools in England to promote community cohesion (DfES, 2006b). This duty came into effect on 1 September 2007. Since September 2008 Ofsted has also been required to report on the contributions made in this area. The government publication *Guidance on the Duty to Promote Community Cohesion* (DCSF, 2007c) defines community cohesion as:

> working towards a society in which there is a common vision and sense of belonging by all communities; a society in which the diversity of people's backgrounds and circumstances is appreciated and valued; a society in which similar life opportunities are available to all; and a society in which strong and positive relationships exist and continue to be developed in the workplace, in schools and in the wider community. (p. 3)

The international picture

From an international perspective, the United Nations Convention on the Rights of the Child (UNCRC) (United Nations, 1989) highlights a number of Articles that are relevant to the discussion on valuing diversity and the provision of equality of opportunity for children. In particular, Article 2 of the Convention states that 'each child should enjoy the rights set out in the convention without discrimination of any kind, irrespective of the child's parent's or guardian's race, colour, gender, language, religion, political or other opinion, national or social origin, property, disability, birth or status'.

The Human Rights Act 1998, which has been incorporated into UK law, stipulates a number of rights that every human being is entitled to. A human rights perspective suggests that all people are treated fairly, without discrimination and with equality of opportunity. Public bodies or persons carrying out a public function can be in breach of various articles under the Human Rights Act 1998. In particular, Article 14 prohibits all forms of discrimination and it is imperative that education settings, including early years settings, promote anti-discriminatory practice by adhering to the obligations of the Human Rights Act. The European Commission (EC), in a *Handbook on Equality Data* (Makkonen, 2006: 11), affirmed its commitment to tackling discrimination and ensuring equality for all, in a strategy document entitled 'Non-discrimination and equal opportunities for all – A framework strategy'. This strategy affects all countries in the European Union, including the UK. The Handbook makes interesting reading and provides a powerful statement about equal opportunities:

> Denial of equal opportunities comes at a high price for those concerned and the society at large, as discrimination prejudices the rights and opportunities of individuals, leads to the wasting of human resources, and causes social disintegration. Furthermore, given Europe's current demographic tendencies – low birth rate, ageing population and thus a shrinking workforce – equal treatment is no longer only a question of social justice but also of economic necessity. (Makkonen, 2006: 11)

The international movement of people across national and international borders for economic, political and social reasons has created an increase in immigrants coming into the UK. The Refugee Council defines an asylum seeker as one who 'has left their country of origin and formally applied for asylum in another country but whose application has not yet been decided' (Refugee Council, 2013).

In the UK, a refugee, according to the same source, is a person whose application for asylum has been successful and who is allowed to stay, having proved that they have a 'well-founded fear of being persecuted' should they return home (Refugee Council, 2013). There appears to be no official figure about asylum seeking and refugee children in the UK, however, according to Rutter (2006), there were about 60,000 refugee and asylum seeking children in the UK who were of school-going age but refugee children are underrepresented in early years provision due to being less likely to access the provision. There is also further evidence by Rutter and Hyder (1998), suggesting that refugee populations have more children under 5 years of age than the general population.

Implications for early years practitioners

The range of legal and policy frameworks on the subject of anti-discrimination and inclusion is vast and covers a range of specific issues. Early years practitioners will, as part of their training, be expected to learn and understand these concepts and the implications for professional practice. Additionally, early years practitioners can be held accountable for any behaviours and attitudes that are not aligned with legislation and which are likely to bring the profession into disrepute. Anti-discriminatory legislation and policy will set boundaries and parameters for professionals during their work with children and will also serve as guidelines for best practice.

Parents, families and carers of children will be able to use relevant legislation as a kind of 'quality assurance' tool in determining the extent to which their provider is working to promote the inclusion of children within their settings. Early years practitioners should promote a culture of openness and trust, in which children can share their fears and hopes for the present and the future. In talking about difference, professionals need to be aware of the language they use to describe children who are different, as children in their care will pick up such language.

Professionals will need to be aware that certain groups of children, for example asylum seeking and refugee children, who access their provision may require additional support in understanding the culture, expectations, procedures and regulations in the UK. Early years practitioners are required to promote equality of opportunity for the children and families they work with and can do this by:

- ensuring equal access by children, carers and families to resources and available learning opportunities
- receiving training to enable them to challenge discrimination firmly and with confidence
- being aware of their duties towards disabled children and the implications of the Disability Discrimination Act 1995 on their work with children

- being aware of and changing practices, policies and procedures that might unintentionally discriminate against children with disabilities
- liaising with health visitors and other health professionals about the health needs of the refugee and asylum seeking children in their care.

Barriers to equal opportunities

Despite being grounded in policy and legislation, it can be difficult to practise in an inclusive way and, whether by intent or sheer misjudgement, practitioners can find themselves in difficult situations which are likely to create unhealthy working environments. This section will briefly outline some of the barriers to achieving equal opportunities for children in the early years sector. According to Brown (2001), the main barriers to achieving equal opportunities for children include the following:

- Being uninformed – being unaware of equal opportunities policy and how it affects children can be a significant barrier to achieving equity within the early years setting. Professionals are required to engage in ongoing development which continues to challenge their thinking and their practice.
- Being insensitive – as unique individuals, our attitudes and behaviours are shaped by our values, beliefs and life experiences, some of which may result in professionals being insensitive to the needs and emotional wellbeing of the children they work with. Being sensitive to a particular issue will convey the message to a child that professionals are interested in and concerned about their wellbeing and development, whereas insensitivity is likely to result in children feeling unimportant and helpless.
- Individual stereotypes – we are all social beings who learn from our environment and experiences and these shape our thought processes and the way in which we view the world. Early years practitioners are not value-free and will invariably hold stereotypes about certain groups of people and individuals and take these with them into practice (Siraj-Blatchford, 1994). For example, assumptions about certain groups in society will create barriers to the provision of equal opportunities for children in these groups.

Overcoming the barriers

Lynch (1987) argues that it is possible to educate teachers and staff in schools on prejudice reduction by way of acquiring the relevant principles of social justice and respect for all people. It is also critical that early years staff demonstrate positive attitudes – a willingness and sense of commitment towards overcoming any barriers to achieving equal opportunities for children they work with. By so doing, the barriers to achieving equal opportunities for children will be minimised and possibly less difficult to overcome. Strategies towards overcoming these barriers include the following.

Encourage open debate and discussion

Open and honest debate and discussion should be encouraged within the workplace, and practitioners should feel safe and able to share their anxieties around issues of diversity to enable a learning environment which is open to a sharing of experiences and skills in the area of difference within the early years setting. Reflection around practitioners' own understanding of diversity and the implications for children in their care should be encouraged. These kinds of reflective exercises could be done within the wider context of a team meeting or training event but also on a more individualised and formal level within supervision.

Promote regular interaction/collaboration between parents and professionals

Early years practitioners should engage in regular interaction and collaboration with parents and carers of the children in their care in order to dispel some of the stereotypical views they might hold about certain people and groups of people. This will also promote an understanding of parents' and carers' motivation and ability to engage in other activities involving their children. It will be unhelpful, for example, to stereotype and label some groups of parents as unengaging or hard to reach without actually experiencing this first hand. Whitmarsh's (2011) study of asylum seeking mothers' interaction with early years provision concluded that a multiplicity of factors such as limited language skill and unfamiliarity with the host country created what was perceived by professionals as hard-to-engage attitudes.

Maintain a reflective and reflexive approach

Often the two words reflective and reflexive are used interchangeably, but they can mean different things. Reflection usually occurs after the event or situation and it involves professionals understanding, analysing, evaluating and reviewing their practice in relation to the children they work with. Reflexivity is ongoing throughout the practice event or situation during which a practitioner considers the impact of their values and assumptions about others on their practice.

Being reflexive when working with children and their families, according to Robinson and Diaz (2006: 169), involves the deconstruction of 'tolerance' to one of 'respect'. This is an important strategy to overcome barriers to equality of opportunities for children because practitioners begin to examine themselves and their practice, which hopefully leads to changes being made wherever necessary. The value of reflective practitioners in early years settings has also been highlighted in the Nutbrown Review (2012b).

Staff composition

Early years staff teams should as closely as possible reflect the diversity of the wider community and societies in which we live. This will not only send a strong message to children and their families and carers, but will also provide role models for many of the children who access the provision. The Nutbrown Review (2012b) has identified the need for an increase in the numbers of men in what is largely perceived as a female-dominated profession.

Creative use of resources

Another means of overcoming barriers to equal opportunities in early years settings is to provide resources that will suit a wide range of children. For example, provide toys that can be used by able-bodied as well as disabled children, games that can be used by children of either gender and books, videos and music that reflect different cultural and ethnic communities.

Also, involve families and carers in activities within the provision to reinforce a commitment to equal opportunities and the diversity of skills, expertise and knowledge provided by families and carers of children. For example, an early years provision that encourages parents and carers, of either gender and any ethnicity, to support group activities or volunteer within the school or provision will send a strong message about their commitment to equality of opportunity for the benefit of the children.

Ouseley and Lane (2006) identify further ways through which early years practitioners can overcome the barriers to providing equality of opportunity to children. A summary of these is given below:

1. Professionals will need to ensure that all children are given the equal opportunity to learn and develop in an environment that is free from discrimination, stereotyping and labelling.
2. Professionals should be conversant with and able to apply the legal framework that governs diversity, including the Equality Act 2010, the Human Rights Act 1998, the United Nations Convention on the Rights of the Child, the Equality Act 2006, the Children Act 1989 and 2004, and the Childcare Act 2006.
3. It is imperative that early years practitioners adopt a social justice approach to their work. This would involve adopting and promoting an attitude of fairness, equality and opportunities for children to achieve their maximum potential. A social justice perspective encourages people to work towards equipping children with the tools needed for a successful and fulfilling adult life.

4. Every child should be encouraged to develop the full range of cognitive, behavioural and critical awareness skills.
5. Early childhood settings and classrooms should celebrate diversity not only through the décor and visual aids but also through open, honest and age-appropriate discussions. In so doing, the view by Park (2011) that diversity is seen and not always heard in early childhood environments can be challenged.

It is imperative that all professionals working with children are aware of the legal framework and policies that underpin diversity and equality of opportunity for children. Aspects of the relevant legislation and policy have been explored in this chapter. An understanding of and commitment to promoting inclusion and social justice is crucial, if it is to be achieved. Children in early years require guidance and positive experiences of human values that accept and embrace diversity among people. There is a clear role for parents and carers, early years practitioners and the wider community to ensure that children grow and develop tolerance, understanding and appreciation of diversity in contemporary society.

 Research in context

Miller, R. and Pedro, J. (2006) 'Creating respectful classroom environments', *Early Childhood Education Journal*, 33 (5): 293–9.

Miller and Pedro (2006) examine the concept of 'respect' in early childhood classroom settings and environments and propose that respect encourages appreciation and genuine tolerance of others' worldviews and cultures and can enhance the learning experiences of all involved. They argue that teachers are the primary vehicle through whom children learn the value of respect and appreciation for a range of differences that exist. They offer a 'respectful classroom inventory' (p. 297) which outlines responsibilities for teachers, individual children and the class as a whole. These responsibilities include a demonstration that they understand the words respect, dignity, courtesy, individuality and uniqueness and that children 'work well together regardless of ethnicity and/or ability' (p. 297). It is being proposed that this sort of framework can be a useful strategy in understanding diversity.

Chapter summary

This chapter has sought to provide a basis for critical reflection on the part of early years practitioners about inclusion and equal opportunities for children. The government has shown a strong commitment to issues of inclusion and requires professionals in this field of work to adhere to and promote inclusion in their places of work. This can be achieved through an examination of professionals' own values, views, experiences and attitudes to difference and through 'unlearning' some of the potentially divisive and unhelpful attitudes and views that they may hold about certain groups in our society (Siraj-Blatchford, cited in Pugh and Duffy, 2006). The Equality and Human Rights Commission, which was created through the merging of the Commission on Racial Equality (CRE), the Disability Rights Commission (DRC) and the Equal Opportunities Commission (EOC) from 2007, has sought to further promote respect for diversity, and seeks to promote equality and human rights for all, reduce inequality, build positive relations, eliminate discrimination and ensure the fair participation of all people in society (see the Equality and Human Rights Commission website, www.equalityhumanrights.com).

Diversity should be promoted in all early years settings, regardless of the nature and scope of difference in a given area. It is not acceptable to deny the promotion of diversity with the excuse that particular early years settings have little or no enrolment from minority communities. For settings where there are no children of black or minority ethnic heritage, for example, it is the provider's responsibility to ensure that the decor, teaching and play aids represent a diverse world in whichever way is helpful to the children.

The aim of promoting diversity should be to enable children to appreciate difference as they grow and develop into citizens of a diverse country and world.

The Introduction to the Statutory Framework for the Early Years Foundation Stage (DfE, 2012d) begins with the words 'Every child ...'. The significance of these words cannot be overemphasised and serves as a firm commitment to provide for all children services and settings that promote equality and discourage discriminatory practices.

The following quote sends a strong message to all about difference and diversity:

> As individual practitioners we cannot make the world free of inequalities and a safe place to be, but we can do our very best to ensure that our early years settings are small models of what we would like the world to be. (Lane, 2007: 1)

Questions for reflection and discussion

1. Consider your personal values, beliefs and attitudes about diversity and social justice and explore where these came from and how they have shaped your identity.
2. How easy is it to challenge discriminatory attitudes and behaviours by colleagues?
3. Why is it important for early years practitioners to have a social justice perspective?

Recommended reading

Brown, B. (1998) *Unlearning Discrimination in the Early Years*. Stoke-on-Trent: Trentham Books.

Coombe, V. and Little, A. (1986) *Race and Social Work: A Guide to Training*. London: Tavistock Publications.

Robinson, K.H. and Diaz, C.J. (2006) *Diversity and Difference in Early Childhood Education*. Maidenhead: Open University Press.

Thompson, N. (2006) *Anti-discriminatory Practice*, 4th edn. Basingstoke: Macmillan.

Recommended websites

www.equalityhumanrights.com
The Equality and Human Rights Commission

www.refugeecouncil.org.uk
The Refugee Council

Want to learn more about this chapter? Visit the companion website at **www.sagepub.co.uk/walleranddavis3e** to access podcasts from the author and child observation videos.

6

Inclusive Practice for Children with Special Educational Needs (SEN)

Christine Hickman and Kyffin Jones

> ### 🔑 Key chapter objectives
>
> - To consider the historical and legislative profile of special educational needs provision
> - To discuss the concept of inclusion in relation to young children with special educational needs
> - To consider advocacy and the voice of the child
> - To discuss how the individual needs of pupils with special educational needs may be met
> - To acknowledge the importance of a multi-agency approach

This chapter will discuss the issues surrounding the inclusion of children with special educational needs in the early years. Inclusion as a term and philosophy will be defined and discussed within a historical and legislative context in relation to special educational needs. Case studies will be used to demonstrate a range of provision for a range of needs. While the importance of a multi-agency approach is commented upon, the main focus is an educational perspective. A range of themes relating to the field of special educational needs (SEN) will be introduced and the importance of emphasising the need to adopt a highly individual and sensitive response, one that pays heed to the child's own identity and perspective, will be stressed.

Recognising the voice of the child

'I had a really great time. Nobody talked to me all night!' (Michael, aged 7). Michael illustrates one of the underlying principles of the education of children with SEN – the notion that how they see the world and what is important to them are individual and might differ from adults' reality. Michael has Asperger's syndrome, which is characterised by impairment in social interaction (Blakemore Brown, 2001), and for him an enjoyable night at his local youth club entailed being completely ignored by his peers. This gave him the space to read his favourite science textbooks uninterrupted. What is clear, however, is that without a firm understanding of Michael's identity, both our assumptions and our interventions will not be accurate and might even be detrimental. The notion of advocacy for young people with SEN, and for those unable to strongly articulate their wishes and feelings about decisions that affect them, has gathered pace (Franklin and Knight, 2011). All children, regardless of any communication need, should be involved in the planning and reviewing of their care (DCSF, 2011, cited in Franklin and Knight, 2011: 5 *sic*). While this chapter recognises that specific disorders and conditions can be linked to general strategies and good practice, it encourages the reader to look more widely than simple labels and categories in order to optimise interventions. It also urges the early years practitioner to recognise and value the unique voice of the child and to be flexible, open and creative to ensure that this voice is heard and interpreted. This is an important consideration that should be seen in tandem with more general factors and principles.

To extend this notion, it is true that an understanding of the principles of conditions such as Asperger's syndrome might in some way aid the practitioner, but they are worth nothing without a clear understanding of the individual's perspective. If Michael is to be a fully functioning and included member of society, his inclusion is in some way dependent on our skills to understand him as much as his skills to fit in with us. In this regard, inclusion is an emotional state and one that demands negotiation and compromise on behalf of all players. The individual's opinion and perspective on his or her education must be recognised, regardless of our assumptions concerning their ability to provide such an opinion.

Inclusion, therefore, is not simply the debate about pupils with SEN being educated in mainstream schools, nor is it the tendency to focus on the 'excluded' (Nutbrown and Clough, 2006); it is about the role society has in including all children irrespective of their background or circumstance.

It is clear therefore that issues of equality, human rights and individuality are central to such a rationale, and education is only one part of the picture. The drive towards inclusive education has to be seen in a wider societal context if it is to be meaningful and successful. In other words, inclusion should be less about teachers and pupils and more about the responsibilities of all citizens. The Charity Commission (2008) describes how social inclusion tackles social *exclusion* by empowering those who suffer from the results of inequality and disadvantage (as a result of circumstances the individual is born into or as a result of their own particular circumstances), and by providing equality of opportunity. Increasingly, the view that inclusion is wider than special educational needs and synonymous with diversity and equal opportunity has become prevalent, articulated in the curriculum requirements for state schools, which stress that teachers should provide opportunities to achieve for all '*boys and girls, pupils with special educational needs, people from all social and cultural backgrounds, people from different ethnic groups including travellers, refugees and asylum seekers and those from diverse linguistic backgrounds*' (DfE, 2011d). In this definition inclusion is seen in parallel with inclusivity and social diversity, with the pupil firmly at the heart of the equation. This sentiment is expressed by Loreman et al., who assert that, 'Schools, after all, primarily exist to meet the educational needs of the students not the other way around. Meeting those needs then is fundamental to the work done by schools' (2010: 3).

As mentioned previously, there has been a need to bring together the differing perspectives and domains within the field of early years. Inclusion is promoted by careful, joint planning, utilising a broad range of expertise from a range of professionals in a cohesive manner. The experiences of John (see case study on p. 122) illustrate the need for the concept of inclusive practice to be taken beyond the realms of the mainstream versus special school debate.

Legislative policy and framework – with particular reference to England

It is clear from the wealth of literature on the subject that the movement towards inclusive education has been part of the educational scene in Britain for many years (Booth and Ainscow, 1998; Dyson and Millward, 2000; Wolfendale, 2000; O'Brien, 2001; Roffey, 2001; Tassoni, 2003; Jones, 2004; Ainscow et al., 2006; Hodkinson and Vickerman, 2009; Warnock and Norwich, 2010). Some maintain that it can be mapped back to the Education Act 1944 which extended the right to education to most (but not all) of Britain's children, as Stakes and Hornby (1997: 24) highlight:

> Children with SEN were to be placed in one of eleven categories of handicap: blind, partially sighted, deaf, partially deaf, epileptic, educationally subnormal, maladjusted, physically handicapped, speech defective, delicate and diabetic. The 1944 Act required that LEAs had to ascertain the needs of children in their area for special educational treatment. It indicated that this should be undertaken in mainstream schools wherever possible.

It is important to note that, at this time, disability was firmly categorised into medical subgroups and that the remit of education was to treat rather than educate. Subsequent reports such as that by the Warnock Committee (DES, 1978) highlighted the principle of integrating children with disabilities and developed the process of obtaining a statement of special educational need – in effect, a contract between pupil and educational provider based on careful assessment. The findings of Baroness Warnock and her team helped inform the subsequent 1981 Education Act. A greater emphasis was given to the education of children with special needs during the 1980s and early 1990s and this culminated in the implementation of the Code of Practice for Special Educational Needs in 1994, updated in 2001. At the time, this was the most prescriptive guidance on special needs to have been issued by the UK government. It aimed to expand the roles and responsibilities of schools and local education authorities (LEAs) highlighted in the 1981 Education Act. This trend of redefining SEN provision has continued and during the past two decades has gained momentum and evolved considerably.

The Code of Practice (DfES, 2001a) stresses that 'provider' means all settings which early years children may attend, therefore adherence to such guidelines impacts upon a wide range of professional practice. The early years have specified strands in the Code: *Early Years Action* and *Early Years Action Plus*. According to Drifte (2001: 4), 'both stages involve individualised ways of working with the child, including the implementation of IEPs (Individual Education Plans), on a gradually increasing level of involvement'.

Curriculum 2000 contains an inclusive statement concerning the provision of effective learning opportunities for all pupils. It sets out three principles that are essential to developing a more inclusive curriculum:

1. Setting suitable learning challenges.
2. Responding to pupils' diverse learning needs.
3. Overcoming potential barriers to learning and assessment for individuals and groups of pupils (QCA, 2000).

Every Child Matters (DfES, 2004c) outlined five outcomes for children of all ages: be healthy, stay safe, enjoy and achieve, make a positive contribution and achieve economic wellbeing. This agenda illustrates the government's aim to work with practitioners within a 'conceptual–philosophical framework' (Wolfendale and Robinson, 2006) and to create a more resolute coordinated package of support. The intention of bringing together services into single settings is one that most parents of children with disabilities welcome. For example, a child with a combination of difficulties could find themselves with as many as 315 different service-based appointments over a period of nine months (DfES, 2007b). The importance of early intervention and assessment, coordinated service provision and working with families for children with special needs and disabilities was underlined in the DfES and DH (2003) guidance *Together from the Start*. The inception of Every Disabled Child Matters (EDCM), a campaign set up to advocate for the rights of disabled children and their families, has underlined the strength of feeling by this group of stakeholders. Such campaign objectives as every family being entitled to a key worker on diagnosis, and every extended school and children's centre to deliver a full range of services to disabled children, are on the EDCM agenda (EDCM, 2006).

Removing Barriers to Achievement (DfES, 2004b) links the notion of the five outcomes for children with the needs of children with SEN. It echoes the intentions of collective responsibility for the child with SEN. The revised Early Years Foundation Stage (EYFS) documentation has provided practitioners with guidance and advice on supporting children's learning, development and welfare (DfE, 2012d). The fact that children learn and develop in different ways and at different rates is stressed, which has great relevance for the inclusion debate. Linking in to the outcomes of Every Child Matters, one of the aims of the EYFS is 'providing for equality of opportunity and anti-discriminatory practice and ensuring that every child is included and not disadvantaged because of ethnicity, culture or religion, home language, family background, learning difficulties or disabilities, gender or ability' (DfES, 2007a: 7).

Aiming High for Disabled Children: Better Support for Families (DfES, 2007d) set out the government's aim for all children to have the best start in life and ongoing support for them and their families so that they may reach their full potential. The three areas of (i) access and empowerment, (ii) responsive services and timely support and (iii) improving quality and capacity are considered to be the priority areas to improve outcomes for disabled children (DfES, 2007b). The thrust for joined-up care and support, involving a range of professionals, will necessitate action concerning staff training as awareness levels and more specific training are prioritised (DfES, 2007b). A common thread throughout this documentation and policy is the need for meaningful parental involvement. Wolfendale and Robinson (2006) underline the essential role that parents and families play. EDCM (2006) has the right of parents and families to shape service delivery at its heart. The previous government's intention to have long-term change in children's services was set out in the Children's Workforce Strategy (DfES, 2005a) and the Multi-Agency Toolkit (DfES, 2005c). The overarching aim of such documentation was the consolidation of good practice in training and working procedure, with the emphasis on support for multi-agency working. While this has gone on for many years, many would admit it was organised and implemented on an ad hoc basis.

The Labour Government, in power from 1997 to 2010, identified inclusion into mainstream school as the key to educating students with behavioural, emotional and social difficulties (BESD) and other special educational needs. Consequently, a number of policy changes were implemented by the Labour administration (HM Government, 2001; DfES, 2001a, 2001b, 2001c, 2004b) to increase the rights for children with SEN including BESD to receive their education in mainstream school (Burton and Goodman, 2011: 134). The White Paper *Excellence in Schools* (DfEE, 1997) was followed by the Green Paper, *Excellence for All Children*, published in September of the same year. These documents highlighted a clear shift in traditional policy towards children with disabilities. Such shifts can also be seen in the context of wider societal values reflected in the establishment of the Equality Act 2010 (HM Government, 2010). This aimed to streamline approaches to tackle disadavantage and discrimination and put disability on an equal footing with other groups and individuals within society. The educational landscape has changed considerably since the Education Act of 1944. Merely providing a school place for children with special needs is no longer acceptable; the quality of that education has to be second to none. The right for disabled children to access coordinated and accessible services was now at the heart of the inclusion agenda. The 1995 Disability Discrimination Act (DDA), for example, makes specific reference to steps being taken to prevent children with disabilities from being treated less favourably than other pupils, and to the provision of access for all children (HM Government, 1995b). In 2009 the Lamb Inquiry examined how parental confidence in the special educational needs education system could be improved (DCSF, 2009). The Conservative–Liberal Democrat Coalition brought with it a promise of an 'education revolution' (Gove, 2010, cited in Goodman and Burton, 2012). The proposals for a new approach to identifying SEN in England, a single assessment process to replace the statementing process and to bring together health, education and social care support, further empowering parents, including having the option of a personal budget are all part of the government's vision for SEN (DfE, 2011e). However, increasing autonomy over admissions, combined with the coalition's wish to 'prevent the unnecessary closure of special schools, and remove the bias towards inclusion' (HM Government, 2010: 29), indicates a move towards more discrete, specialist provision for students with SEN and away from inclusive provision (Burton and Goodman, 2011: 134).

Therefore, the coalition's education policies have major implications for the inclusion of students with SEN in England into mainstream schools. For example, the Academies Act 2010 raises a number of concerns over the future of SEN provision in the context of an educational climate where the prevailing move is towards localism, independence and autonomy (Hatcher, 2011; Skelton and Francis, 2011). As Goodman and Burton (2012) consider, 'as more schools become academies and receive their funds direct from central government rather than via the Local Authority, the LA funds for SEN services will decrease. Furthermore, there is a risk that the autonomy possessed by academies will materialise in unfair admissions procedures by which students with particular SEN such as challenging behaviour may not be admitted for fear that these students will impact negatively on assessment outcomes' (Norwich, 2010, cited in Maddern, 2010).

Defining inclusion

Inclusive policies have been found increasingly higher up the agenda of the UK government, local education authorities and individual schools. This is due in some part to the United Nations Educational, Scientific and Cultural Organization (UNESCO) Salamanca statement on principles, policy and practice in special needs education published in 1994. This statement urged national governments to pursue inclusive educational practices for all children and is still considered to be a key milestone in policy.

It is the consensus of many educationalists (for example, Goodman and Burton, 2010) that the goal of inclusive education is a worthy one but the degree to which it has been achieved is open to debate (Wedell, 2005). It leads us to ask two questions. First, what do we mean by inclusive education or 'inclusion', and second why do we need it? Finding a concrete definition of inclusion can be difficult and it is clear that confusion abounds, affecting providers, parents and the pupils themselves. As Ainscow et al. (2006) assert, inclusion is difficult to define and it is used inconsistently:

> Inclusion may be defined in a variety of ways. Often, however, explicit definitions of the term are omitted from publications, leaving readers to infer the meanings it is being given for themselves. (Ainscow et al., 2006: 14)

The Centre for Studies on Inclusive Education (CSIE) is an independent educational charity set up in 1982. In their literature, they define inclusion as 'disabled and non-disabled children and young people learning together in ordinary pre-school provision, schools, colleges and universities, with appropriate networks of support' (CSIE, 2000: 1).

Such a short definition belies the incredibly far-reaching, controversial and challenging task of the inclusion movement. Essentially, the CSIE is advocating the end of segregated education and with it the traditional model of special education in this country. It follows that there must be a compelling argument behind this radical approach if one is to answer the second of the above questions. Why do we need inclusion? Again, the CSIE (2000) answers this in a succinct and direct way – 'because children – whatever their disability or learning difficulty – have a part to play in society after school; an early start in mainstream playgroups or nursery schools, followed by education in ordinary schools and colleges is the best preparation for an integrated life' (CSIE, 2000: 2). The case for inclusion is often made not on the basis of its efficacy but on the basis of the human rights of young people with SEN to have the same educational opportunities as other children and thus to be included in mainstream schools (Florian, 2008, cited in Goodman and Burton, 2011: 134). Historically, the term 'integration' was used for including children with SEN in mainstream settings. This has now shifted to the term 'inclusion'. However, if we are to define the words we could argue that many settings are still integrating as opposed to including:

> If school personnel talk about extra adaptations or services to help the child fit into a classroom, it is integration. References to overcoming problems, acquiring functional abilities and support worker for the child will be used. Look at the Individual Education Plan (IEP). If the IEP focuses on strategies to help a child fit into a classroom, this is integration. Inclusive schools and classrooms talk about helping everyone. School personnel will emphasise how the classroom/school will be changed to support the

success of a child. The talk will be about how the extra adaptations and services will benefit everyone. When looking at the IEP, strategies will be used to adapt and improve the classroom so that all students achieve success. Inclusion is about helping everyone. (Harman, 2013: 1)

Early intervention is an essential component to any debate on early years and inclusion (Mortimer, 2002). This is typified by the example of Ashlyn (see case study on pp. 121–2). Both Ashlyn and her parents benefited from the intervention of a Portage worker. Portage is a home visiting educational service for pre-school children with additional support needs and their families. Supporting the family is a central aim (National Portage Association, 2013). Due to the introduction and implementation of strategies, as well as awareness raising in respect of the diagnosed condition, this family was able both to address the child's immediate needs and develop a positive ethos towards the notion of having a child with a disability. As the DfES (2007d: 35) observes: 'Early support for disabled children and their families is essential to prevent problems such as deteriorating health, family stress and breakdown, children potentially being placed in care, and deteriorating emotional and social development for disabled children and their siblings'. The Allen Report (Allen, 2011) recommends regular assessments of all pre-school children, focusing on their social and emotional development. Early intervention will improve the lives of vulnerable children and help break the cycle of 'dysfunction and under-achievement' (Allen, 2011).

In this respect, the English government's agenda includes healthy living, community support, multi-agency working and a focus on families (DfE, 2011c, 2012c). Initiatives such as Education and Health Action Zones and Sure Start are examples of these ideals (Wolfendale, 2000: 149). However, the success of the action zones has been open to debate (Ofsted, 2010). The Department for Education consultation on the core purpose of children's centres conducted in 2011 recognises there is still work to be done in establishing effective partnerships with health and social care colleagues, but the majority of stakeholders agree that the centres help improve outcomes for the most disadvantaged (DfE, 2012h). The Foundation Stage curriculum in England has been cited as a reason for the improving outcomes for young people (Tickell, 2011).

Models of disability and the role of special schools

If large numbers of children with SEN are in specialist provision, i.e. 2.8% of children in all schools in England in 2012 (DfE, 2012a), we need to ask why. This has resonance for the very young child with a disability, whose future may seem to be firmly placed in a specialist setting. The answer to this question might lie in the dominant position of the medical model. In this model, the child's needs are defined in medical terms and the idea that these children have different and exclusive needs is perpetuated.

Also implicit in the medical model are the notion of impairment and the idea that problems are predominantly found within the child. Inclusion is aided by the use of educational terminology, such as 'learning difficulty', or 'barriers to learning', rather than reliance on categories ('autistic child') or medical labels. However, there is often a strong desire for a diagnosis and its subsequent 'label', as that is seen to be the route to support and funding for the child. It is here we see the areas of health and education both involved with a child, and where we would aim to see multi-agency working and partnership. The Early Years Development and Childcare Partnerships (EYDCP) brought opportunities for a coming together and joining up of different settings, services, agencies and disciplines (Mortimer, 2002: 47).

Hall (1997: 74) describes the causal link between the medical model and segregated specialist education thus:

> The medical model is only able to see the child and his impairments as the problem, with the solution being to adapt the child and his circumstances to the requirements of the world as it is. All of the adjustments must be made to the lifestyle and functionality of the child. Hence a range of prosthetic devices will be offered, along with a separate educational environment and transport to facilitate attendance. The notion that the world might need to change hardly arises because the child *has* and *is* the problem.

The final sentence of the above quote is important and outlines the argument of the Disability Movement, which has gained momentum in both the global and national arena. This argument advocates the use of the social model of disablement. Such a model is concerned with environmental barriers, and the notion that it is these barriers that disable people, therefore disability is seen as a socially created problem (Gelder, 2004). The Disability Movement makes it clear that the effective removal of impairments is rare, but a great deal more can be achieved by removing those barriers, which include not only the physical environment, but also associated policies and societal attitudes. The lack of a culture of participation for disabled children is recognised as being a barrier to effective inclusion (Franklin and Knight, 2011). These sentiments hit a global audience with the London 2012 Paralympic Games building upon the notion that the games 'play a major part in changing attitudes by emphasising achievement rather than impairment, by accelerating the agenda of inclusion' (Gold and Gold, 2007: 133).

This sentiment was made law within the provisions of the Special Educational Needs and Disability Act (HM Government, 2001) and *Support and Aspiration: A New Approach to Special Educational Needs and Disability* (DfE, 2011e). This has wide implications for the inclusion of children who were excluded from mainstream institutions for reasons of accessibility. Accessibility mirrors our interpretation of inclusion as a varied and individual concept. What is required is a broadening of the concept of access to include the complex and unique barriers to learning and their impact on the individual child.

Sainsbury (2000), an adult with autism, is aware of the debates regarding identity, inclusion and disability rights and advocates a wide interpretation of these factors to meet the particular needs of those on the autistic spectrum. This is demonstrated by her definition of access and what constitutes an optimum learning environment for pupils with Asperger's syndrome: 'we don't need ramps or expensive equipment to make a difference for us; all we need is understanding' (Sainsbury, 2000: 9). This is illustrated very well by the staff training in John's school (see case study on p. 122).

Although the social model is now favoured above the medical model by many disabled people and their advocates, it is also true that for a great number of educationalists, parents and children, the segregated model has a lot of defenders. Jenkinson (1997: 10) categorises the perceived advantages, which are broken down into practical and economic factors, together with specific effects on disabled and non-disabled children. She highlights the efficiency of necessary aids and equipment, specialist teachers and ancillary services being located in one place. This complements the perceived benefits to the students found in smaller classes with more one-to-one attention and a curriculum pitched at an appropriate level. With the introduction and development of a more flexible early years curriculum in the Foundation Stage in England, it is thought by some that even when segregated provision may be the long-term option, the child will be successfully included in the early years (Wolfendale and Robinson, 2006; Tickell, 2011). If, as cited earlier, the EYFS is providing for equality of opportunity as a core intention, then we might hope that children in the early years will be able to experience an inclusive start to their education. The principle of the unique child (DfES, 2007a: 8) and the notion of personalised learning (DCSF, 2008a) are key features of a system that is guided by individualised learning, likewise the value placed on the *enabling environments* whereby the actual fabric of the class or setting can be used to create a bespoke and meaningful milieu and atmosphere (Duffy, 2010: 100).

 Research in context

Sebba, J. (2011) 'Personalisation, individualisation and inclusion', *Journal of Research in Special Educational Needs,* 11 (3): 205–10.

The article by Sebba discusses issues of personalisation, individualisation and inclusion and recognises both difficulties and tensions related to terminology together with positive aspects of personalised learning.

Increasingly in the UK context, the nature of devolved government has entered into consideration. Wyn Siencyn and Thomas (2007) note there have been changes that have led to some differences between Wales and England. Whilst SENDA 2001 makes provision for both Wales and England, and Wales has a SEN Code of Practice, it is interesting to note that the term Additional Learning Needs (ALN) is gradually replacing SEN as the preferred term (Wyn Siencyn and Thomas, 2007). Parents whose first language is not

English also felt there were barriers to support for early identification and inclusion, a point recognised by the Welsh Assembly Government in *Iaith Pawb:* the National Action Plan for a Bilingual Wales (Welsh Assembly Government, 2003). In Scotland, the Education (Scotland) Act 1980 was still guiding provision for children with SEN until the Additional Support for Learning (Scotland) Act 2004 came into place (Carmichael and Hancock, 2007). The overall aim is for full integration and inclusion of all children, although specialised care and education is recognised as being necessary for some children (Carmichael and Hancock, 2007). From this, we can see that while there are some similarities between practices throughout the UK, there are also some significant differences and we should not assume that English provision is generalised.

It is fair to say that the majority of professionals in specialist provision feel they are working in the best interests of the children they teach. In many respects, 'special education' is seen as a worthy profession with established models of good practice and pedagogy. Any suggestion that they are helping to deny disabled children basic human rights or perpetuating institutional discrimination would be denied by many. A more cynical observation would be that it is in the interests of the two branches of education to remain distinctive, preserve the status quo and consolidate their expertise and influence. As Gelder notes, 'An inclusive approach may meet resistance from specialists in special schools because they feel their expertise is being overlooked. There may be resistance from teachers and practitioners from mainstream services, because they feel ill equipped to implement inclusive practice' (DfES, 2004, cited in Gelder, 2004: 105).

Hindrances to inclusion

Despite, over the past decade, the introduction of a number of policies aimed at moving forward the inclusion agenda, belief in the benefits of inclusion for students with SEN is by no means unanimous (Burton and Goodman, 2011: 134). Government policy in England seems to be increasing its scrutiny of student attainment and performance-related indicators with the publication of school league tables (Gabriel, 2004). Wedell (2005: 5) comments that the rigidity of the education system does not aid inclusion and that Ofsted (2004) reported that nearly all schools felt restricted by the national curriculum despite the inclusion statement. To some teachers, inclusion is perceived as a hindrance to these factors as it is often felt that inclusion is merely the opposite of exclusion. As a result, many teachers see the acceptance of children with emotional and behavioural problems into their class as synonymous with inclusion and to the detriment of their mainstream peers.

Social inclusion can therefore cause a great deal of anxiety in schools, as staff might be reluctant to consider issues of behaviour within the context of special needs: 'Teachers in normal schools may be willing to accommodate the "ideal" child with special needs in their classroom – the bright, brave child in a wheelchair – they will still want to be rid of the actual "average" child with special needs – the dull, disruptive child' (Tomlinson, 1982: 80). Even though it is now thirty years old, this quote still has resonance, and we could question how much progress in attitudes has been made. As Goodman and Burton (2010: 234) state:

> the concerns raised by teachers regarding the inclusion of students with BESD not only match concerns identified in current government policy but are also evident in policies introduced 20 years earlier. The reiteration of very similar issues within policies over the last 20 years suggests that the difficulties associated with including students with SEN into mainstream schools have shown little improvement.

The aim of special schools sharing specialist skills and knowledge to support inclusion has a patchy national profile, and many parents still have concerns that their child's needs will be met at their local mainstream school. However, Ofsted found that pupils with even the most severe and complex needs are able to make outstanding progress in all types of settings (DfES, 2007b: 12). Ofsted (2010: 4) advised that further changes to the system should not focus on tightening the processes of prescribing entitlement to services but on improving the quality of assessment, ensuring effective additional support, improving teaching and pastoral support early on and, interestingly, ensuring that schools do not identify children as having SEN when they simply need better teaching. The DfE (2011e) have stated that they feel the term 'special educational need' is overused and used to describe low attainment or slow progress.

Fortunately, the concept of education for *all* is a right that is enshrined in law at local, national and international levels. Issues regarding the inclusion of children with SEN are ongoing and often controversial, highlighting the evolutionary nature of this debate. However, we must not lose sight of the fact that in the recent past, many of the children at the centre of this agenda were deemed ineducable. Scholars must recognise the nature of these advances and place the current arguments into this wider historical perspective.

The following case studies demonstrate the experiences of two children in the early years and the varied nature of SEN and support. They show the difficulties facing practitioners involved in setting up appropriate interventions together, with an indication of the areas that require targeting.

CASE STUDY ONE

Ashlyn

Ashlyn was born prematurely and has a diagnosis of cerebral palsy. She is 18 months old. Her parents were devastated when they were given the diagnosis by their GP, and have no idea what the future may hold for them and their daughter.

(Continued)

(Continued)

A referral was made to the local Portage service. This was funded by the LA. Fortnightly visits were set up by the Portage home visitor, whose background was in physiotherapy. In the first visit, Ashlyn was observed and the Portage worker played with her. The Portage checklist was introduced to her parents and they were encouraged to set aside a regular time each day to work with Ashlyn. Written weekly teaching activities were agreed with Ashlyn's parents, based on her priority areas of need. In Ashlyn's case, these were gross motor skills, fine motor skills, self-help and communication/socialisation. The parents then did daily activities with their daughter. This made them feel totally involved in her progress, and they said they felt their knowledge about Ashlyn's condition was greatly enhanced.

New teaching targets were developed over time; each stage was evaluated, taking into account the views of the parents. Ashlyn has made considerable progress. Ashlyn's mother has joined a parent support group which has a toy library. Both parents feel more positive about the years ahead.

CASE STUDY TWO

John

John is 7 years and 10 months old. He has recently been given a diagnosis of autistic spectrum disorder. John attends a large inner-city, mainstream primary school.

John has odd and idiosyncratic speech, which is a feature of Asperger's syndrome. This often has a maturity beyond his years, e.g. 'I find this work tedious in the extreme', or will feature alliteration, which amuses John but annoys or confuses his peers – 'Today is torturous Tuesday, telemetry is tenaciously taught'. Both peers and staff find it difficult to understand what he is saying as he often mumbles or whispers his words and makes little use of eye contact or gesture. He seems to 'switch off' if adults address him directly, or if they talk at length.

John is an avid reader of books, particularly dictionaries and non-fiction books relating to football statistics. As a consequence of his communication difficulties, John is ostracised and bullied by his peers who find him odd.

John has begun to go up to groups of boys at lunch time and forcefully push them, causing them to chase and physically abuse him. Staff have repeatedly told him not to, but this has no effect and John gives the impression he enjoys the chase and insists that he is *playing* with the boys. When they call him names, he turns them into alliterations, which makes this spiral of bullying continue.

Following a meeting with the autism outreach service, a volunteer has come in at playtime and has introduced some playground games, based upon a football theme. He wrote a simple set of rules to accompany each game for the children to refer to. John was excited to read the rules and became animated when the games were played. He tried to direct his peers, and it was noticeable that they were far more accepting of him in this context.

Staff have followed on from this approach in the classroom and have started to write down information for John to refer to. John also has a small selection of prompt symbols to help him remember such social rules as using a person's name to indicate that he is addressing them. He has responded well to this and staff have noticed that he is far more willing to communicate with them. They have also made attempts to use his knowledge of football-related statistics and his knowledge of unusual words to lift his profile within the class. His peers are very impressed with his knowledge, and while they still regard him as odd, they respect his abilities and tolerate his differences.

 Reflection for case studies 1 and 2

- Which aspects of good practice can you identify within these two case studies?

 ### Research in context

Bauminger, N., Shulman, C. and Agam, G. (2003) 'Peer interaction and loneliness in high-functioning children with autism', *Journal of Autism and Developmental Disorders*, 33: 458–507.

The article looks at the relationship between social interaction and loneliness. Whilst not specifically focused on early years, the concepts are transferable and relevant for all children with social interaction difficulties.

Research in context

Jones, K. and Howley, M. (2010) 'An investigation into an interaction programme for children on the autism spectrum: outcomes for children, perceptions of schools and a model for training', *Journal of Research in Special Educational Needs*, 10 (2): 115–23.

The article by Jones and Howley discusses an intervention project for pupils with autism. It highlights the need to individualise intervention strategies and for all stakeholders to work collectively. It recognises that approaches can be optimised if the pupil is an active participant in the process.

Chapter summary

The case studies serve to illustrate the notion that there are aspects of good practice that are generic with regard to the support of these children and work across the board. These include:

- the use of structure and routine
- practitioner language
- visual systems
- individualised motivators
- practitioner awareness and knowledge
- the appropriate and creative use of support staff
- knowledge of the individual child's perspective and sensibilities
- a recognition of the role of other children and peer relationships
- a recognition of the role of parents
- an understanding that inclusion is a negotiated state between all stakeholders
- a commitment to an inclusive philosophy.

It is equally important, however, that strategies are optimised to take account of those individual factors particular to the child. In the second case study, these include the sensitive use of John's football interests and his highly visual learning style.

It is not the purpose of this chapter to provide a 'one size fits all' definition of inclusion, but rather to promote the notion that it is a process that is highly individualised and wider than the issue regarding specialist versus mainstream provision.

Even if we know a considerable amount about the implications of inclusive values for any particular context, we still do not know how best to put them into action, since making sustained principled changes within schools is notoriously difficult. Therefore effective early years practitioners will be those professionals who are able to look beyond labels, diagnoses and particular settings and look to individual factors to ensure the child with SEN is both prepared for, and accepted within, society. In order to do this, the starting point is the child and the wider context of that child's existence. Good inclusive early years practice will see this individual context flexibly and creatively and consider the interplay between individual, environmental and social factors – not in a generic sense but as unique for each child. The key to achieve this is to take clear cues from the child and to be creative in how these cues are interpreted and incorporated into strategies to support and nurture.

Questions for reflection and discussion

1. What are the benefits of early intervention?
2. Consider the current debate regarding the inclusion of pupils whose behaviour presents challenges in mainstream settings. What is your opinion on this aspect of inclusion?
3. How does the legislative framework regarding access issues affect children you know or have worked with?
4. What issues are there in respect of promoting self-advocacy with children who have special educational needs?
5. How should the rights of parents and guardians be taken into account?
6. How can practitioners negotiate individual needs and characteristics within a wider group or social unit?

Recommended reading

Hodkinson, A. and Vickerman, P. (2009) *Key Issues in Special Educational Needs and Inclusion* (Education Studies: Key Issues). London: Sage.

Nutbrown, C. and Clough, P. (2006) *Inclusion in the Early Years: Critical Analyses and Enabling Narratives*. London: Sage.

Warnock, M. and Norwich, B. (2010) *Special Educational Needs: A New Look* (Key Debates in Educational Policy). London: Continuum.

Recommended websites

www.bild.org.uk
The British Institute of Learning Disabilities

www.nasen.org.uk
Nasen is the leading organisation in the UK promoting the education, training, advancement and development of all those with special and additional support needs.

www.ncb.org.uk/earlysupport
Based at the Council for Disabled Children at the National Children's Bureau, Early Support is a core delivery partner for the implementation of the proposals set out in the government's Green Paper *Support and Aspiration: A new approach to special educational needs and disability* (DfE, 2011e).

www.portage.org.uk
The National Portage Association is a home-visiting educational service for pre-school children with additional support needs and their families.

Want to learn more about this chapter? Visit the companion website at **www.sagepub.co.uk/walleranddavis3e** to access podcasts from the author and child observation videos.

Part Three
Learning and Play

7

Play and Creativity

Paulette Luff

 Key chapter objectives

- To explore definitions of play and creativity, in the context of early childhood education
- To identify features of environments that stimulate and enable creativity
- To discuss adults' roles within children's play and creativity
- To debate the use of pedagogical documentation

'Play' and 'creativity' are two important, overlapping, aspects of early childhood theory and practice. Neither 'play' nor 'creativity' can be easily defined but qualities of imagination, exploration, freedom and flexibility are common to both, and this accounts for their significance within Western traditions of early years education. In this chapter, following a short exploration of the terms 'play' and 'creativity', I offer a brief overview of the place of play and creativity within early childhood education. Three aspects of provision for play and creativity are then explored, namely: the affordances of stimulating environments; the role of responsive adults; and the relevance of pedagogical documentation.

Play and creativity within early childhood education

Play is a notoriously tricky concept to grasp and to explain with precision. Janet Moyles (2010) suggests that attempting to do so is analogous to seizing bubbles and she argues that play can be recognised and valued without the need for a precise definition. Indeed, there is no difficulty on the part of adults, or of children themselves, in identifying when play is occurring (Cohen, 2006; Howard, 2010; Moyles, 1989, 2010). A century ago, Joseph Lee (1915) suggested that the term 'play' itself is misleading as it is used by adults to denote something simple and easy and yet play is of the utmost seriousness and importance in the life of a child. Susan Isaacs (1929: 9), writing just a little later, famously expressed a similar sentiment: 'Play is indeed the child's work and the means whereby he grows and develops.'

Isaacs based her arguments for the importance of play upon evolutionary biology, understandings from the emerging field of developmental psychology, including the ideas of Piaget, and also psychoanalytic theory and the importance of play for mental health. Children's play is still studied from a variety of theoretical and professional perspectives (see, for example, Broadhead et al., 2010; Moyles, 2010; Smith, 2010). Our contemporary understandings of play in early years education range from a view of play as open-ended activity that is controlled by the child, without any adult agenda (Santer and Griffiths, 2007), to a contrasting notion of structured 'planned, purposeful play' (DfE, 2012d: 5), carefully designed by adults to meet intended learning goals, as described within the Early Years Foundation Stage curriculum framework in England.

Whether children themselves would include the latter in the category of 'play' is debatable. Research has shown that young children readily discriminate between play and work and identify whether activities are associated with learning. These distinctions between 'play' and 'work' may be based upon emotional cues, such as the level of fun and amount of choice, and environmental cues, such as the location of the activity and whether a specific product has to be created (Howard and McInnes, 2010). Associated findings, showing enhanced task performance following a practice condition in which cues to play were prevalent, indicate the importance of play and playful environments to enhance learning.

There is, indeed, a consensus amongst academics and early years educators that play is important for holistic learning and development and has recognisable characteristics. These include those first identified by Garvey (1977: 5), who considered play to be activity that is: valued by the players; self-motivated; freely chosen; engaging; and having 'certain systematic relations to what is not play'. The curiosity and imagination that children display in their play can also be considered to be characteristics of creativity.

As for 'play', there is no simple agreed definition of 'creativity' in early years education. Like play, creativity is seen to be a typical characteristic of human behaviour. Just as there is evidence from the earliest times and across cultures of children playing, from pre-historic times and in every society creative activities (such as music, movement, dance, image-making and story-telling) have formed an important part of the lives of human beings (Dissanayake, 1992; Nutbrown, 2011). As with play, the study of creativity is inter-disciplinary and informed by different fields of study.

Recent notions of creativity within education, in a UK context, have come from the *All Our Futures* report (NACCCE, 1999) and subsequent policy documents. For example, guidance from the Qualifications and Curriculum Authority (2005) for promoting creativity in primary schools, identified four aspects of pupils' creative thinking and behaviour:

> First, they [characteristics of creativity] always involve thinking or behaving imaginatively. Second, overall this imaginative activity is purposeful: that is, it is directed to achieving an objective. Third, these processes must generate something original. Fourth, the outcome must be of value in relation to the objective. (QCA, 2005: 7)

Arguably, the most influential ideas about creativity in early childhood education in recent years, in England, are those of Anna Craft (2002, 2011). She offers two particularly useful concepts. The first is 'little c creativity' and the second 'possibility thinking'. Little c creativity describes a notion of creativity that differs from the 'high' or 'big C' creativity associated with exceptional talent in the arts. It is, instead, a 'lifewide' (as opposed to 'lifelong') disposition connected with self-direction, resourcefulness, imagination, self-expression and self-actualisation. The attributes of little c creativity are brought together in, and driven by, 'possibility thinking'. Possibility thinking is central to young children's creativity as they constantly generate possibilities in every area of their play and daily experience through asking 'what if?' and 'what can I do with this?' and thus go beyond 'what is' to explore 'what could be'.

Based upon the above definitions and discussion, not all play is creative and not all creativity is playful. There are, however, elements that play and creativity share. In the early years, in both play and creativity there is a focus on process, rather than product; for young children it is the act of playing or creating that is important. Furthermore, processes of play and creativity involve exploration, making meaning and self-expression. The interest and focus of this chapter is where play and creativity intersect, in early childhood activity characterised by choice, motivation, experimentation, experience, imagination, free expression and open-ended possibilities.

In policy and in practice, both play and creativity are considered important for children's holistic development. For example, they are brought into joint focus in Article 31 of the United Nations Convention on the Rights of the Child (UNCRC) (United Nations, 1989), which states: 'That every child has the right to rest and leisure, to engage in play and recreational activities appropriate to the age of the child and to participate freely in cultural life and the arts.' The importance of the implementation of Article 31 for children's wellbeing and development is emphasised in General Comment 17 (United Nations Committee on the Rights of the Child, 2013), together with the need to make provision for spontaneous play and creativity and to promote attitudes in society to support and encourage these types of activity.

Recognition of children's creative potential and their ability to gain knowledge and skills through play is not new. Friedrich Froebel's belief in children's creativity and the importance of engagement with the world through playful practical activity led to the design of educational materials and activities known as 'gifts' and 'occupations'. Exploration of the 'gifts' was intended to support knowledge of creation through an understanding of mathematical concepts of shape and size; the 'occupations' were open-ended items, such as paints and clay, and their use provided opportunities for self-expression (Froebel, 1897).

From the mid-19th century, followers of Froebel who fled persecution in Prussia and came to England were welcomed. Their ideas were highly influential in the development of nursery schooling and the training of early years teachers, and Froebelian ideas and principles became embedded in child-centred approaches to early years education (Lawrence, 1952/2012). Pioneers of early years education, inspired by Froebel and by the emergence of Piaget's theories of cognitive development, promoted play-based experiential learning and opportunities for self-expression in richly resourced indoor and outdoor environments (Isaacs, 1929; McMillan, 1919). Ideas from other theoretical perspectives have also contributed to the valuing of play and creativity in early childhood, including psychoanalytic views of the importance of self-discovery and emotional self-expression (Isaacs, 1933; Manning-Morton, 2006) and sociocultural notions of group participation and the use of tools to extend thinking and support children's imaginative activities (Kozulin, 2003; Vygotsky, 1978).

Reflecting these philosophical traditions, from its inception the national curriculum for early years education in England has recognised the centrality of play and creativity. In the Desirable Learning Outcomes (SCAA, 1996) and the subsequent Curriculum Guidance for the Foundation Stage (QCA, 2000), 'Creative Development' was identified as one of six areas of learning with a focus on the development of children's imaginations and their ability to communicate and to express ideas and feelings in creative ways. When the *Birth to Three Matters* guidance was issued to support work with the youngest children, 'Being Creative' was, similarly, identified and promoted as part of the 'Competent Learner' aspect of the framework (DfES, 2003b). When the frameworks were brought together in a single statutory curriculum document, the 'Early Years Foundation Stage' (DCSF, 2008a) for children aged from birth to 5, creativity remained a key feature:

> Children's creativity must be extended by the provision of support for their curiosity, exploration and play. They must be provided with opportunities to explore and share their thoughts, ideas and feelings, for example, through a variety of art, music, movement, dance, imaginative and role-play activities, mathematics, and design and technology. (DCSF, 2008a: 16)

In the revised Early Years Foundation Stage (EYFS) curriculum framework (DfE, 2012d) the place of play and creativity remains secure. 'Creative Development' is no longer a named area of learning, having been replaced by 'Expressive Arts' with an emphasis upon music, dance, role play, storytelling, drawing, painting and modelling. The relevance of wider opportunities to question, make connections, innovate, problem-solve and reflect is highlighted in the three characteristics of learning. By 'playing and exploring' children learn through investigation and experiences; through 'active learning' children gain concentration, persistence and enjoyment; and in 'creating and thinking critically' children's thoughts are recognised, connections are made and strategies developed for putting ideas into practice (DfE, 2012d: 7).

Whilst expressive arts, creativity and playful learning have an established place in the EYFS framework, there remains concern that full realisation of these key aspects of early childhood education may be compromised by work towards learning outcomes and an emphasis upon the more formal aspects of early literacy and numeracy skills (Early Childhood Action, 2012). Those looking for an alternative contemporary approach to fostering the creativity and self-expression of young children often turn for inspiration to the pre-schools of Reggio Emilia, in Northern Italy. With no written curriculum, listening to children's ideas becomes the starting point for developing projects in which children and their teachers work together to propose and test hypotheses. Loris Malaguzzi suggested that children are well-adapted to working in creative and open-ended ways as 'they have the privilege of not being excessively attached to their own ideas, which they construct and reinvent continuously. They are apt to explore, make discoveries, change their points of view and fall in love with forms and meanings that transform themselves' (Malaguzzi, cited in Gandini, 2012a: 51).

There are several distinctive features of the Reggio Emilia approach that are of particular interest to early childhood educators who are keen to promote creativity. Attention to the children's ideas stems from a positive image of the 'rich child' as a capable protagonist in the learning process. These ideas can be represented in multiple ways as they express understandings through the use of 'the hundred languages of children' (Malaguzzi, cited in Edwards et al., 1998). The 'pedagogy of listening' ensures that the adults are responsive to the children's thinking and also that they document the creative process in order to make learning visible (Rinaldi, 2006). The design and organisation of pre-schools and classrooms is of particular significance within the Reggio Emilia approach, to the extent that the environment is described as 'the third educator' alongside the two class teachers (Gandini, 2012b).

Environments for play and creativity

For many creative adults, including artists, musicians, dancers and writers, physical environments are significant. These may be landscapes that offer inspiration or studio spaces within which to work. In organisations where employees are required to innovate, thought is given to the design of workplaces (Dul and Ceylan, 2011). Similarly, in order for children to be curious and explore, and to express ideas and emotions in different ways, it is important for the places that they inhabit to be stimulating and enabling.

Atefe Makhmalbaf and Ellen Yi-Luen Do (2007) carried out a very small-scale experiment in which they asked children to draw a picture and answer questions in both their home environment and in the children's activity area of a bookstore. They found that in the bookstore context the children (aged between 4 and 6 years) produced pictures with a greater variety of bright colours and displayed a higher degree of complexity and novelty in the objects depicted in their drawings. They deduced that the children were positively influenced by child-friendly environmental characteristics such as space, bright lighting, warm colours, the availability of visual stimuli and the height of the furniture, and argued that these features may influence children's problem solving and creative thinking ability.

Certainly, those of us who aim to encourage young children's play and creativity must identify the kinds of experiences that we want children to encounter and then consider the potential of environments and resources for affording opportunities. Theodora Papatheodorou (2010) proposes that the learning environments that we provide for children are never neutral but reveal the beliefs that we hold, about the child and the curriculum, and shape behaviours and responses. She challenges educators to reflect upon the qualities of playful learning environments and the messages that they convey.

Educators in Reggio Emilia speak and write explicitly about respect for children and the provision of an aesthetically pleasing environment that is seen as the 'third educator', thus recognising the educational benefits that can be gained through learning and teaching areas that are carefully arranged and used. Tiziana Filippini (1990, cited in Gandini, 2012b) suggests that space is a 'container' where explorations and communication may take place but also, more proactively, it offers educational 'content' in terms of the educational messages and stimuli contained within it and the possibilities provided for interactions and constructive learning. For an early years environment to inspire play and creativity, sensory, intellectual and social stimuli must be carefully balanced and thought given to the design and planning of both indoor and outdoor areas. In addition, there should be some flexibility for children to use spaces as they wish.

The organisation of both indoor and outdoor spaces for play and creativity, therefore, has to be given careful consideration. Justine Howard's (2010) research into children's perceptions of play shows that children may differentiate between work and play on the basis of environmental cues, such as whether an activity takes place on a table or on the floor. Outdoor environments, where there are fewer restrictions and more freedom to move and act spontaneously, are more likely to be associated with play. This is important as in play young children exhibit and practise a wider range of behaviours and skills and rehearse problem-solving strategies with greater engagement (Howard, 2010). This resonates with findings from research into optimal experience in adults where a state of 'flow', as described by Mihaly Csikszentmihalyi (2002), is achieved in contexts where there is some free choice.

Other characteristics of 'optimal experience' that offer clues for the quality of early childhood provision include the degree of challenge within the environment matched with individuals' personal skills and levels of engagement (Freire, 2011). Materials and resources are an important part of the environment and culture of an early years setting. Bernadette Duffy (2006: 133) suggests that 'to some degree creativity is resource led'. If items are chosen with care and presented attractively and accessibly then children are invited to explore, play and create and become involved. The case study presented here raises questions about the types of play materials on offer to children and states a case for reclaimed resources.

CASE STUDY ONE

Creative play with open-ended materials

Early Years Professional Kay Fisher describes how she introduced reclaimed resources to the babies and young children in her child-minding setting:

I began by visiting the Pyramid Resource Centre scrap store, in Thurrock, and slowly introduced reclaimed materials alongside the natural materials and everyday household items already present in my setting. I began to remove the plastic manufactured toys, storing them in the shed as I couldn't bring myself to get rid of them completely. One important aspect of working with reclaimed materials is the confidence of the adult to plan for and perceive them as valuable learning resources. All too often it is the adults who are scared of the resources and it is the adults who don't know what to do with them. The children on the other hand play with them as if they were the most expensive toy in the world.

Having worked with the resources for a while now and after spending time observing and evaluating the quality of learning and development opportunities experienced by the children in my care, it is clear to see that these types of resources create a higher quality of learning and engage children across the 0–5 age range for longer, sustained periods of time. The types of resources used so far include cardboard tubes of various sizes, large pieces of industrial foam, shells, pebbles, potpourri balls, ribbons, textiles, cardboard boxes of various sizes, emergency blankets and sectioned trays – to name but a few.

Exciting rare finds have occurred during visits to the scrap store, including a large garage sign with number plates attached and food/cafe advertising boards from IKEA. These types of resources cannot be purchased from any resource catalogue, yet have extended the role play opportunities, investigation, discovery and questioning skills of the children in a noticeable way over such a short period of time. The reclaimed materials present themselves with the readily

(Continued)

(Continued)

attached question of 'What can you do with me?' Problem solving and exploration are natural progressions during the children's play, allowing them opportunities to develop all three characteristics of effective learning. I am finding my planning far more exciting and challenging and the next step is to get creative with storage and the presentation of resources.

Figure 7.1   *Display of reclaimed materials as playthings*

 Reflection for case study 1

- Have you observed reclaimed, open-ended resources in use in early years settings?
- What types of resources are most useful for creative play?

In Reggio Emilia, reclaimed resources from the Remida recycling centre are used in the pre-schools. They are displayed tastefully, reflecting the importance placed upon the design of spaces for children: 'pleasure, aesthetics and play are essential in any act of learning and knowledge-building' (Rinaldi, 2006: 81). In all settings, consideration can be given to the richness of the visual culture that surrounds children. Bowker and Sawyers (1988) identified the importance of children's early experiences of fine art. They suggested that young children should have the opportunity to see and respond to high quality drawings and paintings and could be offered 'ownership' of such images through assisting in the selection of prints to hang on their classrooms walls.

Children's creativity can be nurtured by exposure to the arts and cultural activities within the environment of the early years setting but also enriched by visits to places beyond the nursery walls and gardens. The Henley Review (2012) includes the suggestion that cultural provision should begin in the early years and, before the children are 7 years old, they should be given the opportunity to visit venues such as theatres, cinemas, concert halls, museums, galleries, libraries or heritage sites and to join in with age-appropriate arts activities.

Whether outside the early years setting or within it, the provision of environments that enable children's play and creativity requires thought and often ingenuity on the part of adults. Duffy (2006) suggests that practitioners may audit their settings in order to evaluate the layout and consider whether every area of provision includes relevant materials and resources to promote creativity. Observing how children play and create within available spaces may offer insights for ways to adapt indoor and outdoor environments. Once the physical environment is set up then further thought must be given as to the most effective ways and means of promoting play and creativity.

The role of adults in fostering play and creativity

Supporting children's play and creativity is a skilled task as educators have to strike a delicate balance between facilitation and interference. On the one hand, there is the need for sufficient guidance and support to stimulate children's imaginations and enable creative processes. On the other, there is the risk of harmful intrusion that may stifle originality and self-expression. As John Matthews (2003: 20) states, in his book about children's drawing and painting: 'There are two major mistakes: (1) no support at all, and (2), just as bad, damaging adult interference and domination'. Specific aspects of the adult's facilitating role include: playful pedagogy and the preparedness of adults to become co-players with children; strategies for adults to stimulate and support children's developing ideas; and the practitioner as a creative role model.

Within the Statutory Framework for the Early Years Foundation Stage (DfE, 2012d) a distinction is made between children leading their own play and participation in play activities guided by adults, with a balance between these recommended. In child-led, free play, children have opportunities to investigate, explore and express themselves.

Pat Broadhead's (2010) work offers evidence of the sociability and cooperation, with attendant rich use of language, communication and problem-solving, that can occur during child-directed role play in a 'whatever you want it to be place'. In this type of creative play the role of the adult concerns the provision of the space and open-ended resources and also careful observation to understand what is happening during the play. Adults may also engage in conversations with children, when they have finished playing, in order to further appreciate the nature of the play and the achievements of the children. Talking with children about their play in this way also has the advantage of showing that free play is valued as highly as other activities that might take place in the setting (Broadhead, 2010).

In adult-guided play there is much less scope for children to choose or to take control. The games or activities are prepared by the adult with specific learning opportunities and outcomes in mind. Typical examples of this type of play would include action songs and circle games, organised activities in physical education sessions, or board games and puzzles. Eleni Mellou (1994) describes tutored dramatic play, in which imagination and creativity are encouraged by the teacher through specific drama exercises, and compares and contrasts this with free role play. She concludes that both forms of play involve interaction, imagination and transformation and both have importance for children's creative, emotional and cognitive development.

Whilst both child-led and adult-guided play may be beneficial, children may view the latter as 'work' rather than 'play' (as discussed above). This presents a challenge to adults who aim to foster play and creativity; indeed Angela Anning (2010: 30) suggests that adults are uncertain about their role in play and that 'the holy grail of early years education is to construct a pedagogy of play'. One such pedagogy, centred upon play and playfulness, is proposed by Kathy Goouch (2010). In this approach adults and children engage in mutually directed play. The adult role is as a play-partner and may include: acting as a scribe or narrator, describing the play as it occurs; following the children's intentions and becoming an actor and co-player; mediating where necessary to help solve problems; or simply being there as a physical presence and a listener (Goouch, 2010; Synodi, 2010).

Two key characteristics of mutually directed play are dialogue and co-construction; this links with a view of learning in which ideas and knowledge are developed through social interactions with others. Through playing together and engaging jointly in open-ended activities, adults and children can inspire one another and respond in creative ways. Tina Bruce (2011) suggests that adults in early years settings have daily opportunities to recognise and value children's motivations and interests and to build upon these to encourage and support creativity. Anna Craft (2002, 2011) and her colleagues (Burnard et al., 2006; Cremin et al., 2006; Craft et al., 2012) describe practices where children and adults work together as 'learner inclusive' and characterised by 'possibility thinking'. Possibilities can be generated in all areas of play and learning, as the example of research into 4-year-olds' possibility thinking illustrates (Craft et al., 2012).

Research in context

Enabling 4-year-olds' possibility thinking

Craft, A., McConnon, L. and Matthews, A. (2012) 'Child-initiated play and professional creativity: enabling four-year-olds' possibility thinking', *Thinking Skills and Creativity*, 7 (1): 48–61.

This research set out to investigate how children's creativity/possibility thinking was manifested in child-initiated play; and the role of the practitioner in supporting this.

Influenced by the 5x5x5=Creativity project (Bancroft et al., 2008; and see below in this chapter) and practice in Reggio Emilia, the investigation focused upon the use of adult-initiated 'provocations' as stimuli enabling play and children's narratives.

The research took the form of a collaborative case study in which academics worked with four practitioners at an established inner-London children's centre. The researchers used methods including naturalistic observations, researcher reflections and interviews, yielding data in the form of field notes, digital images and sound-files and journal entries. The practitioner-researchers invited their key children to take part in the 4-week provocation-stimulated project activity (a total of fifteen children all aged 4 years).

The four practitioner-researchers worked in pairs (group one and two). Group one used natural materials (logs, leaves, stones) as provocations and group two used puppets and props. After the play sessions, photographs were uploaded onto a laptop, discussed with the children and shown to parents. At the end of the day the researchers discussed their observations and documented their thoughts.

Analysis focused on episodes of immersive play that were child-initiated and showed evidence of possibility thinking ('what if' and 'as if' thinking). Two key episodes were identified: one outdoors involving provision of cut sections of small tree branches and logs gathered and placed under a cloth for the children to discover; the other indoors involving a set of puppets used for the telling of a familiar story. Analysis was inductive (open-coding seeking emergent categories) and deductive (seeking direct evidence of possibility thinking as defined in previous studies).

Children's creativity was found to be manifest in three sets of behaviours: stimulating and sustaining possibilities (making a 'fire cage'; narrating a crocodile story); communicating possibilities (verbally and through body language); and children's agency, roles and identities (ownership and engagement, enabled by practitioners). Existing features of possibility thinking were observed (including innovation,

(Continued)

(Continued)

being imaginative, self-determination and intentionality) and extended (power of the leading question and risk-taking) and two new aspects were added: 'individual, collaborative and communal creativity' and the 'imaginative dynamic between practitioner and child'.

Practitioners were found to support creativity in child-initiated play in five ways: provoking possibilities; allowing time and space for responses; being in the moment with children; intervening to support, sustain and suspend play; and mentoring in partnership for mutual professional development. Overall the study showed the relationship between practitioner and child creativity in the context of the use of provocations to stimulate changes in practice and children's experiences.

The research into possibility thinking reveals practical methods for guiding the imagination of children in playful ways, in a context where adults developed confidence in offering provocations and observing and reflecting upon the children's responses. Carlina Rinaldi (2006: 120) asserts that 'there is no creativity in the child if there is no creativity in the adult: the competent and creative child exists if there is a competent and creative adult'. In Reggio Emilia, this is offered not only by teachers but through the work of a skilled professional artist, an *atelierista*, in each pre-school to act as a tutor and role model to the children. Pramling Samuelsson et al. (2009) highlight the importance of presenting expressive arts activities for their own sake, rather than as a means to promote social skills or emotional development. They acknowledge that this is difficult for teachers who do not practise art, dance or music themselves and argue that professional development is essential in order for teachers to provide genuine creative opportunities for children.

CASE STUDY TWO

An adult-led creative activity

Nursery owner and manager Sheila Homer offers an observation of an adult-led creative activity with children aged 3 and 4 years, undertaken in a nursery setting:

The six children were gathered around the adult on a large carpeted area in the setting. The adult began by discussing previous activities and displays they had produced on their 'water' theme. The adult said: 'We are going to create a different sort of picture today, not with paints or crayons, but with what is in the bin. We are going to use our imaginations and really think about what we have and what we can do with it. It will be your picture of your choice.' Child A responded: 'It looks like dressing up!' Adult said, 'Good guess, it's materials for us to use.' The adult laid out a large white cotton sheet and said the children could use this like their piece of paper if they were drawing and asked if anyone would like a clipboard and paper to design their picture first. All six children responded with a resounding 'yes'. While the children were designing the adult proceeded to produce other materials, such as card tubes, shells and stones. The children naturally progressed from the designing stage into their creating stage. The adult acted as a facilitator, supporter and guide to the children. She listened and responded to the children and answered their questions with respect. Child A was completely involved as she placed stones and shells in the folds of the materials, talking quietly about the sun and the stars. Children B and C were discussing whales and sharks being under their sea. All six children were involved in the activity: some played independently and some interacted, some questioned the adult and asked for her support and some did not. Every child worked at their own pace on their own creation. The adult showed genuine interest and wonderment at everything the children were doing. The activity went on for almost 30 minutes and I could see the adult finding it difficult to bring it to a closure. She did this by saying: 'Start to think about finishing your creations very soon.' The activity then gradually came to a natural end.

 Reflection for case study 2

- How does the adult in this example support children's creativity?
- Is there evidence of 'possibility thinking'?
- Have you carried out a similar activity with this age group?
- What, if anything, would you have done differently if you were facilitating the activity?

Adults can come alongside children in their play in different ways. One intervention to support creativity is 'sustained shared thinking', defined as: 'any episode in which two or more individuals "worked together" in an intellectual way to solve a problem, clarify a concept, evaluate activities, extend a narrative etc. ... both parties had to be contributing to the thinking and it had to be shown to develop and extend thinking' (Siraj-Blatchford, 2010a: 157). This is a challenging form of interaction requiring skilled participation by the adult. He or she has to tune in to children's activities with genuine interest and judge the right moment at which to pose positive questions to clarify ideas and encourage elaboration. It is inspiring to listen to a genuine co-inquiry in which the adult enters into a dialogue with a child without preconceptions about 'correct answers'. The children's questions, hypotheses and thought processes can also be observed and recorded in ways that make learning visible.

Documenting play and creativity

Creativity in early years settings is often linked, in the minds of practitioners, to showcasing the products of children's creative activities through display. This might be a wall display of paintings, drawings or collage or a table-top exhibition of 3D models. Whilst this may brighten up the early years environment and demonstrate that children's creativity is valued, the main focus is usually on the outcomes and artefacts. An alternative approach is the use of pedagogical documentation. Inspired by practice in Reggio Emilia, this involves carefully observing, listening to and documenting children's experiences during a project or activity. Multiple methods can be used to capture the creative process, including written records, audio and video recording, photographs and drawings. In place of a static display, stages on a genuine learning journey are presented and these can be shared and reviewed by children, parents and staff.

The production of pedagogical documentation is demanding but it has several advantages. What happens during an activity is made visible to the participants and to others, insights can be gained into children's ideas and understandings, and the documentation can form a basis for shared thinking about the activity and be a source for future planning. The short case study from practice shares an experience of experimenting with documenting children's experiences in this way.

CASE STUDY THREE

Documenting investigations of a fish

Lynsey Thomas explains the pedagogical documentation relating to an activity in which children investigated a fresh fish that a member of staff had brought into their pre-school play group:

Our Learning Journey Walls document the whole group's progress and we try to focus our everyday practices on the 'process' rather than the 'product'. For example, our display shows the children's examination of a 'fish': we looked at it, felt it, discussed it, smelt it, painted it, washed it and then looked inside … The language and enthusiasm was endless, enjoyed by both children and staff.

We were able to record children's learning by taking photos, recording vocabulary (captured as speech bubbles) and displaying the children's artwork. Children use the wall daily to tell their friends and family what they did and how they did it.

Figure 7.2   *Documentation of the exploration of a fish*

⭐ **Reflection for case study 3**

- What part does this documentation play in supporting children's creative responses to the fish?

One UK initiative inspired by work in Reggio Emilia and developing the use of pedagogical documentation is 5x5x5=Creativity. 5x5x5=Creativity is an arts-based action research organisation. The name derives from its beginnings as a collaborative project involving five artists, five cultural centres and five educational settings. The focus is upon collecting and communicating evidence about children's creative capacities and so its members describe their activities as 'researching children, researching the world'. Research in this context is 'critical reflective evaluation of action' that becomes a 'habit of mind'. At the heart of this approach, as in early childhood settings in Reggio Emilia, pedagogical documentation plays an important role: 'careful listening, observations and reflection on children's learning give shape to pedagogical thought' (Bancroft et al., 2008: 4).

Similarly, but in a different context, Will Parnell (2011, 2012) reports and reflects in detail on the experiences of a researcher and two studio teachers who experiment with documenting children's creativity in studio spaces in a university laboratory school in the USA. He describes the children's engagement in a project on birds and drawing owls, and highlights the mutual learning between children and their teachers when adults attend closely to what children are thinking and representing. His articles recommended for further reading below exemplify the use and value of documentation as a basis for shared professional learning between the adults, enabling them to further understand and support the children's creative endeavours.

Chapter summary

This chapter has explored play and creativity, two key concepts within contemporary early childhood education, in England and elsewhere. Both ideas need to be thought through carefully in order to provide young children with opportunities to exercise their imaginations and engage in possibility thinking within early years settings. Attention needs to be given to the creation of physical environments that enable creativity and the provision of open-ended materials and resources. Adults who work with young children must consider optimal ways and means of supporting and structuring opportunities for play and creativity in order to foster children's self-expression. One useful strategy for valuing and supporting play and creativity is the use of pedagogical documentation. There is so much to consider in relation to play and creativity that readers are encouraged to use the recommended resources in order to further explore this important topic.

Recommended reading

Broadhead, P., Howard, J. and Wood, E. (2010) *Play and Learning in the Early Years*. London: Sage.
An inspiring book based on research into play, with several chapters relevant to the relationships between play and creativity with useful insights for early childhood studies students and early years practitioners.

Craft, A. (2002) *Creativity and Early Years Education: A Lifewide Foundation*. London: Routledge. A very interesting exploration of the concept of creativity, the nature and value of creativity in young children and the implications of this for early years teachers.

Parnell, W. (2011) 'Revealing the experience of children and teachers even in their absence: documenting in the Early Childhood Studio', *Journal of Early Childhood Research*, 9 (3): 291–309.

Parnell, W. (2012) 'Experiences of teacher reflection: Reggio inspired practices in the studio', *Journal of Early Childhood Research*, 10 (2): 117–33.

These two articles offer a valuable insight into the processes and purposes of pedagogical documentation and its potential for use in illuminating learning and teaching in the early years.

Recommended websites

www.earlyarts.co.uk/
The website for Earlyarts, a national network for people working creatively with children and families in the arts, cultural and early years sectors.

www.5x5x5creativity.org.uk/
The website for the 5x5x5=Creativity independent arts organisation.

Want to learn more about this chapter? Visit the companion website at **www.sagepub.co.uk/walleranddavis3e** to access podcasts from the author and child observation videos.

8

Outdoor Play and Learning

Helen Tovey and Tim Waller

 Key chapter objectives

- To provide an overview of recent literature on outdoor play and learning
- To discuss the reasons why opportunities for outdoor play have become restricted
- To consider the benefits of outdoor play and learning
- To report on findings from an ongoing Outdoor Learning Project

---

We should feed children's natural desire to contact nature's diversity with free access to an area of limited size over an extended period of time, for it is only by intimately knowing the wonders of nature's complexity in a particular place that one can fully appreciate the immense beauty of the planet as a whole. (Hart, 1997: 18, cited in Casey, 2007: 9)

Outdoor play and learning has been a long-standing feature of early years provision and an essential part of the 'nursery tradition', and many practitioners and parents would empathise with Hart's beliefs above. The past twenty years have seen a resurgence of interest in and commitment to the use of outdoor environments in the UK and provision for regular outdoor experience is emphasised in curriculum documents for the Curriculum for Excellence (CfE) in Scotland (Scottish Government, n.d.); for

Northern Ireland (CCEA, 2006); for the Foundation Phase in Wales (Welsh Government, 2013b); and for the Early Years Foundation Stage in England (DfE, 2012d).

However, a clear pedagogy for the use of the outdoors as a site for learning is not well established and the purpose and value of outdoor play can often be misunderstood. Further, many writers have raised concern over the impact of a 'culture of fear' on children's outdoor play (for example, Furedi, 2002; Gill, 2012; Tovey, 2007). This chapter considers what counts as an outdoor play and learning environment and provides a critical overview of the positive benefits of outdoor play for young children. Findings from an ongoing outdoor learning project are discussed in relation to recent literature and research in the field.

Context and rationale

For many parents and early years practitioners, outdoor play is seen as an essential part of a child's healthy development and learning (White, 2011). Outdoor play and learning is used here as an 'umbrella' term to cover a range of children's experiences in different outdoor locations. For young children attending an early years setting in the UK, these opportunities may include:

- play in outdoor areas within the setting
- visits to natural, wild environments, such as woods, forests, beaches and riverbanks not designed or cultivated by humans or community parks and play spaces
- Forest School or nature kindergarten.

Forest School involves regular visits to natural, wild environments usually with a trained Forest School leader. Forest Schools have a long tradition in the UK and in Scandinavia as a way of giving children play and learning experiences in the natural world. By the 1980s, they had become an integral part of the Danish early years programme and influenced the development of the Forest School movement in the UK (Knight, 2009; Maynard, 2007). The Forest School movement has grown substantially in recent years and there are now sites in urban as well as rural areas. Nature kindergartens offer a similar ethos to Forest Schools but are permanently located within a natural, wild environment.

Decline in opportunities for play outdoors

A focus on outdoor environments has renewed importance and urgency in our current climate, given the changing nature of childhood and evidence of the declining opportunities for spontaneous play outdoors. Increase in traffic, a decline in spaces, including local streets for play, and a rapid growth in a 'culture of fear' (Furedi, 2002) have led to declining autonomy for children to be able to play out, visit local play spaces with friends or travel to school unaccompanied. Research by the UK Policy Studies Institute (Shaw et al., 2013), drawing on the seminal studies by Mayer Hillman, highlights the erosion of children's freedom and independent mobility over the last forty years. For example, just 25% of primary-aged children in the UK were allowed to travel to and from school on their own in 2011 compared with 86% in 1971. However, international comparisons with equivalent groups of children show that this decline in freedom is less evident in Germany. For example, half of children in the German research were able to travel home from school on their own at age 7 compared with less than 5% of children in the UK, suggesting that cultural attitudes to risk and safety as well as differences in local environments may play a significant part.

The decline in access to outdoor play spaces has been paralleled by an unprecedented rise in anxiety over children's safety. It appears that parental anxiety and fear of abduction has had the most pervasive effect on children's play (Lindon, 2011). Evidence from a number of recent surveys (Gill, 2012; Lindon, 2011) shows that not only are few parents happy for their children to play outside without an adult present, but that many children are also anxious about the danger of abduction or murder if they play outdoors. Paradoxically there is no evidence to support this fear as incidents of child abduction, although tragic, are extremely rare and have remained largely unchanged over the last forty years or more (Lindon, 2011).

There is evidence that this risk aversion and anxiety has also permeated early years provision. For example, Maynard and Waters (2007) reported that reception teachers' concern about safety was a limiting factor in their provision of outdoor experiences. Tovey (2010) also found that the majority of early years practitioners in her study showed a reluctance to allow risk-taking in play and demonstrated considerable anxiety about possible adverse outcomes. However, a minority of practitioners in the same study celebrated positive risk-taking and were confident in advocating the benefits of adventurous play outdoors, revealing a more positive perspective on risk and challenge outdoors and one more consistent with the approach advocated by early years pioneers such as Froebel, McMillan and Isaacs amongst others.

Where do children play?

There is growing evidence that children spend increasing amounts of time inside the home, which may be at the expense of time spent playing outside. Moss (2012) reports television viewing figures which show that children aged between 4 and 9 spend over 17 hours a week watching television. This together with the growing availability of other screen-based entertainment indicates that children's play is increasingly home-based and sedentary. Parental fears for children's safety, an increase in traffic and changing attitudes to children's play outdoors have all contributed to what Louv refers to as 'well meaning, protective house arrest' (Louv, cited in Moss, 2012: 4).

However, given the choice, it appears that many children would like to be able to play outside. A study comparing the lives of children in the UK with those in Sweden and Spain to investigate why the UK was placed at the bottom of UNICEF's 2007 ranking of children's wellbeing (UNICEF, 2007b), indicated that the lack of opportunity for free outdoor play was a significant contributor to the poor wellbeing of children in the UK (Ipsos MORI and Nairn, 2011).

Why is outdoor play significant?

What is the evidence for the benefits and significance of outdoor play? Tovey (2007: 37) emphasises the crucial importance of the underpinning values of those who create outdoor spaces or accompany children to natural wild spaces. She argues that some learning can only happen outdoors and summarises the *unique* opportunities that outdoor play provides as including:

- the space and freedom to try things out
- an environment that can be acted on, changed and transformed, creating new imaginary worlds
- a dynamic, ever-changing environment that invites exploration, curiosity and wonder
- whole-body, multi-sensory experiences
- the scope to combine materials in ways that are challenging and problematic
- the opportunity to make connections in their learning
- a rich context for curiosity, wonder, mastery and 'what if' thinking
- the space to navigate and negotiate the social world of people and friendships, and to experience disagreement and resolve conflicts with peers
- the opportunity for giddy, gleeful, dizzy play
- the potential for mastery, a willingness to take risks and the skills to be safe
- a wide range of movement opportunities that are central to learning
- experience of the natural world and their place within it
- opportunities for learning in all areas of the curriculum.

For Tovey (2007: 38), few of these benefits can be realised in open, windswept, asphalt-surfaced playgrounds and outdoor play is about *potential* – the potential of outdoor spaces to support, enhance and engage children's imagination, curiosity and creativity and foster their health and wellbeing. Where adults recognise and understand this potential they can then begin to make effective provision even in situations that are far from ideal. Alongside this is a need for practitioners and parents to seek to overcome obstacles, to recognise 'what can be' rather than just accepting 'what is' and to campaign for more appropriate provision.

Health and wellbeing

Play outdoors on a daily basis impacts positively on health, for example on motor development, cardiovascular fitness, bone and muscle strength and children's mental health and feelings of wellbeing (DH, 2011c). A report from the chief medical officers of all four countries in the UK (DH, 2011c) recommends that children under 5 should be physically active for at least 3 hours a day with minimum time spent in sedentary activity. Children over 5 should spend at least 1 hour and up to several hours each day in vigorous, intensive physical activity beyond everyday activity such as walking to school or to the shops. The authors argue that 'children need the freedom to create their own opportunities for active play, lead their own activities, direct their own play and engage in imaginary play' (DH, 2011c: 22).

Such access to physically active play is especially important given the scale of the obesity epidemic. Despite an encouraging small decline in the numbers of overweight and obese children in the UK in recent years, the figures are still cause for concern. The National Child Measurement Programme, for example, reported that 20% of 4- and 5-year-olds in reception classes in England in 2011–12 were overweight or obese (HSCIC, 2012). Significantly, children from disadvantaged backgrounds are much more likely to be obese than those from more wealthy backgrounds (DH, 2011c). However, Hope et al. (2007: 326) caution us against a simplistic view of the 'obesity epidemic'. They argue that there are issues over the measurement and definition of obesity for children using the body mass index (BMI) which take no account of age, sex, ethnicity or level of fitness. Nevertheless there is common agreement in the literature that regular physical activity is good for promoting a longer and better quality of life and that good habits in terms of physical activity start in childhood.

Opportunity for spontaneous open-ended play outdoors is crucial. For example, research by University College, London (Mackett, 2004) found that unstructured play outdoors is one of the best forms of exercise for children. A leading authority on childhood obesity, writing in the *British Medical Journal*, also concluded that 'opportunities for spontaneous play may be the only requirement that young children need to increase their physical activity' (Dietz, 2001: 314).

However, the spaces that children play in are also highly significant. For example, Fjørtoft (2001) investigated the impact of two different environments on children's play in Norway. She compared a group of children playing in a natural forest environment with those playing in constructed playgrounds with more conventional equipment such as swings, slide, climbing houses and sand pits. She measured the motor development and physical fitness of the two groups of children and found that those using the forest environment made more rapid gains in all areas of motor ability and that there were significant differences between the two groups of children in tests on balance, coordination, strength and agility.

Fjørtoft argues that the dynamic and rough natural playscapes afford more challenging play requiring a greater variety of movements. The unpredictable nature of the forest environment with its uneven terrain, obstacles to manoeuvre over and under and varying heights and levels, affords more opportunities for children to extend their limits, and use their bodies in a wider range of movements than in a conventional, more predictable playground environment.

This is important as it suggests that it is not just outdoor play, but particular qualities of an outdoor environment which promote richer, more challenging play and significant health and fitness benefits. This has implications for the sort of outdoor environments we offer children in settings. It also has implications for the frequency of access to rougher terrain beyond the settings, such as that which children experience in visits out to wild, natural environments or Forest Schools.

In the current climate of concern over obesity and levels of physical activity and fitness, there is a danger that inappropriate exercise programmes will be introduced for young children. Burdette and Whitaker (2005), commenting on the US obesity epidemic, argue against such programmes and in favour of a stronger emphasis on active, unstructured outdoor play for both physical health and improved cognitive, social and emotional wellbeing. They argue that 'play' is a more motivating and positive term for use with parents of young children than 'physical activity', 'exercise' or 'sport'. Movement is part of children's very being and it is spontaneous play and exploration that motivate children to move, not 'keeping fit'.

The central importance of movement

Active play outdoors is not just important for children's health and wellbeing, it is also crucial for all aspects of learning. Indeed, our current health concerns may overshadow the importance of movement in cognition. Babies and young children are primed to move. Whole-body, expansive movement is the very being of children and they imagine, explore the world, represent their ideas, communicate, express their emotions and interact with others primarily through movement. Yet all too often children are confined indoors where the opportunities to move expansively, to act on their environment and receive sensory feedback are severely curtailed.

Space to move is a fundamental justification for outdoor play. The larger the space, the more expansive the movements and the opportunities to run, roll, leap, tumble, swing, climb and so on. But movement is much more than physical development. Body, brain and mind are inextricably connected and movement underpins the development of conceptual thought (Athey, 2007). For example, moving headfirst down a slide offers experience of such things as direction, gradient and speed and concepts of headfirst or even headfirst backwards. Swinging on a rope can provide experience of energy, forces, gravity, speed, distance, and cause and effect. These experiences enrich children's understanding and help develop key mathematical and scientific concepts. Research on developmental movement play (Greenland, 2006) shows the importance of a wide variety of movements such as tipping, tumbling, rolling, scrambling and swinging in developing a sense of balance and one's own body in space. Such experiences, Greenland argues, stimulate the proprioceptive and vestibular senses and can have a significant impact on later learning.

The outdoors offer scope for adventure and challenge, and movements that children perceive to be 'scary' such as sliding fast, hanging upside down, balancing along a wobbly plank, swinging fast on a twisted rope or engaging in bouts of rough and tumble play with peers. Kalliala (2006), drawing on Caillois's work, refers to this as 'dizzy play' where the normal body posture is inverted and the players take great delight in playing 'on the edge' of fear and control. Such play allows children to test their limits, push their own boundaries and find out how their bodies work in space, developing confidence and a sense of 'I can do it'. Biologists Spinka, Newberry and Bekoff (2001) suggest that adventurous play is characteristic of play in all mammals and serves as 'training for the unexpected'. They argue that players deliberately put themselves in disadvantageous positions and that novelty and risk add to the intensity and pleasure of the play. Players switch playfully between well-controlled movements and those where they experience being on the edge of out-of-control. Such play, they argue, increases the range and versatility of movements and helps players cope physically and emotionally with unexpected events.

Positive risk-taking and 'staying safe'

A key feature of play outdoors is that children seek to push out boundaries, test their own limits and take risks. The outdoors offer rich potential for such challenging play as it provides the space, freedom and opportunity to explore limits and to be adventurous, whether a toddler crawling down steps or a group of 5-year-olds rolling down a bank.

Stephenson (2003) argues that children seek out and enjoy physical challenges in their play, as a matter of course. She identified a number of components which she believed were significant in 4-year-old children's physical risk-taking: 'attempting something never done before, feeling on the borderline of "out of control" often because of height or speed and overcoming fear' (Stephenson, 2003: 36).

Such play can cause adults considerable anxiety and can lead to outdoor play environments that are far from challenging, where all sources of potential risk and challenge are removed and adults themselves are fearful of accidents and possible blame and litigation. Here risk is viewed as the equivalent of 'danger', as something to be assessed, managed, controlled, removed, and this view has often been most prominent. Yet an alternative view of risk sees it as a positive feature of children's play and learning, indeed of life itself, and part of being alive and being human (Little, 2006; Sandseter, 2009; Tovey, 2007; Waters and Begley, 2007).

The willingness to take risks is an important learning disposition. Research by Dweck (2000) emphasises the importance of what she terms a 'mastery' approach to learning, a disposition to have a go, try something out and relish challenge, in contrast to a 'helpless' approach characterised by fearfulness and fear of failure. When adults repeatedly say to children 'mind out', 'be careful', 'don't do that', 'come down you'll fall', there is a danger that they help shape this 'helpless' attitude to learning by communicating their own anxiety. To have a good disposition to learn requires confidence, competence and willingness to 'have a go'. Play outdoors motivates children to extend their own boundaries, to be adventurous, to explore a little further and to develop a disposition to see challenges as problems to enjoy rather than things to fear.

As Stephenson (2003: 41) points out, there may be 'a fundamental link between a young child's developing confidence in confronting physical challenges, and her confidence to undertake risks of quite different kinds in other learning contexts'. This has important implications for the development of self-esteem and confidence as well as for dispositions for learning.

Risk-taking in play appears to be positively associated with emotional wellbeing, resilience and mental health. Rather than protecting children from risk it seems that exposure to some risks can itself be protective. Kloep and Hendry (2007) draw on Rutter's notion of 'steeling experiences' to argue that mistakes, providing they are not overly disastrous, can offer protection against the negative effects of future failure. Managing fear and uncertainty and holding your nerve when feeling on the edge of 'out of control' are important aspects of emotional wellbeing, resilience and mental health.

There can also be great joy and delight in play where risk itself is the main attraction and motivation to continue. The simultaneous feeling of risk and challenge, fear and exhilaration, control and lack of control can be considered a characteristic of such play, whether in babies' precarious delight at being thrown in the air, or tipped backwards, in young children's joy in balancing along a wobbly bridge or in older children swinging upside down on the end of a rope. Caillois (2001) identifies the 'voluptuous panic' that such play can engender. He argues that such experiences are important elements of group camaraderie, friendship and social cohesion.

However, risk-taking is not all positive. Children can take risks that are inappropriate, that border on recklessness or that put themselves or others at risk of serious injury. As in many areas of learning, children need the support of experienced others who can help them recognise and assess risk for themselves, who can teach safe ways of doing things where appropriate but who also encourage a 'can do' attitude and a positive disposition to adventurous play. Teaching children to assess risk for themselves, for example by testing the strength of a branch before climbing, or using a stick to measure the depth of water in a stream before paddling, is a central part of the Forest School ethos.

A challenge to the zero risk approach to play can be found in Play England and the Play Safety Forum's document 'Managing Risk in Play Provision: Implementation guide' (Ball et al., 2008). Produced for the play sector, it argues for a more balanced approach to risk management that takes into account the benefits as well as the risks. It argues that risk–benefit assessments can support play providers in offering challenging, exciting, engaging play opportunities while not exposing children to unacceptable risk of harm. It cautions against unqualified use of the words 'safe', 'risk' and 'hazard' as they mean different things to different people in different contexts and what can be safe for one child can be a hazard to another. The document has robust legal scrutiny, and is endorsed by the Health and Safety Executive and the government. It provides a positive way forward in confronting the risk-averse culture that has had such a damaging influence on outdoor play in recent years and which paradoxically placed children at increased risk of harm.

The importance of adults

Despite the importance of a challenging environment, research in New Zealand by Stephenson (2003) emphasised that children's hunger for physical challenge was satisfied more through practitioners' attitudes than the provision itself. For example, adults who enjoyed being outside, who were interested in physical play and took a sensitive and liberal approach to supervision, enabled children to find challenges that were experienced as risky but did not put them in a position of hazard (see also The Outdoor Learning Project on p. 157 of this chapter, and Waller, 2011).

Research in Norway by Sandseter (2007, 2009) also noted that when practitioners regard risky play as positive and necessary, they are willing to support children's reasonable risk-taking, even when this exceeds their own tolerance of risk. Tovey's research in England on practitioners' perspectives of risk suggested that where practitioners felt supported within their teams, had a shared approach to risk, challenge and safety outdoors, and understood the benefits of risk-taking, they were confident to offer experiences which included some element of risk and challenge (Tovey, 2010).

Engagement with the natural world

Play outdoors offers direct experience of the natural world. Children can learn *in* nature rather than just *about* nature. Through play outdoors children can be immersed in direct, first-hand experience of nature and can learn about the growth of plants and animals, about the beauty of nature and about the interrelationships of all living things. A close relationship with nature helps children to begin to see their own place in the natural world and to develop a sense of personal and collective responsibility for it.

Through digging, planting, harvesting and other experiences outdoors, children experience the cycles of life and death, growth and decay, recycling and conserving resources in direct and meaningful ways. Nature can be provocative and at times challenging and children can be interested in the rawness as well as the beauty of nature. For example, death can feature as much as life and is often a source of fascination for children.

Louv (2006) presents a range of evidence showing how children are increasingly disconnected from the natural world and even argues that children are suffering from 'nature deficit disorder'. This is an unfortunate phrase, but his intention is not to suggest a medical disorder but rather to use it as shorthand to highlight the human cost of our alienation from the natural world, such as the diminished use of our senses, attention difficulties and higher rates of physical and emotional illness. He refers to research which shows how children and young people who lack direct experience of nature can become fearful of natural landscapes with their wilder, open terrain, and can find natural processes abhorrent or disgusting. This has alarming implications for the future of our planet. As David Sobel, an environmental campaigner, has argued, children need to love nature before they can be expected to save it (Sobel, 1996).

Nature with its constant changes and transformation attracts children's interest and invites their curiosity. It provides the essential first-hand experiences that we know are so important for children's learning and which enrich and nourish children's brains. There are puddles to splash in, leaves to roll in, trees to climb, bushes to hide in and banks to clamber up or slither down. The weather and seasons are in a constant state of flux and children see how a pond freezes in winter, is full of tadpoles in spring and may dry up completely in summer.

Nature can also be reassuringly familiar. In a fast-changing world of instant fixes, nature takes its own time and children learn how to be patient as they wait for the first pod to appear on their runner bean or a snail to emerge from its shell. Benoit argues that this slow pace of nature is important for children to develop 'frustration tolerance' (cited in Jenkinson, 2001) and can be calming and reassuring to children whose lives are less predictable.

Nature also provides a rich context for imaginative play. As a complex, diverse environment it offers multiple opportunities for children to create alternative realities, whether building a den with sticks or creating a car out of a fallen log. Nature offers a plentiful supply of 'loose parts' (Nicholson, 1971, cited in Tovey, 2007), such as leaves, stones, sticks, moss and mud which can be transformed into whatever children want. Incidental features of the environment take on new meanings and children develop a dynamic, reciprocal relationship with the natural landscape. For example, Waller (2007) reports how a mound becomes a mountain to be climbed, a tree with spreading branches becomes the 'octopus tree' and a pond becomes a swamp monster with eighteen heads! These transformations are highly significant in developing more abstract, symbolic, imaginative 'as if' thinking and help develop a rich store of imaginative plots and scripts.

Nature then is not just a background context for play, it is the very essence of it and it is not surprising that it appears that, when given a choice, children prefer to play in natural environments (Armitage, 2001, cited in Tovey, 2007).

In the nineteenth century Friedrich Froebel, the pioneer of kindergartens for young children, argued that children should be immersed in nature so that they can begin to learn about it, understand it and develop an emotional, creative and even spiritual relationship with it. Through this children could begin to develop an ecological understanding of their own place in the natural world and the interrelationship of all living things. However, he also argued that mere contact with nature is not enough.

Many adults as well as children treat nature as one ordinarily treats the air: one lives in it while knowing almost nothing about it. Children who spend all their time in the open air may still observe nothing of the beauties of nature and their influence on the human heart. (Froebel, in Lilley, 1967: 146)

Today, as many children spend longer amounts of time indoors and are increasingly disconnected from the natural world, Froebel's ideas and those of other pioneers of early years provision have renewed importance and urgency. If children can develop a sense of wonder about nature, can see the effect of their actions on things around them and can get to know a small area of nature in deep ways, they are much more likely to want to conserve nature and help shape a sustainable future. The best way of getting to know nature is to play in it, supported by adults who respect and value the natural world, share children's desire to know more about it and can extend children's ecological awareness and environmental responsibilities in meaningful ways.

 ## Research in context

Waters, J. and Maynard, T. (2010) 'What's so interesting about outside? A study of child-initiated interaction with teachers in the natural outdoor environment', *European Early Childhood Research Journal*, 18 (4): 473–83.

'Simply *being outside* is not enough.' It is the way in which adults and children interact which is crucial for learning. This was the conclusion from a research project by Waters and Maynard (2010) looking at the specific elements in the outside environment that attract children's attention and how this attention is shared with adults. The research involved three classes of children aged from 4 to 7 from an inner-city primary school in South Wales as they visited a local country park. The researchers focused on episodes of child-initiated interaction with adults, looking specifically at what children chose to share and talk about with adults.

Certain features of the environment excited children's interest and afforded child-initiated interactions with adults in about a third of the total interactions. These included 'loose parts', such as berries, sticks and plants; features of the landscape, such as puddles, trees and hills as well as sensations like feeling the wind; wildlife, including insects and animals; familiar landmarks; and a category they called 'other', including fantasy elements such as an elf's home or the dinosaur's hiding place. When adults responded and interacted in a way that was in tune with such interests, there was evidence of rich and meaningful conversational exchanges.

The authors concluded that varied, flexible, natural spaces offer educators a wealth of opportunity to build on children's interests across the Foundation Stage Curriculum and rich potential for children's cognitive engagement as well as their physical, health and social development.

Bilton (2012) also noted the rich potential of the outdoors for sustained conversational exchange between adults and children. However, in the particular settings she researched, the majority of the adult-initiated talk was about mundane, domestic matters, such as taking turns on the bikes, sorting out disputes or telling children to stop doing something. There was less evidence of responses that might extend children's thinking or understanding. Children, on the other hand, sought out adults to share things of interest and to show things they had done or made.

Both research studies reveal the potential of the outdoors for rich cognitive engagement between adults and children and both argue that adults must seize these opportunities. They suggest that the physical features of the environment, as well as the overall ethos and principles underpinning its use, have a powerful impact on the opportunities for children's learning.

The Outdoor Learning Project

The Outdoor Learning Project (OLP) started in January 2004 and involves children, staff, parents and students at a nursery school in England. Children are given regular opportunities to play and learn in natural, wild environments such as woodland and river banks, accompanied by adults. This project is ongoing and is currently celebrating ten years of practice and research.

[A similar project was started at a primary school in Wales in January 2005 and was included in the original chapter on outdoor learning in the previous edition of this book. The project in Wales is reported and discussed in further detail by Waller (2007) and Waters and Maynard (2010).]

The OLP is based at a state nursery school located in a mixed housing estate on the outskirts of a large town in the English Midlands area of the UK. Children (aged 3 and 4 years) attend the nursery on a part-time basis (forty children in the morning and forty in the afternoon). The school adheres to the statutory Early Years Foundation Stage (EYFS) (DfE, 2012d). Children normally attend for one year and then transfer to the Reception class of local primary schools. Staff include a head teacher, class teacher, three nursery nurses and three learning support assistants. There is a base ratio of one practitioner to ten children and the children are organised into 'key groups' of around fourteen.

Outdoor learning is an integral part of the curriculum and the large garden area is open for the children to use freely for all but the very end of sessions when the children go into their key groups. The country park used for the project has elements of a 'natural, wild environment'. The park is built around an Edwardian reservoir and arboretum and below the reservoir dam is an area of approximately 52,000 square metres containing woods, open grassland, a purpose-built children's play area on sand, an amphibian pond and a butterfly garden. Visits to the country park are undertaken on one day per week (morning and afternoon), whatever the weather. The children are transported by bus to the park, with the journey lasting approximately fifteen minutes in each direction. The children are accompanied by practitioners, parents and students, allowing for a one-to-one, or one-to-two, adult–child ratio. A programme of visits is organised so that a small group of children (one 'key' group) is taken on each occasion. This allows for an appropriate level of interaction and support for the children at the park and is also designed to have a minimal impact on staffing at the nursery. Additional adults are also needed to support the collection of written observations, video and photographic evidence.

A similar pattern was observed in all years of the project, so far. On the first visit, the children predictably tended to stay together with the adults, spending time exploring a relatively narrow area. After the first visit, the children tended to split into small groups immediately on arrival and go to different parts of the park or woodland. Once familiar with the outdoor environment, the children recorded image-based data revealing an interesting range of both 'social spaces' and 'individual landmarks' (Clark and Moss, 2001, 2005, 2011). As the visits increased, the children re-visited and named familiar places – 'The Octopus Tree', 'Eeyore's Den', the woods, 'The Top of the World', 'The Giant's Bed' (of leaves), 'The Goblin's House' and 'Dragonfly Land', 'The Crocodile Tree', 'The Giant's Den'. Quite often the children used the environment as a context for their imaginative play involving themes such as dinosaurs or goblins (see Waller, 2006, 2007). While the outdoor environment has open access to the public, on many occasions, especially in the winter months, there were no other visitors at the same time, allowing the children complete freedom of space.

Initially, a range of mostly qualitative and some quantitative information was gathered in the form of questionnaires, observations and video and photographic evidence, and an assessment of children's 'Involvement Levels' (Laevers, 1994) was undertaken. In Table 8.1 a comparison of children's involvement levels in the nursery and the country park over a school year is shown, and the average of all the scores over ten years is reported. At the school, each child is observed regularly and a judgement made about involvement levels every half term. The levels are based on the five-point scale devised by Laevers (1994) (see Chapter 11 for more information on levels of involvement). While it could be expected that children's levels of involvement would increase from autumn to summer as they settle in to nursery, the data show that the involvement levels were consistently higher in the country park. For some individual children (in particular, several boys), they were significantly higher in the park.

The OLP study draws on the 'Mosaic approach' for listening to young children described by Clark and Moss (2001, 2005, 2011). The method uses both the traditional tools of observing children at play and a variety of 'participatory tools' with children. These include taking photographs, book making, tours of the outdoor area and map making. 'The Mosaic approach enables children to create a living picture of their lives' (Clark and Moss, 2005: 13). Also, part of the Mosaic approach is to involve adults in

Table 8.1 Children's average involvement levels over the first ten years of the Outdoor Learning Project

Nursery

Autumn term	3.28 (n = 82)
Spring term	3.41 (n = 83.33)
Summer term	3.79 (n = 83.41)
Country park	4.41 (n = 82.44)

Mean involvement scores using Laevers' scale, 1994

gathering information in addition to perspectives from the children (for further discussion, see Waller and Bitou, 2011).

The OLP has so far revealed a wealth of information about the children's views of the outdoor environment, including places they liked and their play with friends. The initial findings from the project were reported by Waller et al. (2004). One feature of these findings was that involvement in the project promoted a high level of reflection on the benefit of giving children opportunities to create their own learning environments. The project therefore became more focused on eliciting children's views and perspectives. Further papers on the methodology and ethics (Waller, 2005a, 2005b) and on young children's geographical literacy (Waller, 2005c) were given. Also, in Waller (2006) and Waller and Bitou (2011), a critical discussion of participatory research methods is offered, while Waller (2007) discusses the construction and development of children's narratives located around their outdoor experiences. Waller (2010a) draws on gender theory to consider how the shared narratives and the image-based data relating to the narratives (recorded by children and adults) both reflect and support the construction of gender in outdoor spaces.

CASE STUDY ONE

Alfie's den – Scenario 1

Children attending a nursery school (aged 3 and 4) had been visiting a woodland environment regularly and had discussed the possibility of making a den. On one visit, an adult suggested that a good place for the den would be deep in the woods next to a large pile of twigs and small branches that could easily be used for constructing a den. Therefore the den was constructed by children collecting twigs and passing them to the adult who placed them in position to organise a den in the conventional 'tent' shape. The children then developed a narrative around the theme

(Continued)

(Continued)

of 'Eeyore's den' and returned to play in the den on subsequent visits. However, during a break from the visits, due to a school vacation, the den was dismantled, and upon seeing this some children became quite upset. The den was hastily constructed in the same manner and the children returned to their previous play patterns.

Alfie's den – Scenario 2

The following year, the nursery involved a new group of children. Alfie had been on several visits to the woodlands and back at school had discussed with practitioners his desire to make a den. They had encouraged him to plan out his idea and helped him to make a list of tools and equipment he might need to take with him in order to build the den. Archie duly collected his equipment at school together in a rucksack and took it with him on his next visit to the park. It was the start of summer and the local weather had been dry for several weeks, so consequently the ground was very hard. Archie enlisted the help of a number of children and they went in search of a location for the den. Having found a location in the woods that they deemed suitable, the children (frequently directed by Archie) started to construct a den that involved placing sticks in the ground and joining them together with string. However, the ground was too hard and the sticks would not push in, nor could they be put in place with the use of a hammer. Archie asked the practitioner what to do and then tried to hammer the ground. The practitioner asked if he was trying to make the ground softer so that he could put the sticks in and then suggested he think what else might make the ground soft. Archie then picked up a water bottle and poured water into the hole for the sticks, thus enabling them to stay in place and complete the den.

Reflection for case study 1

These two different scenarios both involved the building of dens, although the first one was much more adult-directed and was constructed to look like a conventional den.

- What are the different roles of the adult in the two scenarios?
- How much assistance should adults give children in their play?
- Does it matter if Alfie's construction did not have the appearance of a den?

Parents' perspectives

In addition to the vast range of pedagogical documentation recorded by the children and adults, regular focus groups have been held with both parents and practitioners to elicit their views of the benefits and limitations of the OLP. Initially, the staff of the nursery were reluctant to involve parents in the visits to the country park because they felt the parents might discourage the children from climbing trees, taking risks and getting muddy. However, in 2007 a decision was made to encourage parents and grandparents to participate in the OLP, in keeping with the nursery philosophy of family learning (see Athey, 2007). The focus group held with parents in 2010 illustrates the potential and the strength of the child/parent/practitioner relationship.

The comments below demonstrate how the OLP has impacted positively on some parents' views of outdoor spaces:

> I think it involves growing confidence in the environment and themselves. (Dad G2)

> On the first visit I told my daughter not to get muddy and not to climb trees. Then I realised that these things were good for her and that I was wrong not to let her play naturally in the park ... it's only washing after all. (Mum S17)

> Its been a learning experience for me too. (Mum F34)

Later on the discussion moved towards what happens when the children move to primary school (4–11 years):

> Progression to school is a concern because the primary school is much more risk averse. As soon as they get to the school its unlearning – they can't play out when they want. For example there is a small woodland at the edge of the school grounds and the children are not allowed to play there because 'it's too muddy'. (Dad E19)

> They get this fantastic experience in nursery and then it stops when they go to school. My older daughter took a long time to settle because she wanted to be outside all the time and they were not allowed ... I did wonder about sending my son to another [primary] school ... but that's silly because we live next door to this one! (Mum D26)

The comments above are an example of the impact of the project on parents' knowledge and views about outdoor learning and also of how these views have led to transformations of practice. In September 2012 parent governors persuaded the new primary school head teacher to include more outdoor learning in the curriculum and to give all children regular experiences outdoors. Thus the OLP has demonstrated the value of parents' participating with professionals within an articulated pedagogical approach:

> Teachers of young children could make a revolutionary move forward in developing a pedagogy of the early years if they recorded how they conceptualised and shared professional concepts with parents. (Athey, 2007: 206)

Practitioners' perspectives

During the first ten years of the OLP staffing was extremely consistent and the practitioners remained the same throughout (this is a feature of early years professionalism in England, see Hadfield et al., 2012). Regular focus groups involving staff have been held throughout the project. When asked to reflect on the impact of the OLP, staff regularly reported:

- more quality time with children
- uninterrupted communication
- time for response
- children waiting for adult response
- increased staff confidence (in outdoor spaces)
- children being outside more at nursery
- increased information for records
- adult/staff enjoyment.

For example, in terms of pedagogy staff commented:

> We are more relaxed about letting go and not having a set activity ... tuned into children's ideas more. Changed the way we do planning – more flexibility. (EY Practitioner B)

> Our whole attitude to children's learning changed – we started to trust that we could follow the children's learning ... we changed our practice and planning. Staff have gained expertise and become more confident. Children have become more confident to communicate because of the individual attention. (EY Practitioner F)

> We now have a more natural outside area – more imagination and creativity. (EY Practitioner A)

> (Focus Group May, 2009: see Waller, 2007 and 2010a for a wider discussion of pedagogy and the OLP)

However, in 2012 significant changes to the environment in the country park were made by the park rangers due to a combination of the effects of a destructive storm on a dense area of woodland and increased capital funding from local government. What was once a 'wild' natural area, where many children over the years of the OLP had developed a range of interesting narratives, quite often based around specific trees and built dens, etc., was converted into a 'play area' where a large slide and other play equipment were installed and perceived by adults in the OLP to 'dominate' the space.

Staff views on this change are reflected in the following comments at a focus group in June 2012:

> Recently the country park itself has changed – the new play park has become the focus .... children lost exploration and problem solving opportunities. (EY Practitioner R)

When the environment changed [at the country park] we became less enthusiastic about the visits because the children didn't get so much imaginative play. (EY Practitioner E)

Natural areas are best for children's imaginative play and creativity. (EY Practitioner T)

Consequently, in 2013, due mainly to staff concerns about the impact of the changed outdoor environment in the country park, a decision was made to re-locate the OLP to a small area of woodland and field adjacent to the nursery school and local primary school in future. It will be very interesting to record and reflect on the impact of the change of location for the OLP as the project continues.

Over the past ten years the OLP has evolved methods and tools for eliciting the perspectives of young children, aged 3 and 4, in educational settings, drawing on the Mosaic approach (Clark and Moss, 2001, 2005, 2011) and Learning Stories (Carr, 2001). This model demonstrates, firstly, that young children's views about their environment and experiences within that environment are crucial insights and, secondly, that these insights can help implement changes in practice. Evidence from the OLP also suggests that there are significant benefits when young children are given appropriate access to outdoor environments. This is because the outdoor environment affords the space, time and location for children's culture (Corsaro, 2011; Fjørtoft, 2004; Waller, 2006). Image-based data gathered for the project by the children revealed an interesting range of both 'social spaces' and 'individual landmarks' (Clark and Moss, 2001). Also, as the practitioners and children became more confident in the outdoor environment, increased opportunities for prolonged conversation and 'sustained shared thinking' (Siraj-Blatchford, 2004) with children occurred. Thus, the OLP found (like Burke, 2005 and Clark, 2004) that the process of using participatory tools increased our understanding of the children's lives (Waller, 2007).

This ongoing project has helped to widen our understanding of the possibilities of participative approaches and the interrelationship between children's spaces, early years pedagogy and research. It has also started to demonstrate the significant benefits of outdoor learning for both adults and children. Overall, the main goals in the first four years of the project – to give the children an opportunity to interact regularly with natural surroundings and to develop their own independent learning paths and dispositions – were achieved. A further benefit has been the enhanced staff and student awareness of the potential of an outdoor learning environment, not least as a result of the construction of knowledge through shared reflection and collaborative enquiry.

Chapter summary

This chapter has presented an overview of current literature concerning young children's play and learning in outdoor spaces. Drawing on evidence from an ongoing project and the literature, it has attempted to demonstrate the significant benefits of outdoor learning for both adults and children. In particular, concerns over the restricted opportunities for outdoor play due to risk anxiety and the 'culture of fear' (Furedi, 2002) have been considered and set against a much more positive approach which recognises the significant benefits of outdoor play for contact with nature, movement, health, wellbeing and risk-taking. It has been argued that all young children need regular physical activity outdoors to thrive and that their levels of activity impact directly on their physical and mental health. This involves giving children the opportunity to take acceptable risks in their outdoor play. Thus, the perspective taken in this chapter (Gill, 2012; Tovey, 2007; Waters and Begley, 2007) contends that creating risk-free environments is actually dangerous and inhibiting because children do not have the opportunity to develop and demonstrate competence and confidence in their play. Consequently, there are significant implications for the training of early years practitioners who also need to develop confidence in outdoor spaces in order to encourage children to benefit from the experience of taking positive risks in their play.

The significance of adult attitudes to outdoor play has been highlighted as one of the main factors in determining children's access. Experiences of the Outdoor Learning Project (discussed above) suggest that early years practitioners should recognise the significant potential of outdoor learning and, in addition to developing outside play opportunities within their school grounds, they should also consider giving children regular opportunities to experience wild, natural environments. In both these contexts, it appears that practitioners' attitudes and dispositions towards the shared construction of learning are key factors (Waller, 2007). The outdoor environment is therefore viewed as a place that offers a wide range of distinctly unique opportunities and potential for adventurous play and learning.

Questions for reflection and discussion

1. How significant is the attitude of adults (parents and practitioners) towards giving children the opportunity for regular outdoor experience?
2. What is the difference between play and learning in outdoor spaces and indoors?
3. Why has Forest School become so popular in parts of the UK? Should all children be given the opportunity to experience Forest School?
4. What do children and adults gain from regular experience in 'wild' natural environments together?
5. Are there opportunities in your setting, or one you are familiar with, for children to be adventurous in their play? Are there frequent opportunities for play which they find enjoyably scary? If not, why might this be?

Recommended reading

Casey, T. (2007) *Environments for Outdoor Play: A Practical Guide for Making Space for Children*. London: Paul Chapman.

Education 3–13 (2007) 35 (4). Special Issue on Outdoor Play and Learning, November.

Knight, S. (2010) *Risk and Adventure in Early Years Outdoor Play*. London: Sage.

Lindon, J. (2011) *Too Safe for Their Own Good? Helping Children Learn about Risk and Life Skills*. London: National Early Years Network/NCB.

Tovey, H. (2007) *Playing Outdoors, Space and Places, Risk and Challenge*. Maidenhead: Open University Press.

White, J. (ed.) (2011) *Outdoor Provision in the Early Years*. London: Sage.

Recommended websites

www.educationscotland.gov.uk/earlyyearsmatters/t/takelearningoutside.asp
Early Years Matters – Take Learning Outdoors. Useful information and case studies on outdoor learning produced by Education Scotland.

www.freeplaynetwork.org.uk/playlink/exhibition
Places for Play. An exhibition of photos created by Play Link and the Free Play network including useful editorial comment and discussion on risk.

www.playengland.org.uk
Play England. An organisation campaigning for freedom and space to play throughout childhood. The website includes a wide range of resources on play including briefing papers, research reports, good practice guides and case studies as well as news, events and networks.

Want to learn more about this chapter? Visit the companion website at **www.sagepub.co.uk/walleranddavis3e** to access podcasts from the author and child observation videos.

9

Children and Media

Jane O'Connor

 Key chapter objectives:

- To outline the polarised debate around children using media technology
- To look at issues around children's 'consumption' of media – focus on television
- To explore children's use of media products – focus on computer games and the internet
- To reflect on children's production of media and the learning opportunities this may bring
- To consider the impact of media on children's wellbeing and development

Introduction

The explosion of new forms of media technology over the 20th and 21st centuries beginning with radio and television, and progressing more recently to the internet, video games, digital devices and tablets, has changed the way we all learn, play, consume and interact. The issue of whether media technology is damaging or empowering to childhood is polarised in academic and public debate, with young children being a particular focus of concern. On one side it is argued that the educational and social benefits of using social media, accessing the internet, becoming skilled at playing computer games and so on are unprecedented and that children should be engaged with such media from the earliest opportunity and throughout their school years. The opponents of this view come from a more traditional, protectionist perspective and fear that children using new technology, especially screen-based digital media, is harmful as it deprives children of proper social interaction and outdoor play.

This chapter will explore this debate by discussing research and theory in the following three key areas of children and media: children's consumption of media products, their use of media and digital technology and their active production of media.

Children's consumption of media

Concerns around children, particularly young children, being somehow damaged by exposure to inappropriate material and stories and not being able to tell the difference between fantasy and reality, have been around for a long time. For example, the quote below from the philosopher Plato was written 3000 years ago in Ancient Greece:

> And the first step is always what matters most, particularly when we are dealing with those who are young and tender. That is the time when they are easily moulded and when any impression we choose to make leaves a permanent mark ... Then it seems that our first business is to supervise the production of stories, and to choose only what we think suitable, and reject the rest. We shall persuade mothers and nurses to tell our chosen stories to their children and by means of them to mould their minds and characters which are more important than their bodies. The greater part of the stories current today we shall have to reject ... Nor can we permit stories of war and plots and battles among the gods ... Children cannot distinguish between what is allegorical and what isn't, and opinions formed at that age are usually difficult to eradicate or change; we should therefore surely regard it as of the utmost importance that the first stories they hear shall aim at encouraging the highest excellence of character. (Plato, *The Republic*, 2007: 69–70)

These fears for children's moral character, and physical and mental development, have increased as media forms have diversified and expanded over the years, particularly in the 20th century, which saw the introduction of film, radio and television and, later, the internet and digital technology. It is not only the form and content of the media that children are consuming which is cause for concern, but the sheer amount of time they now seem to spend in front of a screen, whether watching television, playing computer games or using the internet. A recent report from the USA found that children between 6 and 11 years spent on average 28 hours a week watching TV/DVDs or playing computer games, and that for 2–5-year-old pre-schoolers this went up to 32.5 hours, as they spent more time in the home (Kaiser Foundation, 2010). Another study, which included 15,000 children aged 6–17 across twelve countries, found that while children in continental Europe watched around two hours' television a day, their counterparts in the UK viewed up to five hours daily (Livingstone and Bovill, 2001).

Various studies have highlighted the potential negative outcomes of children watching television. For example, in a study of 1,300 children, Pagani et al. (2010) found that those who watched most TV as toddlers performed worse at school and consumed more junk food. Another American study found that levels of attention deficit hyperactivity disorder (ADHD) in children increased in line with television viewing (Christakis et al., 2004). As a result of such findings, Australia and the USA have adopted guidelines that advise parents to restrict the viewing time of children under 2 years to no more than two hours a day. However, there is, as yet, no similar recommendation in the UK despite strict guidelines being presented to the government by a prominent psychologist, Dr Aric Sigman, in 2007. Sigman believes children under the age of 3 should not be exposed to TV at all and that those between 3 and 7 should watch no more than 30–60 minutes of TV a day. However, as more and more children also have televisions and access to internet video streams such as YouTube in their bedrooms, control of their youngsters' viewing has become progressively more difficult for adults once their children are beyond toddlerhood.

As established above, there have always been concerns over the potential influence of watching television on children's wellbeing, and one key aspect of this has been in relation to violent behaviour. The fear that watching violent programmes leads children to act more brutally in real life has led to much research which has tried to establish a definitive causal link between children watching violence on screen and behaving aggressively. Albert Bandura's famous Bobo doll study (Bandura et al., 1961), which is described in the 'Research in context' box on p. 176, set the precedent for a multitude of psychological studies which have tried, and failed, to find a definitive answer to this question.

Neil Postman has also raised concerns about the negative impact watching television has on children, and on the very concept of childhood more generally. In his book *The Disappearance of Childhood* (1995) he argues that learning to be literate used to provide a barrier between childhood and the adult world because children had to learn how to read before they could find out about adult themes such as sex and violence. However, he argues that visual media, particularly television, is immediately accessible to all and so removes the boundary between childhood and adulthood, allowing all the secrets of the adult world to be open to children just by looking at a screen. For this reason, Postman has accused television of causing the 'death of childhood'. He also claims that television, even that designed especially for young children, undermines the role of formal education and creates an expectation among the young that they must be constantly entertained. For example, he criticises the American pre-school programme *Sesame Street* on a number of levels, including abdicating parents of their responsibilities to teach their children to read and removing any guilt they may have felt for allowing their youngsters to watch TV over prolonged periods of time:

> Parents embraced 'Sesame Street' for several reasons, among them that it assuaged their guilt over the fact that they could not or would not restrict their children's access to television. 'Sesame Street' appeared to justify allowing a four- or five-year-old to sit

transfixed in front of a television screen for unnatural periods of time. Parents were eager to hope that television could teach their children something other than which breakfast cereal has the most crackle. At the same time, 'Sesame Street' relieved them of the responsibility of teaching their pre-school children how to read – no small matter in a culture where children are apt to be considered a nuisance .... We now know that 'Sesame Street' encourages children to love school only if school is like 'Sesame Street.' Which is to say, we now know that 'Sesame Street' undermines what the traditional idea of schooling represents. (Postman, 1985: 142)

However, it is important to note that there have also been large-scale studies that have found *Sesame Street* to be an effective educator, particularly for socially disadvantaged children (see, for example, Mares and Pan, 2013).

More recent research has taken a cultural studies 'turn' and recognises that children are active participants in creating meaning from TV and interact with television in different ways, depending on their own experiences and the context in which they are viewing. A main proponent of this view is David Buckingham (1996, 2008), who argues that children are not passive consumers of TV, that they interact with the medium in different ways and, importantly, use talk about television to connect with peer groups and construct their own identity. Buckingham's research focuses on the way that children bring different understandings and subject positions to media texts and interpret them in different ways according to their age, ethnicity, gender, social class, personal experience and so on. So, for example, as Buckingham explains:

The extent to which children find a film or a TV programme frightening will depend upon how they perceive and interpret it; and upon the social contexts in which they watch and subsequently talk about it with others. (1996: 136)

That is to say that watching a scary film alone in your bedroom with the lights off may be a completely different experience from watching one with older siblings, parents or friends in a relaxed and safe environment. Clearly then, there is more to watching television than simply trying to control what children watch, either through parental intervention or state regulation. An example of this is the 9pm 'watershed' adhered to by UK channels whereby gruesome or adult content is broadcast later in the evening, although this is obviously becoming more and more irrelevant with increasing opportunities for viewers to watch programmes at a time of their choice.

Given all the negative research into children watching television it is important to note that there is also evidence that television can aid learning, even in very young children. For example, one study that tested whether experience with television helped 6–24-month-old babies learn from it found that some television experience does seem to aid in imitation, though not in word learning (Krcmar, 2011). A similar study found that a group of babies exposed to a 'Baby Einstein' DVD for one month showed greater gains in understood words than the control group who were not exposed to the video (Vandewater, 2011).

Researchers have also tried to establish the ways in which advertising influences children (such as in terms of gender stereotypes in toy adverts), but there has been little agreement on this (Gunter et al., 2005). What is agreed upon is the amount of advertising which even very young children are exposed to, and the increasing commercialisation of childhood whereby many products have multiple tie-ins with films, TV shows, toys, clothes and so on. Marketing to children is now big business because of children's consumption of popular culture through the media (Henry and Borzekowski, 2011).

Children's use of media

Concerns about children's television viewing have been somewhat superseded in recent years by concerns about children's use of media technology, particularly the internet and computer games/games consoles. As Rideout et al. (2003) conclude in their US study of over 1,000 parents of children aged 6 months to 6 years:

> This study has documented a potentially revolutionary phenomenon in American society: the immersion of our very youngest children, from a few months to a few years old, in the world of electronic and interactive media. The impact that this level of media exposure has on children's development is unknown, but one thing is certain: it is an issue that demands immediate attention from parents, educators, researchers and health professionals. (2003: 12)

As a response to such concerns in the UK, the Byron Review (2008) was a major government research study into potential negative outcomes of children playing computer games and using the internet. The review produced a set of recommendations for keeping children safe, including having safe search settings and parental controls on computers and a classification system for video games. However, the implicit assumption that all adults are involved, able and motivated to regulate children's use of such media can be seen as a flaw of the review, which also fails to recognise the frequent 'digital divide' between the generations whereby children are often more skilled and knowledgeable about technology than their parents/carers or even their teachers.

Another response has been to recommend that children are taught at school about using digital technology safely, in much the same way as they might be taught about road safety for example, in order to empower them with the ability to negotiate the digital world in an informed way and the awareness to make choices that protect them from danger (see Media Smart in Recommended websites).

These issues are important, especially when we take into account the huge, and growing, number of children in the UK and worldwide who have access to, and regularly use, the internet. According to an Ofcom UK report (2010), the proportion of children in the UK who do not use the internet at all was found to be only one in four 5–7s (25%), around one in fifteen 8–11s (7%) and a very small proportion of 12–15s (1%).

As well as concerns around children's development and their viewing of 'unsafe' sites, problems around cyber-bullying and paedophile 'stalkers' have been identified as being particularly difficult to control (Whitaker and Bushman, 2009), with more and more children engaging in social media and having personal electronic communication devices. To date, the vast majority of research on children's use of the internet and online technologies has been conducted on teenagers, leaving many unanswered questions about younger children's usage of, and access to, the Web, especially in the domestic environment. School-based use of the internet as an educational resource for younger children has been better documented, however, and research suggests that many settings are utilising the internet in increasingly imaginative ways to engage children in learning and stimulate their creative and problem-solving abilities (Hill, 2010).

In relation to very young children, studies into 3- and 4-year-olds' use of digital technology have highlighted the impact of changes in communication and entertainment technologies on children's learning, identity construction and interactions (Marsh, 2005; Plowman et al., 2010). Attention has also been drawn to the ways in which young children's use of technology is embedded in family life, and is influenced by parental attitudes towards, and familiarity with, screen-based media (Plowman et al., 2010). In essence, the more a family uses digital technology in the home, the more young children will become familiar with it and the more they will become adept at using it themselves. Lemish (2008) conceptualises children's use of media in early childhood as being akin to a 'mediated playground' whereby media becomes part of their taken-for-granted, everyday environment. As she explains it, even from a very tender age:

> They sit on mom's lap in front of the computer, fall asleep on the sofa with dad during a late night show … and play with the keys of sister's mobile phone. Media are as natural to them as are any other features of their everyday environment. They are there to be explored and enjoyed. They are part of being and of growing up. (Lemish, 2008: 153)

Whilst she recognises the concerns that young children's use of media bring up in relation to regular progression of language, communication and social skills, as well as their motor and physical development, she also highlights the benefits the mediated playground can bring. She explains how a majority of parents assign positive values to giving their children an early start with computers and how the interactive nature of the computer experience seems particularly attractive to parents and educators. One interesting experiment with children aged 4–6 found that children were less attentive and less engaged in a computer story when control of the mouse was in the hand of an adult rather than their own (Calvert et al., 2005), suggesting that children benefit more from being actively engaged with a learning task than being a passive recipient of information.

In relation to playing computer games, research and public opinion are also divided. Gee (2005, 2008) has long been an advocate for the learning opportunities which certain genres of video games can bring. For example, a game like *Yu-Gi-Oh* (Konami), an electronic card game played by children as young as 7, involves complex language, vocabulary and thinking skills that are usually associated with much older children, and playing a video game such as *Age of Mythology* (Microsoft) can complement classroom learning and enhance understanding and enjoyment of the topic. He claims that:

> good video games … challenge us to truly integrate cognition, language, literacy, affect and social interaction in our ideas about learning and the organisation of learning inside and outside schools. (Gee, 2005: 6)

However, the violent content of many video games is a point of contention among those who believe that children, especially young children, should not be allowed unrestricted access to video games that could potentially damage their social and psychological wellbeing. For example, Fleming (2008) draws attention to the way in which children seek meaningful representations of the world. He argues that if the images and creatures they see via deeply enthralling computer games are fearsome creations then surely this could impact negatively on their understanding and expectations of life beyond their bedroom door? More extreme arguments have been made that innocent children might be irreparably corrupted or damaged by exposure to video game violence and links have been made in the press to extreme crimes committed by children. For example, the teenage perpetrators of the Columbine High School shooting in 1999 were alleged to have been obsessed with the violent computer game *Doom* (id Software), and the controversial *Grand Theft Auto* (Rockstar North) series of games has continued to concern many with its apparent endorsement of sex with prostitutes, attacking police officers and stealing cars (Kutner and Olson, 2008). Such fears around the unknown consequences of children playing violent video games are encapsulated in the quote below:

> whereas before the children were just 'passive receivers' of screen violence, with video games they push the button, click the mouse, and pull the trigger to initiate carnage and killing. (Grossman and Degaetano, 1999: 3)

Research findings on this issue are not clear, with some claiming to have found negative effects for children who are regular gamers and others who have found none, or have even claimed to have found some positive effects (Critcher, 2008). Overall it seems that 'effects' are assumed rather than proven, making it difficult to make definitive statements as to whether there should be stricter regulations on the games children should be able to buy and use. Currently in the UK and in many other countries, computer games are given an age rating, although how many parents, friends and older siblings allow younger children access to such games anyway is impossible to know.

On a slightly different tack, Palmer (2006) argues that playing video games is bad for children's health as it takes time away from opportunities to play outside in the 'real' world' and in a natural environment. This 'displacement' argument is also used by those who claim that playing computer games replaces frequent social interactions with adults and other children which are so important to children's healthy development (Vandewater et al., 2006). The Japanese phenomenon of *hikikomori* is an extreme example of this whereby a substantial number of young people (mainly boys) in that country are reported to be virtual prisoners in their own rooms, unable to communicate with the world except via a computer screen and totally dependent on their families to bring them food and support their hermit-like existence (Furlong, 2008). *Hikikomori* is, however, a complicated phenomenon that is related to many social issues such as pressure on academic performance and bullying at schools, and not just heavy use of video games and the internet.

It seems that the overriding message in the debate around children's use of media is that of parental guidance, regulation and mediation. As Lemish (2008: 164) has so wisely advised: 'No young child should be left unattended in any playground, let alone one as rich and vast as the media world.'

However, as even very young children become ever more 'media savvy', the 'digital divide' continues to deepen between the generations and access to increasingly extreme games and websites becomes ever easier given the rise in personal touch-screen devices and phones. Parental guidance may not be enough to provide the long-term answer to the concerns and issues raised in this section.

Children's production of media

The potential for even very young children to become media producers due to the accessible nature of digital technology such as digital cameras, video recorders, touch screens and webcams has now been recognised (Burnett, 2010). Learning to be literate in today's society involves developing an understanding of, and familiarity with, electronic literacies as well as traditional print-based text (Hill, 2010). Children are often actively involved in a number of media-based learning and social activities, such as texting, sending emails, making films and engaging in social media. Many children are now also creating their own websites using software such as Textease and Dazzle, either at school or at home, opening up yet more opportunities to connect and learn.

An important piece of research in this area is Waller's (2007) Outdoor Learning Project (OLP), whereby children aged 3–11 were given regular opportunities to play and learn in natural wild environments and record their experiences using video-film and photographs which were co-constructed with adults into learning stories. Digital images and learning stories were also taken home by children to share with their families. As children re-visited and named familiar places, shared narratives evolved around the spaces, which in turn formed the basis of discussion and activity back in the classroom. The design of the OLP was based on the multi-method 'Mosaic approach' which uses both the traditional tools of observing children at play and a variety of 'participatory tools' with children. As Clark and Moss, the originators of the Mosaic approach explain: 'The Mosaic approach enables children to create a living picture of their lives' (2001: 13). Both the adults and children involved in the project reported finding the activities useful and enjoyable, adding support to the concept that even very young children are able to be active participants in the creation of media texts as long as the right sorts of opportunities are open to them. As Waller points out: 'The role of the digital technology, controlled and used by the children, would appear to be significant in the reification/legitimation of shared knowledge' (2007: 197). This suggests that children's production of media has an important role to play in the wider co-construction of knowledge between adults and children and in deepening under- standings of how children integrate new experiences and communicate their ideas to others (see Chapter 8).

Nixon and Comber (2005) also looked at children's video film-making in their study of children and teachers co-constructing movies in two Southern Australian primary classrooms. The project involved writing scripts and producing narrative films. The scripts were based on the children's daily lives, and also inserted back into them, and the films were shown publicly and responded to by a range of audiences. There is also evidence from a project in which aspects of moving image education were introduced at a nursery that even children of 3 or 4 years old are able to develop digital, animated films if they are given appropriate resources and support (Marsh, 2006).

In relation to learning to be literate, concerns have arisen around the distance that seems to be growing between the way reading and writing have been traditionally taught and used in schools (predominantly via paper-based texts), and the kinds of literacies that are embedded in new social practices such as texting and emailing. In order for children to be fully literate in today's media-driven society, it is argued, we must expand both our definition of literacy and the ways in which it is taught and work towards legitimising children's different ways of communicating digitally within official literacy practices.

One interesting study involved 9- and 10-year-old children who were asked to email researchers about a local myth they had invented. This culminated in the production of web pages that featured the children's on-screen writing (Merchant, 2005). The informal style of the emails and the language used demonstrated the differences between formal 'school' writing and writing using digital communication, suggesting that it is becoming increasingly important for schools to make links between com- munications technology, literacy and social interaction in order to properly reflect children's capabilities. As Merchant (2005: 59) states: 'New technology and new writ- ing are here to stay and a curriculum that ignores this fact is an impoverished one.'

Another study looked at primary school-aged children producing PowerPoint slides as the final collaborative activity of an email communication project (Burnett et al., 2006).

The researchers found that the children created 'multimodal' texts in which they used a variety of visual elements, including their own drawings and digital photographs, photographs and images from the internet, cartoons and clipart which they selected and edited. Children reported that as a result of working on the project they became more confident with new technology and learned 'how to use the computer better' (Burnett et al., 2006: 25). The researchers also found positive benefits to the email stage of the project, stating that:

> Using email not only encourages children to communicate, by providing an authentic and responsive audience, but also actively engages them in the use and exploration of a mode of communication in which focused exchanges of information, playfulness and experimentation are essential features. (Burnett et al., 2006: 25)

However, others have expressed disquiet about the use of e-communication in educational settings, suggesting that a medium that clearly works well for informal 'frivolous' social interaction may not necessarily be an effective tool for learning (Leu, 1996).

Despite such concerns, it is clear that the potentialities for children's production of media are only just beginning to be recognised. The power of digital communication to transform literacy practices and the affordances that visual media offer in terms of recording and sharing narratives and experiences are opening up exciting possibilities in the areas of children's learning, imagination and social interactions.

Research in context

Bandura's 'Bobo doll' study

Bandura, A., Ross, D. and Ross, S.A. (1961) 'Transmission of aggression through imitation of aggressive models', *Journal of Abnormal and Social Psychology*, 63: 575–82.

In the 1960s the psychologist Albert Bandura and his colleagues carried out a series of studies on observational learning, demonstrating that aggression can be learned via social interactions. In their most famous study, nursery-aged children were exposed to either a real-life situation or to a film in which an adult knocked down and beat a rubber 'Bobo' doll. The children were then given the opportunity to reproduce the behaviour observed by being moved to a room with some toys including a hammer and a Bobo doll. Once in the room they were watched through a one-way mirror and rated for their aggression. Their responses were compared to those of a control group who had not seen the attack on the doll.

(Continued)

(Continued)

Findings indicated that the children who had watched the adult knocking down and beating the Bobo doll behaved more aggressively than the control group. They were more violent and imitated exactly some of the behaviours they had observed, as compared with children who had not seen the attack or who had watched an adult behaving in a non-aggressive manner.

The 'Bobo doll' study has been quoted frequently over the years as evidence that children should not watch violence on television as it can lead to them behaving more aggressively. However, there have also been many critics of Bandura's methods and findings who argue that the research is not robust enough to be used as evidence that violent programmes on television can be a dangerous influence on children.

CASE STUDY ONE

Education

McFarlane, A., Sparrowhawk, A. and Heald, Y. (2002) *Report on the Educational Use of Games*. London: DfES.

A 2002 government-funded study asked teachers and children in primary schools to evaluate a range of computer games which they used in the classroom to support learning. These games were outside the traditional classroom software group, but had some apparent curriculum relevance or developed particular skills, for example *Age of Empires* (Microsoft) and *Legoland* (Lego Media). Key results were as follows: at Key Stage 2 (7–11 years) 19% of boys and 31% of girls believed that game playing helps with school subjects and 48% reported that 'working as a team' was a skill developed through game playing at school.

Teachers found with younger children that games where the user interface is obvious and no written instructions are needed worked best, as did games with a clear progression and which can be adapted for pupils of different abilities. They rated content learning as low, but there was a recognition across the age ranges that games support the development of a wide range of skills which are essential to the autonomous learner. One KS2 teacher/evaluator said this in relation to *RollerCoaster Tycoon* (Infogrames): 'The main advantage, in educational terms, of this software is the problem solving and co-operative skills that it demands if used in paired/group situations'. Another teacher identified the mathematical benefits of the game: 'The financial burden on the park designer is well emphasised in the game – and the children were learning about budgeting, pricing, saving continuously' (McFarlane et al., 2002: 15).

The report concludes that the greatest obstacle to integrating games into the curriculum is the mismatch between the skills and knowledge developed in games, and those recognised explicitly in the school system.

 Reflection for case study 1

- How much of a role should computer games play in primary schools to support learning in the following areas: literacy; numeracy; problem solving; science?
- What about early years settings? What concerns might parents have about this practice?

CASE STUDY TWO

Pre-schoolers ready for a digital world?

Dan and Jack are both 4 years old and are due to start school in September. Dan lives with his parents and older sister and Jack is an only child. Their parents have very different ideas about the extent to which young children should be engaged with media products. The case studies below describe each child's experience with media before starting their formal schooling.

Dan watches 2–3 hours of television a day. These programmes are generally aimed at his age group, although he also watches some programmes which his parents or older sister have on. He often asks his parents for toys which he has seen advertised on TV or for tie-in products which are linked to films and characters he likes. Dan often plays on a games console with his sister and his father and also has favourite websites on the family laptop which his mum helps him access. He also likes his mum's iPad and knows how to use certain apps for drawing and game playing and how to look at photos and video clips of himself and his family and friends.

(Continued)

(Continued)

Jack's parents disapprove of TV and limit his viewing to one special programme of 20 minutes a day on a non-commercial channel. Jack has many books and lots of traditional toys, which are educational and robust, such as wooden farm animals which he plays with imaginatively. Jack spends a lot of time playing outside in the garden either alone or with his friends. Jack enjoys looking through photo albums and drawing pictures of the people and places he loves.

Reflection for case study 2

- Which child do you think will be more school-ready in September in relation to literacy and numeracy?
- What are the positive aspects of each child's experiences with media so far?
- What issues do these case studies bring up in terms of media literacies?

Chapter summary

As explained in the introduction, debates around children and media are often polarised, with some arguing that the media are detrimental to childhood, removing innocence, damaging children's health and exposing them to inappropriate material, whereas others are quick to praise the benefits and opportunities that the media bring.

This chapter has attempted to provide an overview of an increasingly important topic in Childhood Studies. Due to the broad scope of the subject the chapter was divided into three parts: 'children's consumption of media', 'children's use of media' and 'children's production of media', with each section discussing key issues, themes and research in the area.

In relation to children's consumption of the media, research relating to the potential negative outcomes of children watching television was discussed and the alternative 'cultural studies' approach which sees children as active participants in creating meaning from TV was reflected upon.

In the discussion of children's use of media, concerns around children using the internet and playing computer games were explored, particularly in relation to young children. The learning opportunities which these media offer were also discussed and the 'digital divide' between the generations was highlighted.

In the final section the different ways in which children produce media was discussed with reference to some key studies and projects from the UK, South Africa and

Australia. The importance of children learning media literacies was emphasised, along with concerns that have been voiced around the appropriateness of activities such as e-communication as tools to learn writing.

From the research then, it seems indisputable that new media technologies offer unprecedented opportunities for learning and socialising for children, but there are also concerns as to the impact increased engagement with digital media may have on children's wellbeing and development. As the ever-changing landscape of media technology moves forward these are issues that will continue to impact upon childhood as adults struggle to find the balance between protecting children from the potential dangers of the media, whilst also allowing them to explore and learn about the digital world of which they must be part.

Questions for reflection and discussion

1. In what ways is media technology empowering to children?
2. Do age ratings on films and games, and parental controls on computers go far enough in protecting children from the possible dangers of media technology? What other measures could be put in place?
3. How far do you agree with the cultural studies approach which emphasises the different ways in which individuals interpret and experience visual media? What implications does this have for limiting children's access to media products?
4. Young children today are frequently described as 'digital natives'. What do you understand by this term?
5. Are schools going far enough in ensuring children are media-literate? How could this be measured or assessed?

Recommended reading

Buckingham, D. (2007) *Beyond Technology: Children's Learning in the Age of Digital Culture.* Polity Press.
In this book, Buckingham argues that the divide between children's digital literacy outside school and their experiences of technology in the classroom needs to be bridged.

Burnett, C. (2010) 'Technology and literacy in early childhood educational settings: a review of research', *Journal of Early Childhood Literacy,* 10 (3): 247–70.
This article is a comprehensive review of research into technology and literacy for children aged 0–8.

Gee, J. (2008) *What Video Games Have to Teach Us About Learning and Literacy.* Basingstoke: Palgrave Macmillan.
A controversial look at the positive things that can be learned from video games by a professor of education.

Palfrey, J. (2010) *Digital Natives*. New York: Basic Books.
Palfrey focuses on the first generation of children who have been born into and raised in the digital world and reflects on the world they are creating.

Plowman, L., McPake, J. and Stephen, C. (2010) 'The technologisation of childhood? Young children and technology in the home', *Children and Society*, 24 (1): 63–74.
This article describes a research project looking at how pre-school children use media technology in their home environment.

Recommended websites

www.cbeebies.com
The award-winning BBC website for very young children including television programmes, interactive games and podcasts.

http://childrenyouthandmedia.org/cscym/
The Centre for the Study of Children, Youth and Media was a unique research centre based at the University of London's Institute of Education between 2000 and 2010. The Centre is now closed, and this site represents an archive of its work, last updated in mid-2010.

www.mediasmart.org.uk/
Media Smart is a media literacy programme for 6–11-year-olds, focused on advertising.

www.ofcom.org.uk
See the Ofcom website for information about regulations around UK broadcasting and advertising to children.

http://youthandmedia.org
The Youth and Media project at Harvard University encompasses an array of US-based research, advocacy and development initiatives around children, young people and technology.

Want to learn more about this chapter? Visit the companion website at **www.sagepub.co.uk/walleranddavis3e** to access podcasts from the author and child observation videos.

Part Four
Health, Wellbeing and Protection

10

Child Health

Sharon Smith and Tania Hart

 Key chapter objectives

- To emphasise the importance of early years settings in promoting, protecting and supporting children's physical and emotional health
- To raise the awareness of the importance of supporting the child's family in order that they are better equipped to meet the needs of their child
- To highlight the importance of strong multi-agency partnership working in order to promote good child health and better support the child with complex health needs

If a child's physical and mental health needs are met in the early years, children are more likely to be ready to learn and are more likely to succeed in fulfilling their full life potential. It is also well documented that children learn best and thrive when they are healthy, safe and engaged, therefore it is important that every early years 'setting' has an ethos of promoting, protecting and supporting the wellbeing of children and their families. The Marmot Review (2010: 147) reported:

> The foundations for virtually every aspect of human development – physical, intellectual and emotional – are laid in childhood. What happens during these early years (starting in the womb) has lifelong effects on many aspects of health and well-being.

This chapter begins by describing the current situation of child health in the UK. The first half of the chapter then examines key aspects that relate to child physical health promotion and disease prevention, providing the reader with a better understanding of how primary healthcare practitioners can work in partnership with early years practitioners to support child health. The second half of the chapter looks at child mental health and how the emotional wellbeing of children can be promoted and supported through partnership working.

Evidence (Blair et al., 2003) suggests that children are generally physically healthier than they have ever been and that the health and wellbeing of children in Britain is slowly improving (Maughan et al., 2008; UNICEF Office of Research, 2013). However, there is still some way to go to ensure every child has the best possible chances of fulfilling their full potential in life (UNICEF Office of Research, 2013). This is because there still remain stark and persistent inequalities in health between children from advantaged families and those who are poor, particularly across different ethnic groups and across different parts of the country. In addition, research informs us that Western influences such as diet and sedentary ways of living are putting many of the nation's children at risk of developing serious life-threatening illnesses later in adulthood (Freedman et al., 2007). Statistics also suggest that the emotional health of the nation's children is in need of address (BMA, 2006), as one child in every ten is said to have a significant mental health problem (Green et al., 2005). Of interest is a survey carried out by UNICEF in 2007; this rated the UK at the bottom of a league of industrialised countries for child wellbeing, emphasising that children in the UK were under-educated, unhappy and unhealthy compared with other European countries (UNICEF, 2007b). In 2013 the UK has risen slightly up this league table, however UNICEF UK suggest there is still work to be done in improving health inequalities in Britain (see also Chapter 11).

Wolfe et al. (2011) suggest that England has the worst all-cause mortality rate for children aged 0–14 years in Europe, and is behind other European countries in improving children and young people's health and wellbeing. A report into children and young people's health on behalf of the NHS Confederation in 2012 suggests that providing good health services for children is essential for the future health and wellbeing of an ageing adult population. This is supported by the Royal College of Paediatrics and Child Health (RCPCH, 2011) in identifying how those early life exposures, often affected by disadvantage and deprivation, impact on adult health and on succeeding generations. It is argued that the growing burden of chronic, long-term conditions that have a substantial component of their origins in early life, obesity, diabetes and poor mental health, are placing an intolerable strain on the NHS and adversely affecting the health and economic wellbeing of the nation. The report suggests that new ways of working need to be considered to improve health outcomes and ensure children and young people receive the high quality care they deserve. The Health and Social Care Act 2012 highlights some of these reforms for children and new structures within the NHS, including the emergence of wellbeing boards and the transference of public health responsibilities to local authorities. An important example of this is the Healthy Child Programme (DH, 2009).

Factors such as the ones highlighted above have in recent years seen the advent of a plethora of UK government policy aimed at improving child health. In the main these policies have dictated that services must unite to promote, protect and support the long-term and sustained improvement in children's health and wellbeing. It was New Labour's Every Child Matters agenda (DfES, 2003a, 2004c) and the policy directive known as the National Service Framework (NSF) for Children, Young People and Maternity Services (DH, 2004b), which saw the emergence of stronger working partnerships between health, education, social services and third-sector providers (that is, the voluntary sector, not-for-profit and non-governmental organisations). Services became united by a shared vision driven by a shared policy, this vision being to put child health and safety at the centre of service delivery, ensuring that services work together with children and families. The aim is to ensure that every child is given the best possible chance in life, so that they are more likely to enjoy and achieve, make a positive contribution to society and achieve economic wellbeing (DH, 2004b).

Supporting Families in the Foundation Years (DfE, 2011a) stressed the vital importance of early life, both in its own right and in promoting future life chances:

> The Government's aim is to put in place a coherent framework of services for families, from pregnancy through to age five, which focus on promoting children's development and help with all aspects of family life. (DfE, 2011a: 11)

A particular emphasis on the early intervention principles of this report was published by the Wave Trust in 2013. This report highlights significant messages about effective parenting, evidenced practice with 0–2s and the development of the future workforce to intervene early and effectively with families. When it comes to children's mental health, *No Health Without Mental Health* (DH, 2011a) and *No Health Without Mental Health: Delivering Better Mental Health Outcomes for People of All Ages* (DH, 2011b) detail current government strategies that aim to improve mental health in all ages and people from all backgrounds. All these government strategies continue to advocate close collaborative working practices amongst services in order to improve children's health. Key principles advocated by these policies include:

- The importance of meeting the child's holistic or 'whole' needs; their physical and mental developmental and also addressing their social needs.
- The importance of promoting good health and protecting children against poor health.
- The importance of also taking into account the child's family and wider social influences, such as school or nursery when supporting the child.

Like other services that support children, those working in the early years setting have in recent years made it their business to promote the health of every child they support. This ranges from healthy schools initiatives that aim to promote the health of children, to more strategic partnership working that aims to support the child with more complex difficulty.

Consideration is now given to key aspects of child health promotion and disease prevention with a special emphasis on childhood obesity and maternal health.

Physical health issues

Rising obesity levels in childhood have significant implications for health in later life, as well as impacting adversely on children's peer relationships and self-esteem. Almost one-third of children are either overweight or obese, and without clear action, this could rise to two-thirds by 2050 (Foresight, 2007). Evaluations from the National Child Measurement Programme (NCMP) (DH, 2012a) indicated that 22.6% of Reception-aged children and a third of Year 6 children were overweight or obese. In addition, there are concerns over the appropriateness of their diet and the amount of exercise taken. The cross-government *Healthy Weight, Healthy Lives* strategy (DCSF and DH, 2008; DH Cross Government Obesity Unit, 2009) aims to provide local areas with guidance on how to promote healthy weight and tackle obesity. It is well documented that children and young people learn best and thrive when they are healthy, safe and engaged. Much interest in child health is due to the desire to influence later adult health. Many serious and life-threatening illnesses in adulthood are now seen as having their roots in lifestyle choices with respect to diet, exercise, alcohol and substance use, which originate in childhood (Rigby, 2002). Changing patterns of eating, playing, working, travel and leisure activities have together led to an unhealthy lifestyle for some children that continues into adolescence and adulthood (DH, 2004a). NICE guidance in promoting physical activity for children recommends at least 60 minutes of exercise a day (NICE, 2009). A focus on the whole child also means recognising that health protection and promotion and disease prevention are integral to their care in any setting. The child exists in a context – family, friends and school – and, therefore, it is essential to remember that if care is optimal, and holistic, the child will avoid missing school and will continue to attend school regularly and engage with activities to promote positive social functioning including forming friendships.

Early intervention

The role of primary healthcare practitioners and educationalists is discussed in this chapter in the belief that education and health go hand in hand, with both impacting on children's current and future wellbeing. The support of families, especially those in vulnerable circumstances, and effective parenting interventions are explored. There is increasing evidence to suggest that there is a strong association between aspects of family relationships, parenting behaviour and child behaviour problems

(Johnston and Titman, 2004). It is widely recognised that earlier intervention is more effective and that health visitors and school nurses are in a strategically important position to deliver behaviour treatment, which may be more acceptable to families than a mental health service.

Field (2010) and Allen (2011) advised that more needed to be done to ensure that services are as effective as possible at working together to achieve positive outcomes for children. The Marmot Review (2010) called for universal service provision for families, ensuring that everyone gets services and, in addition, targeted or specialist services should be available to families with complex needs. The importance of effective needs assessment and early intervention is well documented. Children often receive these universal services in a variety of settings and from a wide variety of professionals including health visitors, midwives, GPs, early years practitioners and staff in children's centres. Research evidence suggests that parents value services that are coordinated (Marmot Review, 2010) and value being referred to appropriate specialist services. A well-qualified and highly trained workforce is fundamental to improving health outcomes for children and families.

Evidence from the Wave Trust (2013) suggests that early intervention by midwives or other health engagement at children's centres can lead to:

- reduced incidence of low birth weight and of fetal and postnatal injury
- improved uptake of preventive health care
- a lower risk of poor bonding
- reduced child neglect and abuse.

Health visitors are key to enhancing health outcomes in the early years. The White Paper 'Healthy Lives, Healthy People' (DH, 2010) demonstrates a commitment to developing health visiting services in order to effectively support families and reduce health inequalities. It plans to increase the health visitor workforce in the UK by 4,200 by 2015, thus providing capacity to extend the delivery of the Healthy Child Programme (HCP) and the Family Nurse Partnership. The Healthy Child Programme established in 2009 provides a framework for health promotion from birth to 18 years (DH, 2009).

Following on from *Health for all Children* (Hall and Elliman, 2006) and the National Service Framework (DH, 2004b), the Healthy Child Programme (DH, 2009) is an early intervention and prevention public health programme for children, young people and families. It offers a range of developmental reviews, and health promotion guidance and support with parenting and making healthy choices. It is based on a model of progressive universalism providing services to everyone (universal) and additional services provided according to need.

If effectively implemented, the Healthy Child Programme should lead to:

- strong parent–child attachment and positive parenting, resulting in better social and emotional wellbeing for children
- care that helps to keep children healthy and safe

- healthy eating and increased activity, leading to a reduction in obesity
- prevention of some serious and communicable diseases
- increased rates of initiation and continuation of breastfeeding
- readiness for school and improved learning
- early recognition of growth disorders and risk factors for obesity
- early detection of – and action to address – developmental delay, abnormalities and ill-health
- identification of factors that could influence health and wellbeing in families
- better short- and longer-term outcomes for children who are at risk of social exclusion. (DH, 2009)

Reviewing every child's health at around 2 years of age is a key feature of the HCP that encourages parents, health professionals and early years practitioners to work together, sharing their information and skills. This review can be done in a variety of settings. It is closely linked to the assessment within the EYFS and provides an opportunity to provide a holistic review of the child and family by joining the care focus and the education focus.

The Family Nurse Partnership offers intensive, targeted support to vulnerable first-time young mothers through a structured home visiting programme. Although these family nurses deliver the HCP, there is more focus on the emotional needs and behavioural issues faced by these mothers. As key public health and primary care practitioners, health visitors and school nurses have an important role to play in improving child health and tackling inequalities. Promoting health and wellbeing and preventing illness means tackling the root causes of inequalities. 'Healthy Lives, Healthy People' (DH, 2010) recognised the pivotal roles that health visitors and school nurses play in delivering the HCP. The 'Health Visitor Call to Action' (DH, 2011d) and 'School Nurse Vision and Call to Action' (DH, 2012b) have provided a robust framework for service delivery in public health.

Health needs can be responded to in a variety of ways, including individual and family health programmes – for example, breastfeeding support or counselling for postnatal depression. The provision and promotion of access to information services such as Sure Start programmes, Parentline and health-related websites can have a positive impact on family health need. Community development initiatives can meet local health needs and promote community participation, such as smoking cessation, healthy schools projects and safety schemes.

Health visitors have a strong tradition of working with individuals, families and communities to promote health. Cowley and Houston (2002) recognise the different elements:

- public health programmes at community level
- community development
- group work
- health prevention and promotion with families and individuals.

They maintain a caseload of all families in a local area who have children under the age of 5 years, delivering their service through a combination of individualised home visiting, clinic contacts and community-based activities.

The family in all its diverse forms is the basic unit of society and the place where the majority of health care and preventative work takes place. Health visitors have always played a vital role in promoting family health and supporting parents.

School nurses have an important role to play in improving child health and tackling inequalities (NHS Confederation, 2012). They are involved in a wide range of health-promoting and public health activities. Like health visitors, school nurses are registered nurses with additional training (usually at graduate level), skills and knowledge that enable them to work competently with school-age children in a variety of settings, including schools. They can provide a range of health improvement activities including:

- immunisation and vaccination programmes
- support and advice to teachers and other school staff on a range of child health issues
- support and counselling in positive mental health
- personal health and social education programmes and citizenship training
- advice on relationships and sex education
- working with parents and other professionals to meet a range of health and social needs.

Schools have an important role in providing integrated, quality health promotion activities, in partnership with local wellbeing boards. The National Healthy School Standards (DfEE/DH,1999) were part of the government's strategy to raise educational achievement and address inequalities. A systematic review of healthy schools (Lister Sharp et al., 1999) concluded that school-based health promotion initiatives can have a positive impact on children's health and development. For an example, see the case study below.

CASE STUDY ONE

To increase the number of pupils making healthy lifestyle choices about diet and exercise, 'a Healthy School' infant school employed a supervisor to promote and develop their established 'Huff and Puff' programme. This aims to increase physical activity before and after school, and at lunch and break times. The supervisor planned lunch-time and break activities and oversaw Year 2 pupils who ran the 'equipment loan shop'. The organisation of lunch-time activities, particularly football, was restricted so that pupils could deal more effectively with competitive aspects that led to arguments.

(Continued)

(Continued)

Playground work was supported by the behaviour support services, including a 'life skills' project, so that breaks and lunch times were seen as part of the learning that took place each day. Other changes were introduced, including a reward system for pupils who reached set activity targets, giving them play equipment bought through sponsorship from local business. Pupils recorded their progress in their school diary, enabling parents to share their success.

A school nurse ran drop-in sessions and encouraged pupils to join in out-of-hours sports activities. The tuck shop also underwent a transformation, with a local supplier agreeing to supply a variety of fruit and vegetables for a trial period. If pupils bought 'unhealthy' options, they also had to buy five pence worth of fruit, a move that was supported by parents and encouraged pupils to eat fruit on a regular basis.

A key factor was helping pupils to make the link between eating well, physical activity and feeling good about themselves. The 'Huff and Puff' scheme appealed to pupils who were not previously engaged, including several who were overweight. The number of serious incidents of negative behaviour was halved with the introduction of structure, purpose and rewards to lunch-time play. Pupils were noticeably more tolerant of each other and there was less disruption in lessons. Teachers and midday supervisors noticed greater cooperation between pupils, and senior staff spent less time dealing with negative behaviour.

 Reflection for case study 1

- How would you ensure a holistic approach to healthy lifestyles in your setting?

You may wish to visit the Department of Health Change for Life programme web pages – see 'Recommended websites' below.

Maternal health

The Marmot Review (2010) on health inequalities cited evidence that development begins before birth and that the health of a baby is crucially affected by the health and wellbeing of the mother. Low birth weight in particular is associated with poorer long-term health and educational outcomes (Jefferis et al., 2002). This was further supported by the Royal College of Midwives in 2012 in the report 'Maternal and Emotional Wellbeing and Infant Development' which recognises maternity services as a critical component of health services for children, highlighting the importance of midwives in promoting brain development, and positive parenting.

The Wave Trust (2013) summarises factors that encourage positive development during pregnancy and in the period after birth:

- enjoying a well-balanced diet
- not experiencing stress or anxiety
- being in a supportive relationship – and not experiencing domestic violence
- not smoking, consuming alcohol or misusing illegal substances
- not being in poor physical, mental or emotional health
- not being socioeconomically disadvantaged
- being at least 20 years old
- having a supportive birthing assistant at the birth itself.

While having a new baby is often seen as a very positive experience, it can be both physically and emotionally demanding on the expectant mother, and affect her relationships with others. It is therefore essential that the health, social care and educational services available work effectively and proactively to educate those who are likely to become parents, and to support them during the pregnancy and in the time after birth. The health of the child can be enhanced by increasing the ability of the parents to support the child.

Research in context

Barlow, J., McMillan, A,. Kirkpatrick, S., Ghate, D., Barnes, J. and Smith, M. (2010) 'Health-led interventions in the early years to enhance infant and maternal mental health: a review of reviews', *Child and Adolescent Mental Health*, 15 (4): 178–85.

Increasing recognition of the importance of maternal mental health in optimising the later mental health of a child is explored in a review conducted by a group of researchers led by Jane Barlow from the University of Warwick. This review evaluated a range of interventions/strategies to support the parent–infant relationship during the perinatal period. This study is particularly interesting as it highlights the need for better support in early parenting as this is crucial to the long-term health outcomes of the child.

Nutrition

While good hygiene, home safety and immunisation are important health promotion factors following birth, adequate nutrition is vital to a child's physical and intellectual development. A healthy, balanced diet and regular physical activity are essential for children's health and wellbeing. Feinstein et al. (2008) confirm that eating habits in the years before school are very important because they influence growth, development and academic achievement in later life. What we eat in childhood affects our health – for example, coronary heart disease, diabetes, cancer and bowel disorders in adults can be attributed to the effects of poor diet in the early years, combined with reduced activity levels. Optimal infant nutrition, especially breastfeeding, enhances the health outcomes for children and reduces potential health risks such as gastroenteritis, respiratory disease and obesity (Horta et al., 2007; Quigley et al., 2007). The findings of the Millennium Cohort Study reported an association between breastfeeding and child cognitive development (Quigley et al., 2012).

Almost two-thirds of adults and a third of children in the UK are either overweight or obese (NICE, 2012) and the Government Office for Sciences Foresight Programme (Foresight, 2007) suggests that, without clear action, these figures will rise to almost nine in ten adults and two-thirds of children in 2050. Being overweight or obese can have a severe impact on adult and children's physical weight, and is associated with diabetes, cancer, heart and liver disease. The 2011/2012 evaluation of the NCMP found that a strong positive relationship existed between deprivation and obesity prevalence, particularly in urban areas. Since its establishment in 2006, the NCMP has recorded the height and weight measurements of children in Reception and in Year 6. This has enabled a detailed analysis of the trends in childhood obesity, informed national policy and raised public awareness of the importance of making healthy lifestyle changes. Local authorities have been responsible for the NCMP since April 2013, following the Health and Social Care Act 2012. This has implications for local health promotion and integration of supporting services. The NCMP has been criticised for its approach by utilising 'scare tactics' in its follow-up letters to parents (Mooney et al., 2010). Their findings suggested that the Department of Health should review the wording and approach used in the letter to parents and that a more targeted follow-up was necessary. This is supported by research from *Healthy Weight, Healthy Lives: One Year On* (DH Cross Government Obesity Unit, 2009) that often parents do not see obesity as their child's problem or are aware of the importance of a healthy weight to their child's health. Obesity can also have an impact on mental health and put many pressures on families and society. The Children's Plan (DCSF, 2007a) recognised child obesity as one of the most serious challenges for children and that it is linked to a number of poor outcomes – physical, social and psychological.

Evidence suggests that type 2 diabetes mellitus is starting to be seen in overweight children (Audit Commission, 2010) and cases of rickets are appearing more frequently (Pearce and Cheetham, 2010). Research by the School Food Trust (now the Children's

Food Trust, 2011) suggests that changes in children's diets and lifestyles have resulted in higher consumption of saturated fats, sugar and salt. In addition, many young children eat fewer than the recommended five portions a day of fruit and vegetables (Nelson, 2007).

The National Standards for School Food transformed the way children eat at school but with nearly a quarter of children obese by the time they reach Reception year, specific food and drink guidelines were introduced in 2011 to help early years providers and practitioners (Children's Food Trust, 2011). This helped to support the Early Years Foundation Stage (EYFS) welfare requirement for the provision of healthy, balanced and nutritious food and drink.

> Early Years settings provide an ideal opportunity to help every child eat well, enjoy a varied diet and establish healthy eating habits to take with them into their school years. (Children's Food Trust, 2011: 7)

A cross-government strategy, *Healthy Weight, Healthy Lives* (DCSF and DH, 2008; DH Cross Government Obesity Unit, 2009), was commissioned to focus the prevention and management of excess weight around five themes. These are:

- children: healthy growth and healthy weight
- promoting healthier food choices
- building physical activity into our lives
- creating incentives for better health
- personalised support for overweight and obese individuals.

Success is demonstrated by:

- as many mothers breastfeeding up to six months as possible, with families knowledgeable about healthy weaning and feeding of their young children
- all children growing up with a healthy diet, e.g. eating at least five portions of fruit and vegetables a day
- all children growing up with a healthy weight, e.g. by doing at least one hour of moderately intensive physical activity each day
- parents having the knowledge and confidence to ensure that their children eat healthily and are active and fit
- all schools being Healthy Schools, and parents who need extra help being supported through children's centres, health services and their local community.

Alderton and Campbell-Barr (2005) suggest that the nutrition requirement of children in early years settings is largely overlooked and only considered where the child has a cultural or medical condition. They argue that this lack of nutritional knowledge among early years providers leads them to treat the selection, preparation and serving of food as a stand-alone activity outside the early years curriculum.

Mental health and its link with good social and emotional development in the early years

Mental health is how we think, feel and cope with life. It helps determine how we handle stress, relate to others and make choices. With very young children, their mental health is commonly referred to as social/emotional development (NICE, 2012). Notably research informs us that the biggest factor that shapes a young child's emotional and social development is the adults that influence their life: their parents, teachers and nursery workers (DCSF, 2008c). A child's social and emotional development is complex and wide-ranging, from the ability to form positive relationships or attachments with others, to the child's ability to regulate and control their behaviours, to their ability to problem-solve and use their initiative.

Factors that promote the child's emotional health

Of special interest to researchers in recent years is the question of what makes one child able to cope against the odds and another not. All children from time to time will have to deal with a range of factors that put their emotional development and wellbeing at risk, for example bereavement, parental divorce or separation, trauma, bullying or a life transition such as moving school or moving house. By researching the child who is coping when faced with difficulty, researchers have determined some key factors that can protect a child who is experiencing adversity. This ability to cope is termed by the specialists as resilience and can be defined in simple terms as 'the ability to take hard knocks, to weather the storm and to continue to value oneself whatever happens' (Cooper, 2000: 31).

Research in this area has helped to inform adults as to how they can help children to learn and develop fundamental skills that look to safeguard and strengthen their emotional health, ensuring they have the best possible start in life (DCSF, 2008c). Resilience factors determined by researchers are outlined in Table 10.1 (DfES, 2001c).

Factors that put the child's emotional health more at risk

As well as factors that promote resilience, there are factors that put a child more at risk of emotional problems. These are often varied and complex. For example, there may be factors that make a child more susceptible or more predisposed to emotional development or mental health problems, such as brain injury prior to, during or after birth, or a genetic or biological vulnerability. Other factors may precipitate or bring on the child's mental health problems; these may include: parent neglect, parental

Table 10.1 Resilience factors

Resilience factors in the child	Resilience factors in the family	Resilience factors in the community
Secure early relationships	At least one good parent–child relationship	A supportive extended family
Higher intelligence	Clear, firm and consistent discipline	Good housing
An easy temperament when an infant	Support for education	Successful school experiences
A positive attitude with a good problem-solving approach	Parental harmony	Attending a school with positive policies towards behaviour, attitudes and anti-bullying
A planner who has a belief that they are in control	An absence of severe discord or family conflict	Attending a school with strong academic and non-academic opportunities
Humour		Access to a range of positive sport and leisure activities
Religious faith		Being a member of a religious faith community
The capacity to reflect or ponder		
Better social skills and a good ability to convey empathy to others		

Source: DfES, 2001c

conflict, family breakdown, physical, sexual or emotional abuse, bereavement/loss of a family member or friend, rejecting or hostile relationships or discrimination (Shucksmith et al., 2009). Research also suggests that some factors may perpetuate or exacerbate the child's emotional difficulties – for example, economic disadvantage (Albee, 2006), parental psychiatric illness (Göpfert et al., 2004) and domestic violence (Buckley et al., 2007; Goddard and Bedi, 2010). However, in some cases less obvious traumatic events, such as moving house, the arrival of a new baby or being left for a long time with someone a child does not know, can cause long-term distress.

Signs of emotional distress

All children from time to time feel sad, anxious, angry or upset – this is part and parcel of growing up. However, sometimes abnormalities of emotions, behaviour or social relationships may lead to potentially serious difficulties, risking the child's optimal physical, social and emotional development, which ultimately can result in the child's family unit being disturbed and the child's problems being exacerbated. It is therefore important that adults supporting children note the subtle signs of emotional distress, in order that problems can be identified as soon as possible, as the earlier the child is helped the better the outcome for that child (DH, 2011b).

Young children may manifest their emotional distress in a number of ways, ranging from appetite changes, sleep or elimination problems, or behavioural problems such as excessive 'clinginess', crying, social withdrawal, demanding or destructive behaviour, clumsiness, carelessness or irritability, temper tantrums or hyperactivity, with the child being very hard to control. Another way distress may manifest itself is through psychosomatic problems such as headaches or stomach pains. Other signs of distress may be more subtle, for example loss of confidence, an inability to concentrate or social withdrawal.

Babies do not exhibit the classic symptoms of distress, however they may exhibit poor sleep patterns, difficulties with feeding, restlessness and gastric disturbance. These signs may indicate that the baby is anxious and tense, or distressed and fearful (Young Minds, 2003). Researchers suggest that these emotions need to be responded to with love and empathy by those whom they depend on for survival (Dwivedi and Harper, 2004; Gerhardt, 2004).

More complex mental health difficulty

When it comes to supporting a child with more complex mental health difficulties it is often specialist healthcare practitioners like paediatricians, or those professionals working within Child and Adolescent Mental Health Services (CAMHS), who carry out an assessment ascertaining the child's emotional and behavioural problems. In CAMHS, mental health specialists from a range of disciplines will work together to assess the child and family's needs. They will formulate a treatment package that places an emphasis on providing evidence-based treatments that are individualised to the unique needs of the child and their family (Carr, 2000; Fonagy, 2002). Sometimes mental difficulties in children are diagnosed by noting signs and symptoms that suggest a particular problem or disorder. Behaviours become symptoms when they occur very often, last a long time, occur at an unusual age, or cause significant disruption to the child's and/or the family's ability to function. Firstly, physical illness must be ruled out and then depending on the child's symptoms the illness may be classified or diagnosed. A diagnosis can help practitioners to plan an appropriate treatment programme for the child and the family, as an individualised treatment plan should always be mapped against national guidelines dictated by bodies such as the National Institute of Clinical

Excellence (NICE). These best guidelines issued by NICE are based on extensive research findings.

> Please see the following links which illustrate the NICE guidelines:
>
> For social and emotional wellbeing: early years
> www.nice.org.uk/nicemedia/live/13941/61149/61149.pdf
>
> For attention deficit hyperactivity disorder (ADHD)
> www.nice.org.uk/nicemedia/live/12061/42059/42059.pdf

Outlined briefly below are some common classifications of children's mental health problems. Note that children can manifest with symptoms that fall into one or more of the following classifications. (This list is not exhaustive and is intended to be a brief summary only.)

- *Emotional disorders* – Children with anxiety disorders respond to certain things or situations with fear and dread, as well as with physical signs of anxiety or nervousness such as a rapid heartbeat and sweating (panic or phobic disorders).
- *Mood disorders* – A child's mood may be abnormally lowered, as in the case of depression, or abnormally elevated, as in the case of bipolar depression.
- *Disruptive behaviours* – All children will be naughty; however if a child's behaviour begins to impact negatively on family and school life they may have more serious behaviour issues. The two main types of disruptive behaviour disorders are oppositional defiant disorder (ODD) and conduct disorder (CD). Children with attention deficit hyperactivity disorder (ADHD) can also have behavioural difficulties such as inattention, with difficulty in concentrating, and impulsivity, which can result in them interrupting or talking over others and overactivity whereby the child is restless and fidgety.
- *Pervasive development disorders* – This includes the disorder autism, which affects a child's ability to interact with the world around them. Signs of autism may include poor language development, repetitive behaviours and poor social interaction with other people.
- *Feeding and eating disorders of infancy and early childhood* – These involve intense emotions and attitudes as well as unusual behaviours associated with food and/or weight (e.g. selective eating, food avoidance emotional disorder).
- *Elimination disorders* – These affect behaviour related to the elimination of body waste – faeces (encopresis) and urine (enuresis).
- *Tic disorders* – These can cause a child to perform and repeat sudden involuntary and often meaningless movements and sounds called tics (e.g. Tourette's disorder).

Research in context

Kendall, J., Beckett, A. and Leo, M. (2003) 'Children's accounts of attention-deficit/hyperactivity disorder', *Advances in Nursing Science: Childhood Health and Illness*, 26 (2): 114–30.

In order to better understand and support children with mental health difficulties, it is important that adults have a better understanding of their perspective and their lived experiences of mental health difficulties. A particularly interesting study carried out by a team of researchers in America looked at gathering qualitative data via one-to-one interviews with thirty-nine children and adolescents with a diagnosis of ADHD. The interviews allowed the researchers to explore the children's perceptions and experiences of living with this diagnosed disorder. This is a particularly insightful piece of research because it debates the usefulness of a diagnostic label, the stigma of mental illness and the importance of identifying signs of difficulty early.

The importance of good multi-agency working in promoting and supporting a child's mental health

The promotion of good emotional wellbeing and the prevention of mental health difficulties in children require good multi-agency partnership and collaboration (CAMHS Review, 2008). This ensures that professionals from a wide range of specialties come together to support the child and the family. Professionals from a multitude of backgrounds may work in varying capacities to promote and prevent mental health difficulties in children; for example, teachers may run school-based programmes that look to promote the emotional literacy of pupils. Other practitioners aim to prevent mental health difficulties from arising; for example, by running parent management groups or specialist parenting support groups aiming to help the parent who has a child with troubling behaviours. Other professionals may work together to support the child who is identified with having complex mental health difficulties (see Chapter 16).

When it comes to supporting the child with identified mental health difficulties, treatment approaches vary. Psychotherapy, which can include cognitive behavioural therapy, group therapy or family therapy, may be used to address emotional responses to the mental illness. Creative therapies such as art therapy or play therapy may be helpful, especially with the child who has trouble communicating thoughts and feelings. Medication is occasionally used and is effective with some childhood mental health problems, for example ADHD. In many cases, a successful treatment intervention will ensure that the distressing and disabling effects of mental illness can be minimised and ultimately prevented.

A complication of joint working is that the many agencies supporting children can have different terminology and language. For example, teachers may use terms like social emotional behavioural difficulties (SEBD), whereas this generic term is not readily recognised by mental health specialists. Furthermore, healthcare workers may use diagnostic terms such as attention deficit hyperactivity disorder (ADHD) and psychological language such as attachment disorder, these terms being alien to other agencies such as teachers. Many experts in the field are now calling for a unity in terminology and some have proposed a unified language that uses terms such as promoting resilience and addressing holistic need (Cooper and Jacob, 2011). However, in the interim to achieving this goal it is important that agencies have some understanding of the differing terminology.

The following case study illustrates how Jodie and her family were supported via multi-agency working.

CASE STUDY TWO

Jodie, aged 4 years, is having tremendous problems settling into school. She is experiencing intense anxiety when separated from her parents or even when having thoughts of being separated from her parents. She is frequently complaining of headaches and stomach-aches in order not to go to school. Jodie has also had lots of recurring nightmares which centre on her fear of being separated from her parents. When Jodie's mother has tried to drop Jodie off at school, Jodie has become very distressed and frightened. Mum, when seeing Jodie like this, has also become distraught and tearful. Jodie's school teachers are worried about the school time Jodie is missing and have spoken to Jodie's mother, asking her to see her GP in order to request a referral to CAMHS.

Jodie was assessed by the CAMHS team, who consisted of a psychiatrist, a psychologist and a senior mental health nurse, all of whom felt Jodie was suffering from attachment anxiety. This is a form of anxiety that is often first reported during the early years; it is also common that the child will have fearful thoughts that something terrible will happen to their parents when they are separated from them.

In order to support Jodie and her parents, the following multi-agency treatment package was taken forward by all the agencies involved in Jodie's welfare:

- Jodie would attend CAMHS where a therapist would work with Jodie, encouraging her to express her thoughts and fears through the medium of play. This would allow her to explore and talk about her fears and anxieties. This exploration aims to allow her to see the world in a less frightening way.

(Continued)

(Continued)

- Mum was referred to a parent support group specialising in supporting children with mental health difficulties. (Research suggests that incorporating parents more centrally into the treatment of children with anxiety disorders can be useful in reducing a child's anxiety.) At the parenting support group parents are taught new ways to interact with their children so that the child's fears are not inadvertently reinforced. Parents are also taught ways to give children ample praise and positive reinforcement for brave behaviour.

- It was also very important that the school did their part in supporting Jodie and her parents, as the more school time she missed the harder it would become for Jodie to return. Therefore it was very important that the school was made aware of Jodie's special mental health needs in order that they could make her feel welcomed at school. This ensured that she had empathetic support from her teachers and that they could proactively support Jodie and her mum, providing plenty of praise and encouragement when arriving at school and during the school day when she was exhibiting signs of escalating anxiety.

 Reflection for case study 2

- If you had to support a child like Jodie in your own early years setting how would you empathetically support her and her mum? What could you do?

You may wish to visit some of the recommended web links to help you with this reflective task.

Chapter summary

This chapter has highlighted a range of factors that aim to promote child physical and emotional health within the early years. These include the importance of supporting maternal wellbeing and early intervention in the promotion of health and emotional wellbeing. Effective multi-agency support adopting a holistic approach when working with families and young children is also emphasised. In addition, this chapter encourages the reader to reflect on the importance of early health interventions to support better health outcomes in later life.

Questions for reflection and discussion

1. What role do you play in improving healthier lifestyles for children and their families?
2. What knowledge and skills do you require in order to support a child's physical and mental health needs?
3. Considering the importance of multi-agency working what part do you play in your team in supporting a child with a complex difficulty?

Recommended reading

Claveirole, A. and Gaughan, M. (2011) *Understanding Children and Young People's Mental Health*. Chichester: John Wiley & Sons.
This book provides the reader with a good overview of child and adolescent mental health.

Eapen, V., Graham, P. and Srinath, S. (2012) *Where There is No Child Psychiatrist: A Mental Healthcare Manual*. London: RCPsych Publications.
This book is for those who work abroad where there is no psychiatrist, however it is an excellent resource for anyone working without access to a mental health practitioner.

Hall, D. and Elliman, D. (2006) *Health for All Children*, rev. 4th edn. Oxford: Oxford University Press.
Provides an overview of approaches to health promotion and early identification of illness and disease.

Luker, K., Orr, J. and McHugh, G.A. (2012) *Health Visiting: A Rediscovery*. Oxford: Wiley-Blackwell.
Provides an overview of the role of health visitors in enhancing health outcomes for children and families.

Oates, J. (ed.) (2007) *Attachment Relationships: Quality of Care for Young Children*. Milton Keynes: Open University. Available free of charge from: www.bernardvanleer.org/English/Home/Our-publications/Browse_by_series.html?ps_page=1&getSeries=3.
Attachment is an important part of child development and this booklet explains attachment in a clear, concise way.

Recommended websites

www.bernardvanleer.org/English/Home.html
Based in the Netherlands, this site describes the work of the Bernard van Leer Foundation and aims to improve opportunities for children growing up in difficult social or economic circumstances.

http://effectivechildtherapy.com/
This is a site providing information about evidence-based treatments available to support the mental health of young people.

www.e-lfh.org.uk/projects/healthy-child-programme/
Access this e-learning for health care site for freely available resources to support professionals working with children.

www.hscic.gov.uk/ncmp
Information about the National Child Measurement Programme is available at this site.

www.nhs.uk/Change4Life/Pages/change-for-life.aspx
This is an NHS website aimed at the general public, to promote better health through healthier eating and increased movement.

www.youngminds.org.uk/
Young Minds is a charitable organisation aiming to promote the emotional wellbeing and mental health of young people. They aim to provide support for young people, parents and professionals and the website provides links to a number of resources.

Want to learn more about this chapter? Visit the companion website at **www.sagepub.co.uk/walleranddavis3e** to access podcasts from the author and child observation videos.

11

Wellbeing

Jane Waters

🔑 **Key chapter objectives**

- To critically consider the concept of wellbeing as complex rather than simplistic
- To exemplify aspects of wellbeing within UK policy and practice contexts
- To consider elements of self-esteem in relation to wellbeing
- To consider the implications of a focus on children's wellbeing for the early years practitioner
- To critically consider measures of wellbeing, international comparative literature and national survey data concerning the wellbeing of children in the UK

Introduction: What is wellbeing?

The concept of wellbeing is considered as 'highly variable' (Pollard and Lee, 2002), 'conceptually muddy' (Morrow and Mayall, 2009: 221), 'difficult to pin down' (Statham and Chase, 2010: 4) and is therefore understood to have no agreed definition (Foley, 2008). 'Wellbeing' is a term occurring frequently in policy and practice relating to children, but as Pollard and Lee (2002: 62) suggest, 'well-being is … inconsistently defined in the study of child development'. Wellbeing is generally understood as 'the quality of people's lives' (Statham and Chase, 2010: 1) but when we consider how a concern for children's wellbeing relates to practice this is not enough. The initial section of this chapter aims firstly, to unpick some aspects of the concept 'wellbeing' and, secondly, to critically consider the notion of wellbeing, in order to develop a deeper understanding of what the term may involve.

Historically, wellbeing has been linked to health – the World Health Organization (WHO) (1948) refers to 'well-being' as a concept that defines the global health of a person; 'health is a state of complete physical, mental and social well-being and not merely the absence of disease or infirmity' (1948: 2). Following a significant review of relevant material at the end of the 20th century, Pollard and Lee (2002) describe five distinct domains of child wellbeing that appear in the literature:

- physical
- psychological
- cognitive
- social
- economic.

The *physical domain* includes physical health, rates of growth and knowledge about eating healthily and staying safe.

The *psychological domain* includes mental health, anxiety levels and psychosocial aspects such as self-esteem, confidence and emotion. Roberts (2006) considers emotional wellbeing, and reports on Bird and Gerlach's (2005) description of emotional health and wellbeing as:

> the subjective capacity and state of mind that supports us to feel good about how we are and confident to deal with present and future circumstances. It is influenced by our emotional development and how resilient and resourceful we feel ourselves to be. (p. 6)

Such an understanding of emotional wellbeing would place this within Pollard and Lee's *psychological domain*, though in literature related to early childhood we may be more likely to come across the term 'emotional wellbeing' rather than 'psychological wellbeing'.

The *cognitive domain* includes aspects that are intellectual or school-related; this may include how children feel about school and their academic performance.

The *social domain* includes sociological perspectives such as family and peer relationships, communication skills and the availability of emotional and practical support.

The *economic domain* includes family income and wealth, economic hardship, availability of and access to economic support, such as government benefit systems.

These domains are consistent with current understandings of the range of the concept, particularly if we consider cognitive and economic aspects to be enacted within children's immediate and future lives in the following statement:

> [There is] some emerging consensus that childhood wellbeing is multi-dimensional, should include dimensions of physical, emotional and social wellbeing; should focus on

the immediate lives of children but also consider their future lives; and should incorporate some subjective as well as objective measures. (Statham and Chase, 2010: 1)

As practitioners working with early years children we may be concerned with some or all of these aspects of wellbeing; and clearly domains will overlap and impact upon one another – for example, a family support officer may be more concerned with the economic aspects of a child's wellbeing than the health visitor who may have the physical aspects of the child's wellbeing foremost in his/her mind. The early years practitioner may have social and cognitive aspects of the child's wellbeing as their primary concern. It is important not to lose sight of the global, or holistic, nature of the concept of wellbeing, nor to assume that a positive or negative assessment in one domain necessarily means that the child's wellbeing as a whole corresponds to this assessment.

The concept of wellbeing is not, then, a straightforward one. However, as early childhood professionals and practitioners, it is important to consider how practices in early years settings reflect a particular conceptualisation of wellbeing. We may ask of our policy and practice: does this reflect an *instrumental* or an *holistic* view of wellbeing? The instrumental view can be reflected by considering wellbeing in terms of what children should know about and what skills they should have; for example:

- knowing how to keep safe
- knowing how to eat healthily
- knowing how to keep clean.

The holistic view can be reflected by considering wellbeing in terms of how children experience their lives; for example:

- feeling part of a community
- feeling valued
- having a voice.

Policies and practices adopting either view will impact upon the child's experience within the setting and in the following sections we will consider the importance of being aware of the complex nature of wellbeing and the value of being willing to discuss such complexity within settings.

Wellbeing can be perceived as an individual or 'within-person' (Anning and Edwards, 2006: 55) characteristic. This means that wellbeing can be viewed as something one person has or lacks independently of the wellbeing of other individuals, family or community. This approach, prevalent in UK policy and literature, is not universally applied however. Some international perspectives construct wellbeing as a social concept – a characteristic of the group, rather than the individual. The bi-cultural early years curriculum document of New Zealand, Te Whāriki (Ministry of Education, 1996), states that, 'The wellbeing of children is interdependent with the wellbeing and culture of: adults in the early childhood education setting; whànau/families; local communities and neighbourhoods' (p. 42). The curriculum emphasises the need for all the early years staff to be knowledgeable about, and respectful of, for example, different child-rearing practices and Maori culture. Under the guidance given to practitioners who are working to ensure the wellbeing of young children, it is stated that 'Culturally appropriate ways of communicating should be fostered, and participation in the early childhood education programme by whànau, parents, extended family, and elders in the community should be encouraged' (Ministry of Education, 1996: 42). The implicit understandings of the concept of wellbeing within this document are therefore clear: wellbeing for a community is linked to the respect afforded the group and its practices by others; wellbeing, then, has strong social and cultural links in this conceptualisation.

Critical consideration of wellbeing

McAuley and Rose (2010) have highlighted four major influences on recent understandings of child wellbeing: children's rights, the new sociology of childhood, the ecological perspective and the new science of happiness. These differing 'lenses' (Rogoff, 2003) from which to view children's wellbeing have served to support a critical consideration of the notion of child wellbeing and it is to this that we now turn.

Critical consideration of the concept of child wellbeing, and the policies in place to support it, is essential given the high priority in political, social, economic and educational terms that it is afforded. Critical voices claim that notions of childhood wellbeing imply a *deficit* model of some children's lives and that in order to correct the deficit (be it in physical, social, cognitive or emotional terms) intervention is legitimised. Furedi (2002) and Ecclestone (2007) refer to the *normalisation* of therapeutic interventions in children's lives and argue that society should not accept such intervention uncritically. Craig (2007, 2009) claims that concern for children's wellbeing, and the associated interventions to support it, mean that children are 'protected' from experiencing the range of emotions necessary for development of resilience which is considered a key feature of positive and ongoing educational achievement (Claxton and Carr, 2004; Siraj-Blatchford, 2010c). Watson et al. (2012) have critically considered the concept of wellbeing and put forward the argument that concern for children's wellbeing can lead to 'pathology and therapy, rather than wellbeing' through a process of 'othering' (Watson et al., 2012: 35).

'Othering' includes the creation of a boundary between 'normal' and 'abnormal'; it allows the designation of 'different' and the need to intervene, correct or re-align the difference in order to establish a 'normal' position. This is of concern for practitioners since 'an Other is always pushed aside, marginalised, forcibly homogenised and devalued as [Western] cognitive machinery does its work' (Foucault, 1983: 19). Watson et al. (2012: 109) argue that shallow consideration of individual wellbeing leads to a position where those who are perceived as lacking wellbeing may be singled out as requiring a process of amendment to return to 'normalcy' in order to be 'brought inside'. Such judgements and actions 'other' specific groups of children, and run counter to the philosophy of inclusion, which is about 'engendering a sense of community and belonging' (DfES, 2001b: 8).

The following is an account from an adoptive parent of three children. Each child had a different and challenging very early life history. The case study describes school-based experiences in which the desire to safeguard an aspect of a child's wellbeing has the opposite effect and then contrasts this experience with an approach at home that does not require conformity to a 'normal' position.

1. Lauren (age 5 years) used to like to have a space for her and Paul (age 4 years) to hide in case the police came. The teacher and teaching assistant (TA) did not allow this to take place in the classroom. They reassured her that the police did not come to the school and that she was very safe, intending to comfort her. However, this assertion did not reflect Lauren's experience and she could not process this information cognitively. She was greatly distressed and her wellbeing was negatively affected.
2. Chris liked to take a soft toy to school in his bag each day. When he reached Key Stage 2 this was frowned upon, as the TA thought he should have 'grown out' of it. The toy was the link between home and school and Chris was greatly distressed when he was told to stop bringing the toy to school; his behaviour resulted in me [adoptive parent] being called to school and having to 'track back' to the source of the upset.
3. Paul hates coats/jumpers or anything constrictive (this is a common trait in a child with Asperger's syndrome). At school, teachers insisted that he wore a coat outdoors even though it caused him great distress. The intention was to keep him safe and warm and thus increase his sense of wellbeing but the requirement for compliance to this rule had the opposite effect.

My own experience of maintaining the children's wellbeing is not to consider development as a linear process; but to allow for progression and regression in a positive way. For example, when the children first came to us (aged 5 years, 4 years, 2 years) I let them choose the type of drinking cup they wanted – a bottle, a feeder cup or a beaker. Each time I would put out the drinks in each type of cup and not make any comment on which one was chosen. For months, Lauren (5 years) chose the bottle or the feeder cup. Then, one day, she asked for a Barbie beaker and we rejoiced ...

(Continued)

(Continued)

 Reflection for case study 1

The parent who provided the case study comments: 'sustaining wellbeing might mean being allowed to be different' and reflects:

> 'Our experience has been that the teachers and support staff involved with our children have judged the relationship with the children (and within this the sense of the children's wellbeing) by its similarity to their own experience, either as parents or teachers.

> Crucially, the further the children's experience from their own, the greater has been the need for the educator to enforce compliance and this is seen as a completely justifiable stance. Sometimes, it is seen not only as justifiable but as a moral/ethical duty to make the child 'fit' into school life. At worst, it has been seen as a need to 'correct' something, some fault, generated by the child; the child was considered to be deficient in some way.'

- Is there a tension between practice that seeks to support aspects of children's wellbeing in school and the philosophy of acceptance and inclusion? The podcast associated with this chapter describes a research project exploring 'wellbeing' with a group of EY practitioners, and describes how 'othering' can happen in practice (Waters et al., 2012), despite the best intentions for children's wellbeing.

Wellbeing and policy documents

Children's wellbeing is variably placed within the policy and curricular frameworks of each country in the UK.

In *Scotland* all policy and guidance material related to service provision for children and young people is underpinned by the principles outlined in a nationally consistent approach – Getting it Right for Every Child (GIRFEC) – which has wellbeing 'at its heart' (Scottish Government, 2013). The wellbeing indicators within GIRFEC (namely that children are: nurtured, achieving, healthy, safe, included, responsible, respected and active) indicate that wellbeing is seen as a within-person characteristic but are characterised by both instrumental and holistic aspects of the concept. For the pre-birth to 3 period, Scottish government guidance (Learning and Teaching Scotland (LTS), 2010) emphasises the need for a partnership approach: 'the promotion of health and wellbeing relies on staff, parents and agencies working together to achieve the best start for all children' (LTS, 2010: 55). The focus of attention in the documentation is children's physical health and development, however attention is also paid to the importance of early relationships in very young children's wellbeing and the opportunities they have for movement and play indoors and in green spaces. The Scottish Curriculum for Excellence 3–18 (CfE) includes Health and Wellbeing Outcomes in order that 'children and young people develop the knowledge and understanding, skills, capabilities and attributes which they need for mental, emotional, social and physical wellbeing now and in the future' (Scottish Government, n.d.: 1). An holistic approach to health and wellbeing is promoted in which learners can expect support in developing both holistic aspects of wellbeing, e.g. self-awareness, the ability to manage change and sustain relationships, understanding of personal development; as well as instrumental aspects, e.g. making healthy choices, evaluating risk, knowing what support structures are in place. Scotland, then, appears to have a coherent and explicit policy approach to the promotion of children's wellbeing, underpinned by GIRFEC and enacted through the 0–3 period and the 3–18 Curriculum for Excellence.

Flying Start was launched in *Wales* by the, then, Welsh Assembly Government (WAG) in October 2005 as a programme for birth to 3-year-olds targeted at families in socio-economically deprived areas. In October 2012 the Welsh Government reiterated its support, stating that 'Flying Start is one of the Welsh Government's top priorities' and committing an additional £55million over the next 3 years to the programme (Welsh Government, 2013a). Wyn Siencyn and Thomas (2007) report that this programme 'sees the integration of childcare, early learning, parenting, and health services as one vision for promoting the wellbeing of children in Wales … [and has] … been welcomed as a cornerstone in the WAG's drive to combating child poverty' (2007: 146). Here clear links are being made between a family's economic and cultural capital and children's wellbeing. The statutory curricular document – Foundation Phase: Framework for Children's Learning for 3- to 7-year-olds in Wales (DCELLS, 2008) – places wellbeing 'at the heart' (2008: 15) of the Foundation Phase. The term is linked with children learning about themselves and others, developing their own sense of self-esteem and 'cultural identity' (2008: 15) alongside developing a respect for that of others. The description for the area of learning *personal and social development, wellbeing and cultural diversity* firmly associates an awareness of Welsh cultural heritage with children's sense of identity and wellbeing. Welsh policy, then, appears to place an emphasis on the cultural aspects of children's wellbeing as well as individual aspects – it might be argued that this interpretation of the term involves a consideration of the wellbeing of the collective group as well as the holistic individual.

The provision for the 0–3 age group in *Northern Ireland* is varied and arises from a number of initiatives and services that are independent from one another. These include

Sure Start, HighScope and Toybox, that focus on different approaches or different groups of children; Toybox, for example, has a focus on HighScope-style provision for Traveller children (0–4 years). Each is concerned with young children's wellbeing though this is variably defined and conceptualised for each programme. The early years curriculum, for children 3–5 years, in Northern Ireland does not make reference to children's wellbeing but identifies a related area of learning, 'personal development and mutual understanding', in which pupils 'explore' personal development such as feelings and emotions; dispositions and attitudes to learning; and the importance of keeping healthy and how to keep safe in familiar and unfamiliar environments. In order to further enhance community cohesion in Northern Ireland pupils explore relationships, responsibilities, how to respond appropriately in conflict situations, similarities and differences between groups of people and learning to live as a member of a community (Northern Ireland Curriculum, 2013).

There is currently a campaign, led by Early Years ('the organisation for young children' – Early Years, 2012), calling for a coordinated policy towards the care and education of children in the 0–6 age range in Northern Ireland (Northern Ireland Assembly, 2012). Early Years claim that currently 'We do not have a system of varied childhood education and care in Northern Ireland. We have quite a lot of ongoing separation and a lack of coherence' (NIA, 2012) and have published a manifesto for 'provision of fully integrated early childhood education and care' (Early Years, 2012).

In Northern Ireland the wellbeing of children is tied to their emotional health in policy terms:

> Emotional wellbeing is critical in developing a healthy successful school community, including developing a pupil's social, emotional and behavioural skills. The Emotional Health and Wellbeing; of pupils has been identified as a priority for action at Ministerial level and additional funding has been made available since the start of the 2008/09 financial year to focus on the issue. (DENI, 2013)

The Pupils Emotional Health and Wellbeing (PEHAW) Programme, developed in partnership with stakeholders by the Department for Education in Northern Ireland, contributes to 'resilient emotional health and well being of pupils' (DENI, 2013). This programme is explicitly meant to offer cohesion and consistency across other services related to children's wellbeing; it is described as the 'glue to integrate individual policies/services such as all non-academic and curriculum activities affecting pupils' (DENI, 2013).

In *England* the term 'wellbeing' does not appear in the statutory curricular documentation relating to the Early Years Foundation Stage (EYFS) (DfE, 2012d), which is applicable to children aged 0–5 years. The term 'welfare' is used in association with requirements for children's safeguarding. The EYFS documentation was revised in 2012 in light of the Tickell Review (Tickell, 2011), which suggested an added emphasis on welfare and safeguarding of children (Palaiologou and Male, 2012). The requirements for children's welfare in the EYFS reflect a highly instrumental approach and set out specific procedures related to, for example, use of cameras, staff qualifications, staff:child ratios, provision of snacks and meals, indoor space requirements, risk assessments and record keeping. The early learning goals include children's personal, social and emotional development, and the descriptions reflect within-person characteristics of achievement such as the development of a positive sense of self, confidence, social skills and an understanding of appropriate behaviour in groups.

The stated aim of the EYFS is to prepare children for school: 'It [EYFS] promotes teaching and learning to ensure children's "school readiness" and gives children the broad range of knowledge and skills that provide the right foundation for good future progress through school and life' (DfE, 2012d: 2). It should not be surprising then that the document is instrumental in its approach. Primary schools, most of which cater for children in the EYFS, attend to children's wellbeing under the auspices of government guidance. The social and emotional aspects of learning (SEAL) programme (DfES, 2005b), designed to develop children's social, emotional and behavioural skills in the primary school, was originally funded by the Department for Education and Skills (DfES). The SEAL programme was developed following a review of findings from evaluations of international initiatives with similar aims which indicated that 'multi-component and universal school-based programmes sustained over a period of one year' (Hallam, 2009: 315) can be effective in enhancing wellbeing. Key considerations from the review included the need for modification of the school environment as well as the 'development of adaptive cognitive and behaviour strategies among the children' (p. 315), that is, the explicit teaching of wellbeing-related strategies to children. The SEAL programme is widely used in primary schools in England (Lendrum et al., 2009), is applicable to the EYFS as well as statutory schooling and is focused on five social and emotional aspects of learning: self-awareness, managing feelings, motivation, empathy and social skills. The curriculum materials aim to develop the underpinning qualities and skills that help promote positive behaviour and effective learning. The materials are organised into seven themes which are designed to be implemented across the EYFS and primary school age range and include materials for a whole school assembly and suggested follow-up activities for pupils in different year groups in all areas of the curriculum. The curriculum operates as a spiral, each theme being revisited throughout the primary school (Hallam, 2009). An evaluation of the SEAL programme in its early stages of implementation indicated that particular strengths 'included the introduction of the language of emotion into schools, increased awareness of difficult emotions and the provision of ways and materials to consider them' (Hallam, 2009: 329); an increase in teaching staff confidence in supporting children's emotional and behavioural development was also reported. Where implemented fully, 'the programme promoted whole school engagement, encouraged dialogue about behaviour, attitudes and choices, and was sustainable over time' (p. 329).

SEAL is delivered in three 'waves of intervention' (Lendrum et al., 2009): the first wave involves whole-school adoption of the programme, as evaluated by Hallam (2009) above; the second wave involves short, small-group interventions for children who are thought to require additional support to develop their social and emotional skills (DfES, 2006d); and the final wave of the SEAL programme involves one-to-one intervention with children who have not benefited from the whole-school and small-group provision in a given school.

There have been critical voices about the adoption of the SEAL programme in schools. For example, Craig, writing as the Chief Executive, Centre for Confidence and Well-being in Scotland, warns that SEAL may be 'well-meaning but formally teaching young people social and emotional skills could back-fire and ultimately make their well-being worse, not better' (2007: 2). She sets out a critique of the SEAL materials and philosophy, supported by reference to psychological research, based on a concern that a universal approach such as SEAL assumes that all children are deficient in social and emotional skills. This notion lowers expectations of appropriate behaviours and creates a situation where children's emotional life and their friendships become 'a problem to be solved' (Craig, 2007: 60) by practitioners. These concerns are similarly reflected by Ecclestone and Hayes (2009), who position SEAL within what they deem to be 'therapeutic education' in their critique of approaches taken to emotional and social skill development in the schooling system. The following example demonstrates the critical position taken by these authors and others in this debate:

> The SEAL document [makes] 'calming down' into a problem for all children. Gone is the expectation of calmness – this is now something children have to learn. As soon as we put it in these terms we see that it introduces the idea of failure – of not being able to induce a calm state. It is very easy to see how by going on about how important it is to be calm, rather than providing a context where calm is expected, teachers could unwittingly increase children's feelings of nervousness around not being calm. In short, the focus on calmness could encourage some children to feel anxious and worried about not being calm. (Craig, 2007: 65)

As yet there is little evidence to support these concerns and the SEAL programme is widely used in schools across England. Useful case studies are provided in the now archived National Strategies pages of the online resource TeachFind: www.teachfind. com (e.g. www.teachfind.com/national-strategies/birchwood-case-study-seal-boards).

Self-esteem

Children's self-esteem is a 'key factor not only for their wellbeing but also for learning outcomes' (Roberts, 1998: 161). Self-esteem is a complex concept linked to self-concept; it relates to how children see themselves and how they behave as a result of their self-perception. As Schaffer (1996: 159) points out, self-concept derives from experience which, if perceived as successful, generates feelings of competence, and if perceived as unsuccessful generates feelings of incompetence. Brooker and Broadbent (2003: 33) make an important point about the self-esteem of young children:

> Self-esteem has been described as the value that a child assigns him or herself: attempts to measure or describe it have focused on the disparity between what a child would like to be like and that child's view of how he or she actually is. But in early childhood it principally reflects the value the child perceives he or she has in the eyes of others, particularly those 'significant others' whose opinions count most.

Roberts (2002: 105) argues that the characteristic of acceptance is at the core of self-concept and that 'unconditional acceptance' is critical for positive self-esteem. She suggests 'the sort of acceptance that babies need from parents and other important people is acceptance that is independent of behaviour; without reservations and without judgements' (Roberts, 2002: 5). Such an argument can be taken forward for the older early years child, a point highlighted by the first case study above. Johnston-Wilder and Collins (2008), who consider self-esteem and how it develops alongside a child's sense of identity, suggest that such acceptance is particularly important because 'children can begin to become the people we think they are' (2008: 43). They report on the 'teacher-expectancy effect' (2008: 48), where children tend to behave in ways that reflect the expectation that teachers have of them or support the labels that have been assigned them (either formally or informally). Johnston-Wilder and Collins argue that 'practitioners need to be aware that labels are likely to have consequences' (2008: 49) and that in order to support the development of positive self-esteem 'practitioners can help by working towards positive relationships that display high levels of warmth and low levels of criticism' (2008: 52). In the light of such consideration, an awareness of the practice of 'othering' (Watson et al., 2012), discussed above, is critical in order to avoid creating low expectations of certain groups of pupils.

Research considering factors associated with children who succeed in primary education 'against the odds' (Siraj-Blatchford, 2010c: 463), despite having home backgrounds that are statistically associated with low educational attainment, indicates that high parental expectation and aspiration are significant. Siraj-Blatchford reports that children who demonstrated high attainment reflected their family's high expectation in their aspirations for their own futures. Both the families and the children associated attainment (e.g. at school) with effort; the children demonstrated a belief that their hard work would be rewarded in future success. Siraj-Blatchford (2010c) associates such 'mastery oriented' learner identities (Dweck and Leggett, 1988) with positive learning dispositions:

> When 'mastery oriented' children experience a setback, they tend to focus on effort and strategies instead of worrying that they are incompetent. These dispositions to learn seem to be very powerful and are associated with the development of positive early personal and social identities. Positive dispositions have been found to provide resilience (Werner and Smith, 1982; Claxton, 1999) and to lead to positive lifelong 'learning trajectories' (Gorard et al., 1999). (Siraj-Blatchford, 2010c: 472)

For practitioners, then, there is a need to ensure that such positive learning dispositions are nurtured and supported in the early years environment. Katz defines dispositions as 'habits of mind' (1999: 2) or 'tendencies to respond to certain situations in certain ways' (1999: 2). Examples of dispositions may be friendliness, shyness, curiosity, bossiness, etc. Katz (1999) reminds us that not all dispositions are positive and suggests that practitioners need to attend to the dispositions they want to encourage in the children in their settings – identifying which dispositions are to be strengthened and which to be weakened and creating situations to support certain dispositions above others (Anning and Edwards, 2006). Those dispositions that are seen as positive for children's learning can be viewed as *positive learning dispositions*. Research concerning learning dispositions suggests that fostering positive learning dispositions leads to children becoming more purposeful, successful and less likely to become disaffected (Brooker and Broadbent, 2003). Carr and Claxton (2002) have identified three positive learning dispositions that it may be particularly valuable to strengthen in early years children: resilience, playfulness and reciprocity. Resilience is the disposition to persist with a task even after a set-back, to tackle a learning challenge where the outcome may be uncertain and to persist, even when this is hard work. Playfulness involves the inclination to be creative in response to situations: to tend to notice, imagine and explore alternative possibilities. Reciprocity is the willingness to engage with others, ask questions, communicate ideas and to listen to and take on board the views of others (Carr and Claxton, 2002).

For Katz (1993) some dispositions to learn (such as exploration) are inborn but these can be adversely affected and even destroyed by inappropriate learning experiences. She gives the example of the child who, having been drilled in the methods for decoding words, is able to read but lacks the disposition to do so – and is therefore not 'a reader'. Dispositions are influenced by early experience: Anning and Edwards (2006) suggest that 'these habits of mind are shaped in young children's interactions with others and in the opportunities for being a learner that are available to them, particularly in their families and in early childhood settings' (2006: 55). High quality early learning and care involves supporting and strengthening positive learning dispositions (Carr, 2001; Sylva, 1994).

In practice then, to support children's development of positive self-esteem we need to provide early years environments in which young children's positive dispositions are supported, in which they achieve success and in which they are *genuinely* accepted for who they are.

Measuring wellbeing

Both UNICEF and the OECD have carried out international comparison studies of nation states in terms of various wellbeing measures. The UNICEF report on child poverty and child wellbeing in 'rich' countries reported on data relevant to childhood wellbeing collected from twenty-one countries across six dimensions: material wellbeing; educational wellbeing; health and safety; family and peer relationships; behaviour and risks; and subjective wellbeing (UNICEF, 2007b). The UK position in this study was poor: the UK was ranked among the worst in the developed world for children's wellbeing. Across the six dimensions the UK ranked higher in the child health and safety dimension than in others (12th out of 21), with the educational wellbeing and material wellbeing dimensions being ranked above the bottom four (17th out of 21). The UK ranked very poorly in terms of the quality of children's relationships with their parents and peers (bottom of the table), behaviour and risk-taking (bottom of the table) and subjective wellbeing (20th out of 21). Similarly the Good Childhood Inquiry, published by The Children's Society (2007), coincidentally, reported that 'children's well-being, particularly mental well-being, is lower in the UK than many other European countries' (2007: 5).

The methodology of the UNICEF study has been heavily critiqued as being biased towards data concerning older children; data not being disaggregated by characteristics such as age, sex and ethnicity; key information (e.g. on child protection and children's mental health) being unavailable for many countries, which were then advantaged in the subsequent rating (compared to countries such as the UK for which such data were available); different aspects of a child's wellbeing were given equal weighting and there was an inherent assumption of causal relationships between the factors studied and children's wellbeing (Statham and Chase, 2010).

The OECD conducted a follow-up to the UNICEF study and compared children's wellbeing across all thirty OECD countries (OECD, 2009). The domains being measured were altered to focus on indicators with the most potential to be influenced by government policies. Housing, environment and quality of school life were added, but children's subjective wellbeing was removed. This report avoided ranking countries on a single composite score, as the earlier UNICEF report had done, and the OECD pointed out that 'no OECD country performs well on all fronts' (2009: 21). However, the OECD comparison was subject to some of the same criticisms as those levelled at the UNICEF report (Statham and Chase, 2010). In the OECD report the UK ranking across the indicators varies widely. The UK is placed 4th for quality of school life but 22nd for educational wellbeing, 12th for material wellbeing and 28th for risk behaviours.

Statham and Chase (2010) conducted a thorough review of material related to children's wellbeing in order to provide a 'summary of how wellbeing is conceptualised' (2010: 2). This included consideration of the domains and measures employed to assess child wellbeing within the UK and internationally; and how the views of children and young people are incorporated into work on child wellbeing. They report:

A wide variety of domains and measures are used to assess levels of childhood wellbeing.

The different domains and measures employed make it difficult to make meaningful comparisons of childhood wellbeing across different studies and different contexts.

> The different foci of wellbeing initiatives (for example on needs, poverty, quality of life, social exclusion or children's rights) has implications for the type of policies and programmes that are supported.

> There is some emerging consensus that childhood wellbeing is multi-dimensional; should include dimensions of physical, emotional and social wellbeing; should focus on the immediate lives of children but also consider their future lives; and should incorporate some subjective as well as objective measures. (2010: 2)

The first two points should remain uppermost in our minds when we read about comparative measures of wellbeing, particularly as we recall that wellbeing is a widely used concept but has 'a weak theoretical basis' (Statham and Chase, 2010: 3). It is very important to recognise that the 'force' (Foucault, 1972) of the concept of wellbeing is high – this means that wellbeing measures and international comparisons have significant status internationally; i.e. being ranked in a low position in international ratings for wellbeing can lead to subsequent national policy intervention. Deleuze and Guattari (1994) argue that the *force* of the concept of wellbeing leads to quantitative, shallow indicators being used to assess it, which may be inconsistent with the concept itself.

The international wellbeing measures used in the middle of the 2000–2010 decade indicated that the UK was a poor place in terms of children's wellbeing: headlines such as 'The worst place in the wealthy world to be a child is Britain, the UN has revealed' (Chrisafis et al., 2007) were a common diet provided by media commentary. Kehily (2010) locates such commentary within a public discourse on childhood that 'commonly invoke[s] a notion of "crisis" (2010: 16). She critiques this discourse using a 'lens of late modern social theory' (p. 16) and provides an insight into the pervasive reach of the notion of crisis in the UK and associated concerns about the wellbeing of the human child from fetus to young adult. Kasser (2011), in his analysis of wellbeing in relation to cultural values, argues that the UK's poor performance in international tables of wellbeing can be attributed to the dominance of hierarchical values within society:

> Using archival data from 20 wealthy nations, analyses demonstrated a general pattern that the more a nation prioritizes values for Hierarchy and Mastery and the less it prioritizes values for Egalitarianism and Harmony, (a) the lower is children's well-being in the nation, (b) the more advertising is directed at children, (c) the less generous are national laws regarding maternal leave, and (d) the more CO_2 the nation emits. (2011: 211)

His argument draws on Bronfenbrenner's ecological model of development (1979): 'culture-level values are the values most likely to influence the policies and practices that affect children's interactions with their social world, and thus children's wellbeing' (Kasser, 2011: 207). This work suggests that when we assess and compare measurements of children's wellbeing across nations, and when policies are developed in order to respond to these comparisons, it is important to consider the public discourse and cultural values in which the policies will reside in order to ensure the appropriateness of the policy-level responses.

There is 'little agreement in the research literature on how to best measure child well-being' (Pollard and Lee, 2002: 66). A wide range of measures are employed throughout the research literature including objective measures such as: child case history reviews, educational assessments, medical records and national statistics such as rates of death, drug abuse and suicide. Subjective measures are also used including participants being asked to respond to multiple separate measures such as self-esteem levels, depression and relationships. Pollard and Lee make the point that measures that focus on self-esteem and depression levels and claim that these are measures of well-being, do not *actually* measure wellbeing since they attend to only one aspect of this complex construct: the psychological/emotional aspect. We should similarly guard against looking for a straightforward or simple way to assess the wellbeing of children in our care. What we might look for are ways of gaining an insight into aspects of children's wellbeing and treating these insights as *indicators* rather than *measures* of 'how our children are doing' (Laevers, 2000).

For younger children, Laevers (2000) argues that we can gain an insight into how our children are doing by considering the linked dimensions of 'well being' and 'involvement' (2000: 24) that children display when engaged in activity:

> when we want to know how each of the children is doing in a setting, we first have to explore the degree to which children feel at ease, act spontaneously, and show vitality and self confidence. All this indicates that their emotional wellbeing is 'OK' and that their physical needs, the need for tenderness and affection, the need for safety and clarity, the need for social recognition, the need to feel competent and the need for meaning and moral value in life, are satisfied … The concept of involvement refers to a dimension of human activity. Involvement is linked neither to specific types of behaviour nor to specific levels of development. (2000: 24)

Children experiencing the highest levels of involvement demonstrate their wellbeing (Anning and Edwards, 2006) and are disposed to engage in 'deep level learning' (Laevers, 2000: 20). Wellbeing is described as 'feeling at home, being oneself and feeling happy' (Laevers, 1994: 5). Involvement concerns 'the intensity of the activity, the extent to which one is absorbed' (1994: 5) and is linked to Csikszentmihayli's (1979) 'state of flow', usually experienced, in young children, in play (Laevers, 2000). Laevers developed the Leuven Involvement Scale to support adult observation of children's activity and allow an evaluation of the extent to which a child is involved in their activity; this in turn provides an insight into 'how they are doing' or their wellbeing (Laevers, 2000).

There is a growing consensus that wellbeing measures should include subjective as well as objective and contextual information. Subjective information includes indicators of the child's own health, skills, knowledge, emotional state; whereas contextual information concerns, for example, family structure, income, neighbourhood crime, services and school quality. These measures should be distinguished from one another since 'indicators of contextual variables are extremely important in that they represent critical inputs into the development and wellbeing of children; however, they are not measures of child wellbeing *per se*' (Lippman et al., 2009: 32; see also Ben-Arieh and Frønes, 2011). This last point is critical if we reconsider the negative potential of the process of 'othering' (as discussed above). By ensuring we do not conflate external, contextual measures with assumptions of the quality of children's lived experience, we can try to ensure we do not engage in 'othering' processes by limiting our expectations of children as a result of contextual factors.

UNICEF (2009b) has considered the need to report *positive indicators* for child wellbeing (see also Anderson Moore et al., 2004), including those that are subjectively reported by children themselves (see also Ben-Arieh, 2005; Ben-Arieh and Frønes, 2007). The term *positive indicators* describes 'the competencies, skills, behaviours, and qualities, as well as the relationships and social connections, which foster healthy development across the domains of a child's life' (Lippman et al., 2009: 4). This approach is

> explicitly strengths-based, focusing on cultivating children's assets, positive relationships, beliefs, morals, behaviours, and capacities to give children the resources they need to grow successfully across the life course. (p. 4)

The use of positive indicators reflects a shift from an adult perspective on child wellbeing to a child perspective, and incorporates an explicit acceptance of children's subjective perspectives on their own wellbeing as a preferred method of assessment of their wellbeing.

The Children's Society has undertaken considerable work with children in England to establish what children themselves feel is important to their own wellbeing. The Society uses an index that includes ten aspects of life, chosen because 'they have been identified as important by children themselves, and because our research shows that they are all strongly associated with children's overall wellbeing' (The Children's Society, 2012: 3):

1. Family
2. Home
3. Money and possessions
4. Friendships
5. School
6. Health
7. Appearance
8. Time use
9. Choice and autonomy
10. The future

Children and young people are asked to comment on these ten aspects in an annual review of children's wellbeing in England (Rees et al., 2010). The 2012 report indicates that, in England,

> most children are happy with their lives as a whole, around one in 11 (9%) is not. This amounts to half a million children in the UK aged eight to 15 who have low wellbeing at any given time.

> In many ways, children's wellbeing does not vary that much according to their individual or family characteristics although it does decline with age: around 4% of children aged eight have low wellbeing, compared to 14% of those aged 15. (The Children's Society, 2013: 3)

The Society has drawn up a checklist of six areas for consideration by policy makers designed to help understand the potential impact that policy development may have on children's wellbeing.

> What do children need?

> 1. The conditions to learn and develop
> 2. A positive view of themselves and an identity that is respected
> 3. Enough of what matters
> 4. Positive relationships with their family and friends
> 5. A safe and suitable home environment and local area
> 6. Opportunity to take part in positive activities to thrive.
>   (The Children's Society, 2012: 7)

This document is a useful reference point for any organisation developing policy that may impact upon children's lives.

 Research in context

Adams, K. (2013) 'Childhood in crisis? Perceptions of 7–11-year-olds on being a child and the implications for education's well-being agenda', *Education 3–13*, 41 (5): 523–37. (Published online, January 2012, doi: 10.1080/03004279.2011.613849.)

Adams (2013) undertook a study that aimed to 'achieve empathy with the children in order to see their world as they do' (2013: 526) rather than simply hear the voice of primary-aged children in relation to childhood wellbeing. While this study was conducted with children aged 7–11 years, the findings serve as a critical reminder that wellbeing is a construct and children's voices may challenge dominant adult

(Continued)

(Continued)

understandings of this construct. Adams (2013) reported that though the majority of children in the study came from low-income homes, there was little evidence to suggest that these children felt deprived – no child complained about a lack of material goods. 'There was a natural sense of resilience but also an attitude of aspiration; those who indicated that their parents had economic worries did not automatically consign themselves to the same destiny, instead believing that they could find well paid jobs when they became adults' (p. 12). Children's reflections on their own lives indicated understandings of their wellbeing that offer a contrasting view of childhood to that promoted within a cultural climate of crisis associated with the lives of children.

Chapter summary

This chapter critically considers the concept of wellbeing, presenting it as complex rather than simplistic, and encourages reflection on practice through the inclusion of practice scenarios and the associated podcast. In particular the chapter notes the process of *othering* as an unwanted outcome of simplistic approaches to consideration of children's wellbeing. That wellbeing is variously conceptualised and enacted across the UK is exemplified by reference to policy documents for the early years child. The measurement of wellbeing is critically considered and the limitations of international comparisons highlighted. The most recent thinking concerning how to approach measurement of wellbeing includes subjective assessment by children themselves as well as a focus on contextual factors that can be considered more objective. The development of positive indicators of child wellbeing is highlighted within a rights-based approach to provision for early years children in which their wellbeing is conceptualised as being, in part, constructed by their own voices.

Questions for reflection and discussion

Personal reflection

1. How do I conceptualise child wellbeing?
2. How is wellbeing conceptualised in my area of work and does this reflect or conflict with my own conceptualisation?

Discussion

1. Re-read the parental case study and consider your EY provision. Are there any situations where a child's wellbeing may not have been best served by attention to certain rules, expectations or practices even though these are meant to support children's wellbeing?
2. How can high expectations of all our children be demonstrated in early years settings?
3. How might we better understand 'how our children are doing' by listening to their views on their own wellbeing?

Recommended reading

Adams, K. (2013) 'Childhood in crisis? Perceptions of 7–11-year-olds on being a child and the implications for education's well-being agenda', *Education 3–13*, 41 (5): 523–37. (Published online, January 2012, doi: 10.1080/03004279.2011.613849.)
This article gives a clear overview of the debate concerning the 'childhood in crisis' discourse as well as an accessible research study that sought to access children's voices in a genuine manner.

Craig, C. (2007) *The Potential Dangers of a Systematic, Explicit Approach to Teaching Social and Emotional Skills (SEAL)*. Glasgow: Centre for Confidence and Wellbeing.
This critique of the SEAL programme provides an insight into the concerns of those who are cautious about systematic teaching of wellbeing skills. It is useful to read this and bear in mind the evidential basis for the claims and concerns raised.

Lendrum, A., Humphrey, N., Kalambouka, A. and Wigelsworth, M. (2009) 'Implementing primary Social and Emotional Aspects of Learning (SEAL) small group interventions: recommendations for practitioners', *Emotional and Behavioural Difficulties*, 14 (3): 229–38.
This article offers practical advice for those implementing the small group intervention stage of the SEAL programme and offers an insight into practical considerations that would be relevant to any institutional intervention directed at supporting children's wellbeing.

Statham, J. and Chase, E. (2010) *Childhood Wellbeing: A Brief Overview*. Briefing Paper One. Childhood Wellbeing Research Centre.
This briefing paper offers a clear and concise overview of aspects of a broad literature base concerning children's wellbeing and its measurement.

The Children's Society (2013) *The Good Childhood Report: Summary of Our Findings*. London: The Children's Society.
This (and subsequent) annual publication offers an overview of 'where we are now' in terms of children's wellbeing. While it has an English focus, the findings can serve as a prompt for investigation, intervention or reflection across the UK.

Recommended websites

www.childrenssociety.org.uk/what-we-do/research/wellbeing-1
This website offers a regular update on The Children's Society's work, including the *Good Childhood* reports. It also offers an accessible overview and commentary on related work internationally.

www.oecd.org/statistics/betterlifeinitiativemeasuringwellbeingandprogress.htm
The OECD Better Life Initiative takes an international overview of policy, practice and the lived experiences of global citizens. This initiative asks: 'Are our lives getting better? How can policies improve our lives? Are we measuring the right things?' The OECD Better Life Initiative and the associated work programme seek to answer these questions, helping us to understand what drives the wellbeing of people and nations and what needs to be done to achieve greater progress on an international scale. This is very useful if you are interested in broad, national decision making and the impact of international policies on people's lives.

www.unicef.org.uk/Latest/Publications
The UNICEF website is an essential resource for all those working and interested in children's wellbeing. It offers information and background concerning children's rights and the UNCRC, regularly publishes international materials related to children's wellbeing and is evidence-based in its reporting. This link takes you directly to the publications pages but the entire site is of interest.

Want to learn more about this chapter? Visit the companion website at **www.sagepub.co.uk/walleranddavis3e** to access podcasts from the author and child observation videos.

12

Protecting and Safeguarding Children

Celia Doyle

 Key chapter objectives

- To help the reader understand the nature of safeguarding and protection, including the role of power in definitions of abuse
- To enhance the reader's awareness of the contexts in which abuse can occur
- To help the reader recognise key features of the different forms of abuse, including the targeting and grooming of young children by sex offenders
- To help the reader appreciate how child victims might respond to abuse, and why they do so
- To assist the reader to acknowledge and understand the obstacles to recognition of abuse
- To provide pointers to aspects of intervention including responding to disclosures and recording concerns

Please be aware that you may find some of the material in this chapter emotionally demanding.

This chapter provides an introduction to some of the key concepts that will help early years workers protect children who might be subjected to abuse and neglect. The main emphasis of this chapter is on abuse by people who are responsible for the care of children, particularly parents. As McKee and Dillenburger (2012: 357) write, 'failure to prepare early childhood educators might contribute to ineffective child abuse identification and more importantly, inappropriate response'. Therefore the aim of this chapter is to supplement the training of those studying early childhood and help early years practitioners to gain sufficient understanding of key areas of child protection to enable them to recognise abuse in all its forms and be aware of obstacles to recognition so that they can attempt to circumnavigate them. The focus is on understanding and recognition rather than on policy and procedures. These latter can change, often as a response to a public outcry about a child's death which hits the headlines. Procedures based on the extremes of abuse are sometimes unhelpful for those facing less extreme, 'grey area' cases. While lessons can be learned from high-profile cases such as those of Victoria Climbié (Laming, 2003) and Peter Connelly (Care Quality Commission, 2009), they are not the subtle instances of what can become profoundly damaging occurrences of emotional abuse or parental neglect. This chapter aims therefore to assist practitioners to cope with a range of types of maltreatment.

It is important that all people working with children acquire information about what they are required to do in the event of their suspecting or finding that a child is being abused (Calder and Hackett, 2003). They need to be aware of the procedures specific to their profession, position and locality, such as the All Wales Child Protection Procedures (Welsh Assembly Government, 2007) or the National Guidance in Scotland (Scottish Government, 2010). However, procedures cannot be implemented if a practitioner fails to recognise that maltreatment is occurring.

In more recent years, the case of Victoria Climbié (Laming, 2003) has clearly demonstrated this. Victoria suffered beatings from her aunt, who was her main carer, and the aunt's boyfriend. The post-mortem revealed severe burns on her body and 128 injuries. This abuse therefore did not occur overnight. Her suffering was over an extended period, during which she was seen by a number of officials including hospital staff and social workers. All of them failed to recognise the signs of abuse.

Innumerable public inquiries into the deaths of children have shown that recognising abuse is by no means straightforward (Reder et al., 1993). Munro (2011: 18) has commented that, especially in the early years, professionals and others seeing children do not realise abuse is occurring 'because the signs and symptoms are often ambiguous and a benign explanation is possible'. However, some knowledge of the underlying dynamics in abuse cases will assist recognition and the appropriate implementation of procedures, and help early years practitioners influence intervention to the benefit of the children involved.

Protecting and safeguarding

One of the responses of the UK government to the Laming Report (2003) was the publication of the *Every Child Matters* Green Paper (DfES, 2003a). This recommended changes to children's services to ensure every child has the support he or she needs to:

- be healthy
- stay safe
- enjoy and achieve
- make a positive contribution
- achieve economic wellbeing.

Subsequently, the Children Act 2004 gave effect to these proposals (HM Government, 2004). There are five main parts. Part 1 provided for the establishment of Children's Commissioners to promote the views and interests of children throughout the UK. Other parts related to better integration of the planning and delivery of children's services throughout England and Wales. Northern Ireland has seen the introduction of the Protection of Children and Vulnerable Adults (Northern Ireland) Order 2003. In Scotland a major initiative was 'It's Everyone's Job to Make Sure I'm Alright' (Scottish Executive, 2002) and the Protection of Children Act (Scotland) 2003. The next section looks at the definition of abuse in more detail.

What is abuse?

One of the complexities faced by those trying to intervene in abuse cases is that many concepts are 'socially constructed' (Hallet, 1995). This means that different cultures and societies view behaviours very differently. For example, in relation to slavery, many past civilisations viewed it as perfectly 'normal', whereas in most modern societies, slavery is unacceptable. Similarly, certain types of behaviour towards children, such as denigrating and beating them, are seen as abusive in some cultures, whereas in others, tenets such as 'spare the rod and spoil the child' and 'children should be seen and not heard' form the bedrock of childrearing practices. It is therefore difficult to give precise definitions of 'abuse'. However, a key defining feature is that there is at least one person, usually a parent figure, who is misusing the power they have over the child. There are three necessary conditions for abuse to occur and to reoccur:

1. The abuse of power or failure to use it appropriately
2. The objectification of victims: this can either be at an individual level when abusers fail to see the essential humanity of their victim; or at a societal level such as occurred during the slave trade when 'slaves' were viewed as commodities
3. Silent witnesses: people, including professionals, who may be unwilling to recognise behaviour as abuse, or are unaware of its seriousness; co-victims too frightened to disclose; associates of the abuser who gain vicarious pleasure from the victim's suffering.

Hence:

- Physical abuse is the *misuse of physical power* causing physical and emotional harm to the child.
- Neglect is the *failure to use, or the misuse of physical and resource power* in such a way that it causes damage to the child including physical, social, developmental and emotional harm.
- Sexual abuse is the *misuse of sometimes physical but more often superior expert power* (greater knowledge) to coerce and sexually exploit children.
- Emotional abuse is the *misuse of a range of powers* to undermine and damage a child's sense of self-worth.

This abuse or misuse of power is all the more potent because young children are almost entirely without power. They have little physical power, no status or economic resources and are entirely dependent on the adults who care for them.

Research in context

Enlow, M.B., Egeland, B., Blood, E.A., Wright, R.O. and Wright, R.J. (2012) 'Interpersonal trauma exposure and cognitive development in children to age 8 years: a longitudinal study', *Journal of Epidemiology and Community Health,* doi: 10.1136/jech-2011-20072.

We are gaining increasing insight into how maltreatment in the early years can have an adverse impact on the architecture of the child's developing brain. There is also evidence that chronic or overwhelming stress can have a long-lasting effect, such as damage to neurons in the hippocampus, which is associated with memory. The paper by Enlow et al. (2012) further demonstrates the potentially adverse impact of child maltreatment on the child in the early years.

The researchers tracked a cohort of children from birth to 8 years old. They recruited 206 children and of these 36.5% had suffered abuse, including witnessing serious domestic violence by the age of 64 months. The researchers took account of factors such as the mother's intelligence level, birth weight or birth complications. They found that the children who had been abused had lower cognitive functioning, especially those maltreated before the age of 2. This finding was consistent with many others revealing similar results (see Twardosz and Lutzker, 2010).

Recognising diversity

Maltreated children will come from a variety of backgrounds, representing a range of socioeconomic strata, ethnic groups, religions and cultures. Their families will have varied structures, including households with several generations living together or ones with just one adult. Children and their parents will also have a range of abilities and disabilities.

There are some factors that create additional risks for children with disabilities, especially those who are isolated and totally dependent on very stressed and relatively unsupported parents. Polnay et al. (2007) also point out that disabled children may have limited mobility so cannot readily escape abuse and also might have communication problems that result in an inability to disclose straightforwardly. Therapy might also be more difficult and Kennedy (2002) provides eloquent testimony to the issues facing abused children who are deaf.

Doyle (1998) found that children in families in which a member had a disability were more at risk of emotional abuse. However, it was not always the disabled child who was abused. For some, while their brother or sister with the disability was cared for with great tenderness and consideration, their siblings were the target of all their parents' anger and frustration.

In terms of children from different ethnic groups, there is no clear evidence that children from any particular cultural background are more at risk. Chand (2008) noted that 'mixed heritage, black and black British children are over-represented on child protection registers' and suggested that families in these groups might be being unjustifiably pathologised. However, if children from particular sectors are under-represented, then there is equal concern that abuse in these groups is being ignored because professionals are worried about being thought discriminatory. As Ramon and Hodes (2012: 31) explain, there is a balance to be achieved between the domination of a professional's own cultural definition of child abuse with that of a particular minority's cultural norms which could result in children from a minority culture 'receiving a lesser standard of care and protection'.

In conclusion, diversity needs to be acknowledged but it can add to the complexity of intervention because workers have to avoid condemning childcare practices that are different but not worse than the mainstream, while not leaving children to be harmed by parenting that is not just different but abusive.

Where does abuse occur?

Abuse can occur everywhere, in both private and public arenas, although the more private the arena, the greater the risk of abuse. This means that mistreatment is often located in relatively isolated, private families and institutions. Furthermore, four groupings of factors point towards increased risks to children. These groupings or contexts – which are not always mutually exclusive – are the unexceptional, chaotic, rigid and deviant ones. They are described briefly below.

Unexceptional context

This is a setting in which children's needs are normally met. Unfortunately, a number of crises and stresses mean that the carer/parent can no longer cope. Sometimes, other children in the family continue to be well cared for but, rather like Cinderella, one child is singled out for mistreatment. In other instances, all the children are affected.

Example: A mother with several very young children suffered from severe post-natal depression after the birth of her new baby. Other adults such as her partner and health professionals did not notice that there was a problem. The children became neglected.

Chaotic context

Here, there is a general lack of boundaries. The physical and emotional care of the children is erratic. Similarly, discipline is inconsistent, with the same behaviours sometimes tolerated and at other times harshly punished depending on their carers' moods. Children are often forced to take on adult roles including parenting the parents or acting as sexual partners. Lack of appropriate boundaries and vigilance means that the children are also exposed to avoidable risks, such as unguarded fires or a sex offender's predatory behaviour.

Example: Jane was 6 years old and lived with her mother, her sister aged 3 and baby brother of 18 months. No fathers were in evidence although the mother had a constant stream of casual boyfriends. Jane was regularly left to parent the other children while the mother went out socialising. Jane was beaten for offences such as making the gravy too lumpy when she made the family meal or being too tired to manage a large pile of ironing.

Rigid context

The care of the children is negative, rigid and punitive. The carers have to be in control at all times and worry about losing 'a grip' on the situation if they do not retain all the power. There is an undercurrent of fear, with the parents terrified of anarchy if they give their children 'an inch', while the children are scared of their parents' extreme wrath if they make the slightest error. Babies are often subject to strict routines but most difficulties arise once they are toddling. Their parents are intolerant of the mess, defiance and tantrums, which are an inevitable part of toddlers' natural curiosity and increasing independence.

Example: Mandy, aged 7, and her brother, aged 4, had, since infancy, been subjected to a very harsh regime by their parents. When taken out, they would sit for hours without daring to move, speak, eat, drink or go to the toilet. Most people failed to recognise the abuse but instead congratulated the parents on having such remarkably well-behaved children.

Deviant context

While mirroring any one of the above contexts, the organisation or family system contains one or two people who are seriously damaged and who abuse their power and yet are skilled at exploitation and manipulation. They appear to derive satisfaction from inflicting physical injury and emotional distress, lack empathy and have little remorse. This grouping also includes people who are 'addicted' to hospitals and medical care but present their children rather than themselves for treatment. Their fabrication of illness in their children can be emotionally and physically damaging and, in some circumstances, fatal (Frye and Feldman, 2012; Kucuker et al., 2010).

Example: Many of the most extreme examples have made headline news, such as Victoria Climbié and Peter Connelly. For practitioners working in early years settings the inquiry into sexual abuse of young children at the Little Teds Nursery in Plymouth makes informative reading (Plymouth Safeguarding Children Board, 2010).

Understanding and recognising physical abuse and neglect

This is not the place to detail all the diagnostic signs of abuse. Even experienced paediatricians and other medical specialists find it difficult to determine the exact cause of many injuries, even with the help of sophisticated X-ray and other equipment. However, there are some physical signs of abuse and neglect that can raise a query.

The most obvious are bruises and lesions on the skin of small children. Babies not yet able to roll over or move very far rarely sustain bruising. If they have, then the carers should be able to give a clear explanation that is consistent with the injury. Finger-tip bruising on tiny babies may indicate a carer who is losing control and gripping the child too hard.

When injuries are observed in young children, it is worth asking how they were sustained and whether or not they have been seen by medical staff. To the untrained eye, cigarette burns could be mistaken for a skin condition such as impetigo, but whether the cause is impetigo or burns, the child needs to be examined by a doctor. Conversely, what sometimes looks like bruising on the back or bottom is really 'Mongolian blue spot', a harmless birthmark seen in over 80% of children with a black or Asian heritage (Nieuweboer-Krobotova, 2013).

Neglected children are likely to be more poorly provided for in terms of clothing, toys and food compared to children in the area. Children who are emotionally or physically neglected may also show growth retardation, although there are medical or genetic conditions that delay growth. Non-organic failure to thrive is a diagnosis made when all medical conditions are excluded (Scholler and Nittur, 2012). It can be confirmed when, in the absence of medical treatment, growth charts show children gaining weight whenever in hospital or care and losing it again after returning home.

Understanding and recognising sexual abuse

According to Finkelhor (1984), in order for an incident of sexual abuse to occur, there has to be:

- someone who wants to sexually abuse a young child
- someone who finds a way of overcoming internal inhibitors (their conscience)
- someone who finds a way of overcoming external inhibitors (for example, protective parents, friends)
- someone who finds a way of overcoming the child victim's resistance (which may be to abuse a child too young to resist effectively).

People who molest young children have a sexual predilection for children independent of their gender orientation. If an adult, male or female, is only sexually attracted to other adults, male or female, then there is very little risk of child sexual abuse. However, some people can only relate sexually to children. Here, there is a high risk of abuse and the offenders fit the typical image of a 'paedophile'. There are also adults who do not discriminate sexually between adults and children. They pose a considerable risk but may not be so readily recognised as sex offenders, especially if they have adult partners.

Children may also engage in sexual activities with other children. When one child is coercive and more powerful than the other, either because of age, more knowledge, physical strength or other features, then the activities can be defined as 'abusive' although the value of labelling a child an 'abuser' is debatable (Sneddon et al., 2012; Vizard, 2013).

The ensuing profile of offenders is based primarily on research into adult male sex offenders. The sexual and offending behaviour of both women and young people differs from that of adult males although there is reason to believe that they share many of the characteristics described below.

Sex offenders are preoccupied with their own needs and can see the situation only from their own point of view. However, they can sometimes learn to say the 'right' thing. They may appear to be surrounded by family and friends but these relationships are superficial and often exploitative; frequently offenders use them to reassure or attract others. Many have excellent social skills, appear charming and plausible, and frequently collect labels of respectability in order to disarm others. In contrast, some offenders are 'loners' and clearly have difficulties forming relationships with non-vulnerable adults but relate well to children because they know what will attract them and can play engagingly with them.

Sex offenders do not offend as a sudden whim or 'one-off', rather their assaults are planned. Collecting child pornography is not a harmless diversion; it is often part of the planning process. They will target children and many will have a preference for a child of a particular gender or type, although those outside their target group will still be at risk (Doyle, 1987; Sullivan et al., 2011). Having chosen a victim, they will then 'groom' the child. Some offenders use force and threats but most are patient, gently persuading the child to trust them and to become a 'willing' victim. During the assault they will treat the child as an object for their own gratification, sometimes covering the child's face so that they cannot be reminded of their victim's personality. After the assault, they will again 'groom' the child, using either threats or persuasion to stop the child telling anyone about the abuse.

Most sex offenders have distorted attitudes to children. They believe that even very young children enjoy sexual activities and are ever ready to seduce adults. They will, for example, interpret a small child showing a glimpse of underwear as 'being provocative' and wanting sex. They also view children as objects designed for adults' sexual pleasure (Beech et al., 2013). Often, society supports these attitudes – for example, by objectifying children and referring to the child as 'it'.

When confronted with their offending behaviour, sex abusers say nothing, make excuses ('I was drunk') or try to elicit sympathy ('feel sorry for poor me'). Some become threatening, constantly make formal complaints to thwart investigations or denigrate workers by using sexist and racist innuendos. Finally, sex offending against children is not a behaviour that can be 'cured'. It can be controlled, but only controlled with difficulty (Doyle, 1994; Ho and Ross, 2012).

Understanding and recognising emotional abuse

It is often difficult to define emotional abuse but there are two important aspects. First, emotional abuse consists of both acts of commission – such as verbal abuse – and acts of omission – such as the refusal to praise or encourage a child. Second, there is a misuse of power – parents and other carers exploit their power over the child to actively abuse him or fail to use their power so as to neglect the child's emotional needs. This is illustrated by the following catalogue of emotionally abusive behaviour:

- *Fear-inducing*: this includes holding a child hostage, or creating insecurity by constantly leaving the child with lots of different 'strange' carers.
- *Tormenting:* this includes pretending to break a child's favourite toy or threatening to kill a child's pet.
- *Degrading:* this can be deliberate humiliation, embarrassing a child in front of other people, or denigration and verbal abuse.
- *Corrupting:* this can consist of using children to carry drugs or taking them on burglaries to climb through small windows. It also includes destructive modelling such as the violent father who encourages his young son to treat all women with derision and hit his sister and mother.
- *Rejecting:* rejection can be active, such as telling a child she is unwanted, or passive through the avoidance of emotional warmth, praise or cuddles. Closely allied to this is ignoring behaviour, refusing to give the child any attention.
- *Isolating:* this may be through locking the child away in a room or cupboard for very long periods. It can also include preventing a child from socialising or having any friends.
- *Applying of inappropriate roles*: this can include being made the scapegoat for all the family's ills, being used as a weapon against the other parent or 'the authorities'. It can also mean being overprotected or infantilised or, alternatively, forced to shoulder too much responsibility.
- Another form of emotional abuse which can develop into physical abuse and neglect is the designation of a child as possessed by a spirit. Children of all ages can be accused of witchcraft or of being the conduit of evil spirits, and some children, especially those who are adopted, who have a disability or are from cultures with strong beliefs in witchcraft, will be more vulnerable (Akilapa and Simkiss, 2012; Pearce, 2012).

Emotional abuse can occur outside the family in the form of school bullying or racist taunts by neighbours. It can also be found in every type of family, regardless of race, size, social class or structure. However, children in those families in which there are already a number of stressors are more likely to be emotionally abused (Doyle, 1997).

Understanding and recognising children's reactions to abuse

One of the paradoxes encountered in child protection work is that rather than try to escape from the abuse, even very young children will hide the signs of mistreatment, refuse to disclose and show a high level of attachment to their abusers. This can be explained partly by the natural feelings of love and attachment that small children develop for their carers in order to ensure survival (Bowlby, 1965). However, this does not fully explain why this attachment is maintained in the face of abuse.

It can, nonetheless, be understood if account is taken of the impact of trauma and maltreatment and the psychological process that helps people cope with trauma.

The Stockholm syndrome is a recognised range of protective processes with relevance to abused children. The syndrome was first identified when bank employees were held hostage in Stockholm, and it has been observed in hostage, kidnap, concentration camp, domestic violence and other abuse situations. There are a number of stages that victims go through. However, as with grief processes, these stages are not experienced by everyone, nor in a clearly defined order.

- *Frozen fright*: when confronted by a situation of terror from which there is no flight or fight possible, people 'freeze'. This results in compliance where all the victim's energy is focused on the abuser and is useful because it conserves energy for a time when flight or fight may become possible and compliance is less likely to antagonise the aggressor.
- *Denial*: the initial frozen fright gives way to a sense of unreality – 'this isn't happening to me'. This is a useful temporary state which guards against people being overwhelmed by the terror of the situation. But for some victims of abuse, this can become an entrenched denial of the severity and pain of the abuse, or of the events ever having occurred.
- *Fear and anger*: once reality has sunk in, victims feel fear and anger but it is too dangerous to express these emotions against abusers so victims often project it onto 'outsiders'. Victims believe that they are more likely to survive if their abusers are basically good and care for them – they therefore look for signs of goodness in their abusers and are grateful for any indication of kindness.
- *Depression*: victims also turn their anger against themselves, leading to depression and self-deprecation. They feel useless, worthless and powerless. Having convinced themselves that the abuser is good, they begin to believe that they are being justifiably mistreated because they are bad.
- *Psychological contrast*: the process towards despair or acceptance may be accelerated by psychological contrast, which substantially weakens victims, making them more compliant. It is a well-known form of interrogation and torture. One person acts as the 'good guy' while the other is the 'bad guy'. Alternatively, one person behaves in a kindly manner and then suddenly becomes threatening and aggressive. In abusive homes, one parent may be cruel while the other tries to compensate by being kind. Or, one parent is abusive and then feels guilt, so is very kind to the victim – until the next time.
- *Acceptance*: finally, victims of maltreatment reach a state of acceptance. They no longer question the rights or wrongs of what is happening to them. Children may appear 'well-adjusted' and their behaviour may seem calm and compliant. They may well have an unquestioning acceptance of the values, justification and behaviour of their abusers.

Recognising abuse and the obstacles to recognition

There are aspects of a child's appearance, behaviour, development and statements that might be suggestive of abuse. However, recognition is not straightforward and the final section summarises the obstacles to recognising abuse.

Appearance

This includes injuries where there are inconsistent explanations or ones that do not fit with the injury. Neglect might be present if a child is smaller, more poorly clothed or dirtier than most of the children in the family or area. An over-dressed child or very loose, swamping clothes may be masking emaciation or injuries. Emotional abuse might be present in a child who appears too clean and smart, especially if he or she is very frightened of making a mess. Finally, there should be concerns when a child shows frozen awareness or appears over-anxious.

Behaviour

A child who abuses other children, draws or plays out violent or sexual scenes with peers or toys might be mimicking behaviour they have experienced. Marked changes in behaviour, an inability to concentrate and anxiety about going home are always worth exploring, as is rummaging in bins or stealing food and comfort items.

Development

Any developmental delay can be an indicator of abuse, but equally significant is a sudden regression, such as the child whose language acquisition suddenly declines or the previously continent child who becomes incontinent.

Statements

Children may disclose abuse directly, clearly and frankly but some may start to try to disclose indirectly by asking what appears to be a strange or rather personal question. Disclosure sometimes comes through children writing poems or stories; if the child has been sexually abused, these may be sexually explicit. Evidently, very young children will have difficulty articulating their experiences but children as young as 2 or 3 years old have been able to convey aspects of the abuse they have suffered.

Workers' attitudes

One of the biggest obstacles to recognition is the professional worker him- or herself. Many professionals cannot accept abuse; it is too painful, so they ignore the signs or go out of their way to advance more comfortable explanations. They may also convince themselves that parents would never harm their children and that the whole discourse of child protection is exaggerated. Other professionals are so emotionally exhausted and burnt out that they no longer feel any concern for the child and ignore any potential signs because of the difficulties and challenges it will pose for them.

Problems recognising the signs

The points below summarise why recognising child abuse is not always easy. Sometimes the signs are indistinct, ambiguous or misleading. However, there are other instances where the signs are comparatively clear but professionals fail to acknowledge them due to their own emotional barriers, such as a reluctance to face a child's suffering. Early years workers need to be aware of the following obstacles to recognition so that they do not make assumptions about the presence or absence of maltreatment:

- Appearance, behaviour and developmental problems can be equally indicative of some other distress or worry.
- Many injuries or skin discoloration can also be indicative of an accident, disease process or birthmark.
- Children with certain disabilities, those for whom English is not their first language and pre-verbal children may not have the vocabulary or communication skills to disclose clearly in English.
- A 'nice' family can contain an abuser. Some professionals use checklists, which mislead them because although abuse often occurs in identifiable 'risk' situations, it can also occur anytime, anywhere and in any type of family.
- In some cases, the abuse is 'victim specific', so that carers/parents who seem to be exemplary in relation to their other children can still abuse one particular victim.
- In sexual abuse cases in particular, the skill of the perpetrator in grooming the victim and their potential protectors into silence is considerable.
- There is the phenomenon of the Stockholm syndrome. Children may appear deeply attached to their parents even when being abused by them.
- Professionals may ignore obvious signs because it is too emotionally painful to think about a child's suffering or they are too emotionally exhausted to contemplate the anguish the child has experienced.

- More insidious reasons for professionals denying probable signs of abuse can be because they are overly concerned that they may be 'making a mistake', they are reluctant to 'rock the boat', they do not want to take any responsibility for initiating an investigation or they are worried about damaging their relationships with the parents. They have lost sight of the fact that the child's welfare is paramount.

CASE STUDY ONE

Brook

Brook is a 5-year-old boy who has a sister, Sky, aged 8 and a brother, Dale, aged 2. All three children have the same white mother, Ruby. Sky's father was African Caribbean; he was killed in a car accident when Sky was 18 months old. All that is known of Brook's father is that he was a white man and never lived with Ruby. Dale's father is white and is Ruby's current husband.

Since Brook started school a year ago, he has been a cause for concern. He is much smaller than the other children in his class. Ruby, her husband, Sky and Dale are all well built. Brook's speech is indistinct, his development is generally delayed and he has difficulty concentrating in class. His clothes are always old and worn and he never brings toys from home. Ruby explained that he always breaks his toys and spoils his clothes so that it is not worth buying him new things.

He has frequent bruising to his legs, back and face. His mother says that he is clumsy and often fights with the other children. The staff have noticed his clumsiness in school but he is withdrawn rather than aggressive with both staff and other children. He often appears to be afraid of trying anything new in case he makes a mess or a mistake. When he is asked to draw pictures or talk about home, he always says how much he loves his mother and shows no fear of her.

 Reflection for case study 1

1. Is this a clear-cut case of abuse or could there be alternative explanations for all the various points of concern?
2. What other information – if any – would you need to make firmer or alternative judgements?

There are many indicators of abuse. Brook could be failing to grow, developmentally delayed, fearful of trying anything new and withdrawn because of emotionally abusive behaviour and neglect. The cause of his bruising and general fearfulness could be physical abuse.

The fact that he does not complain about any maltreatment or seem fearful of Ruby and is attached to her is not an indication that he is not abused. Children may become attached to their abusers, directing their fear onto other people or situations.

Nonetheless, his small stature, clumsiness, developmental delay and quiet anxiousness could simply be innate characteristics. We know little about his genetic inheritance, such as the physical size of his father. He may be small because his father was. It would be useful to obtain information about his father if possible.

Although the bruising is suspicious, it could be caused by a combination of falls and bullying by other children. We need to obtain information about the other children and adults in contact with Brook to find out if people other than his parents could be harming him. It is also necessary to exclude any medical condition that might be the cause of his small stature, his clumsiness or a susceptibility to bruising.

Information about his brother and sister could help, although if they are well cared for, it could be that this is a case where one child is singled out for abuse. It is also essential to check that neither parent is known to the police for acts of violence or offences against children.

Responding to disclosures

Throughout the UK and beyond there will be procedures that professionals need to follow if they suspect child abuse. Nothing in this section detracts from the importance of being aware of the procedures that apply to each practitioner and setting and the need to follow these.

Nevertheless, for those working in the early years, suspicion of abuse and eliciting a disclosure is unlikely to be straightforward. Communicating the experience of maltreatment requires several relatively advanced abilities. First, children need to be able to recognise that their experiences are ones of maltreatment and that complaint is legitimate, although younger children will tend to accept parental behaviour as simply 'what happens'. Secondly, if they are made to feel unhappy they may assume that it is because they have done something wrong and will therefore be hesitant about confiding in anyone. Finally, describing abusive experiences requires a fairly sophisticated vocabulary which younger children will not be able to command. Therefore, early years practitioners are less likely to be offered a clear disclosure; rather they will have mounting concerns because of the way children behave, snippets of things they say, observations of the way they relate to others or aspects of their appearance. Early years practitioners see very many non-abused children and therefore they may subconsciously absorb the minute differences in the way maltreated children present. This results in a 'gut' feeling that something is amiss. While this feeling is to be respected, practitioners know that often they need at least some tangible indicators before discussing their intuitive sense of a problem with colleagues.

Most settings, certainly in the UK, will keep records about children. It might be possible in the setting's everyday records to note which days practitioners saw a child looking tired or tearful or playing excessively aggressively. If the official recording system would not be appropriate for the types of reflection an uneasy practitioner might wish to make, then incidents causing unease could be recorded as part of a general reflective diary that practitioners might keep for their own professional development. However, care has to be taken to ensure the child and family's privacy is respected and it is important to reflect on professional boundaries. Practitioners need to be aware that if the case came to court they might be asked how they could remember so clearly that on a particular date a child behaved in a particular way.

When making notes it is important to be precise. For example, the vague phrase 'inappropriately dressed' means little. However a description such as 'walked to nursery all this week, when temperatures outside were less than 2°C, in sandals, shorts, t-shirt and a thin plastic mac' is not a judgement but a factual description which ultimately conveys much more to the reader. Take care also not to record hearsay as fact, so, for example, avoid stating 'mother was drunk' but record more accurately 'I was told by Jay's father that Sam's mother had been drinking heavily'.

Sometimes children will start talking about events which strongly suggest they are being abused although a clear picture will only emerge if the children are allowed to continue to express themselves. Children might start with an opening such as 'I've a big secret to tell you' or if they see a picture of a sad face they might say 'What mummy and daddy do, makes me sad'. It is important to give the child an opportunity to continue with their explanation. As children disclose, their accounts might give rise to feelings of disgust, shock, disbelief or anger in the listener. It is important to remain calm and avoid comments which might appear to be judging the child, the situation, the parents or the perpetrators.

One important principle is that questions should not be asked that could possibly plant ideas. For example, if a child says 'mummy hurt me' the question 'did she hit you?' would be inappropriate because the child might nod or say 'yes' simply to please, or because she does not know what else to say, yet she might not have been hit at all. Instead it is useful to repeat what the child has said with a question in the voice: 'your mummy hurt you?'. The advantage of this is that if you have misheard, the child can correct you – 'No, I said *nanny* hurt me' – but if you heard correctly the child will acknowledge this and may be prompted to carry on with the explanation. Promising to keep secrets also has to be avoided because child protection procedures normally require practitioners to report any suspicions or a disclosure to designated colleagues. It is also wise to steer clear of phrases that minimise the possible serious outcomes of the disclosure, such as 'don't worry, everything will be fine'.

Early years practitioners can usefully allow the child to say or play out whatever is burdening him with empathy and without making him feel guilty. Practitioners need sufficient evidence of concern about actual or possible abuse before passing information on to colleagues. Yet they have to avoid investigating what has happened because that is the role of social workers or the police. This is a difficult line to tread but can be achieved by simply encouraging the child to unburden herself by repeating phrases, giving reassurances that she is doing nothing wrong by disclosing and the practitioner showing through their body language that they are giving their full attention to the child. As soon as possible after the exchange with the child, the events should be recorded as accurately as possible, including date, time, place and who else was present. The matter is then referred immediately to the designated child protection colleague or agency.

Intervention and prevention

Children who have been abused can be offered help on an individual, family and group basis (Doyle, 2012). Much of this therapeutic work is undertaken by specialist therapists. Nevertheless, there is much that non-specialist early years workers can do to assist the healing process or contribute to preventing abuse from occurring. They can, for example, help children directly by encouraging them to recognise in simple and basic ways that they have fundamental rights to care, not to be exploited, not to be bullied and to have access to 'safe' adults.

At the parental level, practitioners are in a position to model good childcare to parents who may be unsure of how to respond to their children. They can advise parents on how to provide caring discipline and boundaries for young children without resorting to aggression and assault. Because early years practitioners relate to lots of parents, they may recognise one who is depressed or not coping well and be able to suggest resources that might help distressed parents.

It is, however, important to work with all the other professionals involved in safeguarding children. This is advocated by government policy (e.g. DCSF, 2010). This means preparing well for multidisciplinary forums such as case conferences, core groups and even courtrooms, being clear about the information that needs to be shared with other professionals, and being confident enough to contribute to these forums. In child protection cases, each individual has part of a jigsaw puzzle – only by putting all the various pieces of information together is a picture of the situation revealed.

Early years workers are the experts in the day-to-day understanding of young children. Not only may they have had academic training in child development but they will be spending many hours in the company of a diverse range of young children. They will consciously or unconsciously be absorbing information about the range of 'normal' baby, toddler or young child behaviours. Consequently, any feelings they have that all is not well with a particular child are likely to have some foundation and their observations are likely to be highly informative. But the majority of early years workers are female and many are young – they therefore do not represent the more powerful sectors of society. Unfortunately, in some multidisciplinary forums, they find their views are disregarded, while the more powerful professions – health, law enforcement, social work, for example – dominate proceedings. It is important that early years workers give voice to their concerns and have the confidence to do so, knowing that they are the experts in the field.

Early years practitioners can help to prevent abuse by being powerful advocates for young children, ensuring that they are not disregarded and are afforded the rights reflected in *Every Child Matters* (DfES, 2004c) and the EYFS of health, safety, enjoyment, achievement and fulfilment. They can also contest any attitudes that objectify children. For example, if they write or talk about children, they can avoid referring to 'the child' (where there is no indication of gender) as 'it'; just as when referring to adults, they can pluralise, i.e. use 'they' or 'he or she'. They can also avoid and even challenge phrases that demonise children (Goldson, 2001), e.g. referring to them as 'little devils' or 'little monsters'.

Finally, research (Doyle, 2001; Doyle et al., 2010) has shown that it is possible for a range of people to increase children's resilience and provide the positive, valuing messages that counter the negative messages inevitably communicated to children by abuse. This is illustrated in the example of Yasmin below.

CASE STUDY TWO

Yasmin

Yasmin is the second of four children. She has a sister, Meena, who is two years older and twin brothers, Kiran and Harish, who are three years younger. Yasmin is now in her twenties. She recalled how she was physically and emotionally abused by her parents and neglected. Starved of love, she was offered affection by a male neighbour who regularly sexually abused her.

She found out that, while her siblings were the offspring of her mother and the person she viewed as her father, she had been the product of a rape by a distant relative. Initially, her mother had been too humiliated and ashamed to tell anyone or seek an abortion. Just before Yasmin's birth, her mother told her husband what had happened. He had been supportive and agreed to keep the rape secret and let others assume that Yasmin was his own daughter. However, neither parent could accept Yasmin nor bond with her; they were both too aware of the circumstances of her conception. Despite their best intentions, they neglected and abused her.

Yasmin's grandmother also lived in the household and provided Yasmin with physical care and showed her affection. This positive relationship enabled Yasmin to thrive and develop a sense of self-worth. In a nursery attached to the local school, the staff realised Yasmin had a very musical ear. This continued when she moved to the Reception class of the school and, throughout her school career, Yasmin was made to feel special by staff, who valued her musical ability and her very lovely singing voice. All the messages from her nursery, school and grandmother were positive. Consequently, Yasmin began to form the view that she was being abused by her parents because they did not understand her talents and resented her special abilities. Although in her teenage years she became depressed, self-loathing and engaged in some self-harm by cutting herself, she had a deep-seated belief that she was valued and worthy. She therefore sought counselling and now feels that her self-esteem is buoyant and her future bright.

Reflection for case study 2

1. What was the role of early years practitioners in Yasmin's life?
2. Could early years practitioners have helped Yasmin without realising she was being abused?

Yasmin had a particular talent that enabled her teachers to value her and all children have some personality features and aptitudes that can be valued. Early years workers can help safeguard children by adopting positive outlooks, valuing all children. Another aspect of the case is that individual staff might have thought that their positive attitude to her could hardly make a difference given the power of her parents. However, the combined, consistent enriching attitudes towards her of the early years practitioners, the teacher and her grandmother made a profound and positive impact on Yasmin.

Chapter summary

This chapter has demonstrated the importance of understanding the underlying dynamics of abuse because the laws, policies and procedures are worth nothing if practitioners do not know *when* to implement them. All people working with young children need to appreciate the nature of abuse, the different contexts in which it occurs and its various manifestations. They need, however, to be sensitive to the diverse forms of family life and not assume that non-mainstream childcare practices are inevitably harmful. However, they will benefit from an understanding of the power that abusers hold over their victims, whether or not those abusers have any power in wider society. They also need to be aware that abused children might, like hostages displaying the Stockholm syndrome, protect those who harm them and deny any mistreatment. Practitioners need to reflect on their practice, questioning whether they might deny that abuse can occur in their particular practice setting because to do otherwise would cause them too much effort or discomfort.

Usually, there will be signs that children are being abused. However, it is important not to underestimate how difficult it can be to identify these. Early years practitioners have to maintain a fine balance between under-reacting by failing to recognise signs, and overreacting by making assumptions of abuse when there are alternative explanations. If a maltreated child discloses, again there is a balance between allowing the child to unburden herself while not engaging in a full investigation. The more knowledge and understanding acquired, the easier it is to achieve a satisfactory outcome.

Questions for reflection and discussion

1. How are concepts of child protection socially constructed?
2. What are the major obstacles to the recognition of child abuse and neglect?
3. Why is the 'Stockholm syndrome' significant?
4. What are the implications of the Laming Report (2003) for all early years practitioners?
5. How does child protection practice benefit from a multidisciplinary approach?

Recommended reading

Doyle, C. (2012) *Working with Abused Children*, 4th edn. Basingstoke: Palgrave Macmillan.
Lindon, J. (2012) *Safeguarding Children and Young People: Child Protection 0–18 Years*, 4th edn. London: Hodder Education.
Rushforth, C. (2012) *Safeguarding and Child Protection in the Early Years*. London: Practical Pre-school Books.

Recommended websites

www.childrenwebmag.com
The website for the Children's Web Mag, an online journal about child welfare

www.nspcc.org.uk
The website for the National Society for the Protection of Children (NSPCC)

Want to learn more about this chapter? Visit the companion website at **www.sagepub.co.uk/walleranddavis3e** to access podcasts from the author and child observation videos.

13

Working with Families

Eunice Lumsden and Celia Doyle

 Key chapter objectives

- To explore what is meant by 'family' within a diverse society and why family is important for children

- To consider the implications of what it means for children when they do not have an identifiable 'family'

- To discuss early years policy initiatives in relation to children and their families

- To acknowledge the relationship between the statutory and the private, voluntary and independent sectors in work with families

The family has a significant place in the lives of children. Enhancing family life and the role of parents in children's lives is an important aspect of British social policy. However, in order to work effectively with young children and their families, early years practitioners need to appreciate what is meant by 'family' within a diverse society and why family is important for children. They will also find it helpful to consider how they can work with and support families within legal and policy parameters, and the implications of what it means for children when they do not have an identifiable 'family'. This chapter opens by exploring the implications of what it means for children whose understanding of family is limited. This is illustrated by the following example of Lily and Lee.

CASE STUDY ONE

Lily and Lee

A play therapist had started working with Lily, aged 6, and her brother, Lee, aged 5. Three days earlier, they had been taken into care and placed with foster carers. The two children were asked by the therapist to draw their family. Lily drew a line of figures. When asked who they were, Lily indicated: Lee, her 'gran', a neighbour, a new teacher, a neighbour's dog, her mother and a worker at a women's refuge. Lee drew his new foster family.

As a child, Lily and Lee's own mother had had no example of secure family life and it was therefore understandable that she was unable to create one for her children. They, in their short lives prior to coming into care, and under the ad hoc arrangements made by their mother, had experienced over twenty different 'homes' and a vast array of casual carers.

Reflection for case study 1

- How far do you feel concern for Lily and Lee, and if you feel concern, why do you do so?
- If you feel any concern for the children, do you feel more for Lily or Lee, or the same amount of concern for both?

This case study of Lily and Lee shows that for some children 'family' is a remote or confusing concept. It also suggests how important it is for children to grow up within some form of recognisable family. Researchers such as Rutter (1981) and Clarke and Clarke (2000) have demonstrated that, while children are not totally dependent on a single mother figure, they do need to be able to form attachments to a consistent group of carers in order to thrive (Schore and Schore, 2008). The family, alongside reliable alternative carers such as childminders or key nursery staff, form the secure base from which children can start to explore the wider world.

Despite the clear indications that in order to develop satisfactorily children need an identifiable, dependable family in the early years, the form it takes can vary. Diverse cultural traditions or socioeconomic and geographical factors can mean that families may live as isolated nuclear units or as large extended families with several generations sharing the same accommodation. Some children have reconstituted families following the death or divorce of a parent and subsequent remarriage or new partnership. Others are in care and have substitute families. Those from Traveller or armed services families may well experience a number of different locations or homes but most have an established, core family. It is through the experience of a 'stable' family life that the family members are able to grow, flourish and meet their full potential.

An understanding and framework of how human needs can be satisfied is provided by the theorists Maslow (1970) and Alderfer (1972). Their theories have been modified and adapted to ensure their relevance to children's development by researchers such as Thompson et al. (2001) and Doyle and Timms (2013). Basically, whatever its nature, as long as a family meets their child's physical requirements and provides love, care, security, safety and a sense of belonging, children will develop well and reach their potential.

Because of the importance of family, most of the world religions and many cultural traditions provide guidelines on how family life and relationships should be conducted; in some states these are adopted or ratified by national governments. In societies such as the UK, there is a wide variety of religions and cultures and a significant proportion of the population espouses no religion, therefore the government, rather than any church or religious authority, intervenes in order to promote optimum family lives for children. The following section looks more closely at the diverse experiences of family life for young children. This chapter will then discuss some of the UK government initiatives. Finally, it will address the relationships between families and those who work with young children and provide services for them.

Family life

Children's experience of family life in the 21st century is one of diversity. There have been many changes to family structure, views about marriage have altered and the composition of society reflects differences of culture, ethnicity and religion (Cleaver, 2006; Gittins, 1993; Lancy, 2013). More recently, there have also been changes in migration patterns to the UK, bringing with them new challenges as children accessing early years services have either had to adapt to a multitude of new experiences or they are the first of their family to be born in their parents' newly adopted country (Crawley, 2006).

This changing demography heightens the importance, for those working with children, of reflection on what is meant by family life and early childhood. The following activity aims to assist in reflections about changes in families and the diversity of family structures.

Activity 1 – The nature of family

Think about a family that you have known for many years:

- What is the structure of the family, e.g. do the children have one mother and one father or do they have several mother or father figures or only one parent? Is the extended family – aunts, uncles, grandparents – in close contact or rarely involved?
- How do you think that family's life has changed over the generations?
- What do you think about the changes?
- How do you think other people would answer these questions?

While the above activity highlights the diversity in families, the next activity examines children's situations in families. The experience of living in a family will vary from child to child. An eldest sibling may even have a different extended family. A grandparent may be alive during the lives of the older children but have died before the birth of a younger one. Some children have a different set of relatives compared to their siblings, for example half-siblings will share only one set of grandparents.

Activity 2 – The place of children in families

Think about what being a child in a family means. Focus on one young child, either from the family you thought of in Activity 1 or another child known to you.

- Is he or she an only child?
- If not, how many brothers and sisters does the child have? Are they 'full' siblings or are they step, adoptive, foster or half-siblings?
- What position in the family is your chosen child – youngest, middle or oldest?
- How many parent figures does the child have?
- Are the key parent figures birth parents, or are they step, adoptive or foster carers? Or is there some other guardianship arrangement in place?
- Are the key parents married? Are they in a civil partnership?
- Have they divorced? If divorced, have they remarried?
- What are the position and key roles of the mother figure/s in the household?
- What are the position and key roles of the father figure/s in the household?
- What roles do grandparents, aunts and uncles or other relatives play in the child's life?

Now having thought about the various dynamics and relationships experienced by the child, try to draw a 'family tree' for your chosen child. Is it straightforward and easy to draw or is it very complicated with a number of criss-crossing lines?

Constructed concepts of children and family

These activities highlight that while we all share the fact that we have been a child and experienced 'childhood', our experience of being a child is unique, and so is our experience and understanding of being parented and what family life entails. It is an experience whose nature is shaped by how a society socially constructs 'childhood', as the following discussion will illustrate.

The way that childhood is constructed is fluid and can be different in different cultures and has also changed over time within cultures (Flinn et al., 2010; Hendrick, 1997). In some societies, 'childhood' is a limited concept (see Chapter 1). Graham (2011), for example, explains that the arguments of Ariès (1962) that in Medieval Europe children were simply seen as small adults raises 'questions about the historical, social and culturally specific nature of childhood shaped by shifting configurations of family and educational institutions'. In some belief systems young children are seen as innocents living in bliss until knowledge of the real world with all its damage and distress intrudes (Ennew, 1986). In contrast, other societies see children as potential soldiers or 'situated as consumers within a global economy' (Flinn et al., 2010: 249). There are cultures that view children as objects belonging to their parents whereas other cultures reject this, as exemplified by the words of the Arab philosopher Kahlil Gibran (1923: 81), who wrote:

> Your children are not your children.
>
> They are the sons and daughters of Life's longing for itself.
>
> They come through you but not from you,
>
> And though they are with you yet they belong not to you.

In modern times there have been moves towards the concept that children are individuals with rights to voice their views, to participation and to be protected. This idea is enshrined in the United Nations Convention on the Rights of the Child (UNCRC). On 20 November 1989, the governments, including the UK, represented at the General Assembly agreed to adopt the convention into international law. It came into force in September 1990. A further consequence of this is that governments signing up to the UNCRC have introduced policies to provide appropriate services for children. The preamble to the articles in the Convention (United Nations, 1989: 1) states:

> Convinced that the family, as the fundamental group of society and the natural environment for the growth and wellbeing of all its members and particularly children, should be afforded the necessary protection and assistance so that it can fully assume its responsibilities within the community, recognising that the child, for the full and harmonious development of his or her personality, should grow up in a family environment, in an atmosphere of happiness, love and understanding.

Within early years settings, recognising and valuing the importance and uniqueness of family life will help early years workers to work with parents, carers and other family members to support the child in the transition into education, maximise their opportunities within it and form a solid foundation to assist them with the next stage of their education.

In 2012, in the UK, there were 13.3 million dependent children (Office for National Statistics, 2012b) and since 1971, the number of children living in lone families has tripled. In 2006, 24% of children were living in lone-parent families and the number of lone-parent households had risen by 30% since 1971 (Office for National Statistics, 2012e). This had increased further by 2012, with nearly 2 million lone families, 92% comprised of mothers and their children. There is also a diminishing number of marriages in England and Wales, with 241,100 recorded in 2010 (Office for National Statistics, 2012c) compared to 480,285 in 1972 (Office for National Statistics, 2012e). Furthermore, it is now estimated that 42% of marriages end in divorce (Office for National Statistics, 2012d). However, it is important to note here that divorce does not always have to be a negative event (Steel et al., 2012).

The above statistics demonstrate that the way in which families live is constantly changing, a situation that impacts on the experience of being a child. For example, for some children the experience of family life is living with one parent during the week and another at weekends. An increasing number of children live in reconstituted families while others, as the case example of Lily and Lee at the start of this chapter illustrates, do not consistently live in families with their birth parents.

Turning now to children, like Lily and Lee, with substitute carers, on 31 March 2012 there were 67,050 children 'looked after' by local authorities in England, an increase of 13% compared to the number in 2008 (DfE, 2012e). A further 5,726 children were looked after in Wales, an increase of 24% since 2007 (Welsh Government, 2012). In July 2011 there were 16,171 looked after children (LAC) in Scotland (Scottish Government, 2012) and 1,838 in Northern Ireland (DHSSPS, 2012). These looked after children will live predominantly with foster carers, though some will be placed with extended family members, usually in an arrangement called Kinship Care. Some looked after children will be adopted and a small number of young people are resident in institutions.

Children living away from their families of origin may have experienced a variety of different types of family life. Some might also have been deemed 'in need' under the terms of the Children Act 1989 or have been subject to a care order. For them, like Lily and Lee, their early lives might well comprise frequent moves between their primary caretaker and foster placements; they thus experience repeated separation, loss and the need to develop multiple new attachments. Fawcett et al. (2004) note that, proportionally, more children with disabilities are in care, compared to those without. They may face additional barriers to satisfactory alternative care. For example, Fawcett et al. (2004: 125) point out that those children 'regarded as having communication difficulties were found to be excluded from participating in discussions about their needs'.

The ecological model of parenting

The previous section has provided an introduction to concepts of 'family' and 'children', the diversity of family structures and changing trends in family life. One model that supports understanding of the parenting task in this context is an ecological model of parenting (O'Sullivan, 2012: 111). The author draws on the work of Belsky (1984, cited in O'Sullivan, 2012) to suggest how parent–child relationships can be understood in an ecological context. There are three domains that need to be explored: the parent, how they have developed and their 'psychological resources'; the child and their characteristics; and finally 'the contextual sources of stress and support'. This last domain includes such things as: who undertakes the parenting tasks; social support; external agencies such as early years settings; and the impact of parents' employment. To illustrate this further, the cases of Sam and Alexander below afford an opportunity to reflect on how children's early life experiences may impact on their capacity for learning and growth, the role of the early years workers in the lives of young children and how an appreciation of the ecological model of parenting can enhance practice.

CASE STUDY TWO

Sam

Sam is 4 years old and has just started school. His parents are separated and he spends the weekdays with his mother, who presents as rather anxious and works part time at the local supermarket. Her parents live in a neighbouring town, her father is disabled and they are unable to offer support. Sam spends weekends with his father, a long-distance lorry driver, who collects him from the After-school Club at school on Friday night and brings him to the Breakfast Club at school on Monday morning, with his weekend bag. After school, Sam stays at the After-school Club until he is collected by his mother at 5pm. In class, Sam is withdrawn and often appears tired. He is having difficulty making friendships and is prone to angry outbursts.

Reflection for case study 2

- What do you think the role of an early years practitioner could be in this situation?
- How does the ecological model of parenting support further understanding of the parent–child relationship?

Sam has just started school and has a very long day, which may make him tired. He also may or may not find it difficult living in two separate homes. His experiences are impacting on how he is settling into school and making relationships with his peers. His frustration appears to be making him angry and all these circumstances will influence his receptiveness to learning. For the early years practitioner, supporting Sam is really important, as is good communication with the practitioners running the Breakfast and After-school Clubs. They also need to talk to Sam's parents about how their son is presenting in the setting. The ecological model of parenting helps those working with the family understand the parenting style and the context in which the family functions.

CASE STUDY THREE

Alexander

Alexander is 4 years old and has just started in nursery school, his fifth early years setting. He will be in the nursery for one term only as he is due to move into a primary school Reception class. He is the subject of a care order and is living in a foster placement. He has been with his current carers since he was 3 years old and an adoptive home is being sought for him.

Alexander and his mother have been known to social services since his birth. At the age of 16 weeks he spent his first period in the care of the local authority; he returned to live with his mother when he was 19 weeks old but went back into care two weeks later. Unfortunately, he could not go to the same foster placement so he was placed with new foster carers. He stayed there for a month and then returned to live with his mother. He remained living with her for the next year, but spent regular periods in respite care because of her mental health difficulties.

At the age of 18 months, he spent a prolonged period in care with another new set of foster carers. He remained there until he was 2 years old, when he returned to live with his mother. Respite care was provided again but with different carers.

(Continued)

(Continued)

At the age of 3 he returned to the care of the local authority, was placed with yet another new foster carer and a care order was granted. He is currently awaiting matching with an adoptive family.

Reflection for case study 3

- What do you think the impact of Alexander's life experiences will have on his transition into a school setting?
- What are the possible implications of his early experiences for his later life outcomes?
- How does the ecological model of parenting support further understanding of the range of relationships Alexander has to negotiate?

There is now considerable evidence that early experiences of abuse and/or a troubled family life can lead to a turbulent adolescence, including drug and alcohol abuse and challenges in adulthood (Allen, 2011; Egeland et al., 2002). Alexander's early years are marked by frequent moves from his mother to foster and respite care. By the age of 4, he has had seven different people responsible for his care and has lived in six different homes. He has also been in five different early years settings. His mother has had mental health difficulties, which would have impacted on her capacity to parent Alexander. His experiences could have led to attachment difficulties because of the number of primary carers he has experienced. The continual changes would have had an impact on his wellbeing and made him insecure. It is clear that Alexander has not been safe and his capacity for enjoyment and achieving has been compromised. It is important that his transition into the Reception class setting is handled sensitively and that he is fully supported, especially as he is likely to move again when an adoptive placement is found for him. It would also be beneficial if all his pictures, photographs and observations were kept to support his understanding of his life story. Early years practitioners need to ensure that they are working as part of the multi-professional team around Alexander to provide excellent levels of communication to support improved life chances. They need to reflect on the support he receives in the setting and ensure that planning gives him opportunities for high quality experiences, the consistency of a key worker and opportunities to develop resilience.

Research in context

Hogg, R., Ritchie, D., de Kok, B., Wood, C. and Huby, G. (2013) 'Parenting support for families with young children – a public health, user-focused study undertaken in a semi-rural area of Scotland', *Journal of Clinical Nursing*, 22: 1140–50.

While social care and education are essential provisions in the early years, the health of growing children is also important and individual parents may not always have sufficient knowledge to maximise their children's health or to overcome health-related problems. The paper by Hogg et al. (2013) explains that more recently one-to-one support for families with young children has moved from a universal service in the UK to one targeted at vulnerable children and families or those with specific health needs. They therefore set up a research project to explore the general health support needs of families with young children and how these might be met through community-based approaches.

The location of the research was a semi-rural part of Scotland and included an area of deprivation. The participants were eleven mothers and one father who volunteered to take part in focus groups. Three of the mothers were in their teenage years and all were white, with English as their first language. A further set of focus groups were held with seventeen professionals working with families with young children from various disciplines covering health, education and social care.

The main theme emerging from the parents' groups was that while having children was rewarding there were a number of challenges, especially when parents had more than one child. If their extended family was not nearby they experienced isolation. The teenage parents had the added burden of a sense that they were being judged negatively. Breastfeeding emerged as a substantial issue, with the feeling that there were strong messages that they should be breastfeeding but insufficient support and advice available.

There was a consensus that help and advice from other parents was particularly helpful, although this could be usefully complemented by information about local resources and group-based interventions from professionals. The teenage parents however sometimes felt they had little in common with older parents so parent groups were less helpful for them.

One important theme emerging from the professionals' groups was the misunderstanding of each other's roles, particularly that of the health visitor. These felt that their caseloads were particularly onerous and they were under pressure to promote breastfeeding. All the professionals acknowledged the importance of

(Continued)

(Continued)

multi-agency working although this only worked well where agencies were accommodated close together.

The researchers concluded that peer support among parents with young children is valued but that they could also benefit from easy access to professional help and advice, particularly in relation to breastfeeding. However, the research showed that neither parents nor other professionals really understood the role of health visitors. Services for families in the future need to include peer support, easy access to professional support and multi-professional working.

Early years policy initiatives and the family

The growth of policies in the early years in England has been profoundly influenced, as Pugh (2005: 31) argued, by the Labour Government (1997–2010) putting 'services for children and families higher on the national agenda than at any time in living memory'. She continued to argue that the policies transpired for three reasons: improved services for children; to support working mothers; and to support parents and carers. Underpinning these policy developments was the drive to reduce poverty and social injustice. As Brooker (2005: 9) argued, measures implemented by the Labour Government (1997–2010) were aimed at:

> better provision for young children, along with tax credits and other financial measures, [this] would enable more young parents to study, train and work; as a result they would become higher earners (and hence, higher tax payers) and better parents; in the process they would become more integrated into society and feel more committed to their communities and perhaps also the national interest.

Therefore, from 1997 to 2010 there was considerable government investment across the UK. This was targeted at improving outcomes and services for children, families and the community. There was a strong commitment to the early years, integrated working (see Chapter 16) and support to enable parents to work by providing a full range of services that were easily accessible. Initially, this was through Early Excellence Centres and then Sure Start local programmes (Sure Start, 2008). Following on from these initiatives was the commitment to provide a children's centre in every community, and push forward the Extended Schools programme (DfES, 2007e), which by 2010 aimed to work with the local authority and other partners to offer access to a range of services and activities that supported and motivated children and young people to achieve their full potential. These services aimed to provide:

- a varied menu of activities, combined with childcare in primary schools
- community access to school facilities
- swift and easy access (referral) to targeted and specialist services
- parenting support.

In England, the Labour Government also put forward their view of proactive support, in *Aiming High for Children: Supporting Families* (DfES, 2007b). They argued for the need for proactive support packages for families. They also contended that children's resilience needed developing and highlighted the requirement to be more responsive to children assessed as 'at risk'.

Alongside these developments was a growing recognition of the importance of the first five years of life to improving later life outcomes (Allen, 2011; Allen and Duncan Smith, 2008). However, the change in UK government in 2010 brought with it a change in policy direction. The Conservative-led Coalition Government shifted the focus from poverty and issues of social exclusion towards early intervention and introduced *Families in the Foundation Years* (DfE, 2011c). While they reaffirmed the importance of the earliest years and evidence-based practice, there was an increased focus on the families' own responsibility and a more targeted approach. An example here was the special focus on the 120,000 'troubled families' identified by the Coalition Government who were taking up a disproportionate amount of tax payers' money (Department of Communities and Local Government, 2013).

If early years provision specifically is considered nationally in the UK, the number of 3- and 4-year olds receiving early years education tripled between 1970/71 and 2005/6, from 21% to 64% (Office for National Statistics, 2012e). The incoming Coalition Government affirmed the commitment to supporting parents with young children and took forward the former Labour Government's pledge to increase free early childhood education and care (ECEC) from 12.5 to 15 hours per week for 3- to 4-year-olds. By 2012, 1,264,420 (96%) of 3- and 4-year-olds were accessing some free early education (DfE, 2012f). The Coalition Government decided to extend the age range for free entitlement, but rather than taking a universal approach it decided to target the most disadvantaged children. Between 10 and 15 hours of free ECEC was to be provided for 20% of the least advantaged 2-year-olds by September 2013, with this being increased to 40% from September 2014 (DfE, 2012g).

In reviewing the previous case studies of Sam and Alexander, the aim of the policy drivers of the former Labour Government was to provide better outcomes through the provision of high quality services based (usually) in one place. For example, Alexander's mother would have been able to access the full range of services offered by a children's centre, including support for herself, parenting classes and early years provision for her son. The change of government in 2010 and world recession means that access to a children's centre and its services cannot be guaranteed (see Chapter 15).

Turning to potential outcomes, in relation to Lily, Lee, Alexander and Sam, the services available to them may have enhanced their overall development and their resilience

(DfES, 2007a; Rutter, 1999). Understanding this is important for those working with children and families because it helps explain the different ways in which children manage their life experiences. Why is it that some adults and children are able to cope with difficult situations and others seem far less able to do so? There is no one answer to this question as it depends on a range of interacting factors and is unique to each individual. Members of one family can all face the same situation but can each handle it very differently. However, early years practitioners can support and lead practice in this area. For example, it is evident from Sam's case study that he is having difficulty in coping with the nature of the divided care he is receiving from his parents. Early intervention in this case could help both his parents see the impact of his shared care and support them in looking at alternative arrangements that are more sensitive to his needs as a 4-year-old making the transition into school.

Home–school/setting partnerships

The rapidly changing landscape of provision in the early years has had an effect upon early years practitioners' relationships with other professionals, the family and the child. The research by Hogg et al. (2013) described above demonstrates some of the issues of working with other practitioners and engaging in work with parents. Ideas of partnership are integral to how policies are translated into practice and to the role of the early years practitioner in supporting children and families within a variety of settings. Central to this is the importance of seeing that the family and early years settings have complementary roles in the provision of early childhood education and care (ECEC), as the following discussion emphasises.

Vygotsky (1956, 1978) highlighted the importance of the child's 'culture', which is far more than ethnicity; it embraces the child's total physical and emotional environment, history and relationships. 'Enculturation is not something that happens to children; it is something that children do' (Miller, 2002: 373). The implications of this are that if the child's home (or homes) and early years settings do not have shared approaches, are distant from each other or are in conflict, then the child's environment will be confusing and could delay rather than enhance development. Rogoff (1990), in extending Vygotsky's ideas, uses the analogy of an apprenticeship between the child, who is learning to solve problems, and the adult or older child who provides implicit or explicit instruction. However, if children are constantly having to adapt to very different forms of 'instruction', that apprenticeship will be disjointed and perplexing rather than enlightening. For this reason, home–setting links and partnership with parent figures are essential.

Rowan and Honan (2005) provide examples of the difficulties of working in partnership, such as the use of 'book boxes'. Here, children take home books from a range of reading schemes and the parents are expected to read these with their children and sign to affirm they have done so. This appears to be the setting/school working with the home. But as Rowan and Honan (2005: 212) remark, 'school reading practices and processes are taken into the home while the home literary practices are ignored'. Brooker (2005: 128) similarly highlights that there are barriers between parents and early years settings, particularly where families are from minority or socio-economically disadvantaged groups. These barriers, however, can be overcome by 'serious and respectful listening and not by a home–school dialogue which assumes the school is always right'. Other families are sometimes described as 'hard-to-reach' for other reasons such as isolation and lack of transport in remoter rural areas and here it might be a matter of resources for outreach workers, although as Cortis et al. (2009) working in Australia found, obtaining sufficiently skilled workers and the funding to pay for them can be a problem. There are also members of families who are difficult to engage, such as fathers. The research by Hogg et al. (2013) described above highlighted this difficulty because, although they sent out invitations to all parents of children aged under 4 years in the designated area, only one father compared to eleven mothers volunteered to participate. In many of the various cultures of the UK, mothers still have the prime responsibility for childcare and fathers tend to be the main breadwinners (Daniel and Taylor, 2001; Potter and Carpenter, 2010). This explains why it might be difficult for fathers to engage readily with settings, particularly when this requires their involvement during weekday working hours. Arguably, rather than parents and families being hard-to-reach it could be argued that some settings are hard-to-reach for some parents if they are geographically distant, unfamiliar or unwelcoming to some parents, particularly those from minority groups, or providing services at times when parents cannot access them.

Despite these concerns and warnings, there are many examples of effective home–setting partnerships. Potter and Carpenter (2010), for instance, outline the inclusion of fathers in Sure Start settings. McDonald (2010) provides a variety of strategies for engaging with disadvantaged families, which, although written for an Australian readership, are applicable elsewhere. A further example of close links between setting and home is the Pen Green Centre in Corby. This is an early years provision for families focusing on community regeneration, together with family support and education for young children, including those in need and with special needs. From its inception in 1983, it has highlighted the importance of finding out from parents what is needed rather than 'imposing a predetermined "neat and tidy" plan' (Whalley, 2001: 128). It operates on the basis of inclusion of parents with parent groups and meetings to inform policy. Parents were encouraged to record their children at home and share these recordings with the staff, while they were also involved in curriculum development at the Centre. The project has also successfully engaged fathers by not only inviting them to the general activities but also running groups at the weekend, such as Dad's Group and Dad's Baby Massage, and having men's circuit training on weekday evenings.

Draper and Duffy (2001) explored the involvement of fathers in early years provision. They experienced the inevitable issue of working fathers who were unable to attend daytime activities. Nevertheless, they found that fathers were committed to their children's development and education and felt the staff were welcoming. However, centre activities and the attitudes of other parents meant that they were reluctant to become directly involved in the centre. A Scottish Government document (2003: para 72) also highlighted that:

> fathers reported that they found family support services almost entirely staffed and attended by women, and however welcoming the service or other users, they felt very isolated. Some of the professionals we interviewed were dismissive of the men they came into contact with.

Fathers of young children face problems that are not an issue for mothers. For example, when out and about with children still needing help with toileting, it is easy for a mother to take her pre-school son into a female public convenience but it is not so acceptable for a father to take his young daughter into the men's toilets. Clearly, when setting policies, practitioners need to ensure that working in partnership extends to fathers as well as mothers. Fathers can usefully be given opportunities to discuss their concerns openly, preferably with other men facing the same issues. In the longer term, the encouragement of more men into early years occupations might help fathers to feel more included.

Another issue highlighted by Draper and Duffy (2001) is the need to address parents' own expectations. They worked at the Thomas Coram Early Excellence Centre, which, like Pen Green, encouraged parental involvement and engagement. However, they found that at another centre, a proportion of parents had very different ideas about 'what is good for children' and were resistant to involvement in the centre. Some came from cultures where nursery provision was extensive but where nursery staff expected the parents to disappear quickly at the start of the session in order to avoid 'upsetting' their children who would then, in the staff's opinion, not be able to concentrate and learn. Parental involvement appeared to them to mean they were questioning the expertise of the centre staff.

An example provided by Anning (1998) endorses the Pen Green philosophy of respecting the expertise of parents, even in the case where parents are struggling or seem vulnerable. Anning describes how the manager of an inner-city early years centre focused on communication between vulnerable mothers and their babies. She wanted to ensure that her staff gained insights into ways of working with parents and children that avoided de-skilling the parents. Jointly with a speech therapist, the manager introduced relaxed but carefully planned workshops and modelled 'motherese' through play with mothers as well as their babies. The mothers learned that their ability to parent was validated rather than being distrusted.

The case study of Alexander further highlights some of the issues for children with substitute families. For Alexander, joining the nursery setting will not be his first transition. He is used to frequent changes, has lived in a number of different families and has had some very challenging early life experiences. He might be aggressive or withdrawn, and have difficulty trusting adults and forming relationships with his peers. Although he has every right to be angry, actions that harm, distress or alienate others will need to be addressed. His early experiences will impact on his learning and any practitioners involved in his education, in the broadest sense, will have to assess his needs to ensure that his learning opportunities are maximised to the full and that early gaps in his learning are identified and addressed. Indeed, part of the role of the early years worker will be to contribute to the Common Assessment Framework (DfES, 2007c) that will assess the needs of children from a multi-professional perspective.

The other issue for early years workers is to recognise that Alexander has different families. He will probably continue to have contact with his mother and his maternal grandparents and any aunts or uncles. Even if there is no mention of a father, Alexander might have a father and a set of relatives on his father's side. He has been with his current foster carers for over a year and at such a crucial stage in his life, that is the transition from baby/toddler to schoolboy, they form an important family for him. However, early years workers may also have to relate to the new adoptive parents. Even if Alexander has not moved in with them during his time in the nursery school or Reception class, he may well be starting to form a relationship with his potential adoptive parents which he might talk about as his 'forever' parents. Recognising and respecting Alexander's divided loyalties and acknowledging the importance of each of these families in his life require skill and understanding on the part of early years workers.

There is one final point to make in relation to home–school/setting partnerships which relates to child protection. Involving parents in their children's learning is hugely beneficial. However, early years workers need to guard against putting their relationship with the parents before the child's welfare in those, albeit few, instances where children are being neglected, physically or emotionally abused or sexually exploited by their carers.

Chapter summary

Family life for children can be very diverse and understanding and valuing the child within the ecological context of their family is important for those working with them. Most early years practitioners are careful not to make assumptions about families and ensure they see each child and their circumstances as unique. However, the chapter provides an additional focus on the further factors impacting on children who do not live with their birth parents.

As the previous discussion has illustrated, family policy has taken on increased significance since 1997, though the change in government in 2010 marked a shift in policy towards a more targeted approach with a focus on early intervention and parents taking greater control over family life. Furthermore, working in partnership with parents has been integral to policy drivers aimed at developing services for children and their families. Links between the home and early years settings and schools are therefore very important to support the child's later life outcomes. This is not just because policies dictate this approach, but because children's development will be adversely affected if there is no harmony between the various spheres of a child's life, especially between the key domains of the family and the wider services with which they are engaged.

Questions for reflection and discussion

1. In what ways do you think your own family life impacts on you as a person?
2. Why do you think it is important for workers in the early years to understand the diversity of family life?
3. How do you think settings can support children who are being looked after and/or are in local authority care?

Recommended reading

Aveni, D. and Perry, A. (2011) *Working with Fathers: Practical and Effective Ways to Increase Father Participation in Early Years Settings.* Crediton: Southgate Publishers.

Guishard-Pine, J., Mccall, S. and Hamilton, L. (2007) *Understanding Looked After Children: Psychology for Foster Care.* London: Jessica Kingsley.

Potter, C. and Olley, R. (eds) (2012) *Engaging Fathers in the Early Years: A Practitioner's Guide.* London: Continuum Publishing Group.

Trodd, L. (ed.) (2013) *Transitions in the Early Years: Working with Children and Families.* London: Sage.

Whalley, M. and Arnold, C. (2013) *Working with Families in Children's Centres and Early Years Settings.* London: Hodder Education.

Recommended websites

www.education.gov.uk/childrenandyoungpeople/families
This Department for Education website link provides access to the latest policy documents related to families.

www.jrf.org.uk/
The Joseph Rowntree Foundation website is a rich source of data and research about poverty and social exclusion.

www.ons.gov.uk/ons/rel/census/2011-census/key-statistics-and-quick-statistics-for-wards-and-output-areas-in-england-and-wales/video-summary-families.html
This is a video summary on the Office for National Statistics website that makes easily accessible 2011 Census data on families and households in England and Wales.

www.parentingresearch.org.uk/publications.aspx
The website of the National Academy for Parenting Research aims to improve the way in which practitioners work with parents. This link is to a range of publications available.

Want to learn more about this chapter? Visit the companion website at **www.sagepub.co.uk/walleranddavis3e** to access podcasts from the author and child observation videos.

Part Five
Professional Working

14

Professional Work in Early Childhood

Denise Hevey

 Key chapter objectives

- To distinguish between mothering/informal caring and professional roles with young children
- To explain the historical context of training and qualifications in childcare
- To understand the difference between teachers with QTS, social pedagogues and Early Years Professionals (EYPs)/new Early Years Teachers
- To identify and debate the characteristics of professionalism

---

Who needs qualifications?

A baby's best option is to be cared for by someone who loves and responds to it. That person does not need 'qualifications'. It may be a parent or relative or a childminder in her own home or a paid nanny who is stable, kind and committed. (Libby Purves, *The Times*, 14 February 2006)

This quote from an article in *The Times* entitled 'Baby, you deserve better' highlights one of the persisting problems in relation to professionalising the childcare workforce – many people who should know better still believe that education and training are not necessary. The 'myth of motherhood' is so pervasive that it is widely assumed that all you need is love and that the experience of being a mother yourself is sufficient to equip anyone (or at least any female) to work with children. 'This ideology of mothering is so widespread, ancient and powerful that it remains, even if one's lived experience does not validate or even correspond to it' (French, 2003: 760). Yet there is substantial evidence to show that good 'mothering' does not come instinctively and can be learned, and that looking after other people's children is considerably different from caring for your own (Clarke and Clarke, 1976; Rutter, 1972; Scarr and Dunn, 1984). Further, when it comes to promoting children's development to its full potential, the level of education and training of staff really makes a difference, as was clearly demonstrated by the findings of the EPPE project:

> There was a significant relationship between the quality of a centre and improved outcomes for children. There was also a positive relationship between the qualification levels of the staff and ratings of centre quality. The higher the qualifications of the staff, particularly the manager of the centre, the more progress children made. (Sylva et al., 2003: 4)

For as long as childcare is seen exclusively as women's work for which they are genetically predisposed and instinctively pre-programmed, it will continue to be undervalued and underpaid and, worse, children will be denied the benefits of highly trained, professional staff:

> The perpetuation of low pay undermines efforts to raise the quality of the early years workforce and the services it provides. Low pay, low status and a high proportion of females in the workforce interact and reinforce one another. Market failures and gendered conceptions of care work mean that the material reward given to the early years workforce undervalues its economic and social importance. (Cooke and Lawton, 2008: 6)

The history of childcare

To understand how these myths have been created it may be useful to take an historical perspective. As Scarr and Dunn (1984: 52) point out: 'Ideas about motherhood have swung historically with the roles of women.' In pre-industrial societies, work and home were largely combined. Childcare was largely women's work but in the context of extended families who would all take their share. Babies would be taken out to the fields with their mothers, and older children put to work on simple tasks or minding younger ones as soon as they were able (Ariès, 1962). 'Mothers with many children often gave responsibility for a newborn to a daughter of four or five – the only children put to work that early. Most had no regular chores until they were about eight' (French, 2002: 21).

Industrialisation brought change because factories separated work from home and extended families were often left behind as people moved from the countryside into towns and cities. Older children (as young as 8 or 9) were put to work in the mines, mills and factories, younger children were left to fend for themselves on the streets and babies and toddlers were farmed out to wet nurses or minding schools where up to 75% died (French, 2003). Charles Dickens, a great social commentator of the nineteenth century, described the practice of 'baby farming' in his book *Our Mutual Friend*, when Mrs Boffin, seeking to adopt an orphan, visits Betty Higden:

> 'These are not his brother and sister?' said Mrs Boffin. 'Oh dear no, Ma'am. Those are minders.' 'Minders?' the secretary repeated. 'Left to be minded, Sir. I keep a minding-school. I can take only three on account of the mangle. But I love children and four pence is four pence.' (*Our Mutual Friend*, cited in Jackson and Jackson, 1981: 172)

When universal education was introduced in 1870, it wasn't so much to promote children's development and education as to keep working-class children off the streets where they might join gangs and engage in crime. 'Schools were like education factories for poor children. It kept them from being idle and a public nuisance' (Penn, 2005: 114).

By 1900, more than 50% of 3- and 4-year-olds were in school – a level that was not to be achieved again until the 1990s. However, the extent to which they benefited from education was debatable:

> A certified teacher has 60 babies to instruct many of whom are hungry, cold and dirty. They are heavy eyed with unslept sleep. What possible good is there in forcing a little child to master the names of letters and numbers at this age? (Board of Education Inspector's Report 1905, in Penn, 2005: 119)

As a result, the under-5s were excluded from state primary schools, nursery schools were founded by pioneers such as Margaret Macmillan, day nurseries were established largely by enlightened mill owners and the split between nursery education and day care became entrenched. Furthermore, organised childcare was still not available for the majority of working-class families so the gap was plugged by an army of unseen and untrained childminders.

This state of affairs persisted until the Second World War when women were needed to take over men's jobs, childcare was suddenly pronounced by the Ministry of Health as good for children as well as the war effort, and 1,450 wartime nurseries were rapidly established (Scarr and Dunn, 1984). It was during this war that the National Nurseries Examination Board was set up to guarantee basic standards of training (the NNEB Certificate) for the thousands of young, inexperienced and childless girls who were drawn in to work in the wartime nurseries.

It was not until 1948 that the first legislation was introduced to curb the worst excesses of baby farming and to regulate standards of childcare through a registration process (Nurseries and Childminders Regulation Act 1948). By this time, the number of former wartime nurseries had been slashed by half and the government of the day, needing women to give up their jobs to make way for returning soldiers, had conveniently discovered experts to reverse the previous view and declare that childcare was bad for children. Foremost among those experts was John Bowlby whose work contributed to a damning indictment of childcare by the World Health Organisation in 1951. The Report claimed that the use of day nurseries and crèches would inevitably cause 'permanent damage to the emotional health of a future generation' (cited in Rutter, 1976: 154). The history of childcare still resonated in outmoded ideas about early years education and care into the 1990s which had consequences in attitudes to provision of children's services and to training. To caricature: education is good in small doses and is provided by an elite of highly trained teachers; and childcare is bad – really what young children need is the constant presence of their mothers. If they can't have that, then the next best thing is a 'mother substitute' and, of course, you don't need training to be a mother.

National/Scottish Vocational Qualifications

In 1986, a small booklet was published, appropriately entitled *The Continuing Under Fives Muddle* (Hevey, 1986), that tried for the first time to provide an overview of the much neglected area of education and training for work with the under-5s. It concluded that the concept of the child reflected in professional training was partitioned into bits to be educated (teachers), bits to be vaccinated (health visitors) and bits to be cared for (social workers). While the highest-level and best-known qualification available to the majority of childcare workers was the Certificate of the NNEB – pitched at what we would now call level 2 in academic terms – there existed a plethora of other qualifications, some of dubious value, aimed at 16–19-year-olds in schools and colleges. However, there was little in the way of accredited training opportunities for mature students with relevant experience who made up a large section of the workforce. The report was published in the same year as the National Council for Vocational Qualifications (NCVQ) was established for England and Wales, holding out the hope of some rationalisation of qualifications (Jessup, 1991). NCVQ has since undergone a number of transformations and currently regulation of qualifications across multiple awarding bodies in England rests with Ofqual and the Standards and Testing Agency. In Scotland, the Scottish Qualifications Authority performs a similar role working with a single vocational awarding body known as SCOTVEC.

By 1989, the 'Working with Under Sevens Project' had been set up, based at the National Children's Bureau, to develop National Occupational Standards for all those working with young children and their families throughout the UK as a basis for new qualifications at levels 2 and 3 in Childcare and Education. These standards were multidisciplinary, based on articulated values and principles and centred on a core reflecting the active promotion of children's development (rather than passive notions of caretaking). They were quickly adopted by a range of awarding bodies, including SCOTVEC in Scotland. As a result, the NNEB widened its membership base and was transformed into the Council for Awards in Children's Care and Education (CACHE) and the level of its flagship qualification was raised to a level 3 diploma. BTEC/Edexcel also introduced a level 3 diploma in Nursery Nursing for 16–19-year-olds. Perhaps of most significance, the National/Scottish Vocational Qualification (N/SVQ) system of competence-based assessment in the workplace for the first time opened up access to qualifications to thousands of mature women working in playgroups and as childminders (Hevey, 1991).

The role of registration and inspection

The registration of childminders and other childcare providers under the 1948 Act was originally the responsibility of 150 individual local authorities in England which were each empowered to set their own criteria. (Similar arrangements pertained to Wales and Scotland, but with devolution, the regulatory systems have since diverged. The main differences will be identified in this chapter but the detail of variations is too complex to include.) Standards inevitably varied and in some areas registration meant just that – being added to a register. There were no set requirements for the qualification levels of staff and follow-up inspection rarely happened. In 2000, the then Department for Education and Employment issued the first set of National Standards for Under Eights Day Care and Childminding under Part X of the Children Act 1989 (DfEE, 2000), National Care Standards followed from the Scottish Executive in 2002. This included for the first time standardised qualification requirements set at level 3 for the 'registered person', with an additional requirement for a minimum of 50% of other staff to be qualified at least to level 2. These standards were to be nationally enforced through Ofsted which took over responsibility for the regulation and inspection of childcare across England in July 2001 (Baldock et al., 2007; Ofsted, 2002). Changes were also happening in Wales and Scotland where responsibility for funded nursery education stayed with the Education Inspectorates (ESTYN for Wales and HMIE for Scotland), whereas day care became the responsibility of newly created Care Commissions. (A more detailed discussion of the curriculum and regulatory frameworks for early years education and care for each of the nations of the UK is available in Clark and Waller, 2007.) Though not without its critics (Dahlberg et al., 1999), the involvement of Ofsted had a major impact on the sector. It was seen as a strong enforcer that was firmly rooted in education, and the publication of inspection reports acted as a powerful lever on private sector settings that operated in the child-care market place. These changes represented a further important step towards the professionalisation of the early years workforce.

The advent of Foundation Degrees

Meanwhile, the impact of the outcomes-based approach and the vocational relevance initiated by N/SVQs were being extended into Higher Education (HE). In England and Wales, a new type of vocational/academic hybrid award was developed, with a strong work-based component, equivalent in academic terms to the first two years of an undergraduate degree programme. This became known as a Foundation Degree and could be designed and awarded by individual Higher Education Institutions, often in collaboration with local colleges, with support from local employers. (In Scotland, the strong tradition of Higher National Diplomas continued.) The danger was that local responsiveness and diversification would result in a lack of comparability across the country. In 2001, the Sure Start Unit took a strong lead by devising a National Statement of Requirements with endorsement for Foundation Degrees in Early Years that met it. This guaranteed some standardisation of content and quality in return for additional support for students.

Early years provision had begun a rapid expansion in the late 1990s in order to meet government targets for a million extra childcare places and to provide part-time pre-school education for all 3- and 4-year-olds (Baldock et al., 2007). A Nursery Education Grant was payable to a wide range of settings deemed capable of delivering the Foundation Stage (3–5) curriculum, not just primary and nursery schools and classes. (Again, parallel but different curriculum frameworks were developed in Wales, Northern Ireland and Scotland – see Clark and Waller, 2007.) By 2002, the Foundation Degree in Early Years had provided a work-based route to a higher education qualification for the expanding number of experienced staff by then leading the curriculum in early years settings.

CASE STUDY ONE

Kerri left school at age 16 with four GCSEs and no idea what sort of career she wanted. She worked for a while as a shop assistant and then got pregnant. By the age of 21, she found herself married with two children and no prospects. The one thing that she did know was that she loved being with young children.

As soon as her eldest was school age, she got work as a nursery assistant in a community day nursery. She followed their internal training programme and gained NVQ2 in Childcare and Education within 12 months. Gaining the NVQ gave her more confidence in herself as well as in her job. She soon took on extra responsibility and the manager suggested she should do NVQ3 as Ofsted now required this of room supervisors. When the manager left a couple of years later, Kerri took over as the person in charge.

Amongst the training information that she regularly received from the local authority, she spotted an advert for a Foundation Degree in Early Years by day release and the LA adviser said she would get her fees paid. Kerri had never really thought of going to university before but she knew she was good at her job and the entrance requirements were an NVQ3 plus GCSE in English, which she had. She applied and was called for interview which made her very nervous but the tutor was reassuring.

Kerri had never written formal essays before but study skills were a core part of the early stages of the course. She soon discovered that one day per week was only the half of it. She had to put in another six to eight hours a week of background reading and work on her assignments, but thankfully these were all very relevant to her day-to-day work and helped build up her evidence for the Ofsted inspection. She found that when she sat down in the evenings at her kitchen table and opened her books, her two children often joined her to do their homework. It gave her a real kick to think that they were all studying together and that her children now took their own education much more seriously than she had ever done. After two years of hard work, Kerri emerged with a Foundation Degree of which she is justly proud and so were her partner and children when they attended the graduation ceremony and saw her in her gown.

 Reflection for case study 1

Like Kerri, some of you reading this may not have enjoyed study at school and might not have thought that higher education was for you. You might also have been nervous about returning to study after a break. Others will have planned to go to university from the outset.

- What sort of practical support, information and encouragement do you think is most helpful in encouraging good early years practitioners to take that first step towards improving their qualifications?

Children's Workforce Development Council

N/SVQs and Foundation Degrees were part of the wider national strategy for workforce development, with employer involvement through a succession of coalescing Industry Lead Bodies and National Training Organisations and later the Sector Skills

Councils such as SkillsActive for the play, sport and leisure sector. Most of the Sector Skills Councils had a UK-wide remit. Early Years and Childcare was unusual as an 'industry sector' as it was characterised by a mixed economy of provision through the maintained sector (local authority schools and nursery schools), independent schools, voluntary and community groups and private day nurseries and childminders. Within this mix there were few large-scale employers, which made achieving employer representation challenging. For several years the industry sector was represented through the Early Years National Training Organisation (EYNTO), which included national voluntary organisations (such as the Pre-school Learning Alliance and the National Childminding Association) that were membership organisations rather than employers. EYNTO covered an estimated 350,000 to 500,000 workers in England and Wales, but on its own this workforce 'footprint' was not considered big enough. So, in line with the extended responsibilities of the DfES for children's social care under the Every Child Matters agenda (DfES, 2004c), provision was made in the Children Act 2004 to establish a new arrangement for England covering most forms of children's services outside of schools and known as the Children's Workforce Development Council (CWDC). In turn, this linked up with comparable bodies for Scotland and Wales and with related Sector Skills Councils (including SkillsActive for play work and the (then) Training and Development Agency for Schools for the wider schools workforce) via the Children's Workforce Network (Owen, 2006). Arrangements have since gone through further changes and, following the abolition of both the Children's Workforce Network and the CWDC, in 2012 responsibility for the early years' workforce was merged with that for the schools' workforce under the Teaching Agency. As of April 2013, a further merger has taken place to create the National College for Teaching and Leadership.

The government's workforce strategy consultation document, published in early 2005 to coincide with the establishment of the CWDC, set out the broad policy goals in terms of a better integrated and qualified workforce with a climbing frame of recognised qualifications and greater flexibility for workers to transfer from one job to another across the whole sector (e.g. from play work to early years or to social care of children). This document included a specific proposal for establishing graduate leadership of early years and childcare settings, reflecting the findings of one of the first large-scale, longitudinal studies of Effective Provision of Pre-school Education (EPPE – Sylva et al., 2003). This research had demonstrated conclusively in a UK context that better quality provision led to better outcomes for children and that in turn the quality of provision was largely dependent on the qualification levels of staff, especially those of the setting leader/manager (see quote at the beginning of this chapter). At the time of the original research, the only graduate-level qualification relevant to early years work was QTS. However, the consultation invited comments on a broader-based type of professional model akin to the European model of a 'social pedagogue' (Boddy et al., 2007).

Pedagogues, teachers and professionals

The role of social pedagogues with graduate-level education and training is well established in Europe, particularly in Scandinavian countries such as Denmark and Sweden (Einarsdottir and Wagner, 2006). Social pedagogues have a broad-based education and are trained to engage with all aspects of human development and learning and with all age groups from the youngest children to adolescents and the elderly (Petrie et al., 2005). They work in social and residential care settings as well as in day care and in the community where they may be supporting independent living for adults with disabilities or learning difficulties. As such, their training has a particular focus on social–emotional development and life skills and, although they may understand the principles of learning to read, for example, and they may be employed in classrooms alongside teachers, they are concerned with promoting holistic development rather than with the delivery of a particular education curriculum. In Denmark, formal schooling does not begin until the age of 6 and, although some teachers are also employed in kindergarten, social pedagogues (and pedagogue assistants) dominate services for young children (Eurybase, 2006/07). The word 'pre-school' is anathema in Danish eyes because the ethos of childcare and kindergarten is to value the child's experience of the present rather than to see their present experience as a preparation for school (a human being not a 'human becoming' – Qvortrup et al., 1994).

By comparison, the tradition and philosophical approach of teacher education was and is very different from that of social pedagogy and focuses more on cognitive and specifically educational aspects of development for children aged 3–7 in the early years (or 5–11 primary phase). In England, teacher training is undertaken typically through a university-taught first degree with integrated professional training (BEd with QTS) or through a one-year intensive Professional/Post Graduate Certificate in Education following on from a first degree. Students undergo extensive placements in a variety of schools where they are visited and assessed on a regular basis. In their first year of employment, before registration is confirmed, all Newly Qualified Teachers (NQTs) have an entitlement to ongoing supervision and support. More recently, alternative models of work-based training are being provided through Schools Direct in designated schools and in 2013 the 'Teach First' scheme was extended to early years, enabling high-achieving graduates to be employed immediately as teachers in disadvantaged areas.

In 2006 the government of New Zealand decided to aim for a largely graduate workforce in early years settings based on a 'new teacher' model. This extended the age range downwards from traditional teaching and provided greater breadth in terms of children's family/community context, but the primary focus was on delivering a structured curriculum and on preparing children for formal schooling as the next stage in the education process (Ministry of Education, 2002). 'New teachers' were employed on the same terms and conditions of service as traditional teachers – a policy that was admirable in terms of equity but the additional costs incurred meant that early years suddenly became one of the major issues in the New Zealand general election of 2007.

In contrast, the policy direction for England, confirmed in the government's response to the Children's Workforce Strategy Consultation issued in 2005 (DfES, 2005a), was to propose a new form of multidisciplinary Early Years Professional Status (EYPS) with more commonality with a social pedagogue. EYPS was to be conferred on graduates with relevant knowledge and experience across the birth to 5 age range and able to: 'lead practice in the Early Years Foundation Stage (EYFS), support and mentor other practitioners and model the skills and behaviours that safeguard and promote good outcomes for children' (CWDC, 2006: 6). This was quickly followed by the publication in Scotland of the Standard for Childhood Practice (Quality Assurance Agency for Higher Education, 2007b) and the launch of new graduate-level qualifications for early years and childcare professionals capable of working across a broad age range (Scottish Social Services Council, 2008).

EYPS was initially promoted as broadly equivalent to Qualified Teacher Status for those working in the private, voluntary and independent (PVI) sector, which Ofsted had shown to be of more variable quality than the maintained sector. Early Years Professionals (EYPs) would focus exclusively on the birth to 5 age range and, in line with the community orientation of many early years settings, would adopt a more holistic approach to children's general health, wellbeing and development and to supporting families in their parenting roles as well as promoting educational outcomes. There were different pathways to achieving EYPS depending on previous qualifications and experience, but all culminated in a nationally prescribed assessment against thirty-nine National Standards with a system of external moderation to ensure national consistency. First piloted in Autumn 2006, EYPS was rolled out from 2007 and fully funded as part of the Labour Government's workforce strategy. The implementation strategy, which gave priority to flexible routes for up-skilling the existing workforce, proved highly successful in enabling some 11,000 experienced early years practitioners to qualify as EYPs by 2012. However, the initial promise of parity with teachers' status never materialised and teachers remained employed on distinct, nationally agreed terms and conditions of service which make them better paid than other workers in the early years sector. Those with Qualified Teacher Status may be deployed in later stages of primary schools (Key Stages 1 and 2), not just in nursery classes, which gives added flexibility for employment in small schools. In contrast, despite incentives provided under the Graduate Leader Fund, EYPs had no guarantee of pay and conditions commensurate with their graduate qualifications or professional responsibilities. Rather than being entitled to additional support, supervision and further development opportunities as in an NQT year, EYPs were expected to be capable of leadership from day one and had no automatic entitlement to additional support and supervision. Although EYPs could lead nursery classes in independent schools operating on the same 1:13 ratio as qualified teachers, employment in maintained schools was restricted to that of teaching assistant or instructor. Yet qualified primary teachers with little or no formal training in the birth to 5 age group were able to work in early years settings across this age range. Unfortunately, confidence in the value of EYPS itself was undermined by these differences and restrictions.

CASE STUDY TWO

After gaining a Foundation Degree, Kerri went back to university for a third year to do the EYPS Undergraduate Practitioner Pathway leading to an ordinary degree plus EYPS status – the only nationally recognised professional qualification for work with under-5s. The award was made by an eminent speaker at an evening reception in front of more than 150 representatives from early years settings across the region who cheered and clapped because they recognised the hard work that went into it. This achievement is something that Kerri would never have dreamed of at 16, and something that would not have been possible for her personally without work-based routes to qualification and without funding for her fees and cover costs for her setting. However, Kerri is concerned about the uncertainty surrounding EYPS and whether her newly accredited expertise will continue to be recognised. She is also considering her own future given that her knowledge and skills are not reflected in what she earns. She doesn't want to leave the early years sector but with her husband's hours being cut and the children getting older, can she afford to stay?

Reflection for case study 2

Do you recognise Kerri's dilemma? Working with young children all day is hard work, both physically and emotionally as well as in terms of the continual challenges to your knowledge and problem-solving skills. Yet many other simpler jobs are better paid and you can leave them behind at the end of the day.

- What aspects of the work do you find most rewarding?
- How would you encourage Kerri to stay?

Two major evaluations relating to the impact of EYPS were funded in the middle of the decade (Hadfield et al., 2012; Mathers et al., 2011) but neither had reported when a new coalition government took power in May 2010 and all previous policies concerning early years immediately came under review.

Bringing the story up to date

Unlike Scandinavian countries, where the provision of high quality early years services staffed by well-qualified professionals is considered by all to be a basic entitlement for children and families, in the UK political parties are divided about the extent to which the state should intervene in family life and childcare markets. Hence, with every change of government come major changes to policies and funding for both early years provision and related training and qualifications. After three successive terms of Labour government with a strong commitment to expanding universal early education and childcare provision, to establishing children's centres in every disadvantaged neighbourhood and to central government support for the training of early years staff up to graduate level, the newly elected Conservative–Liberal Democrat government of May 2010 had very different ideas.

The first action of the new administration was particularly symbolic in changing the name of the key government department from the Department for Children, Schools and Families (DCSF) to the Department for Education (DfE). Immediately all references to the Every Child Matters agenda started disappearing from websites and it became clear that educational targets would be what drove the new department's strategy rather than wider considerations for multi-agency working and the holistic needs of children and families.

Within the first few months the government had issued new guidance for Sure Start Children's Centres that removed the requirement to provide full day care and for children's centre staff to include two EYPs. They also quietly abandoned the target for all full day care settings to be graduate-led by an EYP by 2015, abolished the ring-fencing of Sure Start and Graduate Leader Funds given to Local Authorities (LAs) and then committed the LAs to year-on-year cuts in their total budgets. At the same time as LAs were being forced to reduce their financial support for education and training, particularly for Foundation Degrees in Early Years, the new policy on student fees forced universities to treble the fees charged. Typically, the total cost of a work-based Foundation Degree over two years was increased from £4,000 to £12,000, putting it out of the reach of many early years workers earning barely above the minimum wage.

With a commitment to reducing bureaucracy and red tape and to deregulation in order to free up markets, the government then set about a 'bonfire of the quangos'. Quango is short for Quasi Non-Governmental Organisation and is the somewhat derogatory term applied to a broad range of arm's-length regulatory and functionally specific bodies that most governments use to enact their day-to-day strategies and targets. The incoming government chose to abolish both the Children's Workforce Development Council and the Teaching Development Agency in favour of a smaller executive agency within the DfE known as the Teaching Agency (TA). It also disposed of the General Teaching Council for England (and incidentally the General Social Care Council) and allocated those regulatory responsibilities for teachers to the Teaching

Agency as well. Hence, overall responsibility for early years workforce development, standards and qualifications passed to the TA alongside that for teachers and the wider schools workforce.

At a time of financial crisis and austerity measures the new government was necessarily concerned to ensure value for money and focus on targeted rather than universal services. However, despite ideological reservations, the commitment to extending free nursery education as a universal service for all 3- and 4-year-olds to 15 hours over 33 weeks was retained, and a roll-out of free places for 2-year-olds in the most disadvantaged areas begun. Meanwhile a number of major reviews had been commissioned, each of which impinged on early years services and, to a greater or lesser extent, on workforce development and qualifications for the sector.

In 2010 Frank Field's report further endorsed the accumulating evidence that high quality, graduate-led, early years services can have a significant impact on improving the life chances of the most disadvantaged children and he advocated that 'The Foundation Years' be recognised and funded on a par with primary, secondary and tertiary phases of education. In 2011, Dame Claire Tickell's report on the Early Years Foundation Stage (EYFS) confirmed the appropriateness of the integrated, play-based curriculum with a primary focus on physical, social/emotional and communication development as well as cognitive development and suggested ways of reducing the complexity of targets and assessment. She also advocated graduate leadership of all settings delivering the EYFS, along with a minimum qualification requirement of level 3 for all early years staff in the longer term. In 2011, the final report of Graham Allen's review of Early Intervention was heavily influenced by findings from neuroscience in relation to the first 1,001 days from conception and about the importance of consistent, responsive 'parenting' and attachment. He drew on hard research evidence of 'what works' in terms of intervention in families in which children were experiencing difficulties and set this in the context of economic assessments – the Heckman curve (Heckman, 2000) – that every dollar invested during the early years would save four times that amount in necessary interventions later in life. Again, the most effective schemes were those that were led by graduate-level professionals – whether from health or education backgrounds.

In terms of early years workforce development, the most important of all of the reviews was that commissioned in 2011 under Professor Cathy Nutbrown. She was charged with evaluating the 'fitness for purpose' of qualifications at all levels in the early years sector and coming up with recommendations for the future, however her remit specifically excluded the pay and conditions of early years staff. Particular concern had been expressed about the relatively new level 3 Diploma in Work with Children and Young People introduced from 2009 to fit with the CWDC's Integrated Qualification Framework. Basically it was perceived as having gone too far in the direction of core skills and common units shared with other types of workers in children's services, to the extent that the goal of promoting mobility across the wider workforce was being achieved at the expense of sufficient knowledge and expertise to function effectively in a specialist early years context. In addition, the volume of study and practice required for the new-style diploma was too small to translate into a full-time 2-year programme for 16–18-year-olds that would support progression to higher education. There were nostalgic calls to go back to the old NNEB as a 2-year specialist programme with an exclusively early years focus and good practice skills development. However, proponents tend to forget that the Diploma of the NNEB was never recognised as 'A' level-equivalent for progression purposes. Professor Nutbrown's report, published in June 2012, made nineteen recommendations including that the level 3 Diploma should be revised, that progressive targets should be set so that by 2022 all staff in early years settings would hold a minimum of a full and relevant level 3 qualification, and that all settings in time should be graduate-led (Nutbrown, 2012b). Her recommendations were informed by evidence from the Millennium cohort study (Mathers et al., 2007) and the EPPE project (Sylva et al., 2003) but unfortunately, at the time of writing, the final report of the evaluation of the impact of Early Years Professional Status had yet to be published.

 ## Research in context

Hadfield, M., Jopling, M., Needham, N., Waller, T., Coleyshaw, L., Emira, M. and Royle, K. (2012) *Longitudinal Study of Early Years Professional Status: An Exploration of Progress, Leadership and Impact.* Final report for the DfE. CeDARE, University of Wolverhampton (Research Report RR 239c).

In 2009 the CWDC commissioned a longitudinal study of the implementation and impact of Early Years Professional Status from a team of researchers based at CeDARE in the University of Wolverhampton. The final report of this study was published in September 2012 (Hadfield et al., 2012).

Methodology: The study had two main elements. The first was a national survey of those with EYPS in 2009 (1,045 respondents) which was repeated two years later (2,051 respondents). This generated a broad picture of the views and experience of professionals in relation to their career ambitions and prospects, their abilities and confidence in relation to their role and perceived improvements in practice and outcomes for children. Secondly, case studies of thirty early years settings were undertaken using slightly modified versions of the ECERS R and E scales (also used in the Millennium Cohort study and EPPE projects) as more objective measures of practice quality. For the sub-set of six settings, a detailed observational measure of interaction with children, the Practitioner Child Interaction Tool (PCIT), was also applied.

Main findings: Overall just over 90% of those who responded to the surveys were extremely positive about the difference that gaining EYPS had made to them personally in terms of increased knowledge and skills, as well as gains in confidence and in their ability to undertake leadership of the early years curriculum and to undertake practice improvement. Just over 50% felt it had increased their career prospects. However, most felt they lacked recognition of their expertise from professionals outside the sector, although acceptance and recognition from colleagues within the sector improved over the two years between the two surveys.

Most of the twenty-five case study settings in which objective measures of process quality were completed over the two years of the study maintained high standards or showed significant improvements, including a nine that started from a poor quality baseline. This was achieved by the EYPs using very different styles of leadership and support, varying from highly directive transmission of knowledge and skills to highly participative depending on the size and needs of their particular setting and the qualification levels of other staff. The quality of interaction with children proved to be one of the more difficult aspects to improve and was only achieved well in the smaller, tight-knit settings where EYPs were able consistently to model good practice and to closely observe and mentor others.

Conclusion: The researchers concluded that 'Overall across the study Early Years Professionals had a significant impact on the quality of practice' (Hadfield et al., 2012: 86).

Evaluation: This was an important study in terms of accessing the views, perceptions and experiences of those who had undergone training and gained EYPS. It captured a national snapshot at an early point in implementation at which stage those qualifying would have been 'early adopters' and/or those who already had some higher education. By the time of the second survey the population of those with EYPS was changing and becoming more mainstream, including a higher proportion of those who had EYPS as an objective when taking their first steps into higher education. The data from the case study settings using more objective measures of impact and outcomes, though more limited in scale, reinforced the view that Early Years Professionals were having a positive impact and highlighted their skills in adapting approaches to suit the circumstances.

Though wishing to build on EYPS as an initiative, Nutbrown expressed concern that EYPS had not resulted in parity of recognition and status with that of qualified teachers. Indeed, a report by the Institute of Policy Studies had previously identified low pay, lack of progression routes other than into management and the alienating effect of previous approaches to professionalisation that had failed to recognise long-standing experience, as serious blocks to further progress (Cooke and Lawton, 2008). Hence Nutbrown recommended a new form of Early Years Teacher with QTS covering the birth to 7 age range and able to extend the child-centred ethos of early years throughout the Reception class and to support a smoother transition into more formal teaching in Key Stage 1.

In March 2013, the much delayed government response to the Nutbrown Review was finally published in *More Great Childcare* (DfE, 2013b). Proposals included radical revision of the Diploma in Work with Children and Young People to restore the central focus on early years and create a new level 3 award of Early Years Educator (EYE). A new graduate award of Early Years Teacher (0–5) was also announced. Much to Professor Nutbrown's annoyance, the government adopted only five of her nineteen recommendations in full and she issued a scathing rejoinder, entitled 'Shaking the Foundations of Quality', pointing out that:

> Government proposes that Early Years Teachers will be introduced and given a training that covers the years birth to five (not seven as I recommended) … But the early years teachers now proposed by the government will not have QTS, nor will they follow a PGCE, in other words, they will not have the same status as teachers of children over five years. … Because my recommendation on QTS was not accepted, the hoped for parity with primary and secondary school teachers will not be realised. (Nutbrown, 2013: 7)

Failing to establish full parity between the new Early Years Teachers and school teachers with QTS not only restricts the former's potential employability and access to better pay and conditions, but also runs counter to the principles being established throughout most of the rest of Europe and reflected in the recent *Children in Europe* policy paper (Van Laere et al., 2008). Further, although claiming to build on EYPS, the dominant emphasis in the new qualifications on 'school readiness', including reading, writing and arithmetic before the end of the child's fifth year, is also contrary to those principles and to the original concept of a multi-disciplinary, holistic professional occupying a 'new professional space' (Lumsden, 2012) at the intersection of teaching, social work and health visiting.

This change of emphasis from the play-based, child-centred approach towards formal teaching and learning, first evident in revision of the EYFS (DfE, 2012b), is now reflected in the standards for both the Early Years Educator and the new Early Years Teacher (National College for Teaching and Leadership, 2013). However, the school readiness agenda has itself been strongly challenged by authors who have argued that trying to force young children to do 'too much too soon' can have negative consequences for their later educational success (see House, 2011). In addition, Moss (2013) has questioned the whole basis of school readiness as a 'dominant discourse' that values children primarily for their future contribution to the 'knowledge economy', inevitably leading to downward pressure from the hierarchically structured levels of the education system. He puts forward an alternative vision of early years provision, based on ideas from Scandinavia and the pedagogical documentation tradition of Reggio Emilia, involving a community of parents, practitioners and children as active constructors of their own knowledge and experience in a social context. The role of the professional in this alternative model is not to teach but to facilitate development using their professional knowledge and expertise to document and make learning explicit and to support the child's explorations.

At the time of writing, both the proposals and draft standards for the level 3 and level 6 qualifications are still out for consultation in England but the government seems determined to pursue the further 'schoolification' of early years.

Even more controversial was the proposal in *More Great Childcare* (DfE, 2013b) to change staffing ratios for babies from 1:3 to 1:4 and for toddlers up to 1:6 in order to reduce the overall cost of childcare. This met with considerable resistance from early years organisations such as the Pre-school Learning Alliance (PSLA) as well as mothers' organisations such as Mumsnet (Helm and Roberts, 2013). Others writing from an academic perspective have argued that such a proposal is not supported by evidence and that higher ratios undermine the capacity of even well-qualified professional staff to implement what they see as best practice in individualised care and attention, particularly for the youngest children (Elfer and Page, 2013; Page and Elfer, 2013). In addition, Professor Nutbrown was moved to comment:

> The positive impact of raising the quality of level 3 qualifications to make them stronger and more appropriate for work with young children and their families from birth to five will be weakened if ratios are weakened. Reducing the number of adults available to work with very young children will dilute any positive effects on the quality of experiences children could expect to receive. (Nutbrown, 2013: 8)

Characteristics of professionalism

So, what does it mean to be a professional in early years? The term 'professional' brings with it a lot of historical baggage. Historically, the only reputable professions were the church and the law – these were the basis on which the original mediaeval universities were founded. Medicine (originally the province of quacks and barber-surgeons) took time to be recognised and it was not until the 20th century that teaching, nursing and social work became graduate professions and were brought into regulation. In recent years the beginnings of professionalisation of the early years workforce has led to an explosion of interest and books on the subject (Dalli and Urban, 2010; Miller and Cable, 2008, 2011; Miller et al., 2012; Nurse, 2007; Peeters, 2008; Reardon, 2013).

Many contributors to these texts refer to, or have attempted themselves to provide, generic definitions of a profession, most of which contain the following elements:

- a discrete body of knowledge informed by theory, research and evidence, to which the profession itself contributes
- expert levels of skills, competence and practice, often expressed as professional standards and at least in part determined by the profession itself
- graduate-level education and training and a commitment to continuing professional development (CPD)

- a code of ethics and values
- registration or membership of a professional body with a quasi-regulatory function
- personal accountability for high standards of performance built on a degree of autonomy in making professional judgements.

In relation to these factors, EYPS and the new Early Years Teacher Status are located in an intermediate position as nationally recognised statuses but without a related professional or chartered body (such as the British Psychological Society for chartered psychologists) or registration requirement (as is the case for school teachers and nurses). Whereas no one can take a qualification, such as a university degree, away once it has been awarded, a breach of professional regulations or codes of practice can lead to someone being 'struck off' and having their professional status removed, i.e. being barred from practice. This higher level of scrutiny is characteristic of all the more established professions and is put in place to protect the public from malpractice by those in positions of trust. In addition, in the case of EYPS/Early Years Teachers, standards are set externally by government agencies rather than by the profession itself and practitioner-based research is only starting to gain credibility. So, at best, we can say that early years now has a fledgling profession in England that is aspiring to recognition and regulation on a par with established professions.

No one who takes their job seriously, whatever their role or status, would wish to be described as unprofessional, so a corollary of professionalisation of the workforce must be the promotion of *professionalism* in terms of ethical, informed and reflective approaches, across all job roles and levels within the sector, not just for graduate leaders (Paige-Smith and Craft, 2008) – this being an 'inclusive' model rather than the traditional 'exclusive' approach (Nurse, 2007). However, it is difficult for even the best motivated and trained staff to function effectively if they are not supported by effective management, enabling conditions of employment and wider policies that allow them time for reflection, planning, making appropriate professional judgements and keeping themselves up to date.

In 2011 the results of a pan-European study of the competences needed for work in early childhood education and care concluded that it was not enough to focus on the competence of individuals at whatever level, but that competence needs also to be recognised as a feature of the system within which individuals work.

At the level of the individual practitioner, being and becoming 'competent' is a continuous process that comprises the capability and ability to build on a body of professional *knowledge* and *practice* and to develop and show professional *values*. Although it is important to have a 'body of knowledge' and 'practice', practitioners and teams also need *reflective competences* as they work in highly complex, unpredictable and diverse contexts. A 'competent system' requires possibilities for *all* staff to engage in joint learning and critical reflection. This includes sufficient *paid* time for these activities. A competent system includes collaborations between individuals and teams and institutions (pre-schools, schools, support services for children and families, etc.) as well as 'competent' governance at policy level (Peeters and Urban, 2011: 21).

This idea of a 'competent system' thus represents the wider systems context that enables individuals to function effectively as professionals in interaction with others: 'In practice, therefore, professionalism is not a possession of an individual, regardless of the level of their formal qualifications; it is always the result of interaction and shared meaning-making' (Dalli and Urban, 2010: 150).

The concept of a 'critical ecology' of a profession takes these ideas even further and borrows from ecological systems theory (Bronfenbrenner, 2009) with the early education and childcare professional at the centre of a series of overlapping and nested systems from micro or local, to macro or national/government policy or even global levels (Dalli and Urban, 2010; Urban, 2012; Urban et al., 2012). At the same time it envisages a bottom-up, rather than just top-down, flow of information, practice evidence and knowledge creation so that the emerging professions in early years are able to resist and challenge government policy imperatives and contribute to their own development and those of the communities they serve.

So, what does it *really* mean to be a professional in early years? For me, professionalism in early years at a personal level means recognising and accepting that:

- working with young children and their families is skilled work for which every worker at all levels needs education and training
- skills and competence alone are not enough – aspiring professionals need indepth, underpinning knowledge and understanding to know when and how to apply them
- many different roles and agencies are involved in work with children and families – aspiring professionals need to understand, respect and value their different contributions and to recognise when another's expertise is needed
- children and families vary in their social, cultural and economic backgrounds as well as in individual abilities, dispositions and health needs – aspiring professionals need to know and appreciate this broader context
- equity and equality do not mean treating every child or family the same but each according to their need
- a professional approach means taking responsibility for the quality of one's own work, reflecting on what has been done and working out what could be done better
- aspiring professionals are committed to ethical practice, act as a role model and lead and support the development of others
- aspiring professionals recognise the need to go on learning and take responsibility for keeping themselves up to date, i.e. undertaking continuing professional development (CPD).

However, on the basis of the most recent thinking about the critical ecology of a profession it seems clear that the notion of professionalism is not just to be considered at a personal level. So, maybe we need to add another couple of factors to this list:

- aspiring professionals are entitled to be supported in their development and in their day-to-day practice by a competent system of management, governance and policies that allow them the time, resources and respect to carry out their roles according to professional standards
- aspiring professionals are able to exercise their professional judgement and be confident enough to challenge policy imperatives that they judge not to be in the best interests of the children or communities they serve.

Chapter summary

This chapter has shown that attitudes to work with young children have changed over time and that a range of qualifications is now available to validate knowledge, skills and competence at different levels. Graduate leadership is increasingly seen as essential for all early years settings, much in the same way that the professionalisation of teachers, nurses or social workers has progressed from largely unqualified through certificate/diploma to graduate-level requirements. One major difference is that, in the case of the early years sector, professionalisation has started to happen much later and much faster than in comparable areas with expectations for leaders changing from level 3 to level 6 (or in Scotland CPA at level 9 in the Scottish Curriculum and Qualifications Framework) in less than a decade. Another is that pay and conditions for Early Years Professionals and the new Early Years Teachers remain poor and are not commensurate with those of other, established professions.

Professionalising the early years workforce starts with debunking the 'myth of motherhood' and moving to a situation in which everyone is expected, and expects, to take a professional approach to their work – engaging in education, training, reflective practice and personal development in ways that are appropriate to their roles (Paige-Smith and Craft, 2008). It means a 'climbing frame' of qualifications through which individuals can progress and develop or broaden their knowledge and skills (Abbott and Hevey, 2001). However, individual competence and professionalism alone are not enough to achieve the highest quality of provision. Individual professionals need to be supported by competent systems of management, governance and wider policies and given the resources and respect to operate in professional ways. They may also need to be prepared to challenge systems that are not serving the best interests of the children, families and communities they serve.

Questions for reflection and discussion

1. If, most of all, babies need carers who are sensitive and responsive to their needs, why should anyone need training?
2. What are the similarities and differences between a teacher with QTS, a social pedagogue and an Early Years Professional/new Early Years Teacher?

3. Should all those who work in early years be considered professionals? If not, why not?
4. What do you think are the most important characteristics of a profession?

Recommended reading

Dalli, C. and Urban, M. (eds) (2010) *Professionalism in Early Childhood Education and Care: International Perspectives*. London and New York: Routledge.

Einarsdottir, J. and Wagner, J.T. (eds) (2006) *Nordic Childhoods and Early Education*. Greenwich, CT: Information Age Publishing.

Van Laere, K., Lund, S.G. and Peeters, J. (2008) 'Young children and their services: developing a European approach. Principle 8: Valuing the work: a 0–6 profession and parity with school teachers'. A Children in Europe policy paper. Available at: http://www.vbjk.be/nl/node/2872

Recommended websites

www.education.gov.uk/nationalcollege
The National College for Teaching and Leadership site includes up-to-date information about developments in teaching and leadership. The professional development section details schemes available through the college.

www.ofsted.gov.uk
The Ofsted (Office for Standards in Education and Childcare for England) site includes an Early Years and Childcare section, and statistical information about inspections can be accessed from the site.

Want to learn more about this chapter? Visit the companion website at **www.sagepub.co.uk/walleranddavis3e** to access podcasts from the author and child observation videos.

15

Joined-up Thinking in Practice: An Exploration of Professional Collaboration

Eunice Lumsden

 Key chapter objectives

- To discuss policy drivers for integrated practice in children's services and the development of inter-agency collaboration
- To examine the language of collaboration
- To consider the characteristics of effective communication
- To consider the barriers to integrated working
- To discuss the place of training and the inclusion of service users

This chapter supports the reader in developing their understanding about the importance of professionals and agencies working together to achieve positive outcomes for children and families. Discussion will consider the challenges presented to multi-professional working by political ideology and shifting policy landscapes. There will be a focus on the complex language of working together, who should be involved in collaborative partnerships, the ingredients of effective communication and the reasons why working outside professional boundaries will remain problematic. It also considers the role of initial training for early years practitioners in developing the key skills required for collaborative practice and the introduction of an inter-disciplinary graduate professional in the early years.

Integrated working and policy

This section considers contemporary policy in relation to integrated working. Discussion will provide an overview of policy developments in England, their interrelationship with other policy initiatives, the impact of political change to a Conservative-led Coalition Government in 2010 and world recession on the direction of travel embedded by the former Labour Government (1997–2010).

Agencies working together is not a new concept; it has been observed in practice ever since the protection of children has been the subject of state intervention. Professionals have historically worked together to provide services and to share information (DH, 1991; HM Government, 1989; Fitzgerald and Kay, 2007; Hill et al., 2012; Loxley, 1997; Smith, 2013a). The foundations of contemporary practice stem from the Children Act 1989 and the guidance provided in *Working Together Under the Children Act* (DH, 1991). Indeed, working interprofessionally is embedded in health and social care professional training (Barrett et al., 2005) and Early Childhood Studies degrees have interdisciplinary knowledge as central to curriculum development (Quality Assurance Agency for Higher Education, 2007a). There are also numerous examples of effective inter-agency initiatives and inter-disciplinary teams working in health, education and social care settings – for example, the Child and Adolescent Mental Health Services (CAMHS), children's centres and early excellence centres, such as Pen Green in Northamptonshire (Carnwell and Buchanan, 2005; Housley, 2003; Leiba, 2003; Littlechild and Smith, 2013; Lloyd et al., 2001; Pinkerton, 2001; Thompson, 2003; Whalley, 2001).

Whilst it is important to recognise the strengths that integrated working brings, it is also important to acknowledge and continually work on the challenges. One of the common factors identified in child death inquires is the difficulty that professionals have in working together to safeguard children, especially in relation to communication and information sharing (Davies and Ward, 2012; Laming, 2003, 2009; Munro, 2011). It was the death of 8-year-old Victoria Climbié, on 25 February 2000, that required both the government and professionals to refocus on the importance of working together. She had been sent by her parents in Africa to live with her aunt in England in the belief that it would enhance her life chances. Her death provided the political driver that legally required effective integrated working. Consequently, high on the political agenda of the former Labour Government and enshrined in legislation was the importance of integrated services and, by implication, the need for improved collaboration between professionals (HM Government, 2004). In fact, integrated services were at the heart of the Every Child Matters agenda (DfES, 2004c) (see later discussion about the impact of political change on this agenda), and the Children Act 2004 provided the legal framework to facilitate the programme of change. The Act received royal assent on 15 November 2004 and purported to herald a new era of services for children and families in England and Wales. To meet the challenge, the Labour Government introduced the following change agenda to overhaul and improve service provision for children and their families:

- the improvement and integration of universal services in early years settings, schools and the health service
- more specialised help to promote opportunity, prevent problems and act early and effectively if and when problems arise
- the reconfiguration of services around the child and family in one place – for example, children's centres, extended schools and the bringing together of professions in multidisciplinary teams
- dedicated and enterprising leadership at all levels of the service, and the development of a shared sense of responsibility across agencies for safeguarding children and protecting them from harm
- listening to children, young people and their families when assessing and planning service provision, as well as in face-to-face delivery. (DfES, 2004c: 4)

In order to promote this direction of travel, a plethora of policy initiatives was introduced aimed at embedding multi-professional working and the integrated provision of universal services for children and families. The Every Child Matters agenda (DfES, 2004c) provided the policy framework for the development of, for example, the *Common Core of Skills and Knowledge for the Children's Workforce* aimed at all people working with children and families (DfES, 2005a) and workforce reform that became central to the facilitation of change. The *Integrated Qualifications Framework* (CWDC [Children's Workforce Development Council], 2008) aimed to ensure mobility for all those working in the children, young people and families sector by 2010. However, post-2010 both the *Common Core Skills* and the qualifications framework disappeared from the national policy agenda, though this was not formally communicated to the workforce. Furthermore, despite being enshrined in legislation, the language of the Every Child Matters agenda was removed from the policy language by the Coalition Government when they took office in 2010. Practitioners were charged with embracing the policy direction set out in *Supporting Families in the Foundation Years* (DfE, 2011a).

The Labour Government had proposed new ways of working together. The *Framework for the Assessment of Children in Need and their Families* (DH, 2000) aimed to enhance the multi-professional approach with children and young people most in need (Butcher, 2002; Walker, 2008). The assessment was conducted by a social worker with a focus on early intervention through collaborative practice. (This framework was replaced in March 2013 by the assessment requirements included in *Working Together to Safeguard Children* [HM Government, 2013 – see later discussion].) The early intervention policy direction was supported further by the introduction of the Common Assessment Framework (CAF) (DfES, 2004a; DfE, 2012a), a holistic assessment of children and young people aimed at identifying needs at a very early stage that can only be undertaken with the full consent of the family. Unlike the assessment of children in need, the CAF assessment can be undertaken by any professional working in universal services (Walker, 2008) and aims for families to have only one point of contact with services, hence a Lead Professional is appointed to coordinate the assessment. CAF assessments are becoming more embedded across England, though one of the challenges has been the overburdensome administrative demands. Such demands were challenged in the Munro Review of child protection (Munro, 2011) and as a result the electronic CAF was removed (DfE, 2011b).

Alongside these developments, the Labour Government introduced *Working Together to Safeguard Children* (DCSF, 2006, 2010). This documentation provided guidance for professionals involved in safeguarding children. The Coalition Government decided to revisit the documentation, launching a consultation in 2012 (Workingtogetheronline, 2012) and new guidance, *Working Together to Safeguard Children* (HM Government, 2013), was published in March 2013. This reaffirmed the importance of integrated working for everyone working with children to ensure their safety. The new guidance stressed the importance of early intervention and the need for all professionals working with children and their families to recognise their role in intervening early, the importance of 'early help assessments' (HM Government, 2013: 12) and that professionals and agencies should share information as early as possible.

Improving the storing and sharing of information between different professionals has been one of the frequent areas raised in serious case reviews (HM Government, 2013). In 2008 the Department for Children, Schools and Families published *Information Sharing: Guidance for Practitioners and Managers* (DCSF, 2008d) and the Children Act 2004 introduced *ContactPoint*. This aimed to provide a central holding point for information on all children and young people and should have been in place by 2009. However, the introduction of a database holding information on all children was controversial and the project was decommissioned in 2010 by the incoming Coalition Government (DfE, 2010). The latest *Working Together to Safeguard Children* (HM Government, 2013) reinforces the guidance about information sharing contained in *Information Sharing: Guidance for Practitioners and Managers* (DCSF, 2008d). This guidance presented 'Seven Golden Rules' for practitioners to follow:

1. Remember that the Data Protection Act is not a barrier to sharing information but provides a framework to ensure that personal information about living persons is shared appropriately.
2. Be open and honest with the person (and/or their family where appropriate) from the outset about why, what, how and with whom information will, or could, be shared, and seek their agreement, unless it is unsafe or inappropriate to do so. Seek advice if you are in any doubt, without disclosing the identity of the person where possible.
3. Share with consent where appropriate and, where possible, respect the wishes of those who do not consent to share confidential information. You may still share information without consent if, in your judgement, that lack of consent can be overridden in the public interest. You will need to base your judgement on the facts of the case.

4. Seek advice if you are in any doubt, without disclosing the identity of the person where possible.
5. Consider safety and wellbeing: base your information-sharing decisions on considerations of the safety and wellbeing of the person and others who may be affected by their actions.
6. Necessary, proportionate, relevant, accurate, timely and secure: ensure that the information you share is necessary for the purpose for which you are sharing it, is shared only with those people who need to have it, is accurate and up-to-date, is shared in a timely fashion, and is shared securely.
7. Keep a record of your decision and the reasons for it – whether it is to share information or not. If you decide to share, then record what you have shared, with whom and for what purpose. (DCSF, 2008d: 11)

One way in which the agenda of integrated services for children and families in England was translated into practice was through the rapid development of children's centres, initially through the Sure Start initiative (Glass, 1999) and then by the expansion of the programme in 2003 with the aim that every neighbourhood would have a children's centre by 2010. This development was unprecedented, and the way in which each centre was visualised varied across the country, with different counties having a variety of models. For example, some centres are attached to schools, others to private, voluntary and independent (PVI) settings, some are being purpose-built and others, often in rural areas, bring together different settings under the umbrella of a 'virtual' children's centre. Considerable research into the variable impact of children's centres is now available (Blewett et al., 2011; Messenger, 2013; National Evaluation of Sure Start, 2012; Ofsted, 2009), however, in 2010, the incoming Coalition Government removed the ring fencing of money to local authorities and this, alongside the austerity measures, has led to some local authorities closing or curtailing the services provided by children's centres (Blewett et al., 2011).

 Research in context

The National Evaluation of Sure Start (NESS) took place between 2001 and 2012. All the research reports can be found at: www.ness.bbk.ac.uk/

It is important to note here that early childhood was placed at the forefront of the integration agenda because it crosses different disciplines and agency boundaries. Furthermore, the strong focus on raising standards in the early years meant that early years practitioners would be instrumental in developing the workforce that would be responsible for implementing the evolving policy into practice. The need to have more 'joined-up' working and services was taken a step further by the Childcare Act 2006

(DfES, 2006c). This saw the removal of any distinction between education and care for the youngest children, the introduction of the Early Years Foundation Stage (DCSF, 2008a; DfES, 2007a), which had partnership working as a central theme, and introduced Early Years Professional Status, which had both collaboration and contributing to multi-professional teams included in the initial and revised standards (CWDC, 2006; DfE, 2012b; Teaching Agency, 2012). The Early Years Professional marked an important change in the professional landscape; for the first time government formally involved itself in imposing a new profession on the workforce; furthermore the Early Years Professional (EYP) was an integrated not segregated professional working at the intersection of health, social care and education (Lumsden, 2012). However, government involvement also made Early Years Professionals susceptible to political change. The incoming Coalition Government in 2010 initially maintained the development of Early Years Professional Status, however, despite the huge financial investment in the development of this new integrated graduate profession, the political drivers for school readiness, less expensive childcare and arguably making their own political mark, led to a shift in policy (DfE, 2013b). The Early Years Professional was to be renamed the Early Years Teacher, working with young children from birth to 5, and the Early Years Professional Status standards were to be revised to bring them more in line with teaching standards (DfE, 2013b) (see Chapter 14).

It is important to highlight for the reader at this point that for students and practitioners in the early years, the period 1997–2010 was an exciting and challenging time, as government policy that involved 'joined-up thinking' and collaborative working became integral for improved outcomes for all children. Organisations working with children had a duty to work in partnership and there was an integrated framework for inspection to ensure that policy became reality (DfES, 2004c). Whilst the Coalition Government affirmed the importance of the earliest years, early intervention and integrated working, changes in policy direction have reinforced the challenges facing the early years as policy has become more enmeshed with politics. Consequently, the early years workforce needs to critically engage with policy to ensure that the holistic needs of the youngest children remain centre stage.

The language of collaboration

Regardless of experience, you will find that the language of collaboration is varied, and there is not necessarily a common understanding of what the different terms encompass and who is included in the collaboration process. In practice, the terms partnership, collaboration, inter-agency work, working together and, more recently, integrated working are often used interchangeably and different professionals can have different interpretations of what they mean. Therefore, for the purposes of this chapter, collaboration will be used as an umbrella term embracing the different terminology in common usage.

Over the past thirty years, these terms have evolved to become integral to discussions about how professionals can develop working patterns that meet the complex needs of adults and children, and 1973 saw the government specifically addressing collaboration (DHSS, 1973). Since then, there have been a series of government publications and legislation embracing issues of partnership between professionals and the involvement of service users (DCSF, 2007a; DfES, 2004c; DH, 1991, 2000; Loxley, 1997; Sanders, 2004). Initially, the focus was on health and social care, with child protection procedures being pivotal in the development of collaborative working in relation to children and their families (Calder and Hackett, 2003; DH, 1991; Sanders, 2004). Education has also increasingly become an active player and collaboration between health, social care and education was central to the Labour Government's (1997–2010) policy initiative, Every Child Matters. The message at that time was very clear: professionals and those using the services provided need to be working together more effectively. This message is still the one purported by the Coalition Government.

While this is the current situation, there remains a lack of clarity over what is meant by the terms. Lloyd et al. (2001) provided some useful definitions to assist practitioners in their understanding of the language of working together, that have continued relevance (see Table 15.1). Two terms missing from their original list are 'partnership', though this term is in frequent use in health, social care and educational settings, and 'integrated working'.

Table 15.1   Terminology

Inter-agency working	More than one agency working together in a planned and informal way
Joined-up	Deliberate and coordinated planning and working which takes account of different policies and varying agency practices and values. This can refer to thinking or to practice or policy development
Joint working	Professionals from more than one agency working directly together on a project – for example, teachers and social work staff offering joint group work. School-based inter-agency meetings may involve joint planning which reflects joined-up thinking
Multi-agency working	More than one agency working with a young person, with a family or on a project (but not necessarily jointly). It may be concurrent, sometimes as a result of joint planning or it may be sequential
Single-agency working	Where only one agency is involved but it may still be the consequence of inter-agency decision making and therefore may be part of a joined-up plan
Multi-professional working	The working together of staff with different professional backgrounds and training
Inter-agency communication	Information sharing between agencies – formal or informal, written or oral
Partnership	Professionals working together (see characteristics identified by Harrison et al., 2003)
Integrated working	Where everyone supporting children and young people works together effectively to put the child at the centre, meet their needs and improve their lives. (CWDC, 2008)

Source: Lloyd et al. (2001)

The literature on partnership was reviewed by Harrison et al. (2003: 4), who found 'that there is no single, agreed definition and that sometimes the term is used inter-changeably with the term collaboration'. They suggest that a more helpful approach is to consider the characteristics of partnerships that are successful:

- involve more than two agencies or groups, sometimes from more than one sector (private, public, voluntary), and include the key stakeholders – that is, those who are primarily affected by the problem and/or have a responsibility for developing solutions
- have common aims, acknowledge the existence of a common problem and have a shared vision of what the outcome should be
- have an agreed plan of action or strategy to address the problem concerned
- acknowledge and respect the contribution that each of the agencies can bring to the partnership
- are flexible in that they seek to accommodate the different values and cultures of participating organisations
- consult with other relevant parties that are not in the partnership
- exchange information and have agreed communication systems
- have agreed decision-making structures
- share resources and skills
- involve the taking of risks
- establish agreed roles and responsibilities
- establish systems of communication between partners and other relevant agencies. (Harrison et al., 2003: 4)

In relation to integrated working, current government guidelines suggest the key elements of integrated working are concerned with professionals working together to intervene early, undertake assessments, record and share information, have a Lead Professional who coordinates the work plan and a Team Around the Child which is working with the child and family (DfE, 2012c).

A further factor in the language of working together is the impact of whether inter, multi or trans are used. Sanders (2004) stated: 'These word parts have different meanings. "Inter" means between, implying the link between the two entities; "multi" means many, and "trans" means across' (Sanders, 2004: 180). He goes on to argue that while multi and inter are most frequently used, multi is preferred because it implies more than two in relation to collaboration. Loxley (1997) draws attention to the fact that the only explicit attempt at identifying what is meant by the term was by the Joint Working Group on collaboration between Family Practitioners committees and District Health Authorities (DHSS, 1984). She discusses their view of collaboration as 'mutual understanding and respect for each other's role and responsibility; identifi-cation of areas of common interest and concern; the establishment of common goals, policies and programmes' (Loxley, 1997: 20). Banks (2004) and Whittington (2003) provide useful discussion about this area and consider a continuum of working together. Banks (2004) introduces the different levels of working together: strategic and team/operational. Whittington (2003: 24) adds a further level of intermediate partnership and collaboration. For him, the continuum ranges from separate services that 'collaborate on an ad hoc basis' to care trusts that exemplify organised integrated services.

Banks (2004) also cites the work of Carrier and Kendall (1995) in relation to the useful distinction between multi-professional and inter-professional working. She states: 'multi-professional working, where the traditional forms and divisions of professional knowledge and authority are retained … inter-professional, where there is a willingness to share and give up exclusive claims to specialist knowledge if the needs of service users can be better met by members of other professional groups' (Banks, 2004: 127). As she goes on to argue, many teams are somewhere between these two and the main aim of this approach is a belief in the idea that the service user will receive a better service. While this may be the case, this approach to the delivery of services is not without difficulties, as professionals with different values, cultures, ideologies and professional identities come together (Banks, 2004; Calder and Hackett, 2003; Loxley, 1997). Indeed, research into this area (Banks, 2004: 134) has highlighted that some of the difficulties in professional working together 'are around the incompatibility of the managerial structures, procedures and systems operating in the parent agencies employing the practitioners'. Calder and Hackett (2003: 10) add to this debate and include factors such as different 'background and training', 'varied attitudes to family life', 'stereotypes and prejudices' and 'communication'. The debate becomes more complex when we consider the balance of power between the professionals involved in the collaboration and how this impacts on services being provided. For example, how can different professionals come together and work effectively on the same case when there is a lack of parity in pay scales, work conditions and context? However, there is another layer and one that is arguably the most important in service delivery – that is the diverse needs of the community for whom the services are provided (Leiba and Weinstein, 2003; Loxley, 1997).

Working together therefore is a complex area, bringing together not only the needs, experience and professional identities of those involved but also the complex needs of those requiring services. As Loxley (1997: 49) states:

> If collaboration is to be a reality and not a myth, these differences need to be identified and acknowledged at all levels, so that they may be honestly faced and taken into account when assessing whether collaboration is feasible, and/or the most effective or efficient response.

Accepting that there is no definition that encapsulates all the complexities of collaboration indicates that there may be a case to simplify language associated with working together in order to provide a shared foundation on which to build our knowledge and working practice. Those working with children and their families and those engaging in early childhood studies not only need to have a shared understanding about the different terminology in use (see Table 15.1), but also an understanding of the ingredients of effective collaboration, the range and depth of working collaboratively and the impact of the power imbalances between professional groups and professionals and their clients. With increased government intervention in the professions (Lumsden, 2012) the impact of political ideology also needs to be addressed in relation to all of these areas.

Collaboration in practice

Another area to consider is who is involved in the collaboration. Is it just the professionals, in other words, those who perform the services, or does it include the recipients of their services, namely children and their families? The needs of those who use the services of health, education and social care are so varied that it is essential that they are active participants in the process so that professionals do not make assumptions about what they think their needs are (Leiba and Weinstein, 2003).

Indeed, working in collaboration with service users is recognised by policy makers and is enshrined in legislation such as the Children Act 1989 and 2004 and the United Nations Convention on the Rights of the Child 1989. Therefore, working together should be for the benefit of both the service providers and those using the services. However, despite the area of service-user participation growing in importance, there is still limited research into the impact of service-user involvement or research that has been conducted is not easily accessible (Beresford, 2007, 2013; Leiba and Weinstein, 2003; Shaw, 2000). There is a 'continuing concern about the quality of involvement, tokenism and lack of resources' (Leiba and Weinstein, 2003: 69). This situation must raise questions about how we can ensure a meaningful partnership between providers and 'consumers'. In relation to children and their families, if they are to be seen as active participants in the process with rights to receive services and input in their development, professionals need to recognise and actively value their involvement. The question that needs to be continually asked is: how can we involve the service user in a meaningful way?

One way might be to assume that service users, clients or patients are active participants (Loxley, 1997). Indeed, valuing the service users' understanding and perception of their own needs has been the subject of much debate (Beresford, 2013; Dominelli, 2002; Leiba and Weinstein, 2003). For Leiba and Weinstein, 'service users are the most important participants in the collaborative process' (2003: 63). They view them as the 'experts' on their individual situations who have an opinion to give. They argue that 'one way of preventing carers from feeling marginalised and to make good use of the special understanding they have of the situation is to engage them fully' (2003: 66). However, they highlight that some professionals can feel 'threatened' by this process and some service users 'uncomfortable'. They state that 'these anxieties must be recognised and opportunities provided to talk them through, if they are not to become barriers to change' (2003: 66). Concern about involving service users is also echoed by Thorpe (2004: 22), who discusses the fact that while service-user involvement is seen as positive, there are concerns 'that many policymakers and practitioners are only paying lip-service to the idea of user-driven services'. However:

> If we listen carefully to service users and carers ... one of the things they tell us is that professionals should collaborate more effectively with each other. Absence of inter-professional collaboration causes breakdown in communication, delays in service delivery and general confusion and frustration for service users. (Leiba and Weinstein, 2003: 69)

Beresford (2013: 193) adds further to the debate. In his discussions about service users' views of social work he suggests that the social model used in social work is valued. The interest in service users' 'broader social and situational issues' is welcomed but they often see this lacking in their encounters with other professionals. He argues for professions to reframe their views on service users.

While service users' involvement in the collaborative process is to be valued, the power balance between them and the professionals also needs to be recognised, especially when issues of care and control are at the forefront of working together. As Pinkerton (2001: 251) points out, 'Child Protection work brings into particular sharp relief the difficulties there can be for partnership', a situation that Beresford (2013) and Smith (2013a) concur with. However, this power imbalance is not just evident in social work but in education and health as well. One way that the power imbalance is also highlighted is in relation to the name given to the people with whom professionals work. Indeed, in this chapter, the terms 'client' and 'service user' are interchanged, however they can also be patients or even consumers of our services. An additional complication is the age of the person who is this 'consumer'. If it is a child, at what age can they be involved in the partnership process for the dialogue to be meaningful? It is only too easy to dismiss a child as being 'too young' but even the youngest children can make their voice heard. Therefore, is it the professional with all their knowledge, understanding and training that knows best or the child and/or family being worked with? It is this area of knowledge that adds another area of complication to the collaborative process for both professionals and clients as it can lead to a power imbalance. Different members of the process may not value the role they have to play because they do not have the same qualifications or, indeed, social standing as other members of the partnership.

It is also important to recognise that collaboration needs effective communication. For Thompson (2003: 67), 'effective communication is not simply a matter of personal skills and individual efforts. Rather, it also depends on such important things as organisational systems, cultures and structures.' The specific nature of professional language adds a further complicating factor – different professions have their own language and set of abbreviations which can act as a barrier to communication; the same terminology can mean different things. For example, working in partnership in a school setting may refer to working effectively with parents and, in a social care setting, to working with other agencies and/or clients (Braye, 2000). Consequently, if professionals struggle with communication, how can service users hope to begin to engage in the process of collaboration?

There are, however, examples of positive strategies being developed to facilitate overcoming such language barriers. For example, the Sheffield Care Trust has developed a glossary of jargon for service users participating in council meetings (Thorpe, 2004). Another example is provided by the National Forum of People with Learning Difficulties, where a 'traffic light' card system is used. Everyone at the meeting has three cards: one used to stop people talking over them, one when they do not understand what is being discussed and another when they agree with what is being said (Leeson and Griffiths, 2004). While this method relates to people with learning difficulties, it is a method that could be used with children and adults alike. Indeed, there are many occasions when this system would have benefited my understanding of a multi-professional meeting.

If we are to move forward in relation to participation and actively involving children in the collaborative process, professionals need to reflect on their language and think about different strategies that can be employed to break down the barriers (Thomas, 2000). Indeed, actively including children in this process of simplifying language can bring clarity to the fog in which adults sometimes find themselves. Mission statements are an example here, as many organisations invest a considerable amount of time trying to find ways to summarise their existence. As an observer of a child participation council, it was fascinating to see how one of the young participants reduced a two-paragraph mission statement to four words that encapsulated the meaning of the message succinctly. He went on to state that he could not understand why adults had to use so many words.

Thus, it is not surprising that the language of collaboration and how this collaboration translates into practice is challenging and complex. The growing literature in this area (Draper and Duffy, 2001; Harrison et al., 2003; Leeson and Griffiths, 2004; Littlechild and Smith, 2013; Loxley, 1997; Weinstein et al., 2003) raises issues around definition, interpretation and the interchangeable nature of the language used and who should be involved in the process. Despite the complexities in this area, it is clear that collaboration has been integral to different governments' policies for several decades.

Finally, it is important to raise the impact of policy changes since 2010, which give rise to an important question: if service users' perspectives are used to shape policy, should they be consulted when the policy they have informed is changed? An example here is the Every Child Matters agenda. At the time this was introduced the fact that children had been involved in developing the five outcomes was applauded but were they consulted when the language of this agenda was removed from policy in 2010?

Effective collaboration

If the agenda of change for children is to move forward positively, effective collaboration at all levels must be the goal to strive for. As previously indicated, while working together is not new, the challenge is to explore what the ingredients are that have worked well and use these as the basis for moving forward. There also needs to be acceptance that working in partnership with children and their families is constructive and that the gains from the process outweigh the difficulties that can occur. However, it is also important that this approach should not be used to mask the reasons why difficulties occur. Loxley (1997: 70–1) helpfully reminds us that:

> The appeal of teamwork, just as the appeal of collaboration, enables policy makers to avoid the crucial issues of irreconcilable structures and limited resources by laying on practitioners the responsibility of mitigating their effects, and practitioners can accept it without fully understanding or recognising that it contains unresolved contradictions. The myth serves to disguise the reality with an appealing ideology.

However, if we are to progress, these issues need acknowledging so that participants in the process do not become resentful, resulting in inaction by those involved. Rather, issues need to be aired openly and dealt with, thus freeing up participants to focus on the specific task. This level of openness and honesty may not only help to improve the interpersonal relationships within the collaboration but enable a greater understanding of the positioning of those involved. It is in developing this understanding that degrees in early childhood can really make a difference, as they can provide an arena in which students are able to develop their knowledge and understanding of the different professional roles in relation to children and their families. Students are also afforded the opportunity to develop key skills to take with them into the workplace, as the final section of this chapter will illustrate.

So how can we work towards effective collaboration? In order for the collaborative process to be successful, there needs to be some common understanding between the participants. There also needs to be 'respect, reciprocity, realism and risk-taking' (Harrison et al., 2003: 26). Harrison et al. also usefully suggest that the framework of 'SMART' (specific, measurable, achievable, relevant, timed) has a positive role to play. This allows purpose to be placed on the agenda by the participants at the start – they are then able to consider how they will work together and how this can be measured. Harrison et al. (2003: 15) also liken the start of partnership to 'the first date', and they provide a useful list of issues that participants need to consider (see Table 15.2).

Leeson and Griffiths (2004: 140) provide further insights into the ingredients for successful collaboration, including the importance of 'strengthening the emotional content of the relationship and interactions both inside and outside the working environments'. They also highlight management support, training and the importance of 'breaking down the power struggles among professionals'. These factors are reinforced by Smith (2013b) who concurs with the view I put forward in the previous two editions of

Table 15.2   The first date

Before the meeting	At the meeting	After the meeting
Researching	Clarifying purpose	Finding the decision-makers
Sharing the idea	Recognising mutual advantage	Gaining internal commitment
Planning an agenda	Identifying potential barriers	Drafting an agreement
Exploring the pros and cons	Anticipating how to get over difficulties	Deciding on a funding formula
Cost–benefit analysis	Drafting a proposal	Keeping an open mind

Source: Harrison et al., 2003: 15

this chapter – that there needs to be a shared vision. In the early years this is in relation to a holistic approach to the child where professionals value and understand each other's positioning and relationship with the child and their family. Furthermore, it is important that the role of the 'consumers' of our services – whether children or adults – is valued and integrated into the collaboration process.

The role of training in the early years

At the time of writing the first and second editions of this chapter, there was also a growing recognition of the importance of developing professionals who understand integrated children's services (Higher Education Academy, 2008). It was argued that in the following ten years there could be workforce reforms and a growth of interest in the early years that could mean courses in the early years becoming more established in universities. Furthermore, they could have a pivotal role to play in developing future professionals who have inter-disciplinary knowledge and who understand the importance of working together to improve outcomes for children and their families. This has indeed become a reality with the expansion of Early Childhood Studies degrees, the Early Years Foundation degrees and the introduction of a graduate professional in the early years. Arguably, for the first time it can now be stated that there is a distinct early years profession, albeit one that is controlled at present by government policy rather than the profession itself.

Furthermore, the growth in degrees in the early years has provided a real opportunity for students to engage in the widest debates about the early years from a health, social care and educational perspective. Students have been afforded the opportunity of observing professionals from different working and organisational cultures, with different professional bodies of knowledge, different roles, qualifications and salary scales, coming together to model good multi-professional practice. They also have the opportunity to explore theoretical perspectives and how these are translated into practice. The first case study provides an example of how one role-play assessment item has the potential to develop knowledge and understanding and shift practice that remains with the student into their professional lives.

C A S E   S T U D Y   O N E

One of the issues frequently raised in inquiries into child deaths is the breakdown of communication between the professionals involved. Therefore, those training 'Tomorrow's Professionals' need to ensure that they have a sound knowledge base about the importance of collaborative practice as students and also gain a more tacit understanding to support their future practice. An example of an assessment item that supports this is a Child Protection Conference role play that is embedded in both the Early Childhood Studies degree and the Early Years Foundation degree at the University of Northampton (Higher Education Academy, 2008).

As part of their safeguarding module, students are given the details of a complex safeguarding case, and allocated a role which they have to research. Where possible they have to meet with a professional of the role in practice. They then participate in the conference chaired by a professional conference chair. Students have to reflect on their individual and group learning, the challenges faced throughout the process and the experience of discussing complex issues with the birth family present.

Research into the student experience has found that whilst they find the role play challenging, it changes their perceptions of families in child protection cases and increases their understanding of, and commitment to, multi-professional working. They have greater understanding of the complexities of the decision-making process and the different perspectives of professionals involved. Former students indicate that the learning is sustained into practice and has proven to be invaluable (Lumsden, 2006). This feedback is received year on year.

Reflection for case study 1

Students express a mixture of feelings before and after participating in the conference. Having read the case study, and reflected on the contents of this chapter, how do you think this experience would:

1. Support your understanding of the Working Together to Safeguard Children policy and how it operates in practice?
2. Develop your knowledge about different professional roles in work with children and families?
3. Enable you to understand the benefits and challenges of collaborative working?
4. Explore issues of working collaboratively with service users?

This provides an excellent foundation from which students can build their future careers in children's services. Moreover, it is especially pertinent for those who move forward to undertake the inter-disciplinary professional role in the early years. Arguably these professionals need to recognise that:

> All children have the right to experience a professionalised early years workforce that supports, challenges and inspires those working within it, works in partnership with others and draws on inter-disciplinary knowledge to address inequality and promote all aspects of children's care, health, development and learning. (Lumsden, 2013)

In order to achieve this, the professional needs a range of capabilities. Case Study 2 provides a list of the capabilities that emerged from research into the development of a new graduate professional identity in the early years.

CASE STUDY TWO

Training pathways to achieve Early Years Professional Status began in January 2007. The introduction of an inter-disciplinary graduate professional was an important step forward in the workforce agenda in the early years. It was also the first time that government had involved itself in actually establishing a profession, and, as previous discussion has illustrated, this has made the profession volatile to political change. Doctoral research conducted between 2006 and 2010 into the development of this new integrated professional found that a new professional space with flexible borders was developing at the intersection of health, social care and education, occupied by those with Early Years Professional Status (Lumsden, 2012). One of the areas to emerge from the research was a range of capabilities needed by an inter-disciplinary professional (Table 15.3). These capabilities are not static, rather they present a framework for continuing professional development to support the professional in developing from novice to expert in the early years field.

Table 15.3   **Professional capabilites of an inter-disciplinary graduate professional**

Roles	Knowledge and understanding	Attributes and skills
Advocate for young children	Anti-discriminatory practice	Diplomacy
Advocate for early years	Continuing professional development	Empathy
Change agent		High-level interpersonal skills
Family worker	Early Childhood Education and Care (ECEC)	Highly organised

(Continued)

(Continued)

Roles	Knowledge and understanding	Attributes and skills
Leader	Holistic understanding of the child, their position within the family and community	Leadership
Manager		Principles and values
Parent partner		Reflection
Practice developer	Integrated working	Reflexivity
Role model	Multi-professional working	Supportive
Staff trainer		Team worker
Working with others	Leadership	**Resilience factors**
Colleagues	Management	Adaptable
Agencies	Policy	Committed
Professionals	Transitions	Flexible
Children	Research knowledge	Manages challenge – low status, pay and conditions, lack of understanding of role
Families	Theoretical perspectives	
Safeguarding		Passionate
Special needs		Patient
		Tolerant
		Has a work ethos

Source: Lumsden, 2012

Reflection for case study 2

- What do you think about these capabilities?
- How do you think each area contributes to a being an inter-disciplinary professional?
- Would you add or remove any of the capabilities?

Think about your own professional development:

- How do your current knowledge, skill base and attributes fit with the capabilities?
- How do you think this framework supports your continuing professional development?

Chapter summary

As this chapter has illustrated, working together is not a new concept and there are numerous examples of professionals productively working together. However, the language of collaboration is complex, both in relation to terminology and the players in the process. What is clear is the importance of a shared vision and a willingness to move beyond the complexities to enable an understanding of the aim of the collaboration, how it is going to be achieved and how those involved will know the aim has been met. It is also important that the workforce is resilient, recognises that policy will never remain static and that embedding policy can be compromised by political imperative. For example, the Every Child Matters agenda should have led to improved working partnerships; however the removal of this policy language from the vocabulary of the Coalition Government, alongside changes to early years policy and new guidelines for Working Together to Safeguard Children, highlights the challenges of improving collaborative practice in a shifting policy landscape.

Part of this shifting policy landscape is the new inter-disciplinary graduate professional who should be able to navigate across professional boundaries. How the integrity of this new professional will be maintained with the current policy shift towards revised professional standards more in line with teaching standards is yet to be seen. Arguably, the current shift in policy may be a missed opportunity in really embedding an inter-disciplinary professional in England, who has the professional capabilities required to navigate some of the challenges of collaborative working and improve outcomes for children.

It is also essential that professionals embrace the importance of moving outside the comfort zone of their own professional boundaries. They need to value working in partnership with others, including children and families, to develop a shared meaning for engagement with each other that leads to improved outcomes. One of the most important ways that this process can be facilitated is through continually reviewing and improving the training provided. There needs to be a range of training initiatives that address the needs of a diverse workforce in education, health and social care. Degrees in early childhood provide one pathway; students develop knowledge and understanding about the different roles professionals play in a child's life and the importance of understanding and critiquing policy. Students then have the opportunity to transfer this shared knowledge and understanding into careers in education, health, social care or as a graduate professional specialising in the early years. They then need to develop this knowledge and understanding as they move from novice to expert in their chosen professional pathway.

Finally, the importance of allowing policy to fully embed needs to be recognised by successive governments. The process of political change brings with it the desire to undo the direction of the previous administration. However, this process can lead to the needs of children and families being side-lined and the learning from inquiries into child deaths being forgotten. The importance of professionals effectively working together and having policies that support joined-up thinking in practice in the long term, not just for the term of a government, should be the legacy left by Victoria Climbié.

Questions for reflection and discussion

1. What do you think are the barriers to integrated working?
2. How do you think that training can promote positive collaborative practice?
3. Can children and their carers ever be equal partners in the collaborative process?

Recommended reading

Anning, A., Cottrell, D., Frost, N., Green, J. and Robertson, M. (2006) *Developing Multiprofessional Teamwork for Integrated Children's Services.* Maidenhead: Open University Press.

Davies, J.M. and Smith, M. (2012) *Working in Multi-professional Contexts: A Practical Guide for Professionals in Children's Services.* London: Sage.

Harrison, R., Murphy, M., Taylor, A. and Thompson, N. (2003) *Partnership Made Painless: A Joined Up Guide to Working Together.* Dorset: Russell House.

Hill, M., Head, G., Lockyer, A., Reid, B. and Taylor, R. (eds) (2012) *Children's Services: Working Together.* Harlow: Pearson Education.

Littlechild, B. and Smith, R. (2013) *A Handbook for Interprofessional Practice in the Human Services: Learning to Work Together.* Harlow: Pearson Education.

Recommended websites

www.caipe.org.uk
The website for the Centre for Advancement of Interprofessional Education

www.ness.bbk.ac.uk/
The website for the National Evaluation of Sure Start (NESS)

www.workingtogetheronline.co.uk/resources.html
Workingtogetheronline is the access point for publications and resources linked to Working Together to Safeguard Children

Want to learn more about this chapter? Visit the companion website at **www.sagepub.co.uk/walleranddavis3e** to access podcasts from the author and child observation videos.

16

Leadership and Change Management in Early Childhood

Geraldine Davis

 Key chapter objectives

- To consider how leadership can be effective in improving outcomes for children and families
- To identify the relevance for early childhood of more traditional theories of leadership and management of change
- To consider the effect of graduate status on leadership in early childhood

Introduction

Whether it is the research evidence, the policy literature or general commentary in the professional press, one thing is clear: leadership is very important in early childhood. This chapter reviews the different aspects of leadership that are evident in the literature and in practice in early childhood settings. It includes examples taken directly from practice.

Leadership impacts on many aspects of early childhood including: improving outcomes for children and families; developing a community of practice; developing staff and oneself; working with parents and carers; and developing the quality of education and care in early childhood education settings. The role of the leader in early childhood is not as someone who stands alone at the front, but of someone who is an enabler of others, working with their team to develop leadership in individual team members, so that the whole team moves forward. So even if you do not consider yourself to be in a leadership role, there may well be opportunities for you to use leadership in your practice. If you have not yet had experience of working in a setting, use this chapter to consider the many facets of leadership which the early years leader works with.

This chapter examines aspects of leadership practice that enable positive development of children and families. Leadership theory is important, but much of the traditional theory is only indirectly applicable to early years. Using work with graduate leaders, this chapter considers the value of using theory in leading change in settings. Finally, the chapter examines the impact the graduate leader in early childhood is having, considering the impact on children, but also on communities of practice and on personal development.

The large body of work on reflective practice, which has been adopted across the health and education professional sector, is of real significance for developing as a leader in early childhood education. The new chapter added for this edition (Chapter 18) demonstrates the importance of reflection in developing practice; some aspects of reflective practice are also included here in relation to leadership and change management.

The link between leadership and improved outcomes for children

The emerging views and research into leadership and management in early childhood in the UK in the early 21st century were summarised effectively by Muijs et al. (2004), Siraj-Blatchford and Manni (2006) and later by Dunlop (2008). These reviews demonstrated both increased activity in the development of leaders in early childhood but also concern that there was a lack of authoritative research to act as an evidence base on which to develop new leaders. Sylva et al. (2004), in the Effective Provision of Preschool Education project (EPPE), identified that children progressed better if there was strong leadership in a setting. In their study of early years leadership, Siraj-Blatchford and Manni (2006) identified the collaborative and collective nature of effective leadership in these settings, something which is discussed in more detail below.

In 2011, Whalley drew together some of the key principles of leading and managing in early childhood, and emphasised that when leading change, the focus must be on improving outcomes for children. All members of the early childhood workforce have opportunities to maximise outcomes for children, and so it could be argued that all have a role to play in leadership of practice. Emphasising the 'how' of leadership and management, Whalley (2011) describes the enormous importance of working collaboratively, and encourages this collaboration to be not only with colleagues but also with parents and carers and with the multi-professional team. Case Study 1 provides an example from practice of this collaborative working in a nursery setting. The importance of reflective practice, not just by the leader but also by the team of early childhood workers, is strongly emphasised. Effective reflective practice is seen to include reflection on practice, looking backwards so that previous experiences can inform future practice, but also reflecting in practice, looking at the here and now, so that practice is thoughtful and considered during the doing of that practice. It can be argued that careful planning for early years is a form of reflection for practice, thinking ahead to plan for the best outcomes.

CASE STUDY ONE

'Do you enjoy working here?'

[Thanks to Sandra Davison for providing this case study.]

The above question was directed at one of my staff by a prospective parent viewing our nursery. It was posed outside of my earshot, presumably with the hope of an honest answer. The answer must have satisfied this mother, as she immediately enrolled her child. When the staff member told me of this exchange, I thought what an insightful question it was and resolved to discover why she thought it was important to ask. This mother had worked with children in her capacity as a Forest School leader and had a good understanding of child development and working within a staff team. She said she thought that if the staff were happy and fulfilled in their jobs, this would be reflected in their work with the children and parents, and would in turn translate into happy, achieving children. My philosophy exactly!

As a nursery manager, the wellbeing of the team has always been important to me – to ensure the staff are valued and cared for so that they can do their jobs to the best of their abilities. The challenge is to build a cohesive, successful team made up of very different individuals. The key, I think, is to know every team member very well. This way you can anticipate their probable reactions to events and prepare for them in advance. Before introducing anything new, I try to put myself in their shoes to see how they may feel about it and how they may need to be prepared. It is important to know each staff member's strengths as well as their areas for development. I try to use their strengths to build their self-esteem and give them every support necessary to improve areas where they lack confidence. In my own mind, I aim to think positively, having their strengths at the forefront, and let them know what I think they are. It is good to take every opportunity to genuinely praise a job well done and to often remind staff of the asset they are to the team.

(Continued)

(Continued)

Any positive comments from parents are passed on and everyone's part played in achieving this is acknowledged. Communication is very important. People always become upset and feel they have not been considered when they are not told about something that affects them. A manager needs to always think very carefully about who needs to be told about something.

When problems do occur, as inevitably they will, they are dealt with promptly and everyone involved is encouraged to put forward their point of view. The manager needs to be creative in working towards a compromise, which is, as far as possible, acceptable to all. However, in the end the manager has to demonstrate strong leadership and make the ultimate decision on the path to take.

Our staff members are well trained so that they feel competent and empowered to do their job, but know they will always receive support when needed. The manager is there to serve the needs of the staff as they provide excellent care for the children. The manager needs to trust the staff to carry out the important job they have been given to do, but to take responsibility for enabling them to achieve this. It takes time to build a strong team bond, and time for the manager to gain the respect and loyalty of the staff. Having done so, there is nothing so pleasurable as working and belonging in this way, producing job satisfaction for staff, with low turnover, good results with happy children reaching their full potential, and supportive parents.

Oh, by the way, the answer to the question was: 'I love working here.'

 Reflection for case study 1

- What does the case study suggest about the way in which leadership operates in this setting?
- What are the strengths of this form of leadership?
- If you were a member of this team, how might this form of leadership impact on your work with children?

But what is the purpose of this collaborative and reflective working? Whalley (2011) emphasises the importance of improving outcomes for children and families, specifically through two mechanisms: leading changes in pedagogical practice and leading changes in inclusive practice. Leadership is now considered for these two areas of practice.

Pedagogical leadership

In their 2011 paper, Heikka and Waniganayake identify the lack of theory development for pedagogical leadership in early childhood. However, being a leader and developing the ways in which children learn in early childhood settings is now emerging as a significant discussion in the literature. There is some distinction between being a leader of pedagogy and being a leader related to the administrative tasks of the role of the early childhood educator. The difficulty in defining pedagogical leadership is discussed by Heikka and Waniganayake (2011), with issues around the use and origin of terms such as pedagogy explored. These authors base their writing on experiences of leadership of pedagogy in Finland and Australia and provide a useful description of the development of the concept of pedagogical leadership over recent years. Pedagogy in early years is defined by Siraj-Blatchford (2009: 2) as 'the form that teaching takes', including aspects of curriculum decisions, the development of relationships and decisions about teaching and learning. The development of relationships suggests an important role for 'care' in leading pedagogy. Those engaged in early childhood education and care recognise their significant role with the young children in their settings across social, psychological and emotional spheres, as well as within the cognitive sphere. So the early childhood pedagogical leader will be thinking about and planning teaching and learning activities across these spheres, and looking for and taking opportunities in their daily practice to support children's development across these spheres, including ways in which to communicate with and work with families. The holistic nature of early childhood pedagogy has been described by Moss (2006: 32) as comprising of 'learning, care and upbringing'. Thus the family and social context is relevant, relationships are significant, and social and emotional development cannot be separated from the cognitive development of the child. Play is a unifying feature of pedagogy throughout early childhood and the chapters in Part Three of this volume reflect the importance of this.

The importance of the early childhood workforce taking a leadership role, not just at the level of the work setting, but also at a policy level, is emphasised by Heikka and Waniganayake (2011). The need for greater leadership of pedagogy is stressed, to include leadership about how the learning and teaching occur, and acknowledgement that learning occurs in relation to the child and the family.

Speaking from the experience of working with a range of very capable graduate leaders in England, I have positive views of the value of the graduate leader role in empowering the early childhood workforce to lead and manage change. However, one element that is perhaps not sufficiently developed in the leader is the practitioner's own philosophy of pedagogy. My own experience is in setting up and running a Masters programme in Early Years Professional Practice (MA EYPP) for those practitioners who hold graduate leader status. A specific pedagogy module had not been planned as part of this MA. An assumption had been made that the graduate leaders would have considerable knowledge of pedagogy and that this could be used within the leadership modules. However, this was a misconception. Those graduate leaders who had not undertaken Early Childhood degrees had not studied pedagogy, and those that had undertaken these degrees were not able to offer their personal pedagogical philosophy. The MA curriculum was therefore changed, at the request of staff, students and stakeholders, to incorporate a specific module on Early Years Pedagogy, with part of the assessment being a reflection on the graduate leader's own pedagogical philosophy. This module has been running now for a number of presentations. It is consistently rated very highly by the MA students. They value the way in which the module gives the student a much broader and deeper understanding of their own pedagogical beliefs and the way in which these beliefs impact on practice. The students are surprised to find that they have been making assumptions about pedagogy without engaging with it as fully as they can in terms of leadership. Thus the module has a self-development role, which then impacts on the students' role as leaders.

Examples of leadership in practice are provided in Case Studies 1 and 2. The personal pedagogical philosophies which the leaders in these cases demonstrate are clearly evident. As a leader of pedagogy, it is important to support staff to reflect on their pedagogical role and to support the development of staff as they seek to support children. For the individual practitioner, either alone or with support from a mentor, it is helpful to reflect on teaching and learning activities that have occurred during the day's work, to think about what elements of the activities supported the child's development and what opportunities could have been taken to further improve development.

Early childhood leaders are in a relatively unique position in the field of education. It can be argued that in schools, leadership of the curriculum sits with managers rather than with teachers. However, in early childhood settings, the leader may have several roles (including being the teacher) and often works in a very small team with others whose role is to support the development of the child (Heikka and Waniganayake, 2011). The opportunity for pedagogical leadership is clear for the early childhood setting, even within the confines of the government-imposed curriculum – in England, the Early Years Foundation Stage. For example, Davis and Barry (2013) identified that leaders may make many relatively small differences in resources or ways of working that impact positively on learning and hence on outcomes for children in their settings. The lack of hierarchy in the majority of early childhood settings can liberate the early childhood practitioner to influence decisions both administratively and pedagogically.

I would argue that leadership of pedagogy or of inclusive practice draws on the same range of qualities in the early childhood leader. It is the leader's role to ensure they apply leadership across the sphere of their practice. Turning now to leadership of inclusive practice, I have taken the opportunity to consider the value of distributed leadership.

Leadership for inclusive practice, with consideration of distributed leadership

The importance of clear policy development within the early childhood setting to identify the way in which inclusion is viewed and pursued within the setting is discussed by Jones and Pound (2008). These authors highlight the need for a philosophy and rationale, a set of objectives or purposes, and the development of broad guidelines in creating the policy framework within the work setting. Developing and implementing this policy framework requires leadership. Leadership theory identifies that any policy will be more effective if the workforce has the opportunity to contribute to the development of that policy (Daft, 2011). This is particularly true in the early childhood setting (Siraj-Blatchford and Manni, 2006). Thus understanding the law and the regulatory framework, consultation with staff, parents and other stakeholders, and implementing change with a focus on the people who need to implement the policy are significant for the leader in this circumstance. But the leader of inclusive practice has the opportunity to distribute leadership across their staff. There is emerging interest in the use of such distributed leadership in early childhood (Heikka and Waniganayake, 2011; Siraj-Blatchford and Manni, 2006). For example, enabling a specific member of staff to take on the role of coordinator, to attend training and to share what they have learned in that training within the early childhood setting is a starting point for demonstrating that all members of staff have important roles to play within the team. This requires the leader to trust the member of staff to lead on this aspect, to consult appropriately and to enact change agreed within the setting. For the member of staff nominated to take the role of coordinator, there is the opportunity to reflect on the setting with new eyes, and look at individual children and families and how they are included, or indeed barriers to their inclusion. By reflecting on inclusion within the setting, and then sharing that reflection at a staff meeting, inclusion practices can become part of team discussions and support the development of thinking about inclusion; this can then impact on the way in which policy is interpreted in the individual setting.

The collaborative nature of early childhood leadership is again emphasised here; distributed leadership identifies that leadership roles can be shared, but that this model of leadership expects strong team support for the range of leader roles generated. By distributing leadership, the members of staff are empowered to generate and share ideas for changes to practice. This type of leadership requires a leader who is confident enough to share power with the team, and team members who want to participate effectively in that leadership.

Leadership for inclusive practice is a very good example of the value of empowering and enabling the workforce, supporting the workforce to both understand the concepts embodied in inclusion (see Part Two of this volume) and to voice their ideas and concerns. In this way, inclusion is not seen primarily as a set of rules and guidelines, but as an active engagement with everyday practice for the benefit of children and their families. Case Study 3 highlights some of this active engagement, using the example of children's centres. On the MA EYPP, there is a module on Inclusive Practice in Early Childhood Settings. One of the real challenges students have with this module is developing their own philosophical stance on inclusion and recognising the power of this. In my experience, graduate leaders are knowledgeable about the law and national policy for inclusion, and indeed this is addressed within graduate leader education programmes, but they have not always considered their own stance in sufficient detail.

The challenge for leadership for inclusive practice is therefore, in my view, the challenge of engaging all staff in developing and enacting the policy framework within their settings. This requires a particularly skilled leader, who is willing to recognise individual contributions and judge their value from a philosophical viewpoint that is transparent.

Can traditional theories of leadership and change management be useful in early childhood?

Leaders in early years are now beginning to be more confident in identifying themselves as leaders. This contrasts with the situation only a few years ago when Moyles (2006) summarised a number of views indicating the reluctance of early years workers to see themselves as leaders. This move to acknowledge the importance of leadership links with a recognition in the early childhood workforce that leadership is about the whole team (Moyles, 2006) and needs to acknowledge and work with the context and culture of the setting (Dunlop, 2008). The emergence of a view of leadership in early childhood which develops the team and values the different views of team members, demonstrates the increased emphasis on shared and distributed leadership.

Leaders in early childhood are becoming more confident and skilled in the use of reflection to improve practice (Hadfield et al., 2012). The community of practice and increased professional development to support the role of the leader includes a range of opportunities to further develop the leadership role given to the graduate leader. One example of professional development for graduate leaders is study at Masters level, and elements of this are now explored.

Using change management theory, graduate leaders studying for an applied Masters programme in Early Years Professional Practice undertook a small change in their early childhood work setting and considered the value of more traditional theory in supporting that change (Davis, 2012). These Masters students were all leaders in early childhood settings. While no one theory was fully fit for purpose in implementing change in early childhood settings, elements of many theories were of value. The leaders made use of these theories to make changes related to the culture and pedagogy within their settings. The way in which graduate leaders used theories that are often considered as atypical for early years settings is explored below.

The value of a staged model of change, to both plan and work through the change, was clearly important. Staged models of change are just that – identified stages through which change occurs, from the planning and assessment stages through to the implementation and maintenance of the change. There are numerous staged models from which to choose, some more detailed than others. Some of the students found Kotter's eight-step model (1996) most valuable for this, while others preferred Lewin's (1997) three-step model, or a variation of this as more applicable to a smaller work setting. Whatever staged model was chosen, there was clearly a value in using a staged process for detailed planning and implementation of change. For example, the leader could easily assess the progress of the change and identify which elements were in need of further attention. One finding that stood out was the realisation that once the change had been implemented, things could move backwards. The need to maintain the change, continuing to address the barriers to change and reinforce the enablers of the change, was very important and had to be planned from the start (Davis, 2012). I wonder how many of us who have led change have concentrated on planning to make the change, rather than also planning to sustain the change.

The 'trait' model of leadership (Adair, 2009) is sometimes seen as dated and more suited to a corporate setting. Trait models identify particular attributes that leaders have or can develop to make them effective leaders. Writings about such traits tend to identify those of the visionary leader, who is able to lead alone and remain tough and focused, and do not often acknowledge the softer communication skills. However, the characteristics associated with leadership in early childhood settings are sometimes those of the softer skills, such as being nurturing and sympathetic (Aubrey, 2011), although a range of leadership traits is often needed to implement change. The leaders indicated that undertaking some self-reflection of their own leadership traits, and what was needed for the change they were considering, was very helpful in identifying where they needed to develop themselves as a leader. This personal development was then planned into the steps of the change. In addition, differentiating the elements of the change that were leadership, and those that were management, helped the leader to understand their own role in leading the change. Thus the leaders were being reflective, thinking about their practice, thinking forward to the needed change and thinking about what skills and abilities they possessed, and what they needed to develop. This analysis also supported the leader in sharing the task of leadership with others in the team, linking to the notion of distributed leadership discussed earlier in this chapter. So while the trait model of leadership is not in itself one to embrace in early childhood settings, elements of it are nevertheless useful in reflecting on one's attributes as a leader.

The leaders found Lewin's (1997) force field analysis useful. This is a way of drawing a picture of the factors in the setting that are helping the change to move forward, and the factors in the setting that are working against the successful implementation of change, in other words being explicit about the forces at work. For example, being able to identify the barriers to change before implementing the change meant that these barriers were considered at the planning stage and taken account of, particularly in the time spent implementing the change and the time spent including staff in decisions and plans related to the change. The importance of seeing the change from the point of view of the individual members of staff was highlighted. One example that has recently come to my attention is that some changes are not identified as major changes when they are proposed. It is only after an attempt at implementation of the change that the scope of the change becomes evident. Early childhood leaders have explained that Lewin's model can be useful at this point to take a new look at the change and the forces operating to support or frustrate that change.

The study (Davis, 2012) also demonstrated the need to be clear who any gatekeeper might be when a change was proposed, and to recognise these individuals at an early stage, so that changes were planned which were realistic and achievable. A gate-keeper is someone who can either enable or block access. For example, a leader of practice may have to go through their employer to get agreement for a change; the employer can therefore act as a gatekeeper and potentially block change. Being aware of gatekeeper roles meant that the leaders considered carefully how to communicate the proposed changes to demonstrate their ability to positively impact on early years practice and outcomes for children. This notion of gatekeepers had emerged from the reading of Easton's Systems Theory (1965) by two of the leaders. Easton's model is sometimes seen to be applicable only to large work settings, but in these cases elements of the theory were useful in small settings.

Leaders reported that change for some members of the team was rather like bereavement, and using Kübler-Ross's work (2009) was useful to determine the stages which an individual might go through in feeling a sense of loss of what was familiar. Kübler-Ross's model focuses on the person experiencing the change or loss. Leaders who used this model were trying to see the change and the impact of the change from the point of view of their members of staff. For example, leaders reported their staff seeing the strengths of the 'old' ways, and taking time to adapt to new ways of work-ing, feeling a sense of loss for what used to be, and the challenge of moving forward to a state where familiarity with the new system meant that there was far less consid-eration of what had been in the past. Being aware of this process enabled the leader to show empathy and understanding, while still moving forward with the change.

In summary, these graduate leaders valued using a staged model, which included thinking about sustaining change after initiating it. They also valued some personal reflection on their own traits or attributes, and ones they may need to strengthen in implementing change. They found it helpful to consider the factors that were driving the planned change forward, and also to consider the factors that were working against successful change. Some of these leaders found it useful to reflect on who might be acting as gatekeeper, and took this into consideration in using the staged model of change. The leaders also clearly began to see that change could be quite challenging for some members of staff, and thinking about the change from the point of view of those members of staff could help the leader to communicate effectively to support those staff undergoing change.

Many of the leaders in this study (Davis, 2012) were surprised at what they learned by considering the use of these theoretical approaches to change. While the leaders were enthusiastic and effective at making changes, they had done far less to consider the importance of maintaining a change once it had occurred, and avoiding the temptation of slipping back into old routines of work. Some had not really considered the strength of feeling in team members of reluctance to change, and how this could negatively impact on both the change itself and the maintenance of the change. What had not been considered was the impact of change on the individual worker. Proposed changes that were clearly for the good of the child or the family had not always been embraced by staff, so that shared leadership was not always easy.

Thus the professional development of these leaders through a Masters degree was having an impact on further developing their professional practice. The link between ongoing professional development and high quality provision in early childhood is highlighted by Aubrey (2011) in her research with the early years workforce in England. The reflective skills and confidence developed by leaders through their graduate leader education (Whalley, 2011) appear to enable leaders in early childhood settings to work independently to determine the value of theoretical models of change management to their own settings. What emerges, however, is that none of the more traditional theories of leadership and change used in the commercial context recognises the complexity of the early childhood work setting, even though Kagan and Hallmark (2001) identified some of the wide range of roles and responsibilities of leadership in early childhood more than a decade ago. Many of the theories are valuable, but only when used with an understanding of the collaborative nature of the early childhood setting, and the focus on improving outcomes for children and families (see Case Study 2 as an example). They should not be used as a means of imposing managerialism or managing levels of performance in early childhood settings, as they do not fit with the overall aims of early childhood education and care. Rather, they should be used as a means of personal reflection for the leader of practice. The early childhood setting is complex and its purposes are not aligned to the traditional commercial context. Some of these complex aspects of early childhood settings are now discussed in relation to the role of the graduate leader in early childhood.

What difference does a graduate make to leadership in early childhood?

Sylva et al. (2004), in the EPPE project, identified that children's progress was better and that the quality of the childcare setting improved with an improvement in the qualifications of staff. Many academics and practitioners in early childhood were keen to see the changes that occurred in 2006 in England with the introduction of Early Years Professional Status (EYPS), the graduate leader. There are now some 11,000 staff with EYPS working in settings in England. Their effectiveness has been evaluated by Hadfield et al. (2011, 2012) at a national level, and by Davis and Barry (2013) and Davis and Capes (2013) at a county level. The graduate leaders have developed communities of shared good practice, which are effective in developing staff and settings to improve outcomes for children and for the wider community. These communities of practice include informal and formal networks of early childhood workers. It is clear that often professional development opportunities have been the trigger for the development of such networks, meeting other people who are keen to get the best outcomes for children and families and sharing ideas with them about the detail of improving practice.

Three main findings emerge from the research by Davis (Davis and Barry, 2013; Davis and Capes, 2013) into the impact of graduate leader status. Graduate leader status provides the practitioner with confidence to use their existing knowledge and experience in new ways, empowering them to make changes. The focus of activity in the early years setting changes from the short-term to the longer-term goals in relation to the development of the child and the family within the community and with the multi-professional team. There is greater emphasis on development of staff so that staff gain greater understanding of why things are done the way they are; staff are developed as reflective practitioners. Findings from this study are described below.

Gaining confidence was evidenced by reference to examples of change the EYPs had made since gaining graduate leader status. The confidence afforded the leaders by undertaking graduate leader education meant that clear decisions were made about training needs within settings, and about accessing this training. Tied to this, the leaders were involving staff in training provided outside the setting, and giving these staff the responsibility of bringing their learning and ideas back to the setting at a weekly meeting. Thus the graduate leader was confident in accessing appropriate training but also in empowering the other members of the team. In a similar way, resources were sought more pro-actively, so that the child's long-term development took precedence over the appearance of the setting. One example given here was the desire to purchase outdoor equipment that was colourful and bright but could only be used by one child at a time, and the actual decision to purchase equipment that could be used by more children to encourage physical and mental development. The graduate leader was identified by participants as empowering in their communication with parents. For example, the graduate leaders were pro-active in seeking opportunities to speak to parents, and pro-active in making information available that would include parents in their child's education. Reflecting on their own practice, graduate leaders stated that they felt much more confident to consider what was good and why it was good, and what needed changing and why. This justification of action, based on improving practice, is considerably different to the model of leadership often presented in the commercial and educational context, where the emphasis may be more focused on administration and measurement of performance rather than on enriching the learning and caring environment. Of course, it could be argued that one cannot measure 'care', but the argument must also be presented that just because something cannot be measured numerically does not mean that it has no value. This is not to devalue the role of measurement, but to recognise its limitations.

CASE STUDY TWO

A reflection from a childminding setting: whose change is it?

[Thanks to a childminder colleague for providing this case study.]

It is my opinion that a leader in early years needs to have a hands-on approach and to be leading from within so that changes can be made through planning, reviewing and implementing: action research. I see the relationship that I have with my colleagues as being as important as those I have with the parents and the children in my setting. Lee (2008) states that the quality of provision resides in the relationships that are within the community of the setting. This needs to go alongside some coaching, giving explanations for why it is we do what we do to promote understanding and build relationships.

My understanding of this has led me to reflect on an incident with an advisor using Brookfield's critical incident lens (1998). Prior to my last Ofsted inspection, I was visited by a support worker who gave me advice enabling me to prepare. One of the things she told me stands out in my memory; this was possibly because I disagreed with her. She suggested that I would not have a successful inspection report unless I created a cosy corner with rugs and cushions for the children to read in. Whilst her idea was a good one in principle, it was not practical in my setting and I had already found ways to provide the children with opportunities to snuggle in, or sit and read a book quietly if they wished. My reflection of why this event had such an effect on me was that the autocratic way in which she made her suggestion annoyed me, as it dismissed my views. Through this approach she was not able to sell her idea to me. This is necessary when trying to implement a change. I have learnt that reflection is self-driven; it needs to come from your own needs or needs that you have identified. For example, in my setting this might be to meet the needs of a group of parents or the children themselves. Change needs to be dictated from within, not dictated by someone else's needs or by

(Continued)

(Continued)

political agendas. I have learnt that it is more appropriate to say 'What do you think you need to do to improve?' rather than 'This is what you should do ...'

I learnt that this experience was not the way I wanted to lead and it made me ensure that I take others' views and opinions into account when making decisions. When I want to make a change it has to be through consultation with others involved. I then make sure that I adapt the change to involve their views. In this way they are also able to take ownership of that change and, consequently, it is more likely to be successful. Our own transformation of learning is a powerful way that we are able to make changes. Commitment and care is my driving force as a graduate leader; I have a passion for the job that I am doing, but this is not always shared by those that I am leading. I therefore need to 'sell' the change to them to ignite their enthusiasm.

 Reflection for case study 2

- In what ways can reflection be used to support the leader in making decisions about changes to practice?
- How can reflection be used effectively if you are working as the sole person in a setting?
- As a member of staff working in an early childhood setting, how is change communicated to you and how do you respond to that communication?

An example of the confidence of the early childhood leader is given in Case Study 2. The graduate leader status is demonstrated through this case study by the leader thinking through and understanding the impact of judgements made, so that changes are not made unless they improve practice. The change proposed could potentially 'tick a box' for the regulator, but could be detrimental for the care of the child.

The study reported above was from a single county in England. The much larger national UK study by Hadfield et al. (2011, 2012) is the first of its kind and is highlighted in the 'Research in context' box in Chapter 14. This study demonstrated a number of findings about the differences that graduate leaders are making to children and families as well as to practitioners. For the 'Research in context' box for this chapter on leadership I have chosen the study by Mathers et al. (2011).

Research in context

Mathers, S., Ranns, H., Karemaker, A., Mody, A., Sylva, K., Graham, J. and Siraj-Blatchford, I. (2011) *Evaluation of the Graduate Leader Fund: Final Report*. Department for Education Research Report DfE-RR144.

Evidence from Siraj-Blatchford and Manni (2006) and Sylva et al. (2004), among others, had already demonstrated the value of a qualified early years workforce but also differences in the workforce between the maintained and the private, voluntary and independent (PVI) sector. From 2006, the then-UK government provided funding to establish graduate leaders in all early years settings by 2015. Between 2007 and 2011, Mathers and the other members of the research team evaluated the use of this funding, particularly in the PVI sector. The researchers visited 238 settings on two occasions, with a two-year gap between visits. On these visits they used the ECERS and ITERS scales to assess the quality of the provision. The research team also undertook twelve case studies. The findings clearly demonstrated the benefits of the funding and the value of graduate leaders. Settings with graduate leaders demonstrated improved quality for the children over the two-year period compared to settings that did not have a graduate leader. Early Years Professional Status was identified as something that added value to the setting, above graduate status alone.

You can read the full study at: www.gov.uk/government/uploads/system/uploads/attachment_data/file/181480/DFE-RR144.pdf

Note: This study was commissioned before the new Coalition Government took office in 2010 and reported in advance of the changes announced by Truss in the *More Great Childcare* report (DfE, 2013b). Please refer to Chapters 14 and 15 for a detailed account of the policy changes that have occurred in recent years.

There is a current dilemma in England though, which is illustrated by Case Study 3. The investment in education and training that has developed graduate leaders has provided confident, capable leaders in early childhood settings. The policy changes being made do not always enable those leaders to be effectively used. For example, the changes in children's centres illustrated by Case Study 3 impact on the ability of staff to sustain relationships with families who may struggle to access the system. A much more holistic approach is needed for the development of leaders and their employment so that they can make the differences they have demonstrated themselves capable of and lead change to improve outcomes for children and families.

CASE STUDY THREE

Change and the children's centre

This case study describes the employment of teachers and graduate leaders in children's centres from the point of view of one teacher who is also a graduate leader.

Phase 1 children's centres were part of the government initiative to support local settings so that better provision could be made for families in disadvantaged areas. Employed on teachers' pay and conditions by the local authority, before the implementation of EYPS, Children's Centre Teachers (CCTs) supported settings within a larger Children's Centre Cluster to engage families and provide a holistic approach to the development of children. The role was one of leading and initiating change using their considerable expertise. The restructuring which occurred meant that CCTs were no longer part of the workforce structure and were lost in 2012.

The requirement for a CCT was relaxed in Phase 2 children's centres, and graduate leaders or teachers were employed, reporting to the coordinator of the centre. This role was different, although recommendations could be made by the person in role; the individual was not able to 'lead' on something unless it met with the vision/instructions of the centre coordinator (who was not necessarily early years trained). Despite this there were successes in improving transition to school, leading transition programmes to enable parents and children to be better prepared for starting school. There was a lot of work to include the families of those who were hard to reach, and there was success in supporting these families, a good example of positive inclusive practice. However, redundancies occurred when the requirement to have a graduate leader or a CCT in the centre was removed.

The overview and experience and knowledge of early years education, and the bigger picture that the graduate leader or CCT possessed, was suddenly lost. There is still a recognised need for the expertise, but not all centres are employing CCTs; in some centres the expertise is to be provided by employing consultants as and when required and when the budget allows. There has been a real investment in continuing professional development (CPD) and many CCTs qualified as graduate leaders and developed their expertise. This is now lost where the roles are redundant. There is a real challenge for leadership here.

Reflection for case study 3

- To what extent are hard-to-reach families able to access early years education in the locality in which you work?

- From your experience, as a leader or a member of a team working with a leader, how can an effective leader support major changes in settings?
- What is happening in your local children's centre? Who leads to enable inclusion of hard-to-reach families?
- Do changes in staffing affect the ability of children's centres to engage in sustained relationships with hard-to-reach families?

Chapter summary

To work effectively as a leader in early childhood, it is essential to work collaboratively and reflectively. The focus on improving outcomes for children and their families through improved pedagogy and inclusive practice is having an impact on the longer-term development of the child. The development of communities of practice is having a broad impact on sharing good practice in how to develop pedagogical and inclusive practice, and how best to involve and collaborate with parents and the multi-professional team.

While the early childhood leader may usefully draw from a range of traditional theories of leadership and change management, leading change in early childhood settings is different. It requires confidence, skill, the ability to reflect effectively on one's own practice and an ability to care for one's colleagues and to recognise the impact of change at the individual level. It also requires vision, tenacity and a willingness to act on one's professional judgement. The confidence afforded by gaining graduate leader status enables the leader to improve practice in small ways, but also to plan for and effect much larger changes in their work settings.

Policy makers need to recognise the strength of leadership within the early childhood workforce, and plan to make best use of this resource in improving outcomes for children.

Questions for reflection and discussion

1. To what extent is your work setting collaborative and reflective? What is your own role in this?
2. Think about your personal philosophy of pedagogy and/or of inclusive practice. Try to summarise your views in a short paragraph on each of these. Think about how your personal philosophy impacts on your role as a leader.

(Continued)

(Continued)

3. Think about a change that you have made, or that has been made, in your setting. Has the change been sustained? Is further planning needed to maintain
or re-establish the change?
4. To what extent are people in your work setting the key to leadership? Is there
potential for sharing some of the roles of leadership? What are the challenges
for the leader of sharing some of the leadership responsibilities?
5. If you do not yet have experience of working in an early years setting, reflect
on the leadership skills you might bring to a setting and the sort of leader who
you would want to work with.

Recommended reading

Davis, G. (2012) 'A documentary analysis of the use of theories of leadership and change by
Early Years leaders', *Early Years: An International Journal of Research and Development*, 32
(3): 266–76.
Hadfield, M., Jopling, M., Needham, M., Waller, T., Coleyshaw, L., Emira, M. and Royle, K. (2012)
*Longitudinal Study of Early Years Professional Status: An Exploration of Progress, Leadership
and Impact*. Final Report for the DfE. University of Wolverhampton, CeDARE. Research
Report RR239c.

Both of these readings report on recent research findings about leadership in early childhood.

Recommended websites

www.ofsted.gov.uk/news/importance-of-leadership-annual-report-of-her-majestys-chief-
inspector-of-education-childrens-servic
This is the link to Ofsted's report on the importance of leadership in early years.

Want to learn more about this chapter? Visit the companion website at
www.sagepub.co.uk/walleranddavis3e to access podcasts from the author and child
observation videos.

Part Six
Research and Reflection

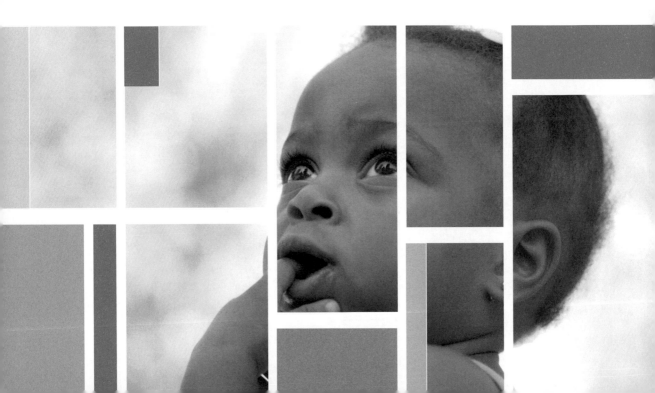

17

Researching Young Children's Worlds

Jane Murray

Key chapter objectives

This chapter explores issues concerning young children and research. It will:

- identify conflicts between children's participation and protection rights
- consider dilemmas and difficulties of judging children's competence in relation to participation

Introduction

In common with many other authors in this volume, this is my third contribution to an edition of *An Introduction to Early Childhood*. Each edition has charted a discourse across significant shifts in perspectives on research and young children's agency. Now, it seems hardly possible to me that my first chapter had the title 'Studying Children' and was primarily concerned with adult studies of children (Murray, 2005). In recent years, the notion of 'evolving capacities' in relation to the youngest children's participation has been increasingly challenged while recognition of children as social actors from birth has gained traction (Alderson et al., 2006; United Nations Committee on the Rights of the Child, 2006). In turn, acknowledgement of young children as already rich and competent has been reflected in research contexts (Harcourt et al., 2011).

Research models predicated on positioning children as objects or subjects have been questioned and new, exciting alternatives valuing young children as co-researchers and researchers are increasingly posited (Christensen and James, 2008). Nevertheless, many of the attempts to position young children as researchers have been predicated on the adults' agenda. Equally, despite progress, children generally remain excluded from the 'rarefied world of the academic' (Redmond, 2008: 17).

This chapter for the third edition considers research and young children and proposes that much of what has been accomplished tends to be tokenistic: primacy is rarely afforded to young children's own, authentic agenda. The chapter opens with a consideration of the nature of research. Discussion centres around research on, about, with and by children (Fielding, 2001) but raises questions about the roles of adults and children in research processes. There is exploration of the proposition that one of the key challenges for adults in recognising children as researchers is that adults often struggle to understand children's behaviours (Bae, 2010). Within the chapter there is consideration of how these issues were encountered and addressed as part of the Young Children As Researchers (YCAR) project (Murray, 2012a).

 Research in context

Murray, J. (2012a) 'An exploration of young children's engagements in research behaviour', PhD thesis. University of Northampton, UK.

The Young Children As Researchers (YCAR) project (Murray, 2012a) adopted participatory, emancipatory and inductive approaches to conceptualise ways that children aged 4–8 years naturally engage during everyday activity in research behaviour that is congruent with professional adult researchers' behaviours.

Participatory methods – including child observation – and the ethics of research with young children were key elements of the study. YCAR conceptualised ways that children aged 4–8 years engage in research activity naturalistically as part of their daily lives. An overview of how this was accomplished is provided in this chapter.

The nature of research

This section considers definitions of research, what counts as research, who does research and who owns it. As a whole, the chapter focuses on early childhood education (ECE) research, which sits at the intersection of educational research and early childhood education and care (ECEC) research (see Figure 17.1).

ECE research includes enquiry focused on numerous disciplines (Bridges, 2006; Teaching and Learning Research Programme, 2012). Among other themes, history,

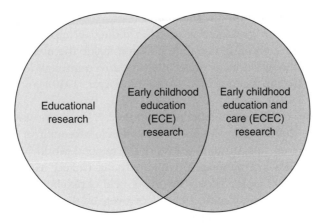

Figure 17.1 *ECE research at the intersection of educational and ECEC research*

philosophy, sociology, psychology, neuroscience, pedagogy, politics, economics, cultural studies, human development and ethics permeate this varied and dynamic field. Whilst being informed by numerous disciplines, ECE research is a relatively new research discipline per se, so this chapter, with its focus on researching aspects of young children's worlds, deconstructs the origins and discourse surrounding ECE research.

Whilst research is described as 'systematic enquiry made public' (Stenhouse, 1975: 142), a 'process of investigation leading to new insights, effectively shared' (REF, 2011) and 'the search for knowledge' (Bassey, 1990: 35), there is no universal definition. Nevertheless, plenty has been written about research. Many ideas informing research now were first documented by the ancient Greeks (Thomas, 2007), yet it can be argued that the Enlightenment period has proved most influential to contemporary research protocols. Hume's 'principle of verification' (1748) has been highly significant: he articulated that for 'learned work' to be considered rigorous, it should comprise 'abstract reasoning concerning number or quantity' or 'experimental reasoning concerning matter of fact and existence' (p. 123). Enlightenment philosophers, including Locke (1690) and Hume (1748), rejected metaphysical accounts in favour of external sensory evidence in their quest to establish a basis for 'truth'.

Reasoning deductively became highly regarded: 'a valid deduction provides a true conclusion when premises leading to that conclusion are true' (Johnson-Laird and Byrne, 1991: 2). Hume (1739) exemplified this proposition through a syllogism: 'All A are B, C is A, therefore C is B'. In other words: all dolls are toys (major premise), Jemima is a doll (minor premise), Jemima is a toy (conclusion). By contrast, in inductive reasoning, the 'truth of the premises need not guarantee the truth of the conclusion'. For example, if you were to walk past a nursery and the only children you could see were in the garden (premise), you might conclude that all the nursery's children were in the garden (conclusion). The premise provides evidential support for the conclusion but does not guarantee its truth in inductive reasoning. This is because there may be a further premise: there are children inside the nursery building whom you cannot see. Although inductive reasoning is derived through logical thought processes, it has tended to be regarded as fallible (Ayer, 1940), and so became less privileged.

Hume's empiricist view was embedded further by logical positivism, which was developed in the 20th century by the Vienna Circle (Neurath et al., 1929). Many Vienna Circle members left Austria because of the Second World War and influenced thinking in universities internationally, particularly the United States. Moreover, there was a strong influence of logical positivism on the field of psychology in US universities, manifesting in behaviourism (Smith, 1986). However, by the middle of the 20th century, logical positivism had been met with significant criticism (Kuhn, 1970; Popper, 1959; Quine, 1953). The rejection of intuition by logical positivism became tempered, leading to interpretive methodologies being recognised as potentially valuable for social science research (Pring, 2000). Furthermore, postmodernist research designs gained momentum (Siraj-Blatchford, 2010b), as did pragmatic approaches (Stenhouse, 1975). A view exists that the bifurcation of research approaches into qualitative and quantitative paradigms presents a 'false dualism' (Pring, 2000) and Glaser and Strauss (1967) attempted to eliminate this divide with grounded theory. Nevertheless, educational and ECE research continue to be characterised by 'scientific and positivistic' as well as 'naturalistic and interpretive' approaches (Cohen et al., 2007: 5). Moreover, positivism has tended to prevail as the privileged underpinning of policy making in educational and ECE fields, despite concerns that it is often ill-suited to the task (Bridges et al., 2009).

This point was reiterated around the turn of the 21st century, when detachment between researcher and researched in educational contexts was observed (Hargreaves, 1996) and the exclusion of practitioners from 'the academy' was explicitly questioned (Ball, 2001). The academy is regarded as a space populated by professional researchers where 'learners and knowledge producers' converge to produce knowledge (Warren and Boxall, 2009: 281), a 'score-keeping world' (Lees, 1999: 382) that sets itself apart from 'the people' (Bridges, 1998). The academy's hegemony has been noted as unhelpful, alongside a suggestion that research might be useful only if it is useful to its users (OECD, 2002). This argument draws on notions of 'knowledge that' and 'knowledge how' (Ryle, 1949); Giddens' proposal (1984) that social science theory is bound into practice, thus different from the theory/practice 'silo' approach prevailing in the natural sciences, condones this view.

Action research (Stenhouse, 1975) attempts to address the division between research and practice; nevertheless, action research has detractors who suggest it lacks scientific rigour and that it is indistinguishable from everyday problem solving (Hodgkinson, 1957). Nevertheless, action research has retained popularity among educational practitioners, perhaps because of its democratic, emancipatory and participatory potential

(Kemmis and McTaggart, 2005). More recently in the field of ECE research, interest has increased in praxeological enquiry – research undertaken by those in the field to gain knowledge of the field, with potential to inform enhancement of that field (Pascal and Bertram, 2012). Nevertheless, work remains to be done to draw together practice and research in educational and ECE research (Biesta, 2007). Particular knowledge production processes, outcomes and groups retain privilege (Brown and Strega, 2005; Foucault, 1989), perpetuating power inequalities (Truman et al., 2000). Within this construction, young children have consistently remained on the margins of the academy (Redmond, 2008).

Young children's roles in research

Distinctions have been made between research *on* children, research *about* children and research *with* children (O'Kane, 2008; Tisdall et al., 2009). Fielding (2001) proposes a continuum, and he indicates a further category – children as researchers (Figure 17.2).

Woodhead and Faulkner (2008) trace the emergence of research *on* children to the late 19th century when Darwin (1872) positioned his own child as a data source. Darwin's work particularly influenced developmental psychology by creating the pattern for objectifying children in research (Gesell, 1925; Watson and Rayner, 1920); this ran contemporaneously with developments in logical positivism (Neurath et al., 1929) and Piaget (1929) perpetuated this model in psychological research. Coady (2010) suggests that such practice locates children as 'curiosities' (p. 73) and there are examples of research *on* children across other disciplines allied with early childhood, including sociology (Tobin et al., 1989) and education (Sylva et al., 1999) as well as early childhood per se (Gillen et al., 2007).

Conversely, children are recognised as subjects in research when they make 'salient' contributions to a research focus (Tisdall et al., 2009: 1). In this role, children become 'active respondents' (Fielding, 2001: 135) and are perceived by adults as 'worthy of study in their own right' (Winter, 2006: 60). When children are positioned as research

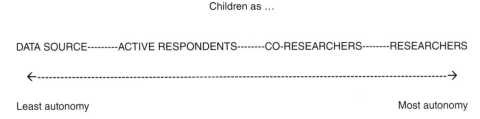

Figure 17.2 *Continuum of children in research (Fielding, 2001)*

subjects, power is shifted from adults towards them (Mandell, 1988). However, the extent and nature of that positioning is predicated on adult 'subjectivities' (Coady, 2010: 73), manifested, for example, in how adults decide what counts as 'salient' in relation to children's contributions. Therefore, in research practices locating children as subjects, adults retain hegemony.

Nevertheless, since new sociologists framed children as active social agents (James and Prout, 1997), discourses surrounding children as co-researchers and researchers have unfolded (Christensen and James, 2008; Harcourt et al., 2011). These discourses suggest that research is inextricably intertwined with practice, policy and theorising concerning children and the juxtaposition of these engagements with adults (James and Prout, 1997; Solberg, 1996). Moreover, new sociological approaches perceive children as 'experts in their own lives' (Langsted, 1994: 29), and have a view of the 'competent and capable child, a rich child, who participates in the creation of themselves and their knowledge' (Dahlberg and Lenz Taguchi, 1994: 2).

Perceptions of the child as an active social agent align with recognition of children's capabilities: 'alternative functionings the person can achieve and from which he or she can choose one collection' (Sen, 1993: 31), where a functioning is 'being or doing what people value and have reason to value' (Alkire and Deneulin, 2009: 22). Appadurai (2006) posits that research can be regarded as 'a specialised name for a generalised capacity, the capacity to make disciplined inquiries into those things we need to know, but do not know yet' (p. 167). Furthermore, Appadurai (2006) proposes that research is a right. If children wish to engage in research activity, it can be argued that they value doing so for their own reasons and, in that case, the rights argument can be applied to young children's ownership of research and engagement as co-researchers and researchers. This argument is reinforced by Articles 12 and 13 of the United Nations Convention on the Rights of the Child, which articulate that children have the right to be involved in decisions that affect them, the right to express their views freely and 'to seek, receive and impart information and ideas of all kinds' (United Nations, 1989).

Whilst research may be regarded as a kind of participation right, the qualities of participation seem variable (Arnstein, 1969; Hart, 1992; Percy-Smith and Thomas, 2010). This idea has congruence with Fielding's continuum (2001), positioning children in different research roles. Aligning further with the notion of participation as a relative concept is consideration of *capacities*. The World Bank (2010) defines capacity as 'fully operational', yet Article 5 of the UNCRC (United Nations, 1989) refers to children's 'evolving capacities', a concept claimed to balance children's protection rights with their participation rights, 'in accordance with their relative immaturity and youth' (Lansdown, 2005: ix). Van Beers, Invernizzi and Milne (2006) suggest that adults resort to the notion of evolving capacities when making decisions regarding their exclusion of children from particular features of social life. Yet it has been established that neonates 'have abstract structured knowledge' and apply their experiences to conceptualising (Gopnik, 2011: 129–30). In an appreciation of such capacities, Alderson, Hawthorne and Killen (2006) argue that 'rights partly become real in being respected' (p. 65). Attempts to respect children's rights through research have included participatory and emancipatory models of enquiry.

Freire (1972) has been particularly influential in the emergence of participatory enquiry in social science research. His work with marginalised groups in Brazil led to the development of participatory research oriented to power redistribution, liberation and transformation (Minkler and Wallerstein, 2003). Participatory research has developed into a vehicle for social justice, although it is regarded as an approach, rather than a methodology in itself (Cornwall and Jewkes, 1995). Nevertheless, participatory research is located within the interpretive paradigm (O'Kane, 2008) and Kemmis and McTaggart (2005) suggest it has certain key characteristics: 'shared ownership ... community based analysis of social problems and an orientation towards community action' (p. 560). Participatory approaches that include children and young people have gained popularity in recent years (O'Kane, 2008).

Participatory Rural Appraisal (PRA) has developed as a significant strand of participatory research, providing 'high validity and reliability of information' (Chambers, 1994: 1253), particularly in small-scale local projects where conventional research methods may prove unsatisfactory (Loader and Amartya, 1999). PRA methods are many and varied, including shared walks, group work, discourse and visualisation techniques (Narayanasamy, 2009). O'Kane suggests that PRA is a particularly valuable research approach with children because it has the capacity to involve children authentically and transfer power from adults to children. Punch (2002) adopted PRA techniques including spider diagrams and activity tables in her research with Bolivian children to establish children's movements and activity in their neighbourhood. Equally, development of the participatory 'Mosaic approach' with young children aged 3–5 years was partly based on the PRA technique of collecting detailed data about a locality by walking and talking about it with its inhabitants (Clark and Moss, 2011).

Another popular participatory approach that has proved useful in research with children and young people is Participatory Action Research (PAR) (Ozer et al., 2010). PAR locates power with participants by beginning with a problem identified by participants who then assume the role of co-researchers. In undertaking PAR, participants can enjoy a level of control that enables them to work in partnership to investigate and address the causes of their problem (Maglajlic, 2010). Based on their work with young people on the Youth Participatory Action Research Programme (YPAR), Cammarota and Fine (2008) suggest that PAR is particularly valuable for researching issues experienced by marginalised young people in educational contexts. Moreover, Zeng and Silverstein (2011) adopted PAR techniques with children following the 2008 Beichuan earthquake in China; these included democratic decision making and group play to reify community engagement among children who had lost their family members and homes. Nevertheless, there are limitations to PAR: it assumes that a problem exists and requires significant time for the relationship to develop sufficiently between the 'outsider facilitators' and the co-researchers in order that the research process can proceed smoothly (Chambers, 1994: 1253). Pascal and Bertram (2012) suggest that participatory approaches with children present philosophical, ethical and practical challenges in their reification, notwithstanding the potential advantages they may bestow.

Around the turn of the 21st century a number of adult researchers were exploring the potential of research *with* and *by* children. Based on a number of studies, Kirby (1999) provided guidance to support practitioners 'to carry out, or commission, research involving young researchers' aged 14–25 years (p. 3), advocating that young people 'can become highly competent researchers with time and practice' (p. 51). Equally, Campbell, Edgar and Halsted (1994) explored the potential of 'students as evaluators', in which students aged 10–14 years were 'helped' by adults 'to develop skills in written and oral communication and logic' in order to evaluate their school experiences in New York. In turn, Campbell et al. (1994) influenced Fielding (2001) to develop the 'Students as Researchers Project', in which he and three teaching colleagues in an English secondary school 'made the decision to form a group of students ... who ... would be trained in research and evidence gathering techniques' (p. 125). Later, Kellett (2005) devised the Children as Researchers programme for 'teaching the research process to children' aged 10–14 years, while Cheminais (2012) has provided resources to support school 'senior managers or teachers guiding pupils through the action research process' (p. 1).

It is noticeable that the projects discussed above were conducted with older children and young people. Helm and Katz (2001) suggest that a reason may be that adults regard research as 'easier' to do with older children than with children in early childhood settings (p. 1). This resonates with the view of young children's 'evolving capacities' (Lansdown, 2005; United Nations, 1989). Nevertheless, such projects have also been undertaken with children younger than 5 years. Clark and Moss (2001) developed the participatory Mosaic approach to co-construct data about children's perspectives of their settings. Participatory methods that Clark and Moss (2001) employed with children aged 3–4 years, including mapping, visual methods and child conferencing, have since been adopted by others working with very young children (Fleet and Britt, 2011; Waller and Bitou, 2011). Moreover, the 'project approach' (Helm and Katz, 2001; Katz and Chard, 1989) is an attempt by adults working in early childhood settings to guide research and investigation projects with children aged 3–5 years as a pedagogical tool in the United States.

Emerging from critical social theory (Marx, 1867), emancipatory approaches in research developed as a critical response to power inequalities, particularly logical positivism (Habermas, 1987; Horkheimer, 1937). Diverse ways of framing knowledge began to gain recognition (Gibbons et al., 1994; Polanyi, 1962; Ryle, 1949). Emancipatory approaches have developed particularly strongly in enquiries with marginalised people (Denzin, 2005) because emancipatory research 'seeks to empower' (Letherby, 2006: 88). Habermas (1987) highlights the characteristics of emancipatory approaches as social interaction, equalised relationships, self-reflection and communication free from hegemony, while Kovach (2005) highlights 'collectivity, reciprocity and respect' (p. 28) and Wilson (2001) sees the aim of emancipatory research as to 'reduce existing injustice' (p. 473). The projects outlined above may have shifted power in the research process towards children and young people to some extent – perhaps even by a 'quantum leap' (Fielding, 2001: 125). However, each was predicated on adults overseeing the process, most focused on an agenda that adults instigated or approved, many depended on adults instructing children and young people in orthodox adult research methods and all were disseminated by adults.

For young children to be authentically engaged in participatory research they would need to share power equally with adults while children's emancipatory research would require children to assume power and lead the research process. Isaacs' observation (1944) that the 'factor of epistemic interest and inquiry ... is in every respect the same in the child as in the adult' (p. 322) suggests that this may be possible. Nevertheless, a virtual lacuna exists in relation to valuing young children's own enquiries as authentic research. This situation disregards children as competent (James and James, 2008), rights holders (UNCRC, 1989), experts (Langsted, 1994), capable (Sen, 1993) and 'sophisticated' thinkers (Papert, 1980: 132).

This was the starting point for the Young Children As Researchers (YCAR) project (Murray, 2012a). The YCAR project reconceptualises and reveals young children's authentic, naturalistic behaviours as research on the academy's terms and the remainder of this chapter tells the story of the YCAR project.

The Young Children As Researchers (YCAR) project

During the YCAR study I worked with young children, their parents and practitioners, as well as academics, to explore further how young children might be recognised as researchers. The YCAR project began from the observation that young children appeared marginalised from the academy's privileged research spaces. Rather than training children in established modes of enquiry, YCAR set out to reveal children's own naturalistic behaviours, with a view to exploring whether or not these may be claimed as research. The YCAR study was underpinned by a value orientation committed to social justice for young children in the context of research; social interaction, mutual respect, attempts to equalise relationships and communication among everyone involved were key modes of working (Habermas, 1987; Kovach, 2005; Letherby, 2006). These efforts were not always rewarded with complete success, yet within constraints, the study attempted to confront rather than ignore or comply with power inequalities.

Paradoxically, because this study was my doctorate, from the outset it had to be conducted within the academy's construction (Hall, 1998; Hargreaves, 1996). I was required to present plans ahead of starting and to comply with my institution's ethical – and other – protocols for conducting research. Therefore, the YCAR study's overarching aim and questions had to be mine, not children's, so, in that way, the YCAR project was flawed from the beginning. At the start of the project, as required, I devised an aim:

'To conceptualise ways in which young children aged 4–8 years are researchers and may be considered to be researchers'.

Four questions shaped the study:

1. Within the field of early childhood education and care (ECEC), what is the nature of research?
2. How can a study be conducted to establish Young Children As Researchers?
3. What enquiries are important to young children and how can they engage in them?
4. What support structures might encourage young children to participate in research? What barriers might prevent this?

To foreground children and other participants, I went to the contexts they inhabited and attempted to limit my own perspective by discarding the constraining set of 'conceptual and instrumental tools' provided by a single paradigm (Kuhn, 1970: 37) in favour of framing the YCAR study within a range of 'postmodern epistemologies' (Siraj-Blatchford, 2010b: 199). These included interpretivism, post-positivism, constructivism, critical research and post-structuralism, shaping a model of plural paradigms (Table 17.1) to create a rigorous framework that privileged participants' perspectives over a single methodological rubric. Each component had a key role (see Table 17.1).

YCAR's value orientation was reified further by three principled approaches: participation, emancipation and induction. Discourses surrounding democracy and rights influenced the study (Brown and Strega, 2005; Freire; 1972; United Nations, 1989) through participatory characteristics (Kemmis and McTaggart, 2005). Furthermore, the study's emancipatory approach underpinned critical and pragmatic responses to power inequalities (Habermas, 1987; Kovach, 2005). Finally, YCAR's inductive

Table 17.1   Plural paradigm model

Component paradigm	Role of the component paradigm in the YCAR project
Constructivism	Valuing individual perspectives as truths
Post-positivism	Extending beyond the academy's privileged spaces
Interpretivism	Recognising subjective realities
Critical research	Reifying transformation
Post-structuralism	Recognising participants' views as dynamic

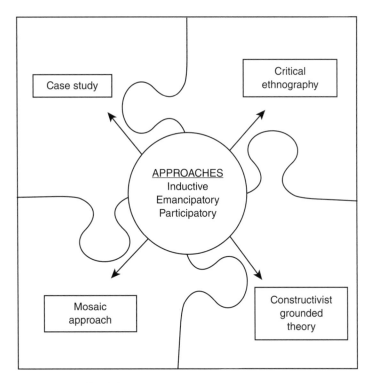

Figure 17.3 *Jigsaw methodology*

approach enabled analysis to emerge from empirical data co-constructed with participants (Charmaz, 2006).

The YCAR study's three principled approaches combined with four single complementary methodologies to form a 'jigsaw' methodology (Figure 17.3). This was useful for maintaining responsiveness to participants' perspectives. It emerged as the study progressed: only grounded theory (GT) was adopted from the start (Glaser and Strauss, 1967), and it accommodated the study's three approaches with ease. Early in the study the decision to adopt GT was refined to constructivist grounded theory (CGT), a GT subset that synergises extant theoretical frameworks with new empirical data (Charmaz, 2006). CGT allowed space for data to be constructed collaboratively in ways that included and valued 'participants' implicit meanings and experiential views' (Charmaz, 2006: 10). Equally, assumptions within CGT that 'we are part of the world we study and … construct our grounded theories through our past and present involvements and interactions' proved valuable for YCAR (Charmaz, 2006: 10). As I had inhabited similar contexts to the YCAR participants (Murray, 2006), the distinction between researcher and researched was minimised. Moreover, constructivism has strongly influenced the ECEC field (DeVries, 2001), so CGT offered further congruence between the study's form and function.

Table 17.2   Three phases of the YCAR project

Phase I	Professional Early Years and Educational Researchers (PEYERs)
Phase II	Children and practitioners in ECEC settings
Phase III	Children and families in their homes

Nevertheless, as CGT is a set of 'principles and practices, not prescriptions' (Charmaz, 2006: 9), it quickly became evident that some additional structure for data construction would be necessary. Charmaz (2006) recognises this issue and advocates ethnography alongside CGT but the YCAR study's focus on social justice indicated *critical* ethnography (CE) (Carspecken, 1996; Thomas, 1993). Reflexivity with participants is common to both CGT and CE and to the Mosaic approach (MA) (Clark and Moss, 2011), which was adopted to provide structure for children and adults not only to construct, but also to interpret, data collaboratively. 'Descriptive case study' (Bassey, 1999; Yin, 2012) completed the 'jigsaw', facilitating practical coordination of YCAR across multiple home and school sites, whilst retaining each site's individual characteristics.

Because of the study's democratic value orientation, ethical considerations permeated the form *and* function of the study, which was conducted according to the British Educational Research Association (BERA) (2004) ethical guidelines (now updated to 2011), with adherence to literature concerning ethical practices in ECEC research (Alderson and Morrow, 2004). The study was framed in three stages, designed to co-construct data with participants:

Phase I

I reasoned that if aspects of young children's activity could be shown as congruent with activity the academy recognises as research, the academy might find it difficult to justify its exclusion of young children. Therefore, initial sampling (Charmaz, 2006) indicated Professional Early Years and Educational Researchers (PEYERs) as Phase I participants. Nine PEYERs participated in interview conversations (Charmaz, 2006) and five engaged in a focus group (Creswell, 2008). All had previously worked in children's services. Given there exists no universal definition of research in the literature, Phase I focused on identifying the nature of educational and ECEC research. Rather than a definition, a taxonomy of thirty-nine research behaviours emerged (see Table 17.3).

The PEYERs ranked the research behaviours and identified exploration, finding solutions, conceptualisation and basing decisions as the four 'most important' so these were prioritised within the YCAR study. Furthermore, the PEYERs indicated that theoretical sampling should include young children, their parents and practitioners.

Table 17.3   Research behaviour framework

Researchers ...

1.	Seek a solution	21.	Investigate
2.	Want to explore	22.	Enquire
3.	Explore with an aim	23.	Test and check
4.	Explore without an aim	24.	Are systematic
5.	Explore with an aim that changes during the process	25.	Are objective
6.	Explore with a fine focus	26.	Base decisions on evidence
7.	Explore broadly	27.	Use processes that are fit for purpose
8.	Find out why things happen	28.	Can replicate process
9.	Find out how things happen	29.	Can replicate output
10.	Examine problems	30.	Use and apply findings in new contexts
11.	Develop better understanding of the world through exploration	31.	Believe what they are doing is good
12.	Increase knowledge	32.	Are focused on their chosen activity
13.	Find a solution	33.	Reflect on process
14.	Go beyond instinct	34.	Reflect on results
15.	Gather data	35.	Do no harm
16.	Build on others' work	36.	Participate with others
17.	Take account of context	37.	Communicate what they are doing
18.	Plan	38.	Can communicate what they have done
19.	Conceptualise	39.	Make links
20.	Question		

Phase II

Three multi-modal case studies (Clark and Moss, 2011; Yin, 2012) were co-constructed with 138 children and their practitioners in ECEC settings in an English Midlands town. Initially, a number of challenges relating to access, gatekeeping and voluntary, informed consent had to be navigated, including withholding of consent for capturing photographs and video footage in one setting (Murray, 2011). Each setting case study was undertaken over six half-days and three full days. The participant profile is shown in Table 17.4.

I worked as a volunteer teaching assistant (TA) in each ECEC setting to build an understanding of the culture in each through 'thick description' (Ryle, 1968), to equalise power relationships in an attempt to move towards 'insider' status (Griffiths, 1998) and to access authentic, naturalistic data (Pellegrini et al., 2004). Nevertheless, gaining insider status was not wholly successful.

Multiple methods were adopted for the co-construction of data (Table 17.5). Drawing on Clark and Moss (2011), this enabled participants to contribute in ways they deemed suitable and to ensure those contributions were appropriately valued.

Table 17.4   Phase II participant profile

	Number of children	Ages of children	Gender share of children	Number and gender share of practitioners	Most recent Ofsted inspection grade	Predominant pedagogic model
Ash setting	32	7–8 years	20 boys 12 girls	3 [1M, 2F]	2 [Good]	Formal
Beech setting	46	4–5 years	23 boys 23 girls	8 [8F]	2 [Good]	Open framework
Cherry setting	60	4–5 years	40 boys 20 girls	6 [1M, 5F]	2 [Good]	Open framework

Table 17.5   Multi-modal methods

Multi-modal methods	Field notes	Interview conversations
Observations	Focus groups	Informal discussions
Documents	Children's artefacts	Photographs
Video recordings	Audio recordings	Research behaviour framework (RBF) analysis sheets

Source: Clark and Moss (2011)

Within the jigsaw methodology's structure, in accordance with CGT processes (Charmaz, 2006), data were constantly compared and evaluated against the research behaviour framework (RBF) in a recursive process. Categorisation and coding of data with participants indicated seventeen children for closer involvement (Table 17.6) who presented clearly and often with research behaviours (see Table 17.3).

Naturalistic observations were recorded with particular focus on these children. Children contributed artefacts, and in Ash and Beech settings most participants took photographs and were involved in the capture of video footage. Practitioners and children engaged with me in focus groups, interview conversations and informal discussion, addressing the nature of research and analysis of primary data (Charmaz, 2006). Using the same filtering process that indicated the seventeen focus children (Table 17.6), Phase II data then suggested two children from each setting who were likely to wish to go on to co-construct further rich data with their families at home (Table 17.7).

Phase III

Initial interview conversations were arranged with families at home to discuss the project. Here, I deliberately established 'outsider' status so families retained power

Table 17.6   Phase II setting 'focus' children

Setting	Pseudonym	Girl	Boy	Age (yr) during setting fieldwork	Home language
Ash	Annie	√		7	
	Billy		√	8	
	Costas		√	8	English
	Demi	√		8	
	Edward		√	8	
	Florence	√		8	
Beech	Gemma	√		5	
	Harry		√	5	English/French
	India	√		5	
	Johnny		√	5	
	Kelly	√		4	English
	Laura	√		5	
Cherry	Martin		√	5	
	Nora	√		5	
	Oscar		√	5	
	Pedro		√	5	Turkish
	Querida	√		4	English

and intrusion was minimised (Griffiths, 1998). I explained and implemented ethical procedures (Alderson and Morrow, 2004; BERA, 2004), provided resources, ensured the children and their families were confident with data collection methods, then handed over data collection to the children and families. Naturalistic behaviour was emphasised as the preferred context for data collection (Pellegrini et al., 2004). Second visits were arranged with each family for a month later to share, discuss, review and analyse multi-modal data in interview conversations and focus groups (Charmaz, 2006).

Analysis was guided predominantly by Charmaz's model for constructivist grounded theory (2006) but complemented by aspects of analysis common to the other three methodologies (Table 17.8).

Data interpreted by children, practitioners and parents 'in action' and 'on action' – and by PEYERs 'on action' (Schön, 1983) – informed further analysis undertaken until a level of 'saturation' was reached (Charmaz, 2006). The analysis and interpretation procedure was lengthy and complex, and whilst participants engaged willingly, their engagement with the full process would have imposed significantly on their everyday lives – an unethical situation (BERA, 2004). Therefore participants' analysis and interpretation were time-limited and the perspectives they provided early in the process were adopted as 'guiding ideals' (Blumer, 1969). This enabled

Table 17.7   Home 'focus' children

	Ash setting		Beech setting		Cherry setting
Pseudonym	Annie	Billy	Gemma	Harry	Martin
Gender	Girl	Boy	Girl	Boy	Boy
Age (yr) during home fieldwork	8	8	5	5	5
Living with ...	Mother Father	Mother Father Sister (9)	Mother Father Brother (8)	Mother Father Brother (4)	Mother Father Sister (4)
Description of home	Modern, detached, 4 bedrooms, garden, on a development in an established English Midlands town	Modern, detached, 4 bedrooms, garden, on a development in an established English Midlands town	Modern, detached, 4 bedrooms, garden, on a development in an established English Midlands town	Modern, detached, 4 bedrooms, garden, on a development in an established English Midlands town	Modern, detached, 4 bedrooms, garden, on a development in an established English Midlands town
Home language	English	English	English	English/French	English
Social class category (MRS, 2006)	A	A/B	B	A	A/B
Family	A	B	C	D	E

Table 17.8   The recursive process of Phase II and III analysis and interpretation

		Transcribe data and apply numerical codes			
	CGT analysis and interpretation methods (Charmaz, 2006)	**Critical ethnography analysis and interpretation methods**		**Mosaic approach (Clark and Moss, 2011)**	**Case study (Bassey, 1999; Yin, 2012)**
		Carspecken (1996)	**Thomas (1993)**		
Constant comparison	Early memo-writing	Preliminary reconstructive analysis		Child conferencing/ listening	
	Initial coding	Reconstructive analysis Dialogic data generation			
	Focused coding	Dialogic data generation			
	Categories	Discovering system relations			
	Axial coding	Discovering system relations	Repeated thinking		Analytic statements
	Advanced memo-writing	Reconstructive analysis			
	Theoretical coding	Discovering system relations		Listening	
		Using system relations to explain findings			

me to complete the time-consuming task of analysis and interpretation in an ethical manner that maintained rigorous alignment with participants' perspectives according to the process in Table 17.8. Within advanced memos, the four prime research behaviours were defined and discussed in relation to extant literature. Through theoretical coding in the final stages of analysis, ninety-two codes spread across the four research behaviours were distilled to nine epistemological factors evidenced in the naturalistic behaviours of young children participating in the YCAR study (Figure 17.4).

The final element in the YCAR study's co-construction of data was deconstructing and evaluating each of the epistemological factors through comparative critical discussion, synthesising findings with extant literature in hundreds of vignettes (Charmaz, 2006). This process attempted to recognise and understand the exposed sophisticated

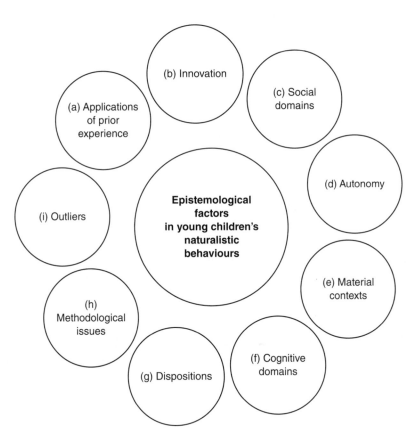

Figure 17.4 *Epistemological factors in young children's naturalistic behaviours*

processes adopted by children in their everyday activities (Bae, 2010). It also revealed congruence between many of the children's natural everyday activities and the four research behaviours deemed 'most important' by academy members. To exemplify these outcomes, two case studies are outlined below.

CASE STUDY ONE

Gemma and the measuring stick

Examples of '(d) Autonomy' relating to children's explorations – one of the nine epistemological factors in young children's research behaviours – were manifested when children *developed their own agenda* (a category within the research behaviour '*explore*').

One day at home, Gemma (girl, aged 5) developed her own agenda when she explored autonomously how to make a measuring stick from two wrapping paper card tubes. At the outset, Gemma asked her mother if she could use two tubes and sticky tape. She then taped the tubes together to make the measuring stick and used pens to add the measuring units. Gemma then tested her measuring stick by asking her brother to stand next to the tube to gauge his height and, finally, she told her mother what she had done.

During this experience Gemma developed her own agenda by examining materials and combining them to construct a measuring stick, aligning with Stebbins' (2001) criteria for exploration in social science research. To pursue her agenda, Gemma had 'space' to operate as an agent, whilst maintaining interdependence with her family (Moss and Petrie, 2002). This activity is congruent with Piaget's view of children as active agents who combine perception and activity to construct new understanding (1969). A number of studies suggest that play can provide a context for children's social agency, provided that the play is 'owned' by the children who construct and engage in it (Markström and Halldén, 2009); Gemma's activity here appears to resonate with these findings.

★ Reflection for case study 1

- What support do adults need to provide so that young children can develop their own agenda and achieve autonomy through exploration?

CASE STUDY TWO

Johnny's wristwatch

During the present study, when they engaged in *conceptualisation* as research behaviour, children sometimes seemed to *plan* as a sub-category of '(f) Cognitive domains'.

One day, during free-flow play in Beech setting, Johnny (boy, 5 years) appeared passive as he watched another child who wore a watch. Subsequently he collected a strip of paper (2.5cm x 12cm), glue and scissors which he took to the writing table and Johnny went on to create a facsimile of a wristwatch made from paper, 'infusing [his] own intentions – [his] own meanings – into objects and actions' (Dyson, 1997: 14).

Young children often plan their solutions '*in action*' (Cox and Smitsman, 2006): in the 'here and now' (Graue and Walsh, 1995). However, here, Johnny appeared to plan *ahead* of action; following apparent inactivity, which later appeared to be observation, he autonomously engaged his 'initiative, involvement and relative control' (Helm and Katz, 2001: 2). Johnny appeared to combine his prior experience of a wristwatch in combination with mental activity to create his facsimile watch, indicating a posteriori conceptualisation (Kant, 1787; Scruton, 2001).

 Reflection for case study 2

- A posteriori conceptualisation occurs when we combine experience with mental activity to make judgements (Kant, 1787; Scruton, 2001). Reflect on your experiences of young children playing: thinking back now, might you have observed them engaging in a posteriori conceptualisation?

Conclusion

The YCAR study was characterised by a value orientation committed to social justice for young children in the context of research. That orientation was pursued through inductive, emancipatory and participatory approaches and a methodology that was reflexive to participants. The form of the YCAR project matched its function. As a result, the YCAR project revealed new understanding of some of the sophisticated ways in which young children behave.

The YCAR study established that participating young children aged 4–8 years could – and did – engage in research behaviours recognised by the academy as congruent with those displayed by adult researchers (see Table 17.9). Given the study's inductive approach, the argument for this is based on deductive logic: a 'valid deduction yields a conclusion that must be true given that its premises are true' (Johnson-Laird and Byrne, 1991: 2). Paradoxically, deductive logic is the academy's dominant methodology (Hanna, 2006).

YCAR produced a plausible account suggesting that children aged 4–8 years engage in research activity naturalistically as part of their daily lives and that this activity is congruent with professional adult researchers' behaviours.

Table 17.9   Young children as researchers

The research behaviour framework (RBF) is populated with behaviours that academy members identify as research	**Major premise**
YCAR children are engaged in behaviours on the RBF	**Minor premise**
Children are engaged in research	**Conclusion**

Chapter summary

This chapter has explored issues concerning young children and research. It has considered the nature of research and young children's roles in research. Conflicts between children's participation and protection rights have been considered and the chapter has provided an overview of the Young Children As Researchers (YCAR) project (Murray, 2012a). The YCAR project confronted the dilemmas and difficulties of judging children's competence in relation to participation, by focusing on children's naturalistic behaviours and exploring their congruence with adult researchers' behaviour.

Questions for reflection and discussion

Look again at the research behaviour framework in Table 17.3. Consider:

1. What can parents do to encourage young children to engage in research behaviour at home?
2. What can practitioners do to encourage young children to engage in research behaviour in their early childhood settings?
3. What barriers might young children encounter as they attempt to engage in research behaviour?

4. Can you think of some examples of research behaviour you have seen in children from birth to 8 years?
5. Can you think of some tensions inherent in ensuring young children are accorded both their protection and participation rights?

Recommended reading

Alderson, P. (2008) *Young Children's Rights.* London: Jessica Kingsley.
This book provides further critical discussion on young children's provision, protection and participation rights.

Harcourt, D., Perry, B. and Waller, T. (eds) (2011) *Researching Young Children's Perspectives: Debating the Ethics and Dilemmas of Educational Research with Children.* Abingdon: Routledge.
This edited book critically examines the complex area of research with young children.

Meltzoff, A.N. (2011) 'Social cognition and the origins of imitation, empathy and theory of mind', in U. Goswami (ed.), *The Wiley-Blackwell Handbook of Childhood Cognitive Development,* 2nd edn. Malden, MA: Wiley-Blackwell, pp. 49–75.
Psychologist Andrew Meltzoff explores the central problem of social cognition and why it is important in human development.

Murray, J. (2012b) 'Young children's explorations: young children's research?', *Early Child Development and Care,* 182 (9): 1209–25.
Further output from the YCAR study, this paper focuses specifically on young children's naturalistic explorations as research behaviour.

Recommended websites

www.crae.org.uk/
The website for the Children's Rights Alliance for England, which lobbies for the protection of children's rights.

www.open.ac.uk/researchprojects/childrens-research-centre/
The website for the Children's Research Centre.

www.unicef.org/crc/
Information concerning the United Nations Convention on the Rights of the Child.

Want to learn more about this chapter? Visit the companion website at **www.sagepub.co.uk/walleranddavis3e** to access podcasts from the author and child observation videos.

18

Reflective Practice

Caroline Jones

 Key chapter objectives

- To identify the key features of reflection and reflective practices
- To consider the factors influencing the process of reflective practice
- To explore the links between reflective practices and professionalism in early childhood education and care
- To highlight case studies and research relating to reflective practice
- To conceptualise reflective practice from a sociocultural historical perspective

Introduction

It is widely accepted that early years practitioners are expected to reflect on practice in a number of ways and that reflective practice is a vital aspect of working with young children (Craft and Paige-Smith, 2011). Even new practitioners are expected to be given time to reflect on their practice, to link it to their understanding of theory and to be able to discuss their reflections with more experienced colleagues (Nutbrown, 2012a). This chapter critically examines the notion of reflective practice in the context of early childhood provision. It is based on the premise that reflective practice is no longer an option for those working with children but should be considered as 'a political and a social responsibility' (Bolton, 2010: 11), belonging to all those involved in early childhood policy and practice. It is important to acknowledge from the outset that understandings of reflective practice are constantly evolving and there is no clear consensus on the meaning of the terms reflection, reflective practice or indeed reflective practitioner. The first part of this chapter reminds readers about traditional understandings of reflective practice, primarily concerned with 'thinking about practice' and reflecting 'in' and 'on' practice (Dewey, 1933; Schön, 1987). The reader is then invited to explore some more recent research, theoretical frameworks and definitions. Building on existing knowledge, it is emphasised that reflective practice is not merely a useful tool for improvement through self-evaluation and professional development, but a complex, dynamic process, an integral part of leadership and the professional identities of early childhood practitioners. Using case studies and drawing on research in context, readers are provided not only with an overview of the key features of reflection and reflective practices, but also stimulated to further reflection – 'the opening up of a problem space' – on the points raised throughout the chapter (Engestrom, 1993, cited in Craft and Paige-Smith, 2008: 90).

Reflective practice, as a value, is inevitably influenced by the broader sociocultural and historical perspectives on early childhood curricula and pedagogy, a point developed later in the chapter. By supporting readers to reach a deeper understanding of reflective process and identify further opportunities for reflection, this chapter must also engage in 'meta-reflection' or reflection on reflection, in order to make the process of reflection explicit (Appleby, 2010).

The chapter concludes that reflective practice should not be understood as a simple cyclical, linear or static state. Rather it is a constantly tangled tapestry, an evolving process of weaving theory and practice, a position, an open-ended state of mind, involving collaborative interactions between a range of professionals, parents, policy makers and early years practitioners, each operating in their own unique contexts.

Reflective practice, traditional meanings and understandings

Reflective practice is difficult to conceptualise as reflection can take many different forms. Taken literally, the adjective 'reflective' describes a physical process, the capability of a surface to reflect light or sound and create a reflection. The use of the word 'reflective' can also describe a mental process, the capability of individuals to engage in deep thought and to create a reflection of a social situation. During the process of reflection perceptions of the situation or practice may change and develop. The notions of reflection and reflective practice in the educational arena are not new or confined to education. Healthcare professionals use models of reflection based on traditional and contemporary understandings of the process (Davies, 2012; Gibbs, 1988; Johns, 1995; Newton, 2000). However, the growth of policy interest in early childhood and the expansion of services have resulted in a renewed emphasis on reflection as part of the drive for change and ongoing improvement in early childhood education and care. Reflection and reflective practice have become culturally embedded in professional dialogue, not only in early childhood but also in the compulsory, higher education and lifelong learning sectors. It is also worth noting here that reflective practice is not exclusive remit of education but is increasingly debated and applied in a range of contexts, including private and public business services and industries. What does reflective practice involve and why is it important? Can it be taught or is it a personal attribute? Does it really have the assumed potential to transform practice or contribute to the vision of a world-class workforce?

The theoretical origins of reflective practice can be traced back to Dewey (1933), one of the most influential of modern thinkers on education who offers an early critique of the technicist view of the world. Dewey was concerned with building a fair and democratic society and made an interesting distinction between two different types of professional actions. First is what he termed 'routine action', in other words, 'we have always done it like this' actions or practices based on habit and tradition. The dominant factor for these actions is usually an externally perceived authority. By definition, these actions and practices are fairly static or unchanging. Secondly, in contrast with routine action, Dewey noted that some professional actions are persistently and carefully considered and justifications developed for them. This 'reflective action' is a more flexible action involving a willingness to engage in self-evaluation and professional development. Dewey (1933) offered an early systematic approach to reflection, suggesting that it stems from identifying a problem and in attempting to resolve the issue, change or development takes place. This can then be evaluated and continued or discontinued. Dewey highlighted five consecutive and distinct steps in this thinking process:

- a felt difficulty
- its location and definition
- suggestion of a possible solution
- development by reasoning
- further experiment and observation leading to acceptance or rejection of the development.

This provided the first of many cyclical models attempting to represent reflective practice. In arguing for what he called 'fluidity' of thought, Dewey (1933) implied that teachers or those working with children cannot simply rely on things just because they have been done in the past. He pointed out that there is unlikely to be one right way to do something and that practitioners need freedom to be adaptable or to use their 'reflective intelligence' to find out what works and what does not, through adopting a problem-solving approach. Dewey describes reflective thinking as turning a subject over and over in your mind and giving every aspect of practice, policy and educational organisation serious consideration. This analytical and reflective style of thinking drew attention to the complexity of working with children, rather than simply focusing on technical aspects such as curriculum planning and delivery.

Fifty years later, Donald Schön (1983, 1987) was also critical of technical rationalism. He again emphasised the complexity of the teaching role, and highlighted the need to understand the unique problems that face practitioners in real situations involving real people. In suggesting that professional action is continuous and complex, Schön developed the notion of 'professional artistry' (1987: 22). More specifically, he pointed out that professionals face unique circumstances and make decisions based on previous experiences, therefore reflection is a process embedded 'in' and 'on' practice. This well-known conceptual framework for thinking about reflection is worth revisiting in view of its significant contribution to the debate on reflective practice and its relevance when related specifically to early childhood. It can be summarised as:

1. Reflection *in* action: thinking, feeling and behaving automatically or on your feet; being spontaneous and creative during an actual event or practice.
2. Reflection *on* action: retrospective thinking: thinking immediately or later after the event, how you could have done things differently or would do things differently in the future.

Certainly, many of the practices in early years settings stem from familiar routines and patterns of activity. These are drawn from a repertoire of intuitive knowledge and skills, acquired by reflection and experience, referred to by Schön as 'knowledge-in-action'. This type of knowledge is rarely shared in discussion or in writing. It is experiential knowledge that is so familiar that practitioners may cease to be aware of it. It has been likened to the experienced car driver, driving without consciously thinking about the intricate details of the manoeuvres (Jones and Pound, 2008). Schön's model suggests practitioners should slow down and think in order to develop knowledge and become aware of the tacit knowledge incorporated into routine practices. This is equally applicable at the planning stage, in other words, reflecting before practice as well as during or afterwards.

With reference to primary teaching, Pollard and Tann (1993) developed these ideas, identifying six key characteristics of reflective practice. These have been adapted below, to apply to early childhood contexts:

1. Reflective practice implies an active concern with aims and consequences, as well as technical efficiency.
2. Reflective practice can be applied in a cyclical or spiralling process, in which practitioners monitor, evaluate and revise their own practice.
3. Reflective practice requires competence in methods of enquiry, to support the development of competence.
4. Reflective practice requires attitudes of open-mindedness, responsibility and wholeheartedness.

5. Reflective practice is based on professional judgement, informed by self-reflection and insights from educational disciplines.
6. Reflective practice, professional learning and personal fulfilment are enhanced through collaboration and dialogue with colleagues.
   (Adapted from Pollard and Tann, 1993: 9–10)

These characteristics draw attention to reflective practice as a collaborative, dialogic process of refining and developing practice, based on professional knowledge, experience, competence and inclusive attitudes. They support the idea that reflective practice should not be viewed in a purely technical sense, but instead seen as an informed process of open-ended questioning and learning in order to gain deeper insights into the meanings of their experiences. Since then, there have been many attempts to conceptually theorise reflective practice and understand the process of reflection. These have continued to characterise reflective practice, using cyclical or linear models, based on stages or levels of analysis, to enable reflection. Most of these models depict a widely held view of reflective practice, as being a relatively straightforward cycle of action, evaluation, reflection and more action leading to improvement. The increasing number of attempts to represent reflective practice have only served to confuse rather than clarify, leading to 'muddles in the models' which could result in failure or, even worse, 'significant damage' to education (Bolton, 2010: xx). Muddles in the models may lead to lack of engagement and dissatisfaction.

Models such as those in Figure 18.1 fail to take account of wider internal and external factors that may hinder or constrain practitioners in their endeavours to reflect and improve. The models commonly assume a capacity on the part of practitioners to mediate, adapt, articulate and reframe their own practice. They fail to acknowledge that many practitioners are not trained or formally qualified to a level that demands questioning, analytical thinking and reflection, and levels of knowledge and experience vary considerably within and between settings. Even where staff are formally qualified, a review of early education and childcare and qualifications identified that the content of the qualifications does not always equip practitioners with the necessary knowledge needed to provide high quality care and early education or to support ongoing professional development. The final report of the *Nutbrown Review* suggested that continuing professional development (CPD) should be a priority for all those who work with young children (Nutbrown, 2012b).

Writing with reference to health professionals, Newton (2000) highlighted the importance of the work environment as either conducive to or a potential inhibitor of reflective practice. Her study of student nurses identified that the amount and type of clinical experience influenced their apparent ability to reflect (Newton, 2000). Less qualified and less experienced practitioners may feel uncomfortable or unsure and could need considerable support from experienced mentors or leaders of practice, in identifying how and what to reflect upon. Nutbrown (2012b) recommended that all new early years practitioners should have professional support in

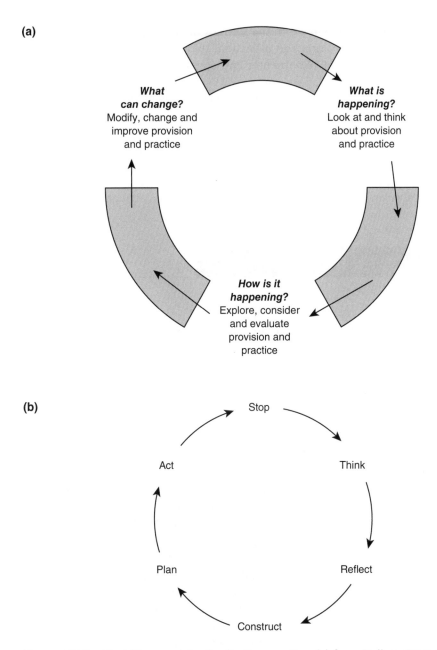

(a)

What can change?
Modify, change and improve provision and practice

What is happening?
Look at and think about provision and practice

How is it happening?
Explore, consider and evaluate provision and practice

(b)

Stop

Think

Reflect

Construct

Plan

Act

Figure 18.1 *Muddling models of reflective practice: (a) from Hallett, 2013: 33; (b) from Tarrant, 2013: 52*

their first six months of employment, in the form of mentoring. Davies (2012) again makes the link between mentoring and reflection, stating that the process of reflection forms an 'integral part' between mentor and mentee, and is reliant on effective mentoring (Davies, 2012).

The revised Statutory Framework for the Early Years Foundation Stage (EYFS) (DfE, 2012d) acknowledged the need for ongoing supervision, training and support by imposing a new requirement on providers to conduct staff appraisals in order to identify training needs, and secure opportunities for continued professional development for staff.

At this point readers might find it useful to refer to the case study below and consider how it is linked to traditional models and ideas concerning reflective practice.

CASE STUDY ONE

Snack time

It was 'tidy-up time' at Rocking Horse pre-school group. 'Tidy-up time, children', said Sharon, deputy supervisor, as she put the tidy-up song on the CD player. Children scurried around, putting all the toys away in the right boxes until the music stopped. 'Children, stop now and listen. Go and wash your hands, then sit down at the tables for your snack', instructed Sharon. Whilst Sharon supervised the tidying up and handwashing, Jackie, an assistant, set out the tablecloth, snacks, cups and plates. She placed a plant in the centre of the table and name cards were positioned at the places where the children were expected to sit. Jackie chose a child to give out the snack of the day and poured out the drinks. Children could choose milk or water. Each child had to say please and thank you, and wait until they were all finished before getting ready to go outside to play. It was viewed by the two staff as a lovely part of the day, an opportunity for the children to sit and eat as a group, an opportunity to recognise their names and to talk socially for 15 minutes. It also gave time for staff to have their own cup of tea.

Jane, the pre-school supervisor, was studying for her Early Years Foundation Degree. She had read some research that suggested the curriculum should emerge from the children's interests. She was aware that the EYFS (DfE, 2012d) emphasised the importance of giving children choices and not frequently interrupting their play in order for them to join whole-group adult-directed activities. The course had prompted her to think about the daily routine in her own setting. On reflection, she realised it was rather rigid and controlled by adults. Much of the day children were doing what they were told to do and going where they were told to go. She reflected on the various elements of the routine and felt there was room for improvement.

She decided to change the long-established snack-time routine, and introduce an 'independent snack time' that she had heard about from one of her fellow students. Jane discussed this with her colleagues and, although they were somewhat resistant, they agreed to introduce the new routine and see how it worked. In the new routine an adult with two child 'helpers' set up a 'snack trolley', and a table (still with cloth and plant), for an hour each session. This trolley had the choice of snack, drinks, cups, plates and name cards. Once it was ready for use, one child told the other children that the snack bar was open. Children continued playing until they decided they wanted their snack. Jane hovered by the handwashing area to ensure they washed their hands. Children could then help themselves from a choice of two snacks and drinks from the trolley. They sat at the small snack table placing their names in the basket. Staff told those children who needed reminding that the snack bar would be closing just before tidying away the trolley. Children put their dirty plates in the washing-up bowl and went back to play, wherever they wished, when they had finished.

Reflection for case study 1

- How are Schön's 'reflection on action' and 'knowledge in action' reflected in this scenario?
- Can you identify any of Pollard and Tann's key characteristics of reflective practice?
- How do each of the cyclical models in Figure 18.1 relate to the processes taking place in the case study?
- What were the consequences of Jane's reflections for staff, children and parents?
- How might Jane have introduced this change to staff, children and parents?
- What were the potential challenges facing Jane in this scenario?
- Why might it be important to document this change?
- What changes could be made within this or your own professional context in order to allow children more choices and control?

Theory, knowledge and reflective practice

Jane, perhaps unwittingly, was engaged in a complex level of reflection. Forde and O'Brien (2011) suggest that reflection involves adopting a questioning approach to practice, including a critical dimension in order to promote change. Brookfield (1995: 29–39) refers to this as questioning or 'hunting' assumptions using four critically reflective lenses:

1. Practitioners' own autobiographies
2. The 'eyes' of learners
3. The perspectives of colleagues through critical dialogue or conversations
4. Information from theoretical literature

Elements from all four of these lenses can be seen in the case study. Firstly, there is Jane's own background, position and experience as a student sharing practice with fellow students and reading research. Secondly, Jane thought about the snack routine through the eyes of the children. In critically analysing the children's experiences she realised that their play was being interrupted, they had no choice as to when they ate their snack and they were simply expected to conform to a pre-determined routine. Thirdly, she considered her colleagues' views in the discussion about changing the routine. Finally, she used her newly acquired theoretical and experiential knowledge to reflect on and develop practice in order to improve the quality of the children's experiences. Ghaye (2011) suggests that this type of reflection should be deliberate and is crucial for future improvement to take place:

> Improvement cannot take place unless we learn from experience. Failure to do this is resigning ourselves to being prisoners to our past. Reflection-on-practice is an intentional action; the intention is to improve the quality of educational experiences through rigorous reflection of the learning that has accrued as a consequence of engaging reflective practices of one kind or another. (Ghaye, 2011: 297)

Parnell confirms that reflection is a way of weaving theory and practice and points out that the ability to 'question and grapple with what exists before our very eyes is sharpened with reflection' (Parnell, 2012: 119). However, this is dependent on practitioners having extended their own knowledge through being aware of the latest research and participating in dialogue with their colleagues. As Craft and Paige-Smith (2011: 3–4) point out, early years practitioners are increasingly expected to be involved with the body of knowledge about their practice and this 'involves a level of theoretical understanding about children's learning and participation in early years settings, and being able to reflect on how the literature, policy, and theory relate to practice'. Taking this point further, it has been suggested that reflecting on practice not only involves relating practice to theory but actually developing new theory. Moss (2011), drawing on Rinaldi's (2006) 'pedagogy of listening', suggests that the concept of reflective practice can be understood as 'a rigorous process of meaning-making, a continuous process of constructing theories about the world, testing them through dialogue and listening, then reconstructing those theories' (Moss, 2011: xiv). From this perspective the idea of reflective practice makes significant demands on the practitioner. Far from simply reflecting in or on their own practice for improvement in the immediate sense, reflective practitioners require a complex array of critical skills, professional knowledge and attributes. The professional identity of a reflective practitioner is related to a desire to make meaning of their experiences.

In the research project outlined below, the three practitioners involved declare themselves to be reflective practitioners as they claim to 'practice learning and teaching in reflection, action and reflective action' (Parnell, 2012: 117). This study into reflective practices was conducted in the United States and is worthy of further consideration.

The research box provides further detail of this research study.

 Research in context

Parnell, W. (2012) 'Experiences of teacher reflection: Reggio inspired practices in the studio', *Journal of Early Childhood Research*, 10 (2): 117–33.

This research, part of a larger study, set out to explore if deliberate conversations and collaboration sessions that look back as they move forward, help practitioners in their role as co-learners with children, make meaning of their experiences, before, through and after the experience. It asked how the process of looking back helps move practice forward. The research took place in a remodelled school, with two creative teaching spaces designated as studios, inspired by the Reggio Emilia approach. The phenomenological research aimed to use collaborative reflection to give meaning to lived experiences and describe the experiences before developing theories to explain them. The research question was: 'How can reflective practice help us make meaning of our experiences in the early childhood studio?' (p. 117). The author, a teacher–educator, acted as a researcher-participant, co-researching with the two studio teachers, reflecting alongside them to make meaning of their experiences in the studios. Working with small groups of children these teacher–researchers intentionally co-learn with children, in the one studio session about making family faces and in the other about creating birds and nests. The research paper illuminates how practitioner reflection can be supported and enhanced by including children as part of the process. Rinaldi's (2006) ideas on pedagogical listening underpin the data collection and analysis.

Numerous data were collected using a qualitative approach and eclectic methods, including field notes, journals, video and audio recordings, e-journals

(Continued)

(Continued)

and reflective sessions, listening and living in the experiences. The data were segmented into themes and categories, and three discussions were analysed in detail from multiple perspectives. The results were analysed and described using pertinent extracts from the data with extensive collaboration, dialogue and interrogation of reflection. The study provides detailed insights into the complexity of the process of reflection and its potential as a means of understanding practices. Using e-journal extracts, Parnell's research illustrates how teacher reflection can be uncomfortable, good, emotional, individual, relational, collaborative and value-driven. Problems can arise and lead to more reflection. Parnell recalls wondering how practitioners know what to do when faced with competent children, how practitioners work as partners with a child in scaffolding their learning and development. He describes being propelled 'forward through living in questions, rather than answering them' (p. 124). One teacher in the study made the point that reflection involves not only the teacher and the child but can also be valuable in connecting to parents. Parnell reminds the reader that 'Remembering to double and triple back around on our experiences with others allows us to see other points of view and allows others into our meaning of experiences' (p. 126). This is evident in a discussion about how other teachers in the centre viewed the studio and the frustrations of the studio teachers in that they felt misunderstood.

By the end of the study, the three co-researchers had brought together their learning, their documentation through reflective dialogue. Through a collaborative and collegial process of reflection, the research team came to believe 'in a school which practices a strongly held set of values, such as the one of teacher-reflection' (p. 131). The researcher was prompted to make a life-changing decision, to change his role from administrator to one of pedagogical director, using reflection to develop the school context and carve a '*third mind* (intersubjective spaces) for meeting up to work within each other's thinking, and grapple in the labor of loving children and school community'. These experiences, he concludes, will move them into the '*unknowing*, wondering what comes next' (pp. 131–2) in the process of reflection.

The reflective practitioner: professional identities

Parnell's study was dependent on the willingness of the practitioners to expose themselves to minute, detailed scrutiny and demonstrates the potential power of reflective practices. The reflective practitioners were at the heart of the process. They appear to be rather like archaeologists digging through layers of earth, exploring at deeper and deeper levels but not knowing what they will find next and having to examine their findings, subjecting them to further scrutiny. Moss (2007) warned against a narrow definition of reflective practitioners. He suggested that early childhood settings may be seen primarily as places for 'technical practice: places where society can apply powerful human technologies to children to produce pre-determined outcomes' and that institutions should instead be seen as a place of 'democratic political practice' (2007: 5). Rather than applying such technologies to children, practitioner reflection might be supported and enriched by working with children, listening to them and involving them in the process of reflection.

Developing an identity as a reflective practitioner involves aspiring to be more than a 'worker as technician' (Moss, 2007, 2008, 2011). Instead, Moss called for an early childhood worker to be a 'democratic and reflective professional' who is capable of thinking critically and co-constructing 'meaning, identity, and values' (2008: 125). It is beyond the scope of this chapter to debate in detail the notion of 'professional'. Manning-Morton (2006) contends that 'professionalism' in the early years must also be understood in terms of the day-to-day detail of practitioners'

> relationships with children, parents and colleagues; relationships that demand high levels of physical, emotional and personal knowledge and skill. Therefore, being a truly effective early years professional requires a reflexive interpretation of those relationships not only through the lens of our theoretical knowledge but also through the mirror of our subjective personal histories and our present, feeling, embodied selves. (2006: 42)

Being a reflective practitioner is an inherent part of the professional identity of an early childhood worker, of potential value to the individual as well as to the setting and ultimately the children's learning and development. Osgood (2006) suggests that a professional identity is enshrined in behaviours, about what practitioners may be doing at particular moments in time, rather than a common set of indicators. Leitch and Day (2000) additionally point out that more attention needs to be given to the importance of the role of emotion in understanding and developing the capacities for reflection that facilitate personal, professional and ultimately system change. Moss (2008), on the other hand, sees professional identity as espousing a common core of values, many of which have also been linked with the characteristics of effective leaders (Jones and Pound, 2008).

Reflective practice is about seeing practice though the eyes of others, about questioning things that are taken for granted, but also about how practitioners feel, their understandings (Appleby, 2010). Appleby also talks about 'the ability to think critically and creatively about reflective practice and the confidence and motivation to construct a personal interpretation of what it means for us as individuals in our particular context'. She goes on to suggest that it is possible to examine the 'personal, social and political "assumptions" surrounding what it means to be a reflective practitioner and to reach a position where we as individuals are able to make informed decisions about our practice' (Appleby, 2010: 8–9). However, practitioners do not work in isolation either from their 'community of practice' or from the broader social, cultural and historical context.

Critical reflection is dialogic and requires social connections with other practitioners, parents, children and communities, to share ideas and possibilities.

Parnell's (2012) study identifies a clear connection between the reflective practitioner and a common core of values and beliefs, which may themselves be contested. In bridging the space between personal values and beliefs and professional practices, reflective practice itself becomes a value and an attitude rather than a state, closely linked to views on the purpose of education, the child as a learner, curricula and critical pedagogy. These societal and individual standpoints will impact on the identity of the reflective practitioner, on the role of the adult in promoting learning and development and on whether his or her reflective practice could be described as technical or truly democratic.

The next part of this chapter invites readers to consider their own position on reflective practice.

Reflective practice: a sociocultural historical approach

Reflective practice does not take place in a vacuum. All practice is embedded in a sociocultural historical and political context. Reflective practice at setting level is, to a greater or lesser extent, dependent on dominant values and beliefs in society, at any given point in time and space, about the purpose of education and views on the learner within the sociocultural historical context. A conceptual framework developed by MacNaughton (2003) in relation to curriculum positions on conforming, reforming and transforming society, is now adapted to theorise reflective practice (MacNaughton, 2003). From this standpoint, reflective practice can be viewed not as cyclical or linear but as 'positional' or influenced by, and situated within, a particular societal position on the purpose of education. These positions will impact on the type, purpose and ultimately the depth of reflection that takes place. Is it purely functional, about moderate changes and professional development? Alternatively, has it the potential to lead to a radical overhaul of established patterns of working? Is the perceived purpose of reflection to conform to existing norms, or to reform and possibly transform practices?

Conforming, reforming and transforming

The 'conforming' position is characterised by compliance with rules, and a technical approach to curricula and pedagogy, usually in the form of standards, statutory requirements and non-statutory guidance documents. From this perspective reflective practice is reduced to a tool for ensuring compliance to externally imposed evaluation criteria or for governing early childhood education and care. It is narrowly interpreted as a technical process of ensuring pre-determined outcomes are reached and driven by prescribed linear targets. In other words, reflective practice is focused on 'assessing practitioner's own conformity to externally imposed norms' (Moss, 2011: xvii). From the 'reforming' standpoint, teaching and learning are more flexible, including individualised planning. Education is associated with producing citizens who are free thinkers with the potential to make some changes to society. In this case, reflective practice is a cyclical process, related to individual learning and professional development, to refining and developing practice in a moderate sense. The third, more radical perspective, 'transforming', suggests fundamental change and is related to co-constructed research-based curricula and pedagogy which promote equity in communities. Reflective practice involves dialogue, action-research and reflection on broader contextual and political issues. These three positions are further illustrated in Table 18.1.

The three positions in Table 18.1 are not separate or mutually exclusive. It may be that depending on the context reflective practice oscillates back and forth between

Table 18.1   Three positions: a conceptual framework for thinking about reflective practice

	Purpose of education*	Views on learner*	Curriculum and pedagogy*	Approach to reflective practice
Conforming	To reproduce society, aspire to preserve status quo, produce citizens that accept, respect and conform to social norms	Passive learner, conforming, moves through same developmental stages	Centrally controlled, pre-determined, linear, target-driven, routine, formal, traditional subjects, timetables, focus on summative assessment	Technical approach, evaluation against pre-specified standards of practice, tool for governing early childhood, straightforward traditional linear or cyclical model
Reforming	To promote some minor changes in society for the better, to produce citizens as individual 'free' thinkers	Individual holistic learner, creative thinker, adaptable, able to make independent choices	Locally controlled, developmentally appropriate, flexible pattern to the day, integrated, enabling environment based on child's choices and interests, focus on observational assessments	Individual approach or organisational level, self-evaluative, strives for improvement and professional development, challenges and questions practice, re-interprets and refines
Transforming	To foster radical changes to society, to produce citizens who are critical thinkers and aspire to transform society, aiming for equity and social justice	Powerful, strong, active, participant, decision maker, child has rights	Participatory, co-constructed by communities including child, parent and professionals, anti-biased, inclusive, enabling environment	Democratic, autonomous, self, problem solver, change agent, creative, analytical, critical, questioning Professional, dialogue, documentation, community, collaborative, risk taking, listening, change agent, contesting, open-ended

* These three columns are adapted from MacNaughton, 2003.

all three positions. Alternatively all three may even be evident simultaneously. This indicates that reflective practice is not value-neutral but is in itself a fluid value. The following case study illustrates the potentially transforming impact of reflection on values, attitudes and practices.

CASE STUDY TWO

Promoting inclusion

Swallowfield Primary School had a speech and language unit, housed in a temporary classroom and separate from the rest of the school. Although children came into school for Friday assemblies, there was very little contact between the unit and the mainstream school provision. The new headteacher immediately realised this was exclusive practice and saw the potential to create a more inclusive approach. She held a number of meetings with staff, parents and governors, and consulted the children. Eventually, with support from the local authority, the speech and language provision was totally re-organised. It moved into the main school building and was renamed the ARC (Additional Resource Centre). The timetable was re-organised so children could frequently participate in school events. Deployment of staff was re-organised in order for children in the ARC to access lessons with their peers, when appropriate for each individual child. One child, for example, would go to Numeracy sessions, with a support worker on hand, as his level of attainment in numeracy was well above the average for his age. Other children joined their peers for physical education or topic work. After 12 months it was as if the ARC children were part of the school, albeit still receiving speech therapy and individualised precision teaching in the ARC. Children were registered in their main classroom and became used to coming and going between the ARC and their main classroom. The philosophy of the school changed so parents, children and staff understood that children should be educated in a place where they can learn best. Children knew why they went to the ARC and it was viewed as an entirely positive place to learn. Sign language and visual timetables were introduced throughout the whole school. All the children could sing and sign together in assemblies and school performances. The ethos of the entire school gradually changed and the divide between the 'unit' and the school no longer existed. The local authority used the ARC as an example and a second provision also converted from a segregated unit to a resource centre in a school. Eventually all special school provision across the authority became integrated into mainstream schools.

Reflection for case study 2

- How are leadership, professionalism, and reflection and community interwoven in this example?
- How does this scenario fit into the columns in Table 18.1?
- What impact might the reflection and subsequent change have on children with and without speech and language difficulties?
- How could the experiences described in the case study influence adults' values and attitudes?

Case study 2 highlighted the interactive nature of reflective practice as involving key players, including policy makers, practitioners, children and families. Practitioners are in part accountable and responsible not only for their own actions and values but also for the social, cultural and political contexts they operate within (Bolton, 2010: 11). Transformation can potentially be achieved through reflective enquiry, driven by a combination of child-centred reflection, adult-centred reflection and group reflection within communities and society.

Chapter summary

This chapter has identified some of the key features of reflective practice and confirmed the centrality of reflective practice in early childhood. It has traced the notion of reflective practice from traditional cyclical or linear models to more complex understandings of reflective practice as a dynamic, value-laden and interactive process. Reflective practice has been examined and presented not as a technical, superficial or context-neutral activity, but linked to aspects of leadership, professionalism, change and pedagogy, ultimately influenced by the current sociocultural historical and political contexts. The chapter has acknowledged that reflection is a 'complex concept that has defied consensus on definition although some commonalities exist' (McClure, 2005: 3). It involves the self and is triggered by the questioning of actions, values and beliefs. Case studies and research have illustrated that reflective practice is an ethical, value-driven, emotional, open-ended process where policy and practice are being explored and critically and actively re-interpreted from multiple perspectives. Whilst there will inevitably be constraints facing early years practitioners in their endeavours to become democratic and reflective professionals, Manning-Morton concludes that it is essential to discard the deficit model of early years practitioners and promote 'the professional identity of a critically reflexive theoretical boundary crosser' (2006: 50).

The notion of 'reflective practice' remains lacking in theoretical sophistication, particularly in relation to the social and political dimensions of learning. As well as more practical challenges such as time constraints, the structural diversity of ECEC provision and the legacy of a split between 'childcare' and 'early education' policy and practices, serve to make any universal model of reflective practice a challenge to interpret in practice. Embedded within a turbulent economic and social policy context, Ghaye suggests that reflective practice may at least fulfil its potential to help practitioners make sense of the uncertainty in their workplaces and offer them 'courage to work competently and ethically at the edge of order and chaos' (Ghaye, 2000: 7). As reflective practices are rooted in values and beliefs about what is best for children, supported by knowledge, theory and experience, it is perhaps time to embrace the broader notion of democratic pedagogical enquiry where the reflective practitioner is redefined as a democratic pedagogical enquirer or leader. Nutbrown (2012b: 7) asserts: 'Excellent pedagogical leadership is vital in improving the quality of provision, and all early years practitioners can aspire to be pedagogical leaders.' In future, reflective practice may have outlived its usefulness as it cannot portray the complexity of theory, policy and practice in early childhood contexts. More research is needed into the children's workforce and a radical overhaul will be needed to ensure that the longstanding rhetoric of a world-class, integrated workforce becomes a reality.

Questions for reflection and discussion

1. How can reflective practice enable practitioners to enhance children's experiences?
2. Can you identify the opportunities and constraints for reflective practice in your own context?
3. What are the key characteristics of a democratic and reflective professional?
4. How democratic and reflective would you consider yourself to be?
5. How has reading this chapter impacted on your understanding of reflection as a process of pedagogical enquiry with the potential to transform practice?

Recommended reading

Appleby, K. (2010) 'Reflective practice: reflective thinking', in M. Reed and N. Canning (eds), *Reflective Practice in the Early Years*. London: Sage. pp. 5–23.
A chapter based on students' perceptions, which explores the reality of reflective practice. Appleby uses an easy-to-follow style to unravel some complex ideas on reflection and reflective practice.

Hallett, E. (2013) *The Reflective Early Years Practitioner.* London: Sage.
The book brings together reflective practice and work-based learning. It is aimed specifically at early years practitioners and provides up-to-date, essential reading for anyone studying early childhood programmes that combine vocational and academic learning.

Paige-Smith, A. and Craft, A. (eds) (2011) *Developing Reflective Practice in the Early Years*, 2nd edn. Maidenhead: Open University Press.
This book supports early years practitioners in articulating and understanding their own practice in greater depth. Written in accessible language, it explores professionally relevant aspects of reflective practice, including children's wellbeing, multi-disciplinary working, parent partnership and inclusion.

Parnell, W. (2012) 'Experiences of teacher reflection: Reggio inspired practices in the studio', *Journal of Early Childhood Research*, 10 (2): 117–33.
An inspiring, detailed account of a study in a US Children's Center. The researcher lives the life of the teacher, co-researching with teachers and collecting a range of data, to explore the notion and purpose of reflective practice. An innovative study with results that anyone working in early childhood would find interesting and stimulating.

Want to learn more about this chapter? Visit the companion website at **www.sagepub.co.uk/walleranddavis3e** to access podcasts from the author and child observation videos.

References

Abbott, L. and Hevey, D. (2001) 'Training to work in the early years: developing the climbing frame', in G. Pugh (ed.), *Contemporary Issues in the Early Years: Working Collaboratively with Children*, 3rd edition. London: Sage.

Adair, J. (2009) *Effective Leadership*, 2nd edn. London: Pan Macmillan.

Adams, K. (2013) 'Childhood in crisis? Perceptions of 7–11-year-olds on being a child and the implications for education's well-being agenda', *Education 3–13*, 41 (5): 523–37. (Published online, January 2012, doi: 10.1080/03004279.2011.613849.)

Ainscow, M., Booth, T. and Dyson, A. (eds) (2006) *Improving Schools, Developing Inclusion (Improving Learning)*. London: Routledge.

Akilapa, R. and Simkiss, D. (2012) 'Cultural influences and safeguarding children', *Paediatrics and Child Health*, 22 (11): 490–5.

Albee, G.W. (2006) 'Historical overview of primary prevention of psychopathology: address to the 3rd World Conference on the promotion of mental health and prevention of mental and behavioral disorders, September 15–17, 2004, Auckland, New Zealand', *Journal of Primary Prevention*, 27 (5): 449–56.

Alderfer, C.P. (1972) *Existence, Relatedness and Growth: Human Needs in Organizational Settings*. New York: Free Press.

Alderson, P. (2005) 'Children's rights: a new approach to studying childhood', in H. Penn, *Understanding Early Childhood: Issues and Controversies*. Maidenhead: Open University Press and McGraw-Hill Education.

Alderson, P. (2008) *Young Children's Rights: Exploring Beliefs, Principles and Practice*. London: Jessica Kingsley.

Alderson, P. and Morrow, G. (2004) *Ethics, Social Research and Consulting with Children*. London: Barnardo's.

Alderson, P., Hawthorne, J. and Killen, M. (2006) 'The participation rights of premature babies', in H. Van Beers, A. Invernizzi and B. Milne (eds), *Beyond Article 12: Essential Readings on Children's Participation*. Bangkok: Black and White Publications. pp. 57–65.

Alderton, T. and Campbell-Barr, V. (2005) 'Quality early education – quality food and nutritional practices? Some initial results from a pilot research project into food and nutrition practices in early years settings in Kent, UK', *International Journal of Early Years Education*, 13 (3): 197–213.

Alkire, S. and Deneulin, S. (2009) 'The human development and capability approach', in S. Deneulin and L. Shahani (eds), *An Introduction to the Human Development and Capability Approach*. London: Earthscan. pp. 22–48.

Allen, G. (2011) *Early Intervention: The Next Steps: An Independent Report to Her Majesty's Government*. London: Cabinet Office. Available at: www.dwp.gov.uk/docs/early-intervention-next-steps.pdf

Allen, G. and Duncan Smith, I. (2008) *Early Intervention, Good Parents, Great Kids, Better Citizens*. London: The Centre for Social Justice.

Alwin, D.F. (1990) 'Historical changes in parental orientations to children', *Sociological Studies of Child Development*, 3: 65–86.

Anderson Moore, K., Lippman, L. and Brown, B. (2004) 'Indicators of child well-being: the promise for positive youth development', *Annals of the American Academy of Political and Social Science*, 591: 125–45.

Anning, A. (1998) 'The co-construction by early years care and education practitioners of literacy and mathematics curricula for young children'. Paper presented at the British Educational Research Association (BERA) Annual Conference, Queen's University of Belfast, Northern Ireland, 27–30 August.

Anning, A. (2005) 'Investigating the impact of working in multi-agency service delivery settings in the UK on early years practitioners' beliefs and practices', *Journal of Early Childhood Research*, 3 (1): 19–50.

Anning, A. (2010) 'Play and legislated curriculum', in J. Moyles (ed.), *The Excellence of Play*, 3rd edn. Maidenhead: Open University Press.

Anning, A. and Edwards, A. (2006) *Promoting Children's Learning from Birth to Five*, 2nd edn. Maidenhead: Open University Press.

Anning, A., Cullen, J. and Fleer, M. (eds) (2004) *Early Childhood Education*. London: Sage.

Appadurai, A. (2006) 'The right to research', *Globalisation, Societies and Education*, 4 (2): 167–177.

Appleby, K. (2010) 'Reflective practice: reflective thinking', in M. Reed and N. Canning (eds), *Reflective Practice in the Early Years*. London: Sage. pp. 7–23.

Archard, D. (2004) Children: Rights and Childhood, 2nd edn. London: Routledge.

Arendt, H. (1959) *The Human Condition*. Chicago: University of Chicago Press.

Ariès, P. (1962) *Centuries of Childhood*. London: Cape.

Arnstein, S.R. (1969) 'A ladder of Citizen Partnership', *Journal of the American Institute of Planners*, 35 (4): 216–24.

Athey, C. (2007) *Extending Thought in Young Children: A Parent–Teacher Partnership*. London: Paul Chapman.

Aubrey, C. (2011) *Leading and Managing in the Early Years*, 2nd edn. London: Sage.

Audit Commission (2010) *Giving Children a Healthy Start*. London: Audit Commission. Available at: www.audit-commission.gov.uk/local (accessed 13 July 2013).

Australian Curriculum, Assessment and Reporting Authority (ACARA) (2012) The Australian Curriculum. Available at: www.australiancurriculum.edu.au/ (accessed October 2013).

Australian Government (2013) *National Quality Framework for Early Childhood Education and Care. Canberra: Department of Education*. Available at: http://education.gov.au/national-quality-framework-early-childhood-education-and-care (accessed 2 December 2013).

Ayer, A.J. (1940) *The Foundations of Empirical Knowledge*. London: Macmillan.

Bae, B. (2009) 'Children's right to participate: challenges in everyday interactions', *European Early Childhood Education Research Journal*, 17 (3): 391–406.

Bae, B. (2010) 'Realizing children's right to participation in early childhood settings: some critical issues in a Norwegian context', *Early Years: An International Research Journal*, 30 (3): 205–18.

Badham, B. (2004) 'Participation – for a change: disabled young people lead the way', *Children and Society*, 18 (2): 143–54.

Baldock, P., Fitzgerald, D. and Kay, J. (eds) (2007) *Understanding Early Years Policy*. London: Paul Chapman.

Ball, D., Gill, T. and Spiegal, B. (2008) *Managing Risk in Play Provision: Implementation Guide.* London: Department for Children, Schools and Families.

Ball, S.J. (2001) '"You've been NERFed!" Dumbing down the academy. National Educational Research Forum: "A National Strategy? Consultation paper": a brief and bilious response', *Journal of Education Policy*, 16 (3): 265–8.

Bancroft, S., Fawcett, M. and Hay, P. (2008) *Researching Children Researching the World: 5x5x5=Creativity.* Stoke-on-Trent: Trentham Books.

Bandura, A., Ross, D. and Ross, S.A. (1961) 'Transmission of aggression through imitation of aggressive models', *Journal of Abnormal and Social Psychology*, 63: 575–82.

Banks, S. (2004) *Ethics, Accountability and Social Professions.* Basingstoke: Palgrave Macmillan.

Barlow, J., McMillan, A., Kirkpatrick, S., Ghate, D., Barnes, J. and Smith, M. (2010) 'Health-led interventions in the early years to enhance infant and maternal mental health: a review of reviews', *Child and Adolescent Mental Health*, 15 (4): 178–85.

Barrett, G., Sellman, D. and Thomas J. (eds) (2005) *Interprofessional Working in Health and Social Care: Professional Perspectives.* Basingstoke: Palgrave/Macmillan.

Bassey, M. (1990) 'On the nature of research in education, part one', *Research Intelligence*, BERA Newsletter No. 36, Summer: 35–8.

Bassey, M. (1999) *Case Study Research in Educational Settings.* Buckingham: Open University Press.

Bauminger, N., Shulman, C. and Agam, G. (2003) 'Peer interaction and loneliness in high-functioning children with autism', *Journal of Autism and Developmental Disorders*, 33: 458–507.

Beech, A.R., Bartels, R.M. and Dixon, L. (2013) 'Assessment and treatment of distorted schemas in sexual offenders', *Trauma Violence Abuse*, 14: 54–66.

Ben-Arieh, A. (2005) 'Where are the children? Children's role in measuring and monitoring their well-being', *Social Indicators Research*, 74: 573–96.

Ben-Arieh, A. and Frønes, I. (2007) 'Indicators of children's well-being: what should be measured and why?', *Social Indicators Research*, 84: 249–50.

Ben-Arieh, A. and Frønes, I. (2011) 'Taxonomy for child well-being indicators: a framework for the analysis of the well-being of children', *Childhood*, 18 (4): 460–76.

Bennett, J. (2008) 'Early childhood education and care systems in the OECD countries: the issue of tradition and governance', in Encyclopedia on Early Childhood Development. Centre of Excellence for Early Childhood Development and Strategic Knowledge Cluster on Early Child Development, Montreal, pp. 1–5. Available at: www.child-encyclopedia.com/documents/BennettANGxp.pdf (20 January 2013).

Bennett, J. (2011) 'Introduction: early childhood education and care', in Encyclopedia on Early Childhood Development. Centre of Excellence for Early Childhood Development and Strategic Knowledge Cluster on Early Child Development, Montreal, pp. 1–9. Available at: www.childencyclopedia.com/documents/BennettANGxp2.pdf (25 January 2013).

BERA (British Educational Research Association) (2004) *Ethical Guidelines for Educational Research.* London: British Educational Research Association.

BERA (British Educational Research Association) (2011) *Ethical Guidelines for Educational Research.* London: British Educational Research Association.

BERA SIG (British Educational Research Association Early Years Special Interest Group) (2003) *Early Years Research: Pedagogy, Curriculum and Adult Roles, Training and Professionalism.* Southwell: BERA.

Beresford, P. (2007) *The Changing Roles and Tasks of Social Work from Service Users' Perspectives: A Literature Informed Discussion Paper.* London: General Social Work Council. Available at: http://www.scie-socialcareonline.org.uk/profile.asp?guid=8e16c61c-f925-4123-b330-f12d96b542f1 (accessed 20 March 2013).

Beresford, P. (2013) 'Services-user issues: rights, needs and expectations', in B. Littlechild and R. Smith (eds), *A Handbook for Interprofessional Practice in the Human Services: Learning to Work Together*. Harlow: Pearson Education.

Berk, L. (2007) *Child Development*, 7th edn. Boston, MA: Allyn and Bacon.

Bethke Elshtain, J. (1996) 'Commentary: political children', *Childhood*, 3 (1): 11–28.

Biesta, G. (2007) 'Why "what works" won't work: evidence-based practice and the democratic deficit in educational research', *Educational Theory*, 57 (1): 1–22.

Bilton, H. (2012) 'The type and frequency of interactions that occur between staff and children outside in Early Years Foundation Stage settings during a fixed playtime period when there are tricycles available', *European Early Childhood Education Research Journal*, 20 (3): 403–21.

Bird, J. and Gerlach, L. (2005) *Improving the Emotional Health and Wellbeing of Young People in Secure Care: Training for Staff in Local Authority Secure Children's Homes*. London: National Children's Bureau.

Blair, M., Brown, S., Waterson, T. and Crowther, R. (2003) *Child Public Health*. Oxford: Oxford University Press.

Blakemore, S.J. (2000) *Early Years Learning*. (POST Report 140.) London: Parliamentary Office of Science and Technology.

Blakemore, S.J. and Frith, U. (2005) *The Learning Brain: Lessons for Education*. Oxford: Blackwell.

Blakemore Brown, L. (2001) *Reweaving the Autistic Tapestry*. London: Jessica Kingsley.

Blanchet-Cohen, N. and Rainbow, B. (2006) 'Partnership between children and adults? The experience of the International Children's Conference on the Environment', *Childhood*, 13: 113–26.

Blewett, J., Tunstill J., Hussein, S., Manthorpe, J. and Cowley, S. (2011) *Children's Centres in 2011: Improving Outcomes for the Children Who Use Action for Children Children's Centres*. London: Kings College.

Blumer, H. (1969) *Symbolic Interactionism: Perspective and Method*. Englewood Cliffs, NJ: Prentice-Hall.

BMA (British Medical Association) (2001) *Consents, Rights and Choices in Health Care for Children and Young People*. London: BMJ Books.

BMA (British Medical Association) (2006) *Child and Adolescent Mental Health: A Guide for Healthcare Professionals*. London: BMA.

Boddy, J., Cameron, C., Moss, P., Mooney, P., Petrie, P. and Statham, J. (2007) *Introducing Pedagogy into the Children's Workforce*. London: Thomas Coram Research Institute.

Bolton, G. (2010) *Reflective Practice: Writing and Professional Development*, 3rd edn. London: Sage.

Bondy, B., Ross, D., Sindelar, P. and Griffin, C. (1995) 'Elementary and special educators learning to work together: team building processes', *Teacher Education and Special Education*, 18 (2): 91–102.

Booth, T. and Ainscow, M. (eds) (1998) *From Them to Us: An International Study of Inclusion in Education*. London: Routledge.

Bowker, J. and Sawyers, J. (1988) 'Influence of exposure on preschoolers' art preferences', *Early Childhood Research Quarterly*, 3: 107–15.

Bowlby, J. (1953) *Child Care and the Growth of Love*. London: Pelican.

Bowlby, J. with Ainsworth, M. (1965) *Child Care and the Growth of Love*, 2nd edn. Harmondsworth: Penguin.

Bowles, S. and Gintis, H. (1976) *Schooling in Capitalist America: Educational Reform and Contradictions of Economic Life*. New York: Basic Books.

Bransford, J.D., Brown, A.L. and Cocking, R.R. (2000) *How People Learn: Brain, Mind, Experience and School*. Washington, DC: Academy Press.

Braye, S. (2000) 'Participation and involvement in social care: an overview', in H. Kemshall and R. Littlechild (eds), *User Involvement and Participation in Social Care: Research Informing Practice*. London: Jessica Kingsley.

Bridges, D. (1998) 'Research for sale: moral market or moral maze?', *British Educational Research Journal*, 24 (5): 593–607.

Bridges, D. (2006) 'The disciplines and discipline of educational research', *Journal of Philosophy of Education*, 40 (2): 259–72.

Bridges, D., Smeyers, P. and Smith, R. (eds) (2009) *Evidence-based Education Policy*. Chichester: Wiley-Blackwell.

Brierley, J. (1994) *Give Me a Child until He Is Seven: Brain Studies and Early Education*, 2nd edn. London: The Falmer Press.

Broadhead, P. (2010) 'Cooperative play and learning from Nursery to Year One', in P. Broadhead, J. Howard and E. Wood (eds), *Play and Learning in the Early Years*. London: Sage.

Broadhead, P., Howard, J. and Wood, E. (eds) (2010) *Play and Learning in the Early Years*. London: Sage.

Bronfenbrenner, U. (1977) 'Toward an experimental ecology of human development', *American Psychologist*, 32: 513–31.

Bronfenbrenner, U. (1979) *The Ecology of Human Development: Experiments by Nature and Design*. Cambridge, MA: Harvard University Press.

Bronfenbrenner, U. (2009) *The Ecology of Human Development: Experiments by Nature and Design*. Cambridge, MA: Harvard University Press.

Brooker, L. (2005) 'Learning to be a child: cultural diversity and early years ideology', in N. Yelland (ed.), *Critical Issues in Early Childhood Education*. Maidenhead: Open University Press.

Brooker, L. and Broadbent, L. (2003) 'Personal, social and emotional development: the child makes meaning in the world', in J. Riley (ed.), *Learning in the Early Years: A Guide for Teachers of 3–7*. London: Paul Chapman.

Brookfield, S. (1995) *Becoming a Critically Reflective Teacher*. San Francisco: Jossey-Bass.

Brookfield, S. (1998) 'Critically reflective practice', *Journal of Continuing Education in the Health Professions*, 18: 197–205.

Brown, B. (1998) *Unlearning Discrimination in the Early Years*. Stoke-on-Trent: Trentham Books.

Brown, B. (2001) *Combating Discrimination: Persona Dolls in Action*. Stoke-on-Trent: Trentham Books.

Brown, L. and Strega, S. (eds) (2005) *Research as Resistance*. Toronto: Canadian Scholars' Press.

Bruce, T. (2011) *Cultivating Creativity: Babies, Toddlers and Young Children*, 2nd edn. London: Hodder Education.

Bruer, J.T. (1997) 'Education and the brain: a bridge too far', *Educational Researcher*, 26 (8): 4–16.

Buckingham, D. (1996) *Moving Images: Understanding Children's Emotional Responses to Television*. Manchester: Manchester University Press.

Buckingham, D. (2008) 'Children and media: a cultural studies approach', in K. Drotner and S. Livingstone (eds), *The International Handbook of Children, Media and Culture*. London: Sage. pp. 219–37.

Buckley, H., Holt, S. and Whelan, S. (2007) 'Listen to me! Children's experiences of domestic violence', *Child Abuse Review*, 16: 296–310.

Bundy, C. (1987) 'Street sociology and pavement politics: aspects of youth and student resistance in Cape Town, 1985', *Journal of Southern African Studies*, 13 (3): 303–30.

Burdette, H. and Whitaker, R. (2005) 'Resurrecting free play in young children looking beyond fitness and fatness to attention, affiliation and affect', *Archives of Pediatric and Adolescent*

Medicine, 159: 46–50. Available at: www.childrenandnature.org/uploads/Burdette_LookingBeyond.pdf (accessed 5 April 2013).

Burke, C. (2005) 'Play in focus: children researching their own spaces and places for play', *Children, Youth and Environments*, 15 (1): 27–53. Available at: www.colorado.edu/journals/cye/ (accessed 7 July 2005).

Burnard, P., Craft, A. and Grainger, T. (2006) 'Documenting possibility thinking: a journey of collaborative inquiry', *International Journal of Early Years Education*, 14 (3): 243–62.

Burnett, C. (2010) 'Technology and literacy in early childhood educational settings: a review of research', *Journal of Early Childhood Literacy*, 10 (3): 247–70.

Burnett, C., Dickinson, P., Myers, J. and Merchant, G. (2006) 'Digital connections: transforming literacy in the primary school', *Cambridge Journal of Education*, 36 (1): 11–29.

Burr, R. (2002) 'Global and local approaches to children's rights in Vietnam', *Childhood*, 9 (1): 49–61.

Burr, R. (2004) 'Children's rights: international policy and lived practice', in M.J. Kehily (ed.), *An Introduction to Childhood Studies*. Maidenhead: Open University Press.

Burton, D. and Goodman, R. (2011) 'Perspectives of SENCos and support staff in England on their roles, relationships and capacity to support inclusive practice for students with behavioural, emotional and social difficulties', *Pastoral Care in Education: An International Journal of Personal, Social and Emotional Development*, 29 (2): 133–49.

Butcher, T. (2002) *Delivering Welfare*, 2nd edn. Buckingham: Open University Press.

Byron Review (2008) *Safer Children in a Digital World*. Nottingham: DCSF Publications. Available at: http://education.gov.uk/childrenandyoungpeople/safeguardingchildren/b0022 2029/child-internet-safety

Caillois, R. (2001) *Man, Play and Games* (trans. M. Barash). Urbana, IL: University of Illinois Press.

Calder, M.C. and Hackett, S. (eds) (2003) *Assessment in Child Care: Using and Developing Frameworks for Practice*. Lyme Regis: Russell House Publishing.

Cale, L. and Harris, J. (2011) '"Every child (of every size)" in physical education: physical education's role in childhood obesity', *Sport, Education and Society*, 18 (4): 433–52.

Calvert, S., Strong, B. and Gallagher, L. (2005) 'Control as an engagement feature for young children's attention to and learning of computer content', *American Behavioral Scientist*, 48 (5): 578–89.

Cameron, C. (2006) 'Men in the nursery revisited: issues of male workers and professionalism', *Contemporary Issues in Early Childhood*, 7 (3): 68–79.

Cameron, C. (2007) 'Understandings of care work with young children: reflections on children's independence in a video observation study', *Childhood*, 14: 467–86.

CAMHS Review (2008) *Children and Young People in Mind: The Final Report of National CAMHS Review*. London: Department for Children, Schools and Families and Department of Health.

Cammarota, J. and Fine, M. (eds) (2008) *Revolutionising Education*. London: Routledge.

Campbell, P., Edgar, S. and Halsted, A. (1994) 'Students as evaluators', *Phi Delta Kappan*, 76 (2): 160–5.

Cannella, G.S. (1997) *Deconstructing Early Childhood Education: Social Justice and Revolution*. New York: Peter Lang.

Cannella, G. (1999) 'The scientific discourse of education: predetermining the lives of others – Foucault, education and children', *Contemporary Issues in Early Childhood*, 1 (1): 36–84.

Cannella, G.S. and Greishaber, S. (2001) 'Identities and possibilities', in S. Greishaber and G. Cannella (eds), *Embracing Identities in Early Childhood Education: 'Diversity and Possibilities'*. New York: Teachers College Press.

Care Quality Commission (2009) *Review of the Involvement and Action Taken by Health Bodies in Relation to the Case of Baby P*. London: Care Quality Commission.

Carmichael, E. and Hancock, J. (2007) 'Scotland', in M.M. Clark and T. Waller (eds), *Early Childhood Education and Care*. London: Sage.

Carnwell, R. and Buchanan, J. (eds) (2005) *Effective Practice in Health and Social Care: A Partnership Approach*. Maidenhead: Open University Press.

Carr, A. (ed.) (2000) *What Works With Children and Adolescents? A Critical Review of Research on Psychological Interventions with Children, Adolescents and Their Families*. London: Routledge.

Carr, M. (2001) *Assessment in Early Childhood Settings*. London: Paul Chapman.

Carr, M. and Claxton, G. (2002) 'Tracking the development of learning dispositions', *Assessment in Education*, 9 (1): 9–37.

Carrier, J. and Kendall, I. (1995) *Interprofessional Relations in Health Care*. London: Edward Arnold.

Carspecken, P. (1996) *Critical Ethnography in Educational Research*. London: Routledge.

Casey, T. (2007) *Environments for Outdoor Play: A Practical Guide for Making Space for Children*. London: Paul Chapman.

Catherwood, D. (1999) 'New views on the young brain: offerings from developmental psychology to early childhood education', *Contemporary Issues in Early Childhood*, 1 (1): 23–35.

Centre for Studies on Inclusion (CSIE) (2000) *Index for Inclusion*. Bristol: Centre for Studies on Inclusion.

CERI (OECD Centre for Educational Research and Innovation) (2007) *Understanding the Brain: The Birth of a Learning Science*. Paris: OECD.

Chambers, R. (1994) 'Participatory Rural Appraisal (PRA): analysis of experience', *World Development*, 22 (9): 1253–68.

Chand, A. (2008) 'Every Child Matters? A critical review of child welfare reforms in the context of minority ethnic children and families', *Child Abuse Review*, 17 (1): 8–22.

Charity Commission (2008) *The Promotion of Social Inclusion*. London: Charity Commission.

Charmaz, K. (2006) *Constructing Grounded Theory*. London: Sage.

Cheminais, R. (2012) *Children and Young People as Action Researchers*. Maidenhead: McGraw-Hill/Open University Press.

Children's Food Trust (2011) *Eat Better, Start Better: Towards a Healthy Future for Every Child*. Sheffield: Childrens Food Trust. Available at: www.childrensfoodtrust.org.uk/pre-school/eat-better-start-better (accessed 13 July 2013).

Chrisafis, A., Conolly, K. and Hooper, J. (2007) 'The state of European childhood', *The Guardian*, 14 February. Available at: www.guardian.co.uk/world/2007/feb/14/eu.children?INTCMP=SRCH (accessed 4 January 2013).

Christakis, D., Zimmerman, F., DiGiuseppe, D. and McCarty, C. (2004) 'Early television exposure and subsequent attentional problems in children', *Pediatrics*, 113 (4): 708–13.

Christensen, P. and James, A. (2008) *Research with Children: Perspectives and Practices*, 2nd edn. London: Falmer Press.

City of Toronto (2011) 'Toronto First Duty'. Available at: www.toronto.ca/firstduty/ (accessed 3 November 2013).

Clark, A. (2004) *Listening as a Way of Life*. London: National Children's Bureau.

Clark, A. and Moss, P. (2001) *Listening to Young Children: The Mosaic Approach*. London: National Children's Bureau Enterprises.

Clark, A. and Moss, P. (2005) *Spaces to Play: More Listening to Young Children Using the Mosaic Approach*. London: National Children's Bureau.

Clark, A. and Moss, P. (2011) *Listening to Young Children: The Mosaic Approach*, 2nd edn. London: National Children's Bureau Enterprises.

Clark, A. and Statham, J. (2005) 'Listening to young children: experts in their own lives', *Adoption and Fostering*, 29 (1): 45–56.

Clark, A., Kjorholt, A. and Moss, P. (eds) (2005) *Beyond Listening: Children's Perspectives on Early Childhood Services*. Bristol: The Policy Press.

Clark, M.M. and Waller, T. (eds) (2007) *Early Childhood Education and Care: Policy and Practice*. London: Sage.

Clarke, A.M. and Clarke, A.D.B. (eds) (1976) *Early Experience: Myth And Evidence*. London: Open Books Ltd.

Clarke, A. and Clarke, A. (2000) *Early Experience and the Life Path*. London: Jessica Kingsley.

Claxton, G. (1999) *Wise Up: The Challenge of Lifelong Learning*. London: Bloomsbury.

Claxton, G. and Carr, M. (2004) 'A framework for teaching learning: the dynamics of disposition', *Early Years*, 24 (1): 87–97.

Cleaver, H. (2006) 'The influence of parenting and other family relationships', in J. Aldgate, D. Jones, W. Rose and C. Jeffery (eds), *The Developing World of the Child*. London: Jessica Kingsley.

Coady, M. (2010) 'Ethics in early childhood research', in G. MacNaughton, S.A. Rolfe and I. Siraj-Blatchford (eds), *Doing Early Childhood Research*. Maidenhead: McGraw-Hill/Open University Press. pp. 73–84.

Cohen, D. (2006) *The Development of Play*, 3rd edn. London and New York: Routledge.

Cohen, L., Manion, L. and Morrison, C. (2007) *Research Methods in Education*, 6th edn. London: Routledge.

Cohen, S., Humphreys, B. and Mynott, E. (2001) *From Immigration Controls to Welfare Controls*. London: Routledge.

Cole, M. (1996) *Cultural Psychology: A Once and Future Discipline*. Cambridge, MA: The Belknap Press.

Commonwealth of Australia (2009) *Belonging, Being and Becoming: The Early Years Learning Framework for Australia*. Available at: http://docs.education.gov.au/node/2632 (accessed 5 November 2013).

Commonwealth of Australia (2010) *Educators Guide to the Early Years Framework for Australia*. Available at: http://docs.education.gov.au/node/2938 (accessed 5 November 2013).

Connell, R. (1987) *Gender and Power*. Sydney: Allen & Unwin.

Cooke, G. and Lawton, K. (2008) *For Love or Money: Pay, Progression and Professionalisation in The 'Early Years' Workforce*. London: Institute for Public Policy Research.

Coombe, V. and Little, A. (1986) *Race and Social Work: A Guide to Training*. London: Tavistock Publications.

Cooper, C. (2000) 'Face on: discovering resilience to disfigurement', *The New Therapist*, 7 (3): 31–3.

Cooper, P. and Jacob, B. (2011) *Evidence of Best Practice Models and Outcomes in the Education of Children with Emotional Disturbances/Behavioral Difficulties: An International Review*. Research report no. 7. Trim, Eire: National Council for Special Education. Available at: www.ncse.ie/uploads/1/7_NCSE_EBD.pdf (accessed 20 July 2013).

Cornwall, A. and Jewkes, R. (1995) 'What is participatory research?', *Social Science and Medicine*, 41 (12): 1667–76.

Corsaro, W.A., Molinary, L. and Brown Rosier, K. (2002) 'Zena and Carlotta: transition narratives and early education in the United States and Italy', *Human Development*, 45: 323–48.

Corsaro, W.A. (2011) *The Sociology of Childhood*, 3rd edn. London: Sage.

Corter, C., Bertrand, J., Pelletier, J., Griffin, T., McKay, D., Patel, S. and Ioannone, P. (2006) *Evidence-based Understanding of Integrated Foundations for Early Childhood*. Toronto First

Duty Phase 1 Summary Report. Toronto, Canada: Toronto First Duty. Available at: www.toronto.ca/firstduty/TFD_Summary_Report_June06.pdf (accessed 3 November 2013).

Cortis, N., Katz, I. and Patulny, R. (2009) *Engaging Hard-to-Reach Families and Children*. Canberra: Australian Government.

Council of Europe (1950) *European Convention on Human Rights*. Rome: Council of Europe.

Council for the Curriculum, Examinations and Assessment (CCEA) (2006) *The Revised NI Primary Curriculum*. Belfast: DENI.

Cowley, S. and Houston, A. (2002) 'An empowerment approach to needs assessment in health visiting practice', *Journal of Clinical Nursing*, 11 (5): 640–50.

Cox, R. and Smitsman, W. (2006) 'Action planning in young children's tool use', *Developmental Science*, 9 (6): 628–41.

CRAE (Children's Rights Alliance for England) (2012) *The State of Children's Rights in England*. London: CRAE.

Craft, A. (2002) *Creativity and Early Years Education: A Lifewide Foundation*. London: Routledge.

Craft, A. (2011) 'Creativity and early years settings', in A. Paige-Smith and A. Craft (eds), *Developing Reflective Practice in the Early Years*. Maidenhead: Open University Press.

Craft, A. and Paige-Smith, A. (2008) 'Reflective practice', in L. Miller and C. Cable (eds), *Professionalism in the Early Years*. London: Hodder Education. pp. 87–97.

Craft, A. and Paige-Smith, A. (2011) 'Introduction', in A. Paige-Smith and A. Craft (eds), *Developing Reflective Practice in the Early Years*. Maidenhead: Open University Press/McGraw-Hill Education.

Craft, A., McConnon, L. and Matthews, A. (2012) 'Child-initiated play and professional creativity: enabling four-year-olds' possibility thinking', *Thinking Skills and Creativity*, 7 (1): 48–61.

Craig, C. (2007) *The Potential Dangers of a Systematic, Explicit Approach to Teaching Social and Emotional Skills (SEAL)*. Glasgow: Centre for Confidence and Wellbeing.

Craig, C. (2009) *Well-Being in Schools: The Curious Case of the Tail Wagging the Dog?* Glasgow: Centre for Confidence and Wellbeing.

Crawley, H. (2006) *Child First, Migrant Second: Ensuring that Every Child Matters*. London: ILPA. Available at: www.ilpa.org.uk/publications/ilpa_child_first.pdf (accessed 24 June 2013).

Cremin, T., Burnard, P. and Craft, A. (2006) 'Pedagogies of possibility thinking', *International Journal of Thinking Skills and Creativity*, 1 (2): 108–19.

Creswell, J. (2008) *Educational Research*. Upper Saddle River, NJ: Pearson.

Crimmens, D. and West, A. (2004) *Having Their Say – Young People and Participation: European Experience*. Lyme Regis: Russell House Publishing.

Critcher, C. (2008) 'Making waves: historical aspects of public debates about children and mass media', in K. Drotner and S. Livingstone (eds), *The International Handbook of Children, Media and Culture*. London: Sage. pp. 91–105.

CSIE (Centre for Studies on Inclusive Education) (2000) <to come>.

Csikszentmihayli, M. (1979) 'The concept of flow', in B. Sutton-Smith (ed.), *Play and Learning*. New York: Gardner.

Csikszentmihalyi, M. (2002) *Flow*, 2nd edn. London: Rider.

Cunningham, H. (1995) *Children and Childhood in Western Society since 1500*. Harlow: Longman Group.

CWDC (Children's Workforce Development Council) (2006) *Early Years Professional Prospectus*. Leeds: CWDC.

CWDC (Children's Workforce Development Council) (2008) *Clear Progression 2008: The Next Steps Towards Building an Integrated Qualifications Framework for the Children and Young*

People's Workforce. Leeds: CWDC. Available at: http://media.education.gov.uk/assets/files/pdf/c/integrated%20working%20explained.pdf (accessed 12 February 2013).

Daft, R. (2011) *The Leadership Experience*, 6th edn. Independence, KY: Southwestern/Cengage Learning.

Dahlberg, G. (1985) *Context and the Child's Orientation to Meaning: A Study of the Child's Way of Organising the Surrounding World in Relation to Public Institutionalised Socialisation*. Stockholm: Almqvist and Wiskell.

Dahlberg, G. and Lenz Taguchi, H. (1994) *Förskola och skola och om visionen om en mötesplats* [Preschool and school and the vision of a meeting-place]. Stockholm: HLS Förlag.

Dahlberg, G., Moss, P. and Pence, A. (1999) *Beyond Quality in Early Childhood Education and Care: Postmodern Perspectives*. London and New York: RoutledgeFalmer.

Dahlberg, G., Moss, P. and Pence, A. (2007) *Beyond Quality in Early Childhood Education and Care: Languages of Evaluation*, 2nd edn. Abingdon: Routledge.

Dalli, C. and Mathias, M. (2011) 'Conclusion: towards new understandings of the early years profession: a critical ecology', in C. Dalli and M. Mathias (eds), *Professionalism in Early Childhood Education and Care: International Perspectives*. Abingdon: Routledge. pp. 150–5.

Dalli, C. and Urban, M. (eds) (2010) *Professionalism in Early Childhood Education and Care: International Perspectives*. London and New York: Routledge.

Daniel, B. and Taylor, J. (2001) *Engaging with Fathers: Practice Issues in Health and Social Care*. London: Jessica Kingsley.

Dann, J. (1980) *The Revolution Remembered*. Chicago: University of Chicago Press.

Darwin, C. (1872) *The Expression of the Emotions in Man and Animals*. London: John Murray.

Davies, C. and Ward, H. (2012) *Safeguarding Children Across Services: Messages from Research*. London: Jessica Kingsley.

Davies, S. (2012) 'Embracing reflective practice', *Education for Primary Care*, 23: 9–12.

Davis, G. (2012) 'A documentary analysis of the use of theories of leadership and change by Early Years leaders', *Early Years: An International Journal of Research and Development*, 32 (3): 266–76.

Davis, G. and Barry, A. (2013) 'Positive outcomes for children: Early Years Professionals effecting change', *Early Child Development and Care*, 183 (1): 37–48.

Davis, G. and Capes, P. (2013) Early Years Professional Status Impact Study. Final Report: Achieving Outcomes in Essex. Report for Essex County Council. Anglia Ruskin University. Available at: http://angliaruskin.openrepository.com/arro/handle/10540/295428 (accessed 28 October 2013).

Davis, J.M. (2011) *Integrated Children's Services*. London: Sage.

DCELLS (Department for Children, Education, Learning and Lifelong Skills) (2008) *Foundation Phase: Framework for Children's Learning for 3- to 7-year olds in Wales*. Cardiff: WAG.

Dearing, E., McCartney, K. and Taylor, B.A. (2009) 'Does higher quality early childcare promote low-income children's math and reading achievement in middle childhood?', *Child Development*, 80 (5): 1329–49.

Deleuze, G. and Guattari, F. (1994) *What is Philosophy?* London: Verso Books.

DeMause, L. (1976) *The History of Childhood*. London: Souvenir Press.

Denov, M. (2012) 'Child soldiers and iconography: portrayals and (mis)representations', *Children and Society*, 26 (4): 280–92.

Denzin, N.K. (2005) 'Emancipatory discourses and the ethics and politics of interpretation', in N. Denzin and Y. Lincoln (eds), *Handbook of Qualitative Research*, 3rd edn. Beverley Hills, CA: Sage. pp. 933–58.

DCSF (Department for Children, Schools and Families) (2006) *Working Together to Safeguard Children: A Guide to Inter-agency Working to Safeguard and Promote the Welfare of Children*. Nottingham: DCSF Publications. Available at: http://collections.europarchive.org/tna/20100423085708/dcsf.gov.uk/everychildmatters/resources-and-practice/ig00060/ (accessed 10 February 2013).

DCSF (Department for Children, Schools and Families) (2007a) *The Children's Plan: Building Brighter Futures*. London: DCSF.

DCSF (Department for Children, Schools and Families) (2007b) *A Study into Children's Views on Physical Discipline and Punishment*. Available at: www.endcorporalpunishment.org/assets/childrendocs/UK%20Section58.pdf (accessed 4 November 2013).

DCSF (Department for Children, Schools and Families) (2007c) *Guidance on the Duty to Promote Community Cohesion*. Notttingham: DCSF Publications.

DCSF (Department for Children Schools and Families) (2008a) *Statutory Framework for the Early Years Foundation Stage*. London: TSO.

DCSF (Department for Children, Schools and Families) (2008b) *The Inclusion of Gypsy, Roma and Traveller Children and Young People*. London: TSO.

DCSF (Department for Children, Schools and Families) (2008c) *Social and Emotional Aspects of Development Guidance for Practitioners Working in the Early Years Foundation Stage*. Nottingham: DCSF Publications.

DCSF (Department for Children, Schools and Families) (2008d) *Information Sharing: Guidance for Practitioners and Managers*. London: DCSF and Department for Communities and Local Government. Available at: www.education.gov.uk/publications/standard/publicationdetail/Page1/DCSF-00807-2008#downloadableparts

DCSF (Department for Children, Schools and Families) (2009) *Special Educational Needs and Parental Confidence*. The Lamb Enquiry. Nottingham: DCSF Publications.

DCSF (Department for Children, Schools and Families) (2010) *Working Together to Safeguard Children*. Nottingham: DCSF Publications. Available at: www.education.gov.uk/publications/eOrderingDownload/00305-2010DOM-EN.pdf

DCSF (Department for Children, Schools and Families) and DH (Department of Health) (2008) *Healthy Weight, Healthy Lives: A Cross-Government Strategy for England*. London: TSO.

Department of Education and Science (DES) (1978) *Special Educational Needs: Report of the Committee of Enquiry into the Education of Handicapped Children and Young People (The Warnock Committee)*. London: HMSO.

DES (Department of Education and Science) (1985) *Education for All*. The Swann Report. London: HMSO.

Devarakonda, C. (2013) *Diversity and Inclusion in Early Childhood: An Introduction*. London: SAGE.

DfE (Department for Education) (2010) 'Decommissioning ContactPoint'. LA Update. Available at: www.education.gov.uk/childrenandyoungpeople/strategy/laupdates/a0071073/decommissioning-contactpoint (accessed 17 February 2013).

DfE (Department for Education) (2011a) *Supporting Families in the Foundation Years*. London: DfE. Available at: http://media.education.gov.uk/assets/files/pdf/s/supporting%20families%20in%20the%20foundation%20years.pdf

DfE (Department for Education) (2011b) 'Decommissioning National eCAF'. Available at: www.education.gov.uk/childrenandyoungpeople/strategy/integratedworking/caf/a0072820/nationale-caf (accessed 10 February 2013).

DfE (Department for Education) (2011c) *Families in the Foundation Years*. Evidence Pack. London: DfE. Available at: http://media.education.gov.uk/assets/files/pdf/f/families%20in%20the%20foundation%20years%20-%20full%20evidence%20pack.pdf

DfE (Department for Education) (2011d) 'Including all learners: Diverse needs'. Available at: www.education.gov.uk/schools/teachingandlearning/curriculum/b00199686/inclusion/needs (accessed 30 October 2013).

DfE (Department of Education) (2011e) *Support and Aspiration: A New Approach to Special Educational Needs and Disability.* London: DfE.

DfE (Department for Education) (2012a) 'The CAF process'. Available at: www.education.gov.uk/childrenandyoungpeople/strategy/integratedworking/caf/a0068957/the-caf-process (accessed 10 February 2013).

DfE (Department for Education) (2012b) 'The Early Years Foundation Stage (EYFS)'. General article [updated 26 April 2013]. Available at: www.education.gov.uk/schools/teachingandlearning/curriculum/a0068102/early-years-foundation-stage-eyfs (accessed 28 October 2013).

DfE (Department for Education) (2012c) 'Integrated working'. Available at: www.education.gov.uk/childrenandyoungpeople/strategy/integratedworking/a0068938/integrated-working (accessed 10 February 2013).

DfE (Department for Education (2012d) *Statutory Framework for the Early Years Foundation Stage: Setting the Standards for Learning, Development and Care for Children from Birth to Five.* Runcorn: DfE Publications. Available at: www.education.gov.uk/publications/standard/AllPublications/Page1/DFE-00023-2012

DfE (Department for Education) (2012e) *Children Looked After in England (Including Adoption and Care Leavers) Year Ending 31 March 2012.* London: Department for Education.

DfE (Department for Education) (2012f) 'Provision for children under 5 years of age in England'. Statistical First Release. Available at: www.gov.uk/government/uploads/system/uploads/attachment_data/file/219240/main_20text_20sfr132012.pdf (accessed 17 July 2013).

DfE (Department for Education) (2012g) 'Extending free early education to more two year olds'. Consultation. Available at: www.education.gov.uk/consultations/downloadableDocs/Early%20Education%20Consultation%20Document%20-%203.doc (accessed 4 November 2013).

DfE (Department of Education) (2012h) 'Core Purpose of Sure Start Children's Centres'. Available at: www.education.gov.uk/childrenandyoungpeople/earlylearningandchildcare/a00191780/core-purpose-of-sure-start-childrens-centres (accessed 4 November 2013).

DfE (Department for Education) (2013a) *Working Together to Safeguard Children: A Guide to Inter-agency Working to Safeguard and Promote the Welfare of Children.* London: DfE. Available at: www.education.gov.uk/publications/standard/publicationDetail/Page1/DFE-00030-2013.

DfE (Department for Education) (2013b) *More Great Childcare: Raising Quality and Giving Parents More Choice.* London: DfE. Available at: www.education.gov.uk/publications/standard/publicationDetail/page1/DFE-00002-2013

DfEE (Department of Education and Employment) (1997) *Excellence for All Children: Meeting Special Educational Needs.* London: DfEE.

DfEE (Department for Education and Employment) (2000) 'National Standards For Under Eights Day Care and Childminding.' In *Department For Education And Employment* (ed.). Nottingham: DfEE Publications.

DfEE (Department for Education and Employment) and DH (Department of Health) (1999) *National Healthy School Standards Document.* London. HMSO.

DfES (Department for Education and Skills) (2001a) *Special Educational Needs Code of Practice.* DfES/581/2001. London: DfES.

DfES (Department for Education and Skills) (2001b) *Inclusive Schooling: Children with Special Educational Needs. Statutory Guidance for local education authorities, schools, health and social services in England.* DfES/0774/2001. London: DfES.

DfES (Department for Education and Skills) (2001c) *Promoting Children's Mental Health within Early Years and School Settings.* London: HMSO.

DfES (Department for Education and Skills) (2003a) *Every Child Matters.* Green Paper. London: TSO.

DfES (Department for Education and Skills) (2003b) *Birth to Three Matters.* Nottingham: DfES Publications.

DfES (Department for Education and Skills) (2004a) *The Common Assessment Framework for Children and Young People.* Available at: www.education.gov.uk/publications/standard/ publicationDetail/Page1/CAF-SUPPORT-TOOLS (accessed 17 February 2013).

DfES (Department for Education and Skills) (2004b) *Removing Barriers to Achievement.* London: HMSO.

DfES (Department for Education and Skills) (2004c) *Every Child Matters: Change for Children. Nottingham:* DfES Publications. Available at: http://webarchive.nationalarchives.gov. uk/20130401151715/https://www.education.gov.uk/publications/eOrderingDownload/ DFES10812004.pdf.

DfES (Department for Education and Skills) (2005a) Children's Workforce Strategy. Available at: www. education.gov.uk/consultations/downloadableDocs/5958-DfES-ECM.pdf. (accessed 12 July 2013).

DfES (Department for Education and Skills) (2005b) *Excellence and Enjoyment: Social and Emotional Aspects of Learning (Guidance).* Nottingham: DfES Publications.

DfES (Department for Education and Skills) (2005c) *Multi-Agency Working: Toolkit for Managers of Multi-Agency Teams.* London: TSO.

DfES (Department for Education and Skills) (2006a) *Exclusion of Black Pupils: Priority Review. Getting It Right.* London: DfES.

DfES (Department for Education and Skills) (2006b) *A Short Guide to the Education and Inspections Act 2006.* London: DfES.

DfES (Department for Education and Skills) (2006c) *Working Together to Safeguard Children: A Guide to Inter-agency Working to Safeguard and Promote the Welfare of Children.* Norwich: TSO.

DfES (Department for Education and Skills) (2006d) *Excellence and Enjoyment: Social and Emotional Aspects of Learning: Key Stage 2 Small Group Activities.* Nottingham: DfES.

DfES (Department for Education and Skills) (2007a) *Curriculum Guidance for the Foundation Stage.* Nottingham: DfES Publications.

DfES (Department for Education and Skills) (2007b) *Aiming High for Children: Supporting Families.* London: TSO.

DfES (Department for Education and Skills) (2007c) *Common Assessment Framework for Children and Young People: Practitioners' Guide – Integrated Working to Improve Outcomes for Children and Young People.* Leeds: Children's Development Workforce Council.

DfES (Department for Education and Skills) (2007d) *Aiming High for Disabled Children: Better Support for Families.* Runcorn: DfES/HM Treasury.

DfES (Department for Education and Skills) (2007e) *Extended Schools: Access to Opportunities and Services for All.* Nottingham: DfES Publications.

DfES (Department for Education and Skills) (2007f) *Statutory Framework for the Early Years Foundation Stage.* Nottingham: DfES Publications.

DfES (Department for Education and Skills) and DH (Department of Health) (2003) *Together from the Start: Practical Guidance for Practitioners Working with Disabled Children (Birth to Third Birthday) and Their Families.* Nottingham: DfES Publications.

DENI (Department of Education Northern Ireland) (2013) *Pupils' Emotional Health and Wellbeing.* Available at: www.deni.gov.uk/index/support-and-development-2/pupils-emotional-health-and-wellbeing.htm (accessed 4 January 2013).

Department of Communities and Local Government (2013) *Helping Troubled Families Turn their Lives Around.* Available at: www.gov.uk/government/policies/helping-troubled-families-turn-their-lives-around (accessed 28 March 2013).

DEEWR (Department for Education Western Australia) (2012) http://deewr.gov.au/national-quality-framework-early-childhood-education-and-care-legislation-standards-and-progress (accessed 24 January 2013).

DH (Department of Health) (1991) *Working Together Under the Children Act 1989: A Guide for Inter-Agency Co-Operation for the Protection of Children from Abuse.* London: HMSO.

DH (Department of Health) (2000) *Framework for the Assessment of Children in Need and their Families.* London: HMSO.

DH (Department of Health) (2004a) Best practice guidance for doctors and other health professionals on the provision of advice and treatment to young people under 16 on contraception, sexual and reproductive health. Available at: http://webarchive.nationalarchives.gov.uk/+/www.dh.gov.uk/en/Publicationsandstatistics/Publications/PublicationsPolicyAndGuidance/DH_4086960 (accessed 16 July 2013).

DH (Department of Health) (2004b) *National Service Framework for Children, Young People and Maternity Services: The Mental Health and Psychological Wellbeing of Children and Young People.* London: DH.

DH (Department of Health) (2009) *Healthy Child Programme: Pregnancy and the First Five Years of Life.* London: DH. Available at: http://webarchive.nationalarchives.gov.uk/20130107105354/http://www.dh.gov.uk/en/Publicationsandstatistics/Publications/PublicationsPolicyAndGuidance/DH_107563

DH (Department of Health) (2010) *Healthy Lives, Healthy People: Our Strategy for Public Health in England.* Available at: http://webarchive.nationalarchives.gov.uk/20130107105354/http://www.dh.gov.uk/prod_consum_dh/groups/dh_digitalassets/@dh/@en/@ps/documents/digitalasset/dh_122347.pdf (accessed 20 July 2013).

DH (Department of Health) (2011a) *No Health Without Mental Health: A Cross-Government Mental Health Outcomes Strategy for People of All Ages.* London: DH.

DH (Department of Health) (2011b) *No Health Without Mental Health: Delivering Better Mental Health Outcomes for People of All Ages.* London: DH.

DH (Department of Health) (2011c) *Healthy Lives Healthy People: A Call for Action on Obesity in England.* London: DH.

DH (Department of Health) (2011d) *Health Visitor Implementation Plan 2011–15: A Call to Action, February 2011.* London: Department of Health. Available at: https://www.gov.uk/government/publications/health-visitor-implementation-plan-2011-to-2015

DH (Department of Health) (2012a) *National Child Measurement Programme.* Available at: www.ic.nhs.uk/ncmp (accessed 4 November 2013).

DH (Department of Health) (2012b) *Getting it Right for Children, Young People and Families. Maximising the contribution of the school nursing team: Vision and call to action.* London: Department of Health. Available at: https://www.gov.uk/government/uploads/system/uploads/attachment_data/file/216464/dh_133352.pdf

DH (Department of Health) Cross Government Obesity Unit (2009) *Healthy Weight, Healthy Lives: One Year On.* London: DH.

(DHSS) Department of Health and Social Security (1973) *Report on the Working Party on Collaboration Between the NHS and Local Government.* London: HMSO.

(DHSS) Department of Health and Social Security (1984) *Report of Joint Working Group on Collaboration between Family Practitioner Committees and District Health Authorities.* London: DHSS.

DHSSPS (Department of Health, Social Services and Public Safety) (2012) *Children in Care in Northern Ireland 2010/11*. Statistical Bulletin. Belfast: Community Information Branch, DHSSPS.

DeVries, R. (2001) *Developing Constructivist Early Childhood Curriculum*. New York: Teachers' College Press.

Dewey, J. (1933) *How We Think: A Restatement of the Relation of Reflective Thinking to the Educative Process*. Boston, MA: DC Heath.

Dietz, W. (2001) 'The obesity epidemic in young children: reduce television viewing and promote playing', *British Medical Journal*, 322: 313–14.

Dissanayake, E. (1992) *Homo Aestheticus: Where Art Comes From and Why*. New York: Free Press.

Dominelli, L. (2002) *Anti-oppressive Social Work Theory and Practice*. Basingstoke: Palgrave Macmillan.

Donaldson, M. (1978) *Children's Minds*. Harmondsworth: Penguin.

Doyle, C. (1987) 'Sexual abuse: giving help to children', *Childhood and Society*, 1 (3): 210–23.

Doyle, C. (1994) *Child Sex Abuse: A Guide for Health Professionals*. London: Chapman and Hall.

Doyle, C. (1997) 'Emotional abuse of children: issues for intervention', *Child Abuse Review*, 6: 330–42.

Doyle, C. (1998) 'Emotional abuse of children: issues for intervention'. Unpublished PhD thesis, University of Leicester.

Doyle, C. (2001) 'Surviving and coping with emotional abuse in childhood', *Clinical Child Psychology and Psychiatry*, 6 (3): 387–402.

Doyle, C. (2012) *Working with Abused Children*, 4th edn. Basingstoke: Palgrave Macmillan.

Doyle, C. and Timms, C.D. (2013) *Child Neglect and Emotional Abuse*. London: Sage.

Doyle, C., Timms, C. and Sheehan, E. (2010) 'Potential sources of support for children who have been emotionally abused by parents', *Vulnerable Children and Youth Studies: An International Interdisciplinary Journal for Research, Policy and Care*, 5 (3): 230–41.

Draper, L. and Duffy, B. (2001) 'Working with parents', in G. Pugh (ed.), *Contemporary Issues in the Early Years*. London: Paul Chapman.

Drifte, C. (2001) *Special Needs in Early Years Settings: A Guide for Practitioners*. London: David Fulton.

Duffy, B. (2006) *Supporting Creativity and Imagination in the Early Years*, 2nd edn. Maidenhead: Open University Press.

Duffy, B. (2010) 'The early years curriculum', in G. Pugh and B. Duffy, *Contemporary Issues in the Early Years*, 5th edn. London: Sage. pp. 95–108.

Dul, J. and Ceylan, C. (2011) 'Work environments for employee creativity', *Ergonomics*, 54 (1): 12–20.

Dunford, J. (2010) *Review of the Office of the Children's Commissioner (England)*. London: Department for Education.

Dunlop, A. (2008) 'A literature review on leadership in the early years'. Available at: www.ltscotland.org.uk/Images/leadershipreview_tcm4-499140.doc (accessed 5 May 2013).

Dunn, J. (1988) *The Beginnings of Social Understanding*. Oxford: Basil Blackwell.

Dweck, C. (2000) *Self-Theories: Their Role in Motivation, Personality and Development*. Hove: Psychology Press.

Dweck, C. and Leggett, E. (1988) 'A social-cognitive approach to motivation and personality', *Psychological Review*, 95 (2): 256–73.

Dwivedi, K.N. and Harper, B.P. (2004) *Promoting the Emotional Well-being of Children and Adolescents and Preventing Their Mental Ill Health: A Handbook*. London: Jessica Kingsley.

DWP (Department for Work and Pensions) (2013) *First Release: Households Below Average Income (HBAI) Statistics*. London: DWP.

Dyson, A. and Millward, A. (2000) *Schools and Special Needs: Issues of Innovation and Inclusion.* London: Paul Chapman.

Dyson, A.H. (1997) *Writing Superheroes: Contemporary Childhood, Popular Culture, and Classroom Literacy.* New York: Teachers' College Press.

Early Childhood Action (ECA) (2012) *Unhurried Pathways: A New Framework for Early Childhood.* Winchester: Early Childhood Alliance.

Early Childhood Forum (2003) Definition of inclusion. Available at: www.ncb.org.uk/media/216977/ecf_inclusion_leaflet.pdf (accessed 17 July 2013).

Early Years (2012) *Annual Report 2011–12.* Belfast: Early Years. Available at: www.early-years.org/about-us/docs/annual_report_2011-2012.pdf (accessed 4 January 2013).

Easton, D. (1965) *A Systems Analysis of Political Life.* New York: Wiley.

Ecclestone, K. (2007) 'Resisting image of the "diminished self": the implications of emotional well-being and emotional engagement in education policy', *Journal of Education Policy*, 22 (4): 455–470.

Ecclestone, K. and Hayes, D. (2009) *The Dangerous Rise of Therapeutic Education.* London: Routledge.

ECHRC. Council of Europe (1950) *European Convention on Human Rights.* Rome: Council of Europe.

Edwards, D. and Mercer, N. (1987) *Common Knowledge: The Development of Understanding in the Classroom.* London: Methuen.

Edwards, C., Gandini, L. and Forman, G. (1998) *The Hundred Languages of Children*, 3rd edn. Santa Barbara, CA: Praeger.

Eekelaar, J. (1992) 'The importance of thinking that children have rights', in P. Alston and J. Seymour (eds), *Children's Rights and the Law.* Oxford: Clarendon Press.

Egeland, B., Yates, T., Appleyard, K. and van Dulmen, M. (2002) 'The long-term consequences of maltreatment in the early years: a developmental pathway model to antisocial behavior', *Children's Services: Social Policy, Research and Practice*, 5 (4): 249–60.

Einarsdottir, J. and Wagner, J. (eds) (2006) *Nordic Childhoods and Early Education.* Greenwich, CT: Information Age.

Elfer, P. and Page, J. (2013) Briefing paper response to Coalition proposals on improving quality of childcare, 'More Great Childcare'. Copy available direct from p.elfer@roehampton.ac.uk.

Emilson, A. and Folkesson, A.M. (2006) 'Children's participation and teacher control', *Early Child Development and Care*, 176 (3&4): 219–38.

End Child Poverty Campaign (2008) *Unhealthy Lives: Intergenerational Links between Child Poverty and Poor Health in the UK.* London: End Child Poverty/GMB. Available at: www.endchildpoverty.org.uk/files/Intergenerational_Links_between_child_Poverty_and_poor_health.pdf

Enlow, M.B., Egeland, B., Blood, E.A., Wright, R.O. and Wright, R.J. (2012) 'Interpersonal trauma exposure and cognitive development in children to age 8 years: a longitudinal study', *Journal of Epidemiology and Community Health,* doi: 10.1136/jech-2011–20072.

Ennew, J. (1986) *The Sexual Exploitation of Children.* Cambridge: Polity Press.

Eurybase (2006/07) *General Organisation of the Education System and Administration of Education.* Denmark.

Every Disabled Child Matters (EDCM) (2006) *Getting Rights and Justice for Every Disabled Child.* Available at: www.edcm.org.uk/page.asp (accessed 21 April 2007).

Facer, K. (2011) *Learning Futures: Education, Technology and Social Change.* London: Routledge.

Facer, K. (2012) 'Taking the 21st century seriously: young people, education and socio-technical futures', *Oxford Review of Education*, 38: 97–113.

Facer, K., Furlong, J., Furlong, R. and Sutherland, R. (2003) *ScreenPlay: Children and Computing in the Home*. London: RoutledgeFalmer.

Farson, R. (1974) *Birthrights*. London: Collier Macmillan.

Fawcett, M. (2000) 'Historical views of childhood,' in M. Boushel, M. Fawcett and J. Selwyn (eds), *Focus on Early Childhood: Principles and Realities*. Oxford: Blackwell.

Fawcett, B., Featherstone, B. and Goddard, J. (2004) *Contemporary Child Care Policy and Practice*. Basingstoke: Palgrave Macmillan.

Feinstein, L., Sabates, R., Rogers, I. and Emmett, P. (2008) 'Dietary patterns related to attainment in school: the importance of early eating patterns', *Journal of Epidemiology and Community Health*, 62: 734–9.

Field, F. (2010) *The Foundation Years: Preventing Poor Children Becoming Poor Adults*. Report of the independent review on poverty and life chances. HMG 2010. Available at: http://outdoor matters.co.uk/wp-content/uploads/2011/03/Frank-Field-Report-The-Foundation-Years.pdf

Fielding, M. (2001) 'Students as radical agents of change', *Journal of Educational Change*, 2: 123–41.

Finkelhor, D. (1984) *Child Sexual Abuse: New Theory and Research*. New York: The Free Press.

Fitzgerald, D. and Kay, J. (2007) *Working Together in Children's Services*. Abingdon: Routledge.

Fjørtoft, I. (2001) 'The natural environment as a playground for children: the impact of outdoor play activities in pre-primary school children', *Early Childhood Education Journal*, 29 (2): 111–17.

Fjørtoft, I. (2004) 'Landscape as playscape: the effects of natural environments on children's play and motor development', *Children, Youth and Environments*, 14 (2): 21–44.

Fleet, A. and Britt, C. (2011) 'Seeing spaces, inhabiting places', in D. Harcourt, B. Perry and T. Waller (eds), *Researching Young Children's Perspectives: Debating the Ethics and Dilemmas of Educational Research with Children*. Abingdon: Routledge. pp. 142–62.

Fleming, D. (2008) 'Managing monsters: videogames and the "mediatisation" of the toy', in K. Drotner and S. Livingstone (eds), *The International Handbook of Children, Media and Culture*. London: Sage. pp. 55–71.

Flinn, J.L., Nybell, L.M. and Shook, J.J. (2010) 'The meaning and making of childhood in the era of globalization: challenges for social work', *Children and Youth Services Review*, 32: 246–54.

Foley, P. (2008) 'Introduction', in J. Collins and P. Foley (eds), *Promoting Children's Wellbeing*. Bristol: The Policy Press. p. 312.

Fonagy, P. (2002) *What Works for Whom? A Critical Review of Treatments for Children and Adolescents*. New York: Guilford Press.

Forde, C. and O'Brien, J. (eds) (2011) *Coaching and Mentoring: Developing Teachers and Leaders*. Edinburgh: Dunedin Academic Press.

Foresight (2007) *Tackling Obesities: Future Choices*. Project Report. Available at: http://webarchive.nationalarchives.gov.uk/+/http://www.bis.gov.uk/foresight/our-work/projects/current-projects/tackling-obesities

Fortin, J. (2003) *Children's Rights and the Developing Law*. London: Butterworth.

Foucault, M. (1972) *The Archaeology of Knowledge*. London: Tavistock.

Foucault, M. (1983) 'On the genealogy of ethics', in H. Dreyfus and P. Rabinow (eds), *Michel Foucault: Beyond Structuralism and Hermeneutics*, 2nd edn. Chicago: University of Chicago Press.

Foucault, M. (1989) *The Archaeology of Knowledge*. Abingdon: Routledge.

Francis, M. and Lorenzo, R. (2002) 'Seven realms of children's participation', *Journal of Environmental Psychology*, 22: 157–69.

Franklin, B. (ed.) (2002) *The New Handbook of Children's Rights: Comparative Policy and Practice*. London: Routledge.

Franklin, A. and Knight, A. (2011) *Someone on Our Side: Advocacy for Disabled Children and Young People*. London: The Children's Society.

Freedman, D.S., Zuguo, M., Srinivasan, S.R., Berenson, G.S. and Dietz, W.H. (2007) 'Cardiovascular risk factors and excess adiposity among overweight children and adolescents: the Bogalusa Heart Study', *Journal of Paediatrics*, 150 (1): 12–17.

Freeman, M. (1983) *The Rights and Wrongs of Children*. London: Pinter.

Freire, P. (1985) *The Politics of Education: Culture, Power and Liberation*. Westport: Greenwood Publishing.

Freire, P. (1970) *Pedagogy of the Oppressed*. Harmondsworth: Penguin.

Freire, P. (1972) *Pedagogy of the Oppressed*. Hardmondsworth: Penguin.

Freire, T. (2011) 'From flow to optimal experience: (re)searching the quality of subjective experience throughout daily life', in I. Brdar (ed.), *The Human Pursuit of Well-Being*. Dordrecht, Heidelberg, London and New York: Springer.

French, M. (2002) *From Eve to Dawn: A History of Women Volume II: The Masculine Mystique*. Toronto, Ont: McArthur and Company.

French, M. (2003) *From Eve to Dawn: A History of Women Volume III: Infernos and Paradises*. Toronto: McArthur and Company.

French, J. (2007) 'Multi-agency working: the historical background', in I. Siraj-Blatchford, K. Clarke and M. Needham (eds), *The Team Around the Child: Multiagency Working in the Early Years*. Stoke-on-Trent: Trentham Books. pp. 47–66.

Froebel, F. (1897) *Pedagogics of the Kindergarten*, trans. by J. Jarvis. London: Edward Arnold.

Frones, I. (1994) 'Dimensions of childhood', in J. Qvortrup, G. Sgritta and H. Wintersberger (eds), *Childhood Matters: Social Theory, Practice and Politics*. Aldershot: Avebury.

Frye, E.M. and Feldman, M.D. (2012) 'Factitious disorder by proxy in educational settings: a review', *Educational Psychology Review*, 24: 47–61.

Furedi, F. (2002) *Culture of Fear: Risk Taking and the Morality of Low Expectations*. London: Continuum.

Furlong, A. (2008) 'The Japanese hikikomori phenomenon: acute social withdrawal among young people', *The Sociological Review*, 56 (2): 309–25.

Gabriel, N. (2004) 'Being a child today', in J. Willan, R. Parker-Rees and J. Savage (eds), *Early Childhood Studies*. Exeter: Learning Matters.

Gandini, L. (2012a) 'History, ideas and basic principles: an interview with Loris Malaguzzi', in C. Edwards, L. Gandini and G. Forman (eds), *The Hundred Languages of Children*, 3rd edn. Santa Barbara, CA: Praeger.

Gandini, L. (2012b) 'Connecting through caring and learning spaces', in C. Edwards, L. Gandini and G. Forman (eds), *The Hundred Languages of Children*, 3rd edn. Santa Barbara, CA: Praeger.

Garvey, C. (1977) *Play*. Cambridge, MA: Harvard University Press.

Gee, J. (2005) 'Learning by design: good video games as learning machines', *E-Learning*, 2 (1): 5–16.

Gee, J. (2008) *What Video Games Have to Teach Us About Learning and Literacy*. Basingstoke: Palgrave Macmillan.

Gelder, U. (2004) 'The importance of equal opportunities in the early years', in J. Willan, R. Parker Rees and J. Savage (eds), *Early Childhood Studies: An Introduction to Children's Worlds and Children's Lives*. Exeter: Learning Matters.

Gerhardt, S. (2004) *Why Love Matters: How Affection Shapes a Baby's Brain*. Hove: Brunner-Routledge.

Gesell, A. (1925) *The Mental Growth of the Preschool Child*. New York: Macmillan.

Ghaye, T. (2000) 'Into the reflective mode: bridging the stagnant moat', *Reflective Practice*, 1 (1): 5–9.

Ghaye, T. (2011) *Teaching and Learning through Reflective Practice: A Practical Guide for Positive Action*, 2nd edn. Abingdon: Routledge.

Gibbons, M., Limoges, C., Nowotny, H., Schwatzman, S., Scott, P. and Trow, M. (1994) *The New Production of Knowledge*. London: Sage.

Gibbs, G. (1988) *Learning by Doing: A Guide to Teaching and Learning Methods*. Oxford: Further Education Unit, Oxford Polytechnic.

Gibran, K. (1923 [1995]) *The Prophet* (annotated edn by S. Bushrui). Oxford: Oneworld.

Giddens, A. (1984) *The Constitution of Society*. Berkeley, CA: University of California Press.

Gill, T. (2012) *No Fear: Growing Up in a Risk Averse Society*. London: Calouste Gulbenkian Foundation.

Gillen, J., Cameron, C., Tapanya, S., Pinto, G., Hancock, R., Young, S. and Gamannossi, B. (2007) '"A Day in the Life": advancing a methodology for the cultural study of development and learning in early childhood', *Early Child Development and Care*, 177 (2): 207–18.

Gittins, D. (1993) *The Family in Question*, 2nd edn. London: Macmillan.

Gittins, D. (1998) *The Child in Question*. Basingstoke: Macmillan.

Gittins, D. (2004) 'The historical construction of childhood', in M.J. Kehily (ed.), *An Introduction to Childhood Studies*. Maidenhead: Open University Press and McGraw-Hill Education.

Glaser, B. and Strauss, A.L. (1967) *The Discovery of Grounded Theory: Strategies for Qualitative Research*. New York: Aldine.

Glass, N. (1999) 'Sure Start: the development of an early intervention programme for young children in the United Kingdom', *Children and Society*, 13: 257–64.

Goddard, C. and Bedi, B. (2010) 'Intimate partner violence and child abuse: a child-centered perspective', *Child Abuse Review*, 19 (1): 5–20.

Gold, J.R. and Gold, M.M. (2007) 'Access for all: the rise of the Paralympic Games', *The Journal of the Royal Society for the Promotion of Health*: 127–133.

Goldson, B. (2001) 'The demonization of children: from the symbolic to the institutional', in P. Foley, J. Roche and S. Tucker (eds), *Children in Society: Contemporary Theory, Policy and Practice*. Basingstoke: Palgrave.

Goldthorpe, L. (2004) 'Every Child Matters: a legal perspective', *Child Abuse Review*, 13: 115–36.

Goodman, R. and Burton, D. (2010) 'The inclusion of students with BESD in mainstream schools: teachers' experiences of and recommendations for creating a successful inclusive environment', *Emotional and Behavioural Difficulties*, 15 (3): 223–7.

Goodman, R. and Burton, D. (2012) 'The academies programme: an education revolution', *Education Futures: ejournal of the British Education Studies Association Journal*, 58–78.

Goouch, K. (2010) 'Permission to play', in J. Moyles (ed.), *The Excellence of Play*, 3rd edn. Maidenhead: Open University Press.

Göpfert, M., Webster, J. and Seeman, M. (2004) *Parental Psychiatric Disorder: Distressed Parents and Their Families*. Cambridge: Cambridge University Press.

Gopnik, A. (2011) 'A unified account of abstract structure and conceptual change: probabilistic models and early learning mechanisms', *Behavioral and Brain Sciences*, 34 (3): 129–30.

Gorard, S., Rees, G. and Fevre, R. (1999) 'Patterns of participation in lifelong learning: do families make a difference?', *British Educational Research Journal*, 25 (4): 517–32.

Goswami, U. (2004) 'Neuroscience and education', *British Journal of Educational Psychology*, 74: 1–14.

Graham, M. (2007) *Black Issues in Social Work and Social Care*. Bristol: The Policy Press.

Graham, M. (2011) 'Changing paradigms and conditions of childhood: implications for the social professions and social work', *British Journal of Social Work*, 41 (8): 1532–47.

Graue, M.E. and Walsh, D.J. (1995) 'Children in context: interpreting the here and now of children's lives', in J.A. Hatch (ed.), *Qualitative Research in Early Childhood Settings*. Westport, CT: Praeger. pp. 135–54.

Green, H., McGinnity, A., Meltzer, H. et al. (2005) *Mental Health of Children and Young People in Great Britain, 2004*. Basingstoke: Palgrave Macmillan.

Greenland, P. (2006) 'Physical development', in T. Bruce (ed.), *Early Childhood: A Guide for Students*. London: Sage.

Greeno, J. (1997) 'On claims that answer the wrong questions', *Educational Researcher*, 26 (1): 5–17.

Griffiths, M. (1998) *Educational Research for Social Justice*. Buckingham: Open University Press.

Grossman, D. and Degaetano, G. (1999) *Stop Teaching Our Kids to Kill*. New York: Crown Publishers.

Guardian (2001) Editorial: 'Welcome to the tween age', *The Guardian*, 30 March, p. 15.

Gunter, B., Oates, C. and Blades, M. (2005) *Advertising to Children on TV*. Hillsdale, NJ: Lawrence Erlbaum Associates.

Habermas, J. (1987) *Knowledge and Human Interests*. Cambridge: Polity Press.

Hadfield, M., Jopling, M., Needham, N., Waller, T., Coleyshaw, L., Emira, M. and Royle, K. (2012) *Longitudinal Study of Early Years Professional Status: An Exploration of Progress, Leadership and Impact*. Final report for the DfE. CeDARE, University of Wolverhampton (Research Report RR 239c).

Hadfield, M., Jopling, M., Royle, K. and Waller, T. (2011) *First National Survey of Practitioners with Early Years Professional Status*. Leeds: CWDC.

Hall, B. (1998) 'Knowledge, democracy and higher education: contributions from adult and life-long learning', in W. Mauch and R. Narang (eds), *Learning and Institutions of Higher Education in the 21st Century*. Mumbai: Department of Adult Education and Continuing Education and Extension, University of Mumbai/Hamburg: UNESCO Institute of Education. pp. 17–31.

Hall, D. and Elliman, D. (2006) *Health for All Children*, rev. 4th edn. Oxford: Oxford University Press.

Hall, J. (1997) *Social Devaluation and Special Education*. London: Jessica Kingsley Publishers.

Hallam, S. (2009) 'An evaluation of the Social and Emotional Aspects of Learning (SEAL) programme: promoting positive behaviour, effective learning and well-being in primary school children', *Oxford Review of Education*, 35 (3): 313–30.

Hallet, C. (1995) 'Child abuse: an academic overview', in P. Kingston and B. Penhale (eds), *Family Violence and the Caring Professions*. London: Macmillan.

Hallett, E. (2013) *The Reflective Early Years Practitioner*. London: Sage.

Handley, G. and Doyle, C. (2012) 'Ascertaining the wishes and feelings of young children: social workers' perspectives on skills and training', *Child and Family Social Work*, doi: 10.1111/cfs.12043.

Haney-Lopez, I.F. (2000) 'The social construction of race'. *Critical race theory: The cutting edge*: 163-175.

Hanna, R. (2006) *Rationality and Logic*. Cambridge, MA: The MIT Press.

Haralambos, M. and Holborn, M. (2004) *Sociology, Themes and Perspectives*, 6th edn. London: Collins.

Harcourt, D. (2011) 'An encounter with children: seeking meaning and understanding about childhood', *European Early Childhood Education Research Journal*, 19 (3): 331–43.

Harcourt, D. and Einarsdottir, J. (2011) 'Introducing children's perspectives and participation in research', *European Early Childhood Education Research Journal*, 19 (3): 301–7.

Harcourt, D., Perry, B. and Waller, T. (eds) (2011) *Researching Young Children's Perspectives: Debating the Ethics and Dilemmas of Educational Research with Children*. Abingdon: Routledge.

Hargreaves, D. (1996) 'Teaching as a Research-Based Profession: Possibilities and Prospects'. Teacher Training Agency Annual Lecture. London: Teacher Training Agency.

Harman, B. (2013) *Inclusion/Integration, is There a Difference?* Calgary: Canadian Downs Syndrome Society. Available at: http://www.cdss.ca/images/pdf/general_information/integration_vs_inclusion.pdf (accessed 5 February 2014)

Harms, T., Clifford, M. and Cryer, D. (1998) *Early Childhood Environment Rating Scale*, rev. edn (ECERS-R). New York: Teachers College Press.

Harrison, N. (2011) *Teaching and Learning in Aboriginal Education*. South Melbourne: Oxford.

Harrison, R., Mann G., Murphy, M., Taylor, T. and Thompson, N. (2003) *Partnership Made Painless: A Joined Up Guide to Working Together*. Dorset: Russell House Publishing.

Hart, R. (1992) *Children's Participation from Tokenism to Citizenship*. Innocenti Essays No 4. Florence: UNICEF.

Hatcher, R. (2011) 'Local government against local democracy: a case study of a bid for Building Schools for the Future funding for an academy', in H.M. Gunter (ed.), *The State and Education Policy: The Academies Programme*. London: Continuum.

Hawker, D. (2006) 'Joined up working – the development of children's services', in G. Pugh and B. Duffy (eds), *Contemporary Issues in the Early Years*, 4th edn. London: Sage. pp. 21–34.

Hawker, D. (2010) 'Children's trusts and early years services: integration in action', in G. Pugh and B. Duffy (eds), *Contemporary Issues in the Early Years*, 5th edn. London: Sage. pp. 21–32.

Hayes, A., Weston, R., Qu, L. and Gray, M. (2010) *Families Then and Now, 1980–2010*. Melbourne: Australian Institute of Family Studies. (Available at: http://aifs.gov.au/institute/pubs/factssheets/fs2010conf/fs2010conf.html.)

Heckman, J.J. (2000) 'Policies to foster human capital', *Research in Economics* 54 (1): 3–56.

Heikka, J. and Waniganayake, M. (2011) 'Pedagogical leadership from a distributed perspective within the context of early childhood education', *International Journal of Leadership in Education: Theory and Practice*, 14 (4): 499–512.

Helm, J.H. and Katz, L. (2001) *Young Investigators*. New York: Teachers' College Press.

Helm, T. and Roberts, Y. (2013) 'Parent groups join nurseries to fight new carer ratios', *The Observer*, 28 April.

Hendrick, H. (1997) 'Constructions and reconstructions of British childhood: an interpretative survey, 1800 to the present', in A. James and A. Prout (eds), *Constructing and Reconstructing Childhood: Contemporary Issues in the Sociological Study of Childhood*. London: Falmer Press. pp. 33–60.

Hendrick, H. (2008) 'The Child as a Social Actor in Historical Sources: Problems of Identification and Interpretation'. In, P. Christensen and A. James (eds) *Research with Children: Perspectives and Practices*, second edition. London: Falmer.

Henley, D. (2012) *Cultural Education in England: An Independent Review*. London: Department for Culture Media and Sport and Department for Education.

Henry, H. and Borzekowski, D. (2011) 'The Nag Factor: a mixed methodology study in the US of young children's requests for advertised products', *Journal of Children and Media*, 5 (3): 298–318.

Hevey, D. (1986) *The Continuing Under Fives Muddle; An Investigation of Current Training Opportunities*. London: Voluntary Organisations Liaison Council For Under Fives.

Hevey, D. (1991) 'National vocational qualifications in child care and education. Starting Points No.5: A Series of VOLCUF Briefing Papers'. London: Voluntary Organisations Liaison Committee for Under Fives.

Heywood, C. (2001) *A History of Modern Childhood*. Cambridge: Polity Press.

Higher Education Academy (2008) *Integrating Children's Services in Higher Education (ISE-HE): Preparing Tomorrow's Professional*. Available at: www.swap.ac.uk/docs/projects/icshe_brief-paper.pdf (accessed 17 July 2013).

Hill, M. (2006) 'Children's voices on the ways of having a voice: children's and young people's perspectives on methods used in research and consultation', *Childhood*, 13 (1): 69–89.

Hill, M., Head, G., Lockyear, A., Reid, B. and Taylor, R. (eds) (2012) *Children's Services: Working Together*. Harlow: Pearson Education.

Hill, S. (2010) 'The millennium generation: teacher–researchers explore new forms of literacy', *Journal of Early Childhood Literacy*, 10 (3): 314–40.

HM Government (1989) Children Act 1989 c. 41. London: HMSO. Available at: www.legislation. gov.uk/ukpga/1989/41/contents/

HM Government (1995a) Children (Scotland) Act 1995 c. 36. London: HMSO. Available at: www. legislation.gov.uk/ukpga/1995/36/contents

HM Government (1995b) Disability Discrimination Act 1995 c. 50. London: HMSO.

HM Government (2001) Special Educational Needs and Disability Act. London: TSO. Available at: www.legislation.gov.uk/ukpga/2001/10/contents

HM Government (2003) Criminal Justice (Scotland) Act 2003 asp 7. London: TSO. Available at: www.legislation.gov.uk/asp/2003/7/contents

HM Government (2004) Children Act 2004 c. 31. London: TSO. Available at: www.legislation. gov.uk/ukpga/2004/31/pdfs/ukpga_20040031_en.pdf

HM Government (2006) Childcare Act 2006 c. 21. London: TSO. Available at: www.legislation. gov.uk/ukpga/2006/21/contents

HM Government (2010) The Equality Act c. 15. London: TSO. Available at: www.legislation.gov. uk/ukpga/2010/15/contents

HM Government (2013) *Working Together to Safeguard Children: A Guide to Inter-agency Working to Safeguard and Promote the Welfare of Children*. London: DfE. Available at: www. education.gov.uk/publications/standard/publicationDetail/Page1/DFE-00030-2013.

Ho, D.K. and Ross, C.C. (2012) 'Cognitive behaviour therapy for sex offenders: too good to be true?', *Criminal Behaviour and Mental Health*, 1 (1): 1–6.

Hobbes, T. (1651 [1982]) *Leviathan*. London: Penguin.

Hodkinson, A. and Vickerman, P. (2009) *Key Issues in Special Educational Needs and Inclusion* (Education Studies: Key Issues). London: Sage.

Hodgkinson, H.L. (1957) 'Action research: a critique', *Journal of Educational Sociology*, 31 (4): 137–53.

Hogg, R., Ritchie, D., de Kok, B., Wood, C. and Huby, G. (2013) 'Parenting support for families with young children – a public health, user-focused study undertaken in a semi-rural area of Scotland', *Journal of Clinical Nursing*, 22: 1140–50.

Holt, J. (1974) *Escape from Childhood: The Needs and Rights of Childhood*. New York: E.P. Dutton and Co.

Hope, G., Austin, R., Dismore, H., Hammond, S. and Whyte, T. (2007) 'Wild woods or urban jungle: playing it safe or freedom to roam', *Education 3–13*, 35 (4): 321–32.

Horkheimer, M. (1937) 'Traditional and critical theory', in M. Horkheimer (1972) *Critical Theory: Selected Essays* (trans. M.J. O'Connell). New York: Continuum. pp. 188–243.

Horta, B.L., Bahl, R., Martinés, J.C. and Victora, C.G. (2007) *Evidence on the Long-term Effects of Breastfeeding*. Geneva: World Health Organisation. Available at: www.who.int/maternal_child_adolescent/documents/9241595230/en/index.html (accessed 13 July 2013).

House, R. (ed.) (2011) *Too Much Too Soon? Early Learning and the Erosion of Childhood*. Gloucester: Hawthorn Press.

Housley, W. (2003) *Interaction in Multidisciplinary Teams*. Aldershot: Ashgate Publishing.

Howard, J. (2010) 'Making the most of play in the early years: the importance of children's perceptions', in P. Broadhead, J. Howard and E. Wood (eds), *Play and Learning in the Early Years*. London: Sage.

Howard, J. and McInnes, K. (2010) 'Thinking through the challenge of a play-based curriculum', in J. Moyles (ed.), *Thinking About Play: A Reflective Approach*. Maidenhead: Open University Press.

Hoyles, M. and Evans, P. (1989) *The Politics of Childhood*. London: Journeyman Press.

HSCIC (Health and Social Care Information Centre) (2012) *National Child Measurement Programme England 2011–12 School Year*. London: Department of Health.

Hume, D. (1739/1896) *A Treatise of Human Nature* (ed. L.A. Selby-Bigge). Oxford: Clarendon Press.

Hume, D. (1748 [2000]) 'An enquiry concerning human understanding', in T. Beauchamp (ed.), *David Hume: An Enquiry Concerning Human Understanding*. Oxford: Oxford University Press. pp. 5–123.

Hunter, M. (2004) 'Hearts and minds reluctantly follow as Bill finally completes passage', *Community Care*, 18–24 November, 18–19.

Husband, T. (2012) '"I don't see color": challenging assumptions about discussing race with young children', *Early Childhood Education Journal*, 39: 365–71.

ILO (International Labour Organisation) (2011) International Programme on the Elimination of Child Labour (IPEC). www.ilo.org/ipec/programme/lang--en/index.htm.

Ipsos MORI and Nairn A. (2011) *Children's Well-Being in UK, Sweden and Spain: The Role of Inequality and Materialism*. London: Ipsos MORI Social Research Institute. Available at: www.ipsos-mori.com/researchpublications/publications/1441/Childrens-Wellbeing-in-UK-Sweden-and-Spain.aspx (accessed 4 May 2012).

Isaacs, N. (1944) 'Children's "why" questions', in S. Isaacs, *Intellectual Growth in Young Children*. London: Routledge. pp. 291–354.

Isaacs, S. (1929) *The Nursery Years*. London: Routledge and Kegan Paul.

Isaacs, S. (1933) *Social Development in Young Children*. London: Routledge and Kegan Paul.

Jackson, B. and Jackson, S. (1981) *Childminder*. London: Penguin Books.

James, A. (2009) 'Agency', in J. Qvortrup, W.A. Corsaro and M.S. Honig (eds), *The Palgrave Handbook of Childhood Studies*. Basingstoke: Palgrave Macmillan.

James, A. and James, A. (1999) 'Pump up the volume: listening to children in separation and divorce', *Childhood*, 6 (2): 189–206.

James, A. and James, A. (2004) *Constructing Childhood: Theory, Policy and Social Practice*. Basingstoke: Palgrave.

James, A. and James, A. (2008) *Key Concepts in Childhood Studies*. London: Sage.

James, A. and Prout, A. (eds) (1997) *Constructing and Reconstructing Childhood: Contemporary Issues in the Sociological Study of Childhood*. London: Falmer Press.

James, A., Jenks, C. and Prout, A. (1998) *Theorising Childhood*. Cambridge: Polity.

James, A., James, A. and McNamee, S. (2004) 'Turn down the volume? Not hearing children in family proceedings', *Child and Family Law Quarterly*, 16 (2): 189–202.

Jans, M. (2004) 'Children as citizens: towards a contemporary notion of child participation', *Childhood*, 11 (1): 27–44.

Jefferis, B., Power, C. and Hertzman, C. (2002) 'Birth weight, childhood socioeconomic environment, and cognitive development in the 1958 British birth cohort study', *BMJ*, 325 (7359): 305.

Jenks, C. (1982) *The Sociology of Childhood*. London: Batsford.

Jenks, C. (1996) *Childhood*. London: Routledge.

Jenks, C. (2004) 'Constructing childhood sociologically', in M.J. Kehily (ed.), *An Introduction to Childhood Studies*. Maidenhead: Open University Press.

Jenkinson, J. (1997) *Mainstream or Special: Educating Students with Disabilities*. London: Routledge.

Jenkinson, S. (2001) *The Genius of Play: Celebrating the Spirit of Childhood*. Stroud: Hawthorn Press.

Jessup, G. (1991) *Outcomes: NVQs and The Emerging Model Of Education and Training*. London: Falmer.

Johns, C. (1995) 'Framing learning through reflection within Carper's fundamental ways of knowing in nursing', *Journal of Advanced Nursing*, 22 (2): 226–34.

Johnson-Laird, P.N. and Byrne, R.M.J. (1991) *Deduction*. Hillsdale, NJ: Lawrence Erlbaum Associates.

Johnston, T. and Titman, P. (2004) 'A health visitor-led service for children with behavioural problems', *Community Practitioner*, 77 (3): 90–4.

Johnston-Wilder, S. and Collins, J. (2008) 'Children negotiating identities', in J. Collins and P. Foley (eds), *Promoting Children's Wellbeing: Policy and Practice*. Bristol: The Policy Press.

Jones, C. (2004) *Supporting Inclusion in the Early Years*. Maidenhead: Oxford University Press.

Jones, C. and Pound, L. (2008) *Leadership and Management in the Early Years: From Principles to Practice*. Maidenhead: Open University Press/McGraw-Hill Education.

Jones, K. and Howley, M. (2010) 'An investigation into an interaction programme for children on the autism spectrum: outcomes for children, perceptions of schools and a model for training', *Journal of Research in Special Educational Needs*, 10 (2): 115–23.

Jordan, B. (2004) 'Scaffolding learning and co-constructing understandings', in A. Anning, J. Cullen and M. Fleer (eds) *Early Childhood Education*. London: Sage.

Jordanova, L. (1989) 'Children in history: concepts of nature and society', in G. Scarre (ed.), *Children, Parents and Politics*. Cambridge: Cambridge University Press.

Kagan, S.L. and Hallmark, L.G. (2001) 'Cultivating leadership in early care and education', *Child Care Information Exchange*, 140: 7–10.

Kaiser Foundation (2010) 'Daily media use among children and teens up dramatically from five years ago'. Available at: www.kff.org/entmedia/entmedia012010nr.cfm

Kalliala, M. (2006) *Play Culture in a Changing World*. Maidenhead: Open University Press.

Kaltenborn, K. (2001) 'Family transitions and childhood agency', *Childhood*, 8 (4): 463–98.

Kant, I. (1787) *The Critique of Pure Reason*. Prepared in e-text by C. Aldarondo (2003) Project Gutenberg. Available at: www.gutenberg.org/dirs/etext03/cprrn10.txt (accessed 5 May 2012).

Kasser, T. (2011) 'Cultural values and the well-being of future generations: a cross-national study', *Journal of Cross-Cultural Psychology*, 42 (2): 206–15.

Katz, L.G. (1993) *Dispositions as Educational Goals*. ERIC Digest. ERIC clearing house on Elementary and Early Childhood Education. EDO PS 93 10 (September).

Katz, L. (1999) *Another Look at What Young Children Should be Learning*. ERIC Digest. Available at: www.vtaide.com/png/ERIC/Learning-EC.htm (accessed 15 July 2013).

Katz, L. and Chard, S.C. (1989) *Engaging Children's Minds: The Project Approach*. Norwood, NJ: Ablex Publishing Corporation.

Kehily, M.J. (ed.) (2004) *An Introduction to Childhood Studies*. Maidenhead: Open University Press and McGraw-Hill Education.

Kehily, M.J. (ed.) (2009) *An Introduction to Childhood Studies*, 2nd edn. Maidenhead: Open University Press and McGraw-Hill Education.

Kehily, M.J. (2010) 'Childhood in crisis? Tracing the contours of "crisis" and its impact upon contemporary parenting practices', *Media, Culture and Society*, 32 (2): 171–85.

Kellett, M. (2005) *How to Develop Children as Researchers*. London: Sage.

Kemmis, S. and McTaggart, R. (2005) 'Participatory action research', in N. Denzin and Y. Lincoln (eds), *The Sage Handbook of Qualitative Research*. Thousand Oaks, CA: Sage. pp. 559–604.

Kendall, J., Beckett, A. and Leo, M. (2003) 'Children's accounts of attention-deficit/hyperactivity disorder', *Advances in Nursing Science: Childhood Health and Illness,* 26 (2): 114–30.

Kennedy, M. (2002) 'Disability and child abuse', in K. Wilson and A. James (eds), *The Child Protection Handbook*, 2nd edn. Edinburgh: Harcourt Publishers.

Keskitalo, P., Määttä, K. and Uusiautti, S. (2011) 'Toward the practical framework of Sámi education', *British Journal of Educational Research*, 1 (2): 84–106.

Kimmel, C. and Roby, L. (2007) 'Institutionalised child abuse: the use of child soldiers', *International Social Work*, 50 (6): 740–54.

King, M. (1987) 'Playing the symbols – custody and the Law Commission', *Family Law*, 17: 186–91.

Kirby, P. (1999) *Involving Young Researchers*. London: Joseph Rowntree Foundation/Save the Children.

Kirby, P. and Marchant, R. (2004) 'The participation of young children: communication, consultation and involvement', in B. Neale (ed.), *Young Children's Citizenship: Ideas into Practice.* York: Joseph Rowntree Foundation.

Kjørholt, A.T. (2002) 'Small is powerful: discourses on "Children and Participation" in Norway', *Childhood*, 9 (1): 63–82.

Kloep, M. and Hendry, L. (2007) '"Over-protection, over-protection, over-protection!" Young people in modern Britain', *Psychology of Education Review*, 31 (2): 4–8.

Knight, S. (2009) *Forest Schools and Outdoor Learning in the Early Years.* London: Sage.

Knobel, M. and Lankshear, C. (eds) (2007) *New Literacies Sampler.* New York: Peter Lang.

Kobayashi, A. and Ray, B. (2000) 'Civil risk and landscapes of marginality in Canada: a pluralist approach to social justice', *The Canadian Geographer*, 44 (4): 401–17.

Kotter, J.P. (1996) *Leading Change.* Boston, MA: Harvard Business School Press.

Kovach, M. (2005) 'Emerging from the margins: indigenous methodologies', in L. Brown and S. Strega (eds), *Research as Resistance.* Toronto: Canadian Scholars' Press. pp. 19–36.

Kozulin, A. (2003) 'Psychological tools and mediated learning', in A. Kozulin, B. Gindis, V.S. Ageyev and S. Miller (eds), *Vygotsky's Educational Theory in Cultural Context.* Cambridge: Cambridge University Press.

Krcmar, M. (2011) 'Can past experience with TV help US infants learn from it?', *Journal of Children and Media*, 5 (3): 235–47.

Kübler-Ross, E. (2009) *On Death and Dying.* Abingdon: Routledge.

Kucuker, H., Demir, T. and Oral, R. (2010) 'Pediatric condition falsification (Munchausen syndrome by Proxy) as a continuum of maternal factitious disorder (Munchausen syndrome)', *Pediatric Diabetes*, 11: 572–8.

Kuhn, T. (1970) *The Structure of Scientific Revolutions.* Chicago: Chicago University Press.

Kutner, L. and Olson, C. (2008) *Grand Theft Childhood: The Surprising Truth about Violent Video Games.* New York: Simon and Schuster.

Labbo, L. and Reinking, D. (2003) 'Computers and early literacy instruction', in N. Hall, J. Larson and J. Marsh (eds), *Handbook of Early Childhood Literacy.* London: Sage.

Laevers, F. (ed.) (1994) *The Leuven Involvement Scale for Young Children. Manual and Video.* Experiential Education Series, No. 1. Leuven, Belgium: Centre for Experiential Education.

Laevers, F. (2000) 'Forward to basics! Deep-level-learning and the experiential approach', *Early Years*, 20 (2): 19–29.

Laming, Lord (2003) *Inquiry into the Death of Victoria Climbié.* London: TSO.

Laming, Lord (2009) *The Protection of Children in England: A Progress Report.* London: TSO.

Lancy, D.F. (2013) '"Babies aren't persons": a survey of delayed personhood', in H. Keller and O. Hiltrud (eds), *Different Faces of Attachment: Cultural Variations of a Universal Human Need.* Cambridge: Cambridge University Press. Available at: www.usu.edu/anthro/davidlancyspages/RW_Powerpoints/Babies%20Aren't%20Persons%2010.12.12.pdf (accessed 25 June 2013).

Lane, J. (2007) *Embracing Equality: Promoting Equality and Inclusion in Early Years.* London: Pre-School Alliance.

Langsted, O. (1994) 'Looking at quality from the child's perspective', in P. Moss and A. Pence (eds), *Valuing Quality in Early Childhood Services: New Approaches to Defining Quality.* London: Paul Chapman.

Lankshear, C. and Knobel, M. (2003) *New Literacies: Changing Knowledge and Classroom Learning.* Buckingham: Open University Press.

Lansdown, G. (2001) 'Children's welfare and children's rights', in P. Foley, J. Roche and S. Tucker (eds), *Children in Society: Contemporary Theory, Policy and Practice.* Basingstoke: Palgrave.

Lansdown, G. (2005) *The Evolving Capacities of Children: Implications for the Exercise of Rights.* Florence: UNICEF Innocenti Research Centre.

Lave, J. (1988) *Cognition in Practice*. Cambridge: Cambridge University Press.

Lave, J. and Wenger, E. (1991) *Situated Learning*. Cambridge: Cambridge University Press.

Lawrence, E. (1952/2012) *Friedrich Froebel and English Education* (Routledge Library Editions: Education). London: Routledge.

Learning and Teaching Scotland (LTS) (2010) *Pre-birth to Three: Positive Outcomes for Scotland's Children and Families*. Edinburgh: LTS. Available at: www.educationscotland.gov.uk/Images/PreBirthToThreeBooklet_tcm4-633448.pdf (accessed 4 January 2013).

Lee, J. (1915) *Play in Education*. New York: Macmillan.

Lee, N. (2001) *Childhood and Society: Growing Up in an Age of Uncertainty*. Buckingham: Open University Press.

Lee, W. (2008) 'ELP: empowering the leadership in professional development communities', *European Early Childhood Education Research Journal*, 16 (1): 95–106.

Lee-Hammond, L. (2012a) 'Big expectations for little kids', in B. Down and J. Smyth (eds), *Critical Voices in Teacher Education: Teaching for Social Justice in Conservative Times*. Dordrecht: Springer. pp. 171–84.

Lee-Hammond, L. (2012b) *Walliabup: Connecting Young Children with Culture in the Outdoors*. Video production. Perth, Australia: Burdiya Aboriginal Corporation.

Lee-Hammond, L. (2013) 'Integrated services for Aboriginal children and families', *Australasian Journal of Early Childhood*, 38 (1): 55–64.

Lee-Hammond, L. and Jackson-Barrett, E. (2013) 'Aboriginal children's engagement in Bush School', in S. Knight (ed.), *International Perspectives on Forest School*. London: Sage.

Lees, L. (1999) 'Critical geography and the opening up of the academy: lessons from "real life" attempts', *Area*, 31 (4): 377–83.

Leeson, C. and Griffiths, L. (2004) 'Working with colleagues', in J. Willan, R. Parker-Rees and J. Savage (eds), *Early Childhood Studies*. Exeter: Learning Matters.

Leiba, T. (2003) 'Mental health policies and inter-professional working', in J. Weinstein, C. Whittington and T. Leiba (eds), *Collaboration in Social Work Practice*. London: Jessica Kingsley.

Leiba, T. and Weinstein, J. (2003) 'Who are the participants in the collaborative process and what makes collaboration succeed or fail?', in J. Weinstein, C. Whittington and T. Leiba (eds), *Collaboration in Social Work Practice*. London: Jessica Kingsley.

Leitch, R. and Day, C. (2000) 'Action research and reflective practice: towards a holistic view', *Educational Action Research*, 8 (1): 179–89.

Lemish, D. (2008) 'The mediated playground: media in early childhood', in K. Drotner and S. Livingstone (eds), *The International Handbook of Children, Media and Culture*. London: Sage.

Lendrum, A., Humphrey, N., Kalambouka, A. and Wigelsworth, M. (2009) 'Implementing primary Social and Emotional Aspects of Learning (SEAL) small group interventions: recommendations for practitioners', *Emotional and Behavioural Difficulties*, 14 (3): 229–38.

Lepler, S., Uyeda, K. and Halfon, N. (2006) *Master Contracting with Comprehensive Service Providers: A Tool to Simplify Administration and Promote Outcome-Focused Integrated Services*. Los Angeles, CA: Center for Governmental Research Inc. and UCLA Center for Healthier Children, Families and Communities. Available at: http://eric.ed.gov/?id=ED496854

Letherby, G. (2006) 'Emancipatory research', in V. Jupp (ed.), *The Sage Dictionary of Social Science Research*. London: Sage. pp. 88–90.

Leu, D. (1996) 'Sarah's secret: social aspects of literacy and learning in a digital information age', *The Reading Teacher*, 50: 162–5.

Lewin, K. (1997) *Resolving Social Conflicts: Field Theory in Social Science*. Washington, DC: American Psychological Association.

Lilley, I. (1967) *Friedrich Froebel: A Selection from His Writings*. Cambridge: Cambridge University Press.

Lindon, J. (2011) *Too Safe for Their Own Good? Helping Children Learn about Risk and Lifestyles*. London: National Early Years Network/NCB.

Lippman, L.H., Anderson Moore, K. and McIntosh, H. (2009) *Positive Indicators of Child Well-being: A Conceptual Framework, Measures and Methodological Issues*. Innocenti Working Party Paper: IWP-2009-21. UNICEF.

Lister Sharp, D., Chapman, S., Stewart Brown, S. and Sowden, A. (1999) 'Health-promoting schools and health promotion in schools: two systematic reviews', *Health Technology Assessment*, 3 (22): 1–207.

Little, H. (2006) 'Children's risk-taking behaviour: implications for early childhood policy and practice', *International Journal of Early Years Education*, 14 (2): 141–54.

Littlechild, B. and Smith, R. (2013) *A Handbook for Interprofessional Practice in the Human Services: Learning to Work Together*. Harlow: Pearson Education.

Livingstone, S. and Bovill, M. (eds) (2001) *Children and their Changing Media Environment: A European Comparative Study*. Mahwah, NJ: Lawrence Erlbaum Associates.

Lloyd, E. and Hallet, E. (2010) 'Professionalising the early childhood workforce in England: work in progress or missed opportunity?' *Contemporary Issues in Early Childhood,* 11(1): 75–86.

Lloyd, G., Stead, J. and Kendrick, A. (2001) *Interagency Working to Prevent School Exclusion*. York: Joseph Rowntree Foundation.

Loader, R. and Amartya, L. (1999) 'Participatory rural appraisal: extending the research methods base', *Agricultural Systems*, 62 (2): 73–85.

Locke, J. (1690/1959) *Essay Concerning Human Understanding*. New York: Dover.

Loreman, T., Deppeler, J. and Harvey, D. (2010) *Inclusive Education: A Practical Guide to Supporting Diversity in the Classroom*. London: Routledge.

Louv, R. (2006) *Last Child in the Woods: Saving Our Children from Nature-Deficit Disorder*. New York: Workman Publishing.

Loxley, A. (1997) *Collaboration in Health and Welfare: Working with Difference*. London: Jessica Kingsley.

Lumsden, E. (2006) 'Safeguarding children: developing confidence in working across professional boundaries'. Paper presented at XVIth ISPCAN International Congress on Child Abuse and Neglect, York, UK, September.

Lumsden, E. (2012) 'The Early Years Professional: a new professional or a missed opportunity', PhD thesis, University of Northampton. Available at: http://nectar.northampton.ac.uk/4494/1/1Lumsden20124494.pdf (accessed 23 March 2013).

Lumsden, E. (2013) 'Child Development Professionalism'. Consultation on Early Childhood and Development in the Post 2015 Agenda. UNICEF and Municipality of Turkey, 24–25 January.

Lynch, J. (1987) *Prejudice Reduction and the Schools*. New York: Nichols Publishing.

Mackett, R.L. (2004) *Making Children's Lives More Active*. London: Centre for Transport Studies, University College London.

Macormick, N. (1982) *Legal Rights and Social Democracy: Essays in Legal and Political Philosphy*. Oxford: Clarendon Press.

MacNaughton, G. (2003) *Shaping Early Childhood*. Maidenhead: Open University Press.

MacNaughton, G. (2004) 'Exploring critical constructivist perspectives on children's learning', in A. Anning, J. Cullen and M. Fleer (eds), *Early Childhood Education Society and Culture*. London: Sage.

Macpherson, W. (1999) *The Stephen Lawrence Inquiry: Report of an Inquiry by Sir William Macpherson of Cluny*. London: TSO.

Maddern, K. (2010) 'Tories care about SEN, but will they make it count?', *Times Educational Supplement*, 22 October.

Maglajlic, R.A. (2010) '"Big Organisations" supporting "Small Involvement": lessons from Bosnia and Herzegovina on enabling community-based participation of children through PAR', *American Journal of Community Psychology*, 46 (1–2): 204–14.

Makhmalbaf, A. and Yi-Luen Do, E. (2007) 'Investigating how physical environment might help enhance children's creativity', in IASDR (International Association of Societies of Design Research) Emerging Trends in Design Research Conference, Hong Kong Polytechnic University School of Design, 14 November, Session D Creativity. Available at: www.sd.polyu.edu.hk/iasdr/proceeding/ (accessed 4 March 2013).

Makkonen, T. (2006) *European Handbook on Equality Data*. Paris: European Commission.

Malaguzzi, L. (1993) 'For an education based on relationships', *Young Children*, 11/93: 9–13.

Mandell, N. (1988) 'The least-adult role in studying children', *Journal of Contemporary Ethnography*, 16 (4): 433–67.

Manning-Morton, J. (2006) 'The personal is professional: professionalism and the birth to threes practitioner', *Contemporary Issues in Early Childhood*, 7 (1): 42–52.

Mares, M-L. and Pan, Z. (2013) 'Effects of Sesame Street: a meta-analysis of children's learning in 15 countries', *Journal of Applied Developmental Psychology*. Available at: http://dx.doi.org/10.1016/j.appdev.2013.01.001

Markström, A. and Halldén, G. (2009) 'Children's strategies for agency in preschool', *Children in Society*, 23 (2): 112–22.

Marmot Review (2010) *Fair Society, Healthy Lives*. Strategic Review of Health Inequalities in England post-2010 (Chair Michael Marmot). London: The Marmot Review.

Marsh, J. (ed.) (2005) *Popular Culture, New Media and Digital Technology in Early Childhood*. London: RoutledgeFalmer.

Marsh, J. (2006) 'Digital animation in the early years: ICT and media education', in M. Hayes and D. Whitbread (eds), *ICT in the Early Years of Education*. Milton Keynes: Open University Press.

Marsh, J., Brooks, G., Hughes, J., Ritchie, L. and Roberts, S. (2005) *Digital Beginnings: Young Children's Use of Popular Culture, Media and New Technologies*. Sheffield: The University of Sheffield. Retrieved from: www.digitalbeginings.shef.ac.uk/ (accessed 15 July 2013).

Marsh, J. (2007) 'Digital Beginnings: Conceptualisations of Childhood'. Paper presented at the WUN Virtual Seminar, 13 February. Available at: www.wun.ac.uk/download.php?file=2488_Childrenpaper13Feb.pdf&mimetype=application/pdf. (accessed 11 August 2007).

Marson, D. (1973) *Children's Strikes in 1911*. Oxford: Ruskin College.

Marx, K. (1867) *Das Kapital*. Hamburg: Verlag Meissner.

Maslow, A.H. (1970) *Motivation and Personality*, 2nd edn. New York: Harper Row.

Mathers, S., Ranns, H., Karemaker, A., Mody, A., Sylva, K., Graham, J. and Siraj-Blatchford, I. (2011) *Evaluation of the Graduate Leader Fund: Final Report*. Department for Education Research Report DfE-RR144.

Mathers, S., Sylva, K. and Joshi, H. (2007) *The Quality of Childcare Settings in the Millenium Cohort Study*. Sure Start Research Report SSU/2007/FR.

Matthews, J. (2003) *Drawing and Painting: Children and Visual Representation*, 2nd edn. London: Paul Chapman.

Maughan, B., Collishaw, S., Meltzer, H. and Goodman, R. (2008) 'Recent trends in UK child and adolescent mental health', *Social Psychiatry and Psychiatric Epidemiology*, 43 (4): 305–10.

May, V. and Smart, C. (2004) 'Silence in court? Hearing children in residence and contact disputes', *Child and Family Law Quarterly*, 16 (3): 305–20.

Mayall, B. (1996) *Children, Health and the Social Order*. Buckingham: Open University Press.

Mayall, B. (2002) *Towards a Sociology of Childhood: Thinking from Children's Lives*. Buckingham: Open University Press.

Maynard, T. (2007) 'Adopting the Forest School approach: challenges and changes', in R. Austin (ed.), *Letting the Outside In*. Stoke-on-Trent: Trentham Books.

Maynard, T. and Thomas, N. (eds) (2004) *An Introduction to Early Childhood Studies*. London: Sage.

Maynard, T. and Thomas, N. (eds) (2009) *An Introduction to Early Childhood Studies*, 2nd edn. London: Sage.

Maynard, T. and Waters, J. (2007) 'Learning in the outdoor environment: a missed opportunity', *Early Years*, 27 (3): 255–65.

McAdam-Crisp, J. (2006) 'Factors that can enhance and limit resilience for Children of War', *Childhood*, 13 (4): 459–77.

McAuley, C. and Rose, W. (2010) *Child Well-being: Understanding Children's Lives*. London: Jessica Kingsley.

McClure, P. (2005) *Reflection on Practice: Making Practice-Based Learning Work*. Available at: www.practicebasedlearning.org pdf (accessed 24 April 2013).

McDonald, M. (2010) *Are Disadvantaged Families 'Hard to Reach'? Engaging Disadvantaged Families in Child and Family Services*. Melbourne: Australian Institute of Family Studies.

McFarlane, A., Sparrowhawk, A. and Heald, Y. (2002) *Report on the Educational Use of Games*. London: DfES.

McKee, B.E. and Dillenburger, K. (2012) 'Effectiveness of child protection training for pre-service early childhood educators', *International Journal of Educational Research*, 53: 348–59.

McMillan, M. (1919) *The Nursery School*. London: Dent.

Mellou, E. (1994) 'The case of intervention in young children's dramatic play in order to develop creativity', *Early Child Development and Care*, 99: 53–61.

Merchant, G. (2005) 'Digikids: cool dudes and the new writing', *E-Learning*, 2 (1): 50–60.

Messenger, W. (2013) 'Professional cultures and professional knowledge: owning, loaning and sharing', *European Early Childhood Education Research Journal*, 21 (1): 138–49.

Millei, Z. and Imre, R. (2009) 'The problems with using the concept of "citizenship" in Early Years policy', *Contemporary Issues in Early Childhood*, 10 (3): 280–90.

Miller, L. and Cable, C. (eds) (2008) *Professionalism in the Early Years*. London: Hodder Education.

Miller, L. and Cable, C. (eds) (2011) *Professionalization, Leadership and Management in the Early Years*. London: Sage.

Miller, L., Drury, R. and Cable, C. (eds) (2012) *Extending Professional Practice in the Early Years*. London: Open University and Sage.

Miller, P.H. (2002) *Theories of Developmental Psychology*, 4th edn. New York: Worth Publishers.

Miller, R. and Pedro, J. (2006) 'Creating respectful classroom environments', *Early Childhood Education Journal*, 33 (5): 293–9.

Ministry of Education (1996) *Te Whāriki: Early Childhood Curriculum*. Wellington, NZ: Learning Media Limited. Available at: www.educate.ece.govt.nz/learning/curriculumAndLearning/TeWhariki.aspx

Ministry of Education (2002) *Pathways to the Future: Nga Huarahi Aratiki. A 10-Year Strategic Plan for Early Childhood Education*. Wellington: Learning Media.

Minkler, M. and Wallerstein, N. (eds) (2003) *Community-Based Participatory Research for Health*. San Francisco: Jossey-Bass.

Monk, D. (2004) 'Childhood and the law: in whose best interests?', in M.J. Kehily (ed.), *An Introduction to Childhood Studies*. Maidenhead: Open University Press.

Mooney, A., Stratham, J., Boddy, J. and Smith, M. (2010) *NCMP: Parental Experiences*. London: Thomas Coram Research Unit, Institute of Education, University of London.

Morrow, V. and Mayall, B. (2009) 'What is wrong with children's well-being in the UK? Questions of meaning and measurement', *Journal of Social Welfare and Family Law*, 36 (3): 217–29.

Mortimer, H. (2002) *Special Needs Handbook: Meeting Special Needs in Early Years Settings*. Leamington Spa: Scholastic.

Moss, P. (2006) 'Structures, understandings and discourses: possibilities for re-envisioning the early childhood worker', *Contemporary Issues in Early Childhood*, 7 (1): 30–41.

Moss, P. (2007) 'Bringing politics into the nursery: early childhood education as a democratic practice', *European Early Childhood Education Research Journal*, 15 (1): 5–20.

Moss, P. (2008) 'The democratic and reflective professional: rethinking and reforming the early years workforce', in L. Miller and C. Cable (eds), *Professionalism in the Early Years*. London: Hodder Education. pp. 121–30.

Moss, P. (2011) 'Foreword', in A. Paige-Smith and A. Craft (eds), *Developing Reflective Practice in the Early Years*, 2nd edn. Maidenhead: Open University Press/McGraw-Hill Education. pp. xiii–xviii.

Moss, S. (2012) *Natural Childhood*. London: National Trust.

Moss, P. (2013) 'The relationship between early childhood and compulsory schooling: a properly political question', in P. Moss (ed.), *Early Childhood Education and Compulsory Schooling: Reconceptualising the Relationship*. London: Routledge. pp. 2–50.

Moss, P. and Petrie, P. (2002) *From Children's Services to Children's Spaces*. London and New York: RoutledgeFalmer.

Moss, P., Candappa, M., Cameron, C., Mooney, A., McQuail, S. and Petrie, P. (2003) *Early Years and Childcare International Evidence Project: An Introduction to the Project*. London: DfES.

Moyles, J. (1989) *Just Playing: The Role and Status of Play in Early Childhood Education*. Buckingham: Open University Press.

Moyles, J. (2006) *Effective Leadership and Management in the Early Years*. Maidenhead: Open University Press.

Moyles, J. (2010) *The Excellence of Play*, 3rd edn. Maidenhead: Open University Press.

MRS (Market Research Society) (2006) 'Occupation grouping: a job dictionary'. London: Market Research Society.

Muijs, D., Aubrey, C., Harris, A. and Briggs, M. (2004) 'How do they manage? A review of the research on leadership in early childhood', *Journal of Early Childhood Research*, 2 (2): 157–60.

Munro, E. (2011) *The Munro Review of Child Protection: Final Report. A Child-centred System*. London: Department for Education.

Murray, J. (2005) 'Studying the worlds of young children', in T. Waller (ed.), *An Introduction to Early Childhood*. London: Sage. pp. 106–22.

Murray, J. (2006) 'Conversations with gatekeepers: academic and leadership perspectives on early years' educational research'. Paper presented at the EECERA 16th Annual Conference in Reykjavik, 30 August – 2 September.

Murray, J. (2011) 'Knock, knock! Who's there? Gaining access to young children as researchers: a critical review', *Educate ~*, 11 (1): 91–109.

Murray, J. (2012a) 'An exploration of young children's engagements in research behaviour', PhD thesis. University of Northampton, UK.

Murray, J. (2012b) 'Young children's explorations: young children's research?', *Early Child Development and Care*, 182 (9): 1209–25.

Narayanasamy, N. (2009) *Participatory Rural Appraisal: Principles, Methods and Application*. New Delhi: Sage.

NACCCE (National Advisory Committee on Creativity and Cultural Education) (1999) *All Our Futures: Creativity, Culture and Education*. London: DfEE.

National College for Teaching and Leadership (2013) *Teachers' Standards (Early Years)*. Available at: www.gov.uk/government/uploads/system/uploads/attachment_data/file/211646/Early_Years_Teachers__Standards.pdf

National Evaluation of Sure Start (2012) *Full Report on the Impact of Sure Start Local Programmes on Seven Year Olds and their Families*. London: The Institute for the Study of Children, Families and Social Issues. Available at: www.ness.bbk.ac.uk/ (accessed 23 March 2013).

National Portage Association (2013) Home page. www.portage.org.uk (accessed 9 July 2013).

NCH Action for Children (1996) *Factfile 96/97*. London: NCH.

Ndebele, N. (1995) 'Recovering childhood: children in South African reconstruction', in S. Stephens (ed.), *Childhood and the Politics of Culture*. Princeton, NJ: Princeton University Press.

Nelson, M. (2007) *Low Income and Nutrition Survey*. London: TSO.

Neurath, O., Hahn, H. and Carnap, R. (1929) *Wissenschaftliche Weltauffassung. Der Wiener Kreis*, trans. (1973) P. Foulkes and M. Neurath, 'Scientific World Conception: The Vienna Circle', in O. Neurath (ed. M. Neurath and R.S. Cohen), *Empiricism and Sociology*. Dordrecht: Reidel. pp. 299–318.

Newton, J.M. (2000) 'Uncovering knowing in practice amongst a group of undergraduate student nurses', *Reflective Practice: International and Multidisciplinary Perspectives*, 1 (2): 183–97.

NHS Confederation (2012) *Children and Young People's Health and Wellbeing in Changing Times: Shaping the Future and Improving Outcomes*. London: NHS Confederation. Available at: www.nhsconfed.org/Publications/Documents/Children-and-young-peoples-health-in-changing- times.pdf (accessed January 2013).

NICE (National Institute for Health and Clinical Excellence) (2009) Promoting physical activity for children and young people. NICE Public Health Guidance 17. London: NICE. Available at: http://guidance.nice.org.uk/PH17

NICE (National Institute for Health and Clinical Excellence) (2012) Social and emotional wellbeing: Early Years. NICE Public Health Guidance 40. London: NICE. Available at: http://guidance.nice.org.uk/PH40

Nieuweboer-Krobotova, L. (2013) 'Hyperpigmentation: types, diagnostics and targeted treatment options', *Journal of the European Academy of Dermatology and Venereology*, 27 (Suppl. 1): 2–4.

Nixon, H. and Comber, B. (2005) 'Behind the scenes: making movies in early years classrooms', in J. Marsh, (ed.), *Popular Culture, New Media and Digital Literacy in Early Childhood*. London: RoutledgeFalmer. pp. 219–36.

Norgrove, D. (2011) *Family Justice Review: Final Report*. London: Ministry of Justice.

Northern Ireland Assembly (2012) Committee for Education: Early Years Manifesto: Early Years Strategic Alliance. Available at: www.niassembly.gov.uk/Assembly-Business/Official-Report/Committee-Minutes-of-Evidence/Session-2011-2012/February-2012/Early-Years-Manifesto--Early-Years-Strategic-Alliance (accessed 4 January 2013).

Northern Ireland Curriculum (2013) Foundation Stage Areas of Learning. Available at: www.nicurriculum.org.uk/foundation_stage/areas_of_learning/pdmu/index.asp (accessed 4 January 2013).

Nurse, A.D. (ed.) (2007) *The New Early Years Professional: Dilemmas and Debate*. Abingdon: Routledge.

Nutbrown, C. (2011) 'Conceptualising arts-based learning in the early years', *Research Papers in Education*, 07/11: 1–25. doi: 10.1080/02671522.2011.580365.

Nutbrown, C. (2012a) *Review of Early Education and Childcare Qualifications: Interim Report* (March 2012). London: DfE.

Nutbrown, C. (2012b) *Foundations for Quality: Independent Review of Early Education and Childcare Qualification: Final Report* (June 2012). London: DfE. Available at: www.education. gov.uk/nutbrownreview.

Nutbrown, C. (2013) 'Shaking the foundations of quality? Why "childcare" policy must not lead to poor quality education and care'. Unpublished rejoinder to *More Great Childcare*. Available at: www.shef.ac.uk/polopoly_fs/1.263201!/file/Shakingthefoundationsofquality.pdf (accessed 3 November 2013).

Nutbrown, C. and Clough, P. (2006) *Inclusion in the Early Years: Critical Analyses and Enabling Narratives*. London: Sage.

Oakley, A. (1994) 'Women and children first and last: parallels and differences between children's and women's studies', in B. Mayall (ed.), *Children's Childhoods Observed and Experienced*. London: Falmer.

O'Brien, T. (2001) *Enabling Inclusion: Blue Skies ... Dark Clouds?* London: The Stationery Office.

O'Donnell, S., Lord, P., Sargent, C., Byrne, A., White, E., Gray, J., MacLeod, S. and Brown, D. (2010) *An International Perspective on Integrated Children's Services*. Report commissioned by CfBT Education Trust. Reading, UK: CfBT Education Trust.

OECD (Organisation for Economic Co-operation and Development) (2001) *Starting Strong I: Early Childhood Education and Care*. Paris: OECD.

OECD (Organisation for Economic Cooperation and Development) (2002) *Educational Research and Development in England. Examiners' Report*. CER/CD (2002)10. Paris: OECD.

OECD (Organisation for Economic Co-operation and Development) (2006) *Starting Strong II: Early Childhood Education and Care*. Paris: OECD.

OECD (Organisation for Economic Co-operation and Development) (2009) 'Comparative child well-being across the OECD', in *Doing Better for Children*. Paris: OECD.

OECD (Organisation for Economic Co-operation and Development) (2012) *Starting Strong III: A Quality Toolbox for Early Childhood Education and Care*. Paris: OECD.

Ofcom UK (2010) Children's Media Literacy. Available at: http://stakeholders.ofcom.org.uk/ market-data-research/media-literacy/archive/medlitpub/medlitpubrss/ukchildrensml/ (accessed 19 September 2012).

Office of the Children's Commissioner (2012) 'They never give up on you'. School Exclusions Inquiry. Available at: www.childrenscommissioner.gov.uk/content/publications/content_561

Office for National Statistics (2012a) 2011 Census. Available at: www.ons.gov.uk/ons/guide-method/census/2011/index.html (accessed 16 May 2013).

Office for National Statistics (2012b) Dependent children. Available at: www.ons.gov.uk/ons/rel/ family-demography/families-and-households/2012/stb-families-households.html#tab-Dependent-children (accessed 20 March 2013).

Office for National Statistics (2012c) Marriage summary statistics 2010. Available at: www.ons. gov.uk/ons/datasets-and-tables/index.html?pageSize=50&sortBy=none&sortDirection=none& newquery=marriage&content-type=Reference+table&content-type=Dataset (accessed 20 March 2013).

Office for National Statistics (2012d) What percentage of marriages end in divorce? Available at: www.ons.gov.uk/ons/rel/vsob1/divorces-in-england-and-wales/2011/sty-what-percentage-of-marriages-end-in-divorce.html (accessed 20 March 2013).

Office for National Statistics (2012e) Lone parents with dependent families 2001–2011. Available at: www.ons.gov.uk/ons/rel/family-demography/families-and-households/2011/sum-lone-parents.html (accessed 20 March 2013).

Ofsted (Office for Standards in Education) (2002) *Early Years: Early Days*. In Office For Standards in Education (ed.). London: HMSO.

Ofsted (Office for Standards in Education) (2004) NR 2004 – 126. Available at: http://www.ofsted.gov.uk (accessed 12 December 2004).

Ofsted (Office for Standards in Education, Children's Services and Skills) (2009) *The Impact of Integrated Services on Children and their Families in Sure Start Children's Centres*. London: Ofsted.

Ofsted (Office for Standards in Education) (2010) *Special Educational Needs and Disability Review*. London: Ofsted.

O'Kane, C. (2008) 'The development of participatory techniques', in P. Christensen and A. James (eds), *Research with Children*. London: Routledge. pp. 125–55.

Osgood, J. (2006) 'Rethinking professionalism in the early years: perspectives from the United Kingdom', *Contemporary Issues in Early Childhood*, 7 (1): 1–4.

O'Sullivan, T. (2012) 'Parenting and family relationships in context', in R. Adams (ed.), *Working with Children and Families: Knowledge and Contexts for Practice*. Basingstoke: Palgrave.

Oswell, D. (2013) *The Agency of Children: from Family to Global Human Rights*. Cambridge: Cambridge University Press.

Ouseley, H. and Lane, J. (2006) *Response to the Consultation on a Single Quality Framework for Services to Children from Birth to Five: Every Child Matters: Change for Children*. London: DfES/DWP.

Owen, C. (2003) *Men's Work? Changing the Gender Mix of the Childcare and Early Years Workforce*. London: Thomas Coram.

Owen, S. (2006) 'Training and workforce issues in the early years', in G. Pugh and B. Duffy (eds), *Contemporary Issues in The Early Years*, 4th edition. London: Sage.

Ozer, E.J., Ritterman, M.L. and Wanis, M.G. (2010) 'Participatory action research (PAR) in middle school: opportunities, constraints, and key processes', *American Journal of Community Psychology*, 46: 152–66.

Pagani, L., Fitzpatrick, C., Barnett, T. and Dubow, E. (2010) 'Prospective associations between early childhood television exposure and academic, psychosocial, and physical well-being by middle childhood', *Archives of Pediatric and Adolescent Medicine*, 164 (5): 425–31.

Page, J. and Elfer, P. (2013) 'The emotional complexity of attachment interactions in nursery', *European Early Childhood Education Research Journal*, 21 (4). Available at: www.tandfon-line.com/doi/abs/10.1080/1350293X.2013.766032?prevSearch=page%2Band%2Belfer&searchHistoryKey=

Paige-Smith, A. and Craft, A. (eds) (2008) *Developing Reflective Practice in the Early Years*. Maidenhead: Open University Press.

Palaiologou, I. and Male, T. (2012) 'The implementation of the Early Years Foundation Stage', in I. Palaiologou (ed.), *The Early Years Foundation Stage: Theory and Practice*, 2nd edn. London: Sage.

Palmer, S. (2006) *Toxic Childhood: How the Modern World Is Damaging Our Childhood and What We Can Do About It*. London: Orion.

Papatheodorou, T. (2010) 'The pedagogy of play(ful) learning environments', in J. Moyles (ed.), *Thinking About Play: Developing a Reflective Approach*. Maidenhead: McGraw-Hill/Open University Press.

Papert, S. (1980) *Mindstorms: Children, Computers and Powerful Ideas*. New York: Basic Books.

Park, C. (2011) 'Young children making sense of racial and ethnic differences: a socio-cultural approach', *American Educational Research Journal*, 48 (2): 387–420.

Parnell, W. (2011) 'Revealing the experience of children and teachers even in their absence: documenting in the Early Childhood Studio', *Journal of Early Childhood Research*, 9 (3): 291–309.

Parnell, W. (2012) 'Experiences of teacher reflection: Reggio inspired practices in the studio', *Journal of Early Childhood Research*, 10 (2): 117–33.

Pascal, C. and Bertram, T. (2012) 'Praxis, ethics and power: developing praxeology as a participatory paradigm for early childhood research', *European Early Childhood Research Journal*, 20 (4): 477–92.

Pearce, S.H.S. and Cheetham, T.D. (2010) 'Diagnosis and management of vitamin D deficiency', *British Medical Journal*, 340: b5664.

Pearce, T. (2012) 'Identifying children at risk of abuse linked to belief', *British Journal of School Nursing*, 7 (6): 270–1.

Pearson, G. (1983) *Hooligan: A History of Respectable Fears*. Basingstoke: Macmillan.

Peeters, J. (2008) *The Construction of a New Profession: A European Perspective on Professionalism in Early Childhood Education and Care*. Amsterdam: SWP Publishers.

Peeters, J. and Urban, M. (2011) Competence Requirements in Early Childhood Education and Care: A Study for the European Commission Directorate-General for Education and Culture. Final report of CoRE project. London and Ghent. University of East London and University of Ghent.

Pellegrini, A.D., Symons, F.J. and Hoch, J. (2004) *Observing Children in Their Natural Worlds*. Mahwah, NJ: Lawrence Erlbaum Associates.

Penn, H. (2005) *Understanding Early Childhood: Issues and Controversies*. Maidenhead: Open University Press and McGraw-Hill Education.

Penn, H. (2008) *Understanding Early Childhood: Issues and Controversies*, 2nd edn. Maidenhead: Open University Press/McGraw-Hill.

Penn, H. (2009) 'International perspectives in participatory learning', in D. Berthelsen, J. Brownlee and E. Johansson (eds), *Participatory Learning in the Early Years: Research and Pedagogy*. London: Routledge. pp. 12–25.

Percy-Smith, J. (2005) *What Works in Strategic Partnerships for Children?* Ilford, Essex: Barnardo's.

Percy-Smith, B. and Thomas, N. (2010) *A Handbook of Children and Young People's Participation*. London: Routledge.

Petrie, P., Boddy, J., Cameron, C., Hepinstall, E., Mcquail, S., Simon, A. and Wigfall, V. (2005) 'Pedagogy – a holistic, personal approach to work with children and young people across services.' *European Models for Practice, Training, Education and Qualifications*. London: Thomas Coram Research Institute, University of London, p. 8.

Piaget, J. (1929) *The Child's Conception of the World*. London: Routledge and Kegan Paul.

Piaget, J. (1969) *The Mechanisms of Perception*. New York: Basic Books.

Pianta, R.C., La Paro, K.M. and Hamre, B.K. (2008) *Classroom Assessment Scoring System*. Baltimore, MD: Brookes.

Pinkerton, J. (2001) 'Developing partnership practice', in P. Foley, J. Roche and S. Tucker (eds), *Children in Society: Contemporary Theory, Policy and Practice*. Basingstoke: Palgrave.

Plato (2007) *The Republic*, trans. D. Lee. London: Penguin Classics.

Plowman, L., McPake, J. and Stephen, C. (2010) 'The technologisation of childhood? Young children and technology in the home', *Children and Society*, 24 (1): 63–74.

Plymouth Safeguarding Children Board (2010) *Serious Case Review: Overview Report Executive Summary in Respect of Nursery Z*. Plymouth: Plymouth Safeguarding Children Board.

Polanyi, M. (1962) *Personal Knowledge*. London: Routledge.

Pollard, A. and Tann, S. (1993) *Reflective Teaching in the Primary School*, 2nd edn. London: Cassell.

Pollard, E.L. and Lee, P.D. (2002) 'Child well-being: a systematic review of the literature', *Social Indicators Research*, 61: 59–78.

Pollock, L. (1983) *Forgotten Children – Parent: Child Relations from 1500–1900*. Cambridge: Cambridge University Press.

Polnay, J., Polnay, L., Lynch, M. and Shabde, N. (2007) *Child Protection Reader*. London: Royal College of Paediatrics and Child Health.

Popper, K. (1959) *The Logic of Scientific Discovery*. London: Hutchinson and Co.

Postman, N. (1982) *The Disappearance of Childhood*. London: Comet.

Postman, N. (1983) *The Disappearance of Childhood*. New York: W.H. Allen.

Postman, N. (1985) *Amusing Ourselves to Death: Public Discourse in the Age of Show Business*. London: Penguin.

Postman, N. (1995) *The Disappearance of Childhood*. New York: Vintage.

Potter, C. and Carpenter, J. (2010) 'Fathers' involvement in Sure Start: what do fathers and mothers perceive as the benefits?', *Practice: Social Work in Action*, 22 (1): 3–15.

Powell, A. (2004) 'High court challenge to secret abortions for under 16s; *Daily Mail*. Available at: www.dailymail.co.uk/news/article-312217/Secret-abortions-16s.html (accessed 18 March 2014).

Pramling Samuelsson, I., Asplund Carlsson, M., Olsson, B., Pramling, N. and Wallerstedt, C. (2009) 'The art of teaching children the arts: music, dance, and poetry with children 2–8 years old', *International Journal of Early Years Education*, 17 (2): 119–35.

Preston, J.P., Cottrell, M., Pelletier, T.R. and Pearce, J.V. (2012) 'Aboriginal early childhood education in Canada: issues of context', *Journal of Early Childhood Research*, 10 (1): 3–18.

Pring, R. (2000) *Philosophy of Educational Research*. London: Continuum.

Prout, A. (2003) 'Participation, policy and the changing conditions of childhood', in C. Hallett and A. Prout (eds), *Hearing the Voices of Children*. London: Falmer Press.

Prout, A. (2005) *The Future of Childhood: Towards the Interdisciplinary Study of Children*. London: Falmer Press.

Prout, A. and James, A. (1997) 'A new paradigm for the sociology of childhood?', in A. James and A. Prout (eds), *Constructing and Reconstructing Childhood: Contemporary Issues in the Sociological Study of Childhood*. London: Falmer Press. pp. 7–32.

Pugh, G. (2005) 'Policy matters', in L. Abbott and A. Langston (eds), *Birth to Three Matters: Supporting the Framework of Effective Practice*. Maidenhead: Open University Press.

Pugh, G. and Duffy, B. (2006) *Contemporary Issues in the Early Years*, 4th edn. London: Sage.

Punch, S. (2002) 'Research with children: the same or different from research with adults?', *Childhood*, 9 (3): 321–41.

Quality Assurance Agency for Higher Education (2007a) *Quality Subject Benchmark Statement: Early Childhood Studies*. Mansfield: QAA Publications. Available at: www.qaa.ac.uk/Publications/InformationAndGuidance/Pages/Subject-benchmark-statement-Early-childhood-studies.aspx

Quality Assurance Agency for Higher Education (2007b) *The Standard for Childhood Practice 2007: Scottish Subject Benchmark Statement*. Mansfield: QAA Publications.

QCA (Qualifications and Curriculum Authority) (2000) *Curriculum Guidance for the Foundation Stage*. London: DfES Publications.

QCA (Qualifications and Curriculum Authority) (2005) *Creativity: Find It, Promote It: Promoting Pupils' Creative Thinking and Behaviour across the Curriculum at Key Stages 1 and 2 – Practical Materials for Schools*. London: QCA.

QCA (2007) *Meeting the Challenge: Achieving Equality for All. Single Equality Scheme*. London: QCA. Available at: http://dera.ioe.ac.uk/8096/ (accessed 10 July 2013).

Quigley, M.A., Hockley, C. and Carson, C. (2012) 'Breast feeding is associated with improved child cognitive development', *Journal of Paediatrics*, 160: 25–32.

Quigley, M.A., Kelly, Y.J. and Sacker, A. (2007) 'Breastfeeding and hospitalisation for infection in the United Kindom millennium cohort study', *Pediatrics*, 119 (4): 837–42.

Quine, W. (1953) *From a Logical Point of View*. Cambridge, MA: Harvard University Press.

Qvortrup, J., Bardy, M., Sgritta, G. and Wintersberger, H. (eds) (1994) *Childhood Matters: Social Theory, Practice and Politics*. Aldershot: Avebury.

Raban, B., Ure, C. and Manjula, W. (2003) 'Multiple perspectives: acknowledging the virtue of complexity in measuring quality', *Early Years*, 23 (1): 67–77.

Ramon, S. and Hodes, D. (2012) 'Cultural issues in child maltreatment', *Journal of Paediatrics and Child Health*, 48: 30–7.

Rangahau (2013) Principles of Kaupapa Máori. Available at: www.rangahau.co.nz/research-idea/27/ (accessed 27 January 2013).

Ratner, C. (2000) 'Agency and culture', *Journal for the Theory of Social Behaviour*, 30: 413–34.

RCPCH (Royal College of Paediatrics and Child Health) (2011) *Children and Young People's Health – Where Next?* London: NHS Confederation. Available at: www.rcpch.ac.uk/system/files/protected/page/childrenandyoungpeopleshealth.pdf

Reardon, D. (2013) *Achieving Early Years Professional Status*, 2nd edn. London: Sage.

Reder, P., Duncan, S. and Gray, M. (1993) *Beyond Blame: Child Abuse Tragedies Revisited*. London: Routledge.

Redmond, G. (2008) *Children's Perspectives on Economic Adversity: A Review of the Literature*. SPRC Discussion Paper No. 149. Sydney: The Social Policy Research Centre.

Rees, G., Goswami, H. and Bradshaw, J. (2010) *Developing an Index of Children's Subjective Well-being in England*. London: The Children's Society.

REF (Research Excellence Framework) (2011) *Assessment Framework and Guidance on Submissions* (updated). Available at: www.ref.ac.uk/media/ref/content/pub/assessment-frameworkandguidanceonsubmissions/GOS%20including%20addendum.pdf (accessed 29 October 2013).

Refugee Council (2013) Who's who: definitions. Available at: www.refugeecouncil.org.uk/policy_research/the_truth_about_asylum/the_facts_about_asylum (accessed 30 October 2013).

Reynolds, P., Nieuwenhuys, O. and Honson, K. (2006) 'Refractions of children's rights in development practice: a view from anthropology – introduction', *Childhood*, 13: 291–302.

Rhedding-Jones, J., Bae, B and Winger, N (2008) 'Young children and voice', in G. Macnaughton, P. Hughes and K. Smith (eds), *Young Children as Active Citizens*. Cambridge: Cambridge Scholars Publishing.

Rideout, V.J., Vandewater, E.A. and Wartella, E.A. (2003) *Zero to Six: Electronic Media in the Lives of Infants and Preschoolers*. Menlo Park, CA: The Henry J. Kaiser Family Foundation Report.

Rigby, K. (2002) *New Perspectives on Bullying*. London: Jessica Kingsley.

Riley, J. (ed.) (2007) *Learning in the Early Years*, 2nd edn. London: Sage.

Rinaldi, C. (2006) *In Dialogue with Reggio: Listening, Researching and Learning*. London: RoutledgeFalmer.

Roberts, R. (1998) *Self Esteem and Early Learning*. London: Sage.

Roberts, R. (2002) *Self Esteem and Early Learning*, 2nd edn. London: Sage.

Roberts, R. (2006) *Self Esteem and Early Learning*, 3rd edn. London: Sage.

Robinson, K.H. (2005) 'Doing anti-homophobia and anti-heterosexism in early childhood education: moving beyond the immobilising impacts of "risks", "fears" and "silences" – can we afford not to?', *Contemporary Issues in Early Childhood*, 6 (2): 175–88.

Robinson, K.H. and Diaz, C.J. (2006) *Diversity and Difference in Early Childhood Education*. Maidenhead: Open University Press.

Roche, J. (2001) 'Social work values and the law', in L. Cull and J. Roche (eds), *The Law and Social Work*. Basingstoke: Palgrave.

Roffey, S. (2001) *Special Needs in the Early Years*. London: David Fulton.

Rogoff, B. (1990) *Apprenticeship in Thinking: Cognitive Development in Social Context*. New York: Plenum Press.

Rogoff, B. (1998) 'Cognition as a collaborative process', in D. Kuhn and R.S. Seigler (eds), *Handbook of Child Psychology*, *2*, 5th edn. New York: John Wiley.

Rogoff, B. (2003) *The Cultural Nature of Human Development*. New York: Oxford University Press.

Rose, N. (1992) *Governing the Soul*. London: Routledge.

Rose, S. (1989) *From Brains to Consciousness? Essays on the New Sciences of the Mind*. London: Penguin.

Rosen, D. (2005) *Armies of the Young: Child Soldiers in War and Terrorism*. New Brunswick: Rutgers University Press.

Rowan, L. and Honan, E. (2005) 'Literarily lost: the quest for quality literacy agendas in early childhood education', in N. Yelland (ed.), *Critical Issues in Early Childhood Education*. Maidenhead: Open University Press.

Royal College of Midwives (2012) *Maternal and Emotional Wellbeing and Infant Development*. Available at: www.rcm.org.uk/college/your-career/information-services/resources/ (accessed 13 July 2013).

Royal Society (2011) *Brain Waves Module 2: Neuroscience: Implications for Education and Lifelong Learning*. London: The Royal Society.

Rutanen, N. (2011) 'Space for toddlers in the guidelines and curricula for early childhood education and care in Finland', *Childhood*, 18 (4): 526–39.

Rutter, M. (1972) *Maternal Deprivation Reassessed*. London: Penguin.

Rutter, J. (2006) *Refugee Children in the UK*. Maidenhead: Open University Press.

Rutter, M. (1999) 'Resilience concepts and findings: implications for family therapy', *Journal of Family Therapy*, 21: 119–44.

Rutter, J. and Hyder, T. (1998) *Refugee Children in the Early Years: Issues for Policy-makers and Providers*. London: Save the Children and the Refugee Council.

Rutter, M. (1981) *Maternal Deprivation Reassessed*, 2nd edn. London: Penguin.

Ryle, G. (1949) *The Concept of Mind*. London: Penguin.

Ryle, G. (1968) 'The Thinking of Thoughts: What is "Le Penseur" doing?' University Lectures, No. 18. Saskatchewan: University of Saskatchewan. Available at: http://lucy.ukc.ac.uk/CSACSIA/Vol14/Papers/ryle_1.html (accessed 10 June 2012).

Sainsbury, C. (2000) *Martian in the Playground: Understanding the Schoolchild with Asperger's Syndrome*. Bristol: Lucky Duck Publishing.

Sanders, B. (2004) 'Interagency and multidisciplinary working', in T. Maynard and N. Thomas (eds), *An Introduction to Early Childhood Studies*. London: Sage.

Sandseter, E. (2007) 'Categorising risky play: how can we identify risk taking in children's play?', *European Early Childhood Research*, 15 (2): 237–52.

Sandseter, E. (2009) 'Children's expressions of exhilaration and fear in risky play', *Contemporary Issues in Early Childhood*, 10 (2).

Santer, J. and Griffiths, C. (2007) *Free Play in Early Childhood: A Literature Review*. London: National Children's Bureau.

SCAA (School Curriculum Assessment Authority) (1996) *Nursery Education: Desirable Outcomes for Children's Learning on Entering Compulsory Education*. London: SCAA and Department for Education and Employment.

Scarr, S. and Dunn. J. (1984) *Mother Care/Other Care: The Childcare Dilemma for Women and Children*. Harmondsworth, Middlesex: Penguin Books Ltd.

Schaffer, H.R. (1996) *Social Development*. Oxford: Blackwell.

Scholler, I. and Nittur, S. (2012) 'Understanding failure to thrive', *Paediatrics and Child Health*, 22 (10): 438–42.

Schön, D. (1983) *The Reflective Practitioner: How Professionals Think in Action*. New York: Basic Books.

Schön, D. (1987) *Educating the Reflective Practitioner*. San Francisco: Jossey-Bass.

Schor, J.B. (2004) *Born to Buy: The Commercialized Child and the New Consumer Culture*. New York: Scribner.

Schore, J.R. and Schore, A.N. (2008) 'Modern attachment theory: the central role of affect regulation in development and treatment', *Clinical Social Work Journal*, 36 (1): 9–20.

Scottish Executive (2002) *It's Everyone's Job to Make Sure I'm Alright: Report of the Child Protection Audit and Review*. Edinburgh: TSO.

Scottish Government (2003) *Growing Support: A Review of Services for Vulnerable Families with Young Children*. Edinburgh: TSO. Available at: www.scotland.gov.uk/ Publications/2003/01/15814/13951 (accessed 28 June 2013).

Scottish Government (2010) *National Guidance for Child Protection in Scotland*. Edinburgh: Scottish Government. Available at: www.scotland.gov.uk/Resource/Doc/334290/0109279.pdf (accessed 28 June 2013).

Scottish Government (2012) *Children's Social Work Statistics Scotland*. Statistical Bulletin No. 1. Edinburgh: Scottish Government Statistician Group.

Scottish Government (2013) Wellbeing. Available at: www.scotland.gov.uk/Topics/People/ Young-People/gettingitright (accessed 4 January 2013).

Scottish Government (n.d.) *Curriculum for Excellence: Health and Wellbeing – Experiences and Outcomes*. Available at: www.educationscotland.gov.uk/Images/health_wellbeing_experiences_ outcomes_tcm4-540031.pdf (accessed 4 January 2013).

Scottish Social Services Council (2008) *Investing In Children's Futures: The New Childhood Practice Awards*. Dundee: SSSC.

Scruton, R. (2001) *Kant*. Oxford: Oxford University Press.

Sebba, J. (2011) 'Personalisation, individualisation and inclusion', *Journal of Research in Special Educational Needs*, 11 (3): 205–10.

Sen, A. (1993) 'Capability and well-being', in M. Nussbaum and A. Sen (eds), *The Quality of Life*. Oxford: Oxford University Press. pp. 30–53.

Shaw, B., Watson, B., Frauendienst, B., Redecker, A., Jones, T. and Hillman, M. (2013) *Children's Independent Mobility: A Comparative Study in England and Germany (1971–2010)*. London: Policy Studies Institute.

Shaw, I. (2000) 'Just inquiry? Research and evaluation for service users', in H. Kemshall and R. Littlechild (eds), *User Involvement and Participation in Social Care: Research Informing Practice*. London: Jessica Kingsley.

Shorter, E. (1976) *The Making of the Modern Family*. London: Collins.

Shucksmith, J., Spratt, J., Philip, K. and McNaughton, R. (2009) *A Critical Review of the Literature on Children and Young People's Views of the Factors that Influence their Mental Health*. Glasgow: NHS Scotland.

Sigman, A. (2007) *Remotely Controlled: How Television is Damaging our Lives*. London: Ebury.

Silin, J. (1995) *Sex, Death and the Education of Children: Our Passion for Ignorance in the Age of Aids*. New York: Teachers College Press.

Sims, M., Saggers, S., Hutchins, T., Guilfoyle, A., Targowska, A. and Jackiewicz, S. (2008) *Towards an Indigenous Child Care Plan*. Perth: Centre for Social Research, Edith Cowan University.

Sinclair, R. (2004) 'Participation in practice: making it meaningful, effective and sustainable', *Children and Society*, 18: 106–18.

Siraj-Blatchford, I. (1994) *The Early Years: Laying the Foundations for Racial Equality*. Stoke-on-Trent: Trentham Books.

Siraj-Blatchford, I. (2004) 'Quality teaching in the early years', in A. Anning, J. Cullen and M. Fleer (eds), *Early Childhood Education*. London: Sage.

Siraj-Blatchford, I. (2007) 'The case for integrating education with care in the early years', in I. Siraj-Blatchford, K. Clarke and M. Needham (eds), *The Team Around the Child: Multi-agency Working in the Early Years*. Stoke-on-Trent: Trentham Books. pp. 1–6.

Siraj-Blatchford, I. (2009) 'Early childhood education', in T. Maynard and N. Thomas (eds), *An Introduction to Early Childhood Studies*, 2nd edn. London: Sage. pp. 1–17.

Siraj-Blatchford, I. (2010a) 'A focus on pedagogy: case studies of effective practice', in K. Sylva, E. Melhuish, P. Sammons, I. Siraj-Blatchford and B. Taggart (eds), *Early Childhood Matters: Evidence from the Effective Pre-School and Primary Education Project*. London: Routledge.

Siraj-Blatchford, I. (2010b) 'Mixed-method designs', in G. MacNaughton, S.A. Rolfe and I. Siraj-Blatchford (eds), *Doing Early Childhood Research*, 2nd edn. Maidenhead: Open University Press/McGraw-Hill. pp. 193–208.

Siraj-Blatchford, I. (2010c) 'Learning in the home and in school: how working class children succeed against the odds', *British Educational Research Journal*, 36 (3): 463–82.

Siraj-Blatchford, I. and Manni, L. (2006) *Effective Leadership in the Early Years Sector (ELEYS) Study*. London: Institute of Education.

Skelton, C. and Francis, B. (2011) 'The renaissance child: high achievement and gender in late modernity', *International Journal of Inclusive Education*. DOI:10.1080/13603116.2011.555098.

Smith, A.B. (2007) 'Children and young people's participation rights in education', *International Journal of Children's Rights*, 15: 147–64.

Smith, A.B. (2011) 'Respecting Children's Rights and Agency: Theoretical Insights into Ethical Research Procedures' in, D. Harcourt, B. Perry and T. Waller (Eds). *Young children's perspectives: Debating the ethics and dilemmas of educational research with children*. Abingdon: RoutledgeFalmer.

Smith, L.D. (1986) *Behaviorism and Logical Positivism: A Reassessment of the Alliance*. Stanford: Stanford University Press.

Smith, P.K. (2010) *Children and Play*. Chichester: Wiley-Blackwell.

Smith, R. (2013a) 'Working together: Why is it important and why is it difficult?', in B. Littlechild and R. Smith, *A Handbook for Interprofessional Practice in the Human Services: Learning to Work Together*. Harlow: Pearson Education.

Smith, R. (2013b) 'The drivers and dynamics of interprofessional working in policy and practice', in B. Littlechild and R. Smith, *A Handbook for Interprofessional Practice in the Human Services: Learning to Work Together*. Harlow: Pearson Education.

Sneddon, H., Ferriter, M. and Bowser, A.A. (2012) 'Cognitive-behavioural therapy (CBT) interventions for young people aged 10 to 18 who sexually offend', *Cochrane Database of Systematic Reviews*, Issue 5. Art. No.: CD009829. doi: 10.1002/14651858.CD009829.

Sobel, D. (1996) *Beyond Ecophobia: Reclaiming the Heart in Nature Education*. Great Barrington: Orion Society.

Social Work Reform Board (2012) Building a Safe and Confident Future: One Year On. Improving the Quality and Consistency of the Social Work Degree in England. Available at: www.education.gov.uk/swrb

Solberg, A. (1996) 'The challenge in child research: from "being" to "doing"', in M. Brannen and M. O'Brien (eds), *Children in Families: Research and Policy*. London: The Falmer Press.

Soler, J. and Miller, L. (2003) 'The struggle for early childhood curricula: a comparison of the English Foundation Stage curriculum, Te Whāriki and Reggio Emilia', *International Journal of Early Years Education*, 11 (1): 57–68.

Snodgrass-Godoy, A. (1999) 'Our right to be killed', *Childhood*, 6 (4): 425–42.

Spinka, M., Newberry, R. and Bekoff, M. (2001) 'Mammalian play: training for the unexpected', *The Quarterly Review of Biology*, 76 (2): 141–68.

Spyrou, S. (2011) 'The limits of children's voices: from authenticity to critical reflexive representation', *Childhood*, 18 (2): 151–65.

Stainton Rogers, R. (1992) 'The social construction of childhood', in W. Stainton Rogers, J. Hevey, J. Roche and E. Ask (eds), *Child Abuse and Neglect: Facing the Challenge*, 2nd edn. London: Batsford.

Stainton Rogers, R. and Stainton Rogers, W. (1992) *Stories of Childhood: Shifting Agendas in Child Concern*. Upper Saddle River, NJ: Prentice Hall.

Stakes, R. and Hornby, G. (1997) *Meeting Special Needs in Mainstream Schools*. London: David Fulton.

Statham, J. and Chase, E. (2010) *Childhood Wellbeing: A Brief Overview*. Briefing Paper One. Childhood Wellbeing Research Centre.

Stebbins, R.A. (2001) *Exploratory Research in the Social Sciences*. Thousand Oaks, CA: Sage.

Steel, L., Kidd, W. and Brown, A. (2012) *The Family*, 2nd edn. Basingstoke: Palgrave.

Stenhouse, L. (1975) *An Introduction to Curriculum Research and Development*. London: Heinemann.

Stephenson, A. (2003) 'Physical risk-taking: dangerous or endangered?', *Early Years*, 23 (1): 35–43.

Sturge, C. and Glaser, D. (2000) 'Contact and domestic violence: the experts' court report', *Family Law*, 30: 615–29.

Sullivan, J., Beech, A.R., Craig, L.A.and Gannon, T.A. (2011) 'Comparing intra-familial and extra-familial child sexual abusers with professionals who have sexually abused children with whom they work', *International Journal of Offender Therapy and Comparative Criminology*, 55 (1): 56–74.

Sure Start (2008) Sure Start Children's Centres. [Update 2012]. Available at: www.education.gov. uk/childrenandyoungpeople/earlylearningandchildcare/delivery/surestart/a0076712/sure-start-children's-centres (accessed 21 June 2013).

Sylwester, R. (1995) *A Celebration of Neurones: An Educator's Guide to the Brain*. Alexandra, VA: ASCD.

Sylva, K. (1994) 'School influences on children's development', *Journal of Child Psychology and Psychiatry*, 35 (1): 135–70.

Sylva, K. (2003) *Assessing Quality in the Early Years*. Stoke-on-Trent: Trentham Books.

Sylva, K., Hurry, J., Mirelman, H., Burrell, A. and Riley, J. (1999) 'Evaluation of a focused literacy teaching programme in Reception and Year 1 classes: classroom observations', *British Educational Research Journal*, 25 (5): 617–35.

Sylva, K., Melhuish, E.C., Sammons, P., Siraj-Blatchford, I. and Taggart, B. (2004) *The Effective Provision of Pre-School Education (EPPE) Project: Final Report: Effective Pre-School Education*. London: DfES/Institute of Education, University of London.

Sylva, K., Melhuish, E.C., Sammons, P., Siraj-Blatchford, I. and Taggart, B. (2006) 'The Effective Provision of Pre-School Education (EPPE) Project', in J.J. van Kuyk (ed.), *The Quality of Early Childhood Education*. Arnhem, The Netherlands: Cito. pp. 45–56.

Sylva, K., Melhuish, E., Sammons, P., Siraj-Blatchford, I. and Taggart, B., (2010) *Early Childhood matters. Evidence from the Effective Pre-school and Primary Education* Project. London: Routledge.

Synodi, E. (2010) 'Play in the kindergarten: the case of Norway, Sweden, New Zealand and Japan', *International Journal of Early Years Education*, 18 (3): 185–200.

Tarrant, P. (2013) *Reflective Practice and Professional Development*. London: Sage.

Tassoni, P. (2003) *Supporting Special Needs: Understanding Inclusion in the Early Years (Professional Development)*. Oxford: Heinemann.

Teaching Agency (2012) *Early Years Professional Status Standards*. London: Department for Education. Available at: www.education.gov.uk/publications/eOrderingDownload/eyps%20standards%20from%20september%202012.pdf (accessed 23 March 2013).

Teaching and Learning Research Project (2007) *Teaching and Learning Principles into Practice*. London: Teaching and Learning Research Project and Economic and Social Research Council.

Teaching and Learning Research Programme (2012) *Teaching and Learning Principles into Practice*. London: Teaching and Learning Research Programme and Economic and Social Research Council. Available at: http://www.tlrp.org/proj/index.html

The Children's Society (2007) *Good Childhood Inquiry*. London: GfK NOP (Job no: 451311).

The Children's Society (2008) 'Good Childhood Inquiry reveals mounting concern over commercialisation of childhood', 26 February 2008. Retrieved from: www.childrenssociety.org.uk/whats_happening/media_office/latest_news/6486_pr.html (accessed 1March 2008).

The Children's Society (2013) *The Good Childhood Report: Summary of Our Findings*. London: The Children's Society.

Theobold, M. and Kulti, A. (2012) 'Investigating child participation in the everyday talk of a teacher and children in a Preparatory Year', *Contemporary Issues in Early Childhood*, 13 (3): 210–25.

Thomas, G. (2007) *Education and Theory: Strangers in Paradigms*. Maidenhead: Open University Press/McGraw-Hill.

Thomas, J. (1993) *Doing Critical Ethnography*. Newbury Park, CA: Sage.

Thomas, N. (2000) *Children, Family and the State*. London: Macmillan.

Thomas, N. (2001) 'Listening to children', in P. Foley, J. Roche and S. Tucker (eds), *Children in Society: Contemporary Theory, Policy and Practice*. Basingstoke: Palgrave.

Thomas, N. (2004) 'Law relating to children', in T. Maynard and N. Thomas (eds), *An Introduction to Early Childhood Studies*. London: Sage.

Thompson, M., Grace, C. and Cohen, L. (2001) *Best Friends, Worst Enemies: Understanding the Social Lives of Children*. New York: Ballantine Books.

Thompson, N. (2003) *Communication and Language: A Handbook of Theory and Practice*. Basingstoke: Palgrave.

Thompson, N. (2006) *Anti-discriminatory Practice*, 4th edn. Basingstoke: Macmillan.

Thompson, P. (1978) *The Voice of the Past: Oral History*. Oxford: Oxford University Press.

Thorpe, S. (2004) 'Positive engagement', *Care and Health Magazine*, 73: 22–3.

Tickell, C. (2011) *The Early Years: Foundations for Life, Health and Learning*. London: DfE.

Tisdall, E., Kay, M. and Davis, J. (2004) 'Making a difference? Bringing children's and young people's views into policy-making', *Children and Society*, 18 (2): 131–42.

Tisdall, E.K.M., Davis, J.M. and Gallagher, M. (2009) *Researching with Children and Young People*. London: Sage.

Tobin, J. (2005) 'Quality in early childhood education: an anthropologist's perspective', *Early Education and Development*, 16 (4): 421–34.

Tobin, J., Wu, D. and Davidson, D. (1989) *Preschool in Three Cultures: Japan, China and the United States*. New Haven, CT: Yale University Press.

Tomlinson, S. (1982) *A Sociology of Special Education*. London: R.K.P.

Tovey, H. (2007) *Playing Outdoors, Space and Places, Risk and Challenge*. Maidenhead: Open University Press.

Tovey, H. (2010) 'Playing on the edge: perceptions of risk and danger in outdoor play', in P. Broadhead, J. Howard and E. Woods (eds), *Play and Learning in the Early Years: From Research to Practice*. London: Sage.

Treseder, P. (1997) *Empowering Children and Young People: Training Manual*. London: Save the Children and Children's Rights Office.

Truman, C., Mertens, D. and Humphries, B. (eds) (2000) *Research and Inequality*. London: University College London Press.

Tunison, S. (2007) *Aboriginal Learning: A Review of Current Metrics of Success*. Saskatoon, SK: Aboriginal Learning Knowledge Center.

Tunstill, J., Aldgate, J. and Hughes, M. (2006) *Improving Children's Services Networks: Lessons from Family Centres*. London: Jessica Kingsley.

Turmel, A. (2008) *A Historical Sociology of Childhood: Developmental Thinking, Categorisation and Graphic Visualisation*. Cambridge: Cambridge University Press.

Twardosz, S. and Lutzker, J.R. (2010) 'Child maltreatment and the developing brain: a review of neuroscience perspectives', *Aggression and Violent Behavior*, 15: 59–68.

UNESCO (United Nations Educational, Scientific and Cultural Organization) (2006) *Strong Foundations: Early Childhood Care and Education*. Education for All Global Monitoring Report. Paris: UNESCO.

UNICEF (2004) *The State of the World's Children*. New York: UNICEF.

UNICEF (2005) *The State of the World's Children*. New York: UNICEF.

UNICEF (2006) *The State of the World's Children*. New York: UNICEF.

UNICEF (2007a) *The State of the World's Children*. New York: UNICEF.

UNICEF (2007b) *Child Poverty in Perspective: An Overview of Child Well-Being in Rich Countries*. Report card 7. New York: UNICEF Innocenti Research Centre.

UNICEF (2008a) *The State of the World's Children: Child Survival*. New York: UNICEF.

UNICEF (2008b) *The State of Africa's Children*. New York: UNICEF.

UNICEF (2009a) *The State of the World's Children*. New York: UNICEF.

UNICEF (2009b) 'Positive Indicators of Child Well-Being: A Conceptual Framework, Measures and Methodological Issues'. Innocenti working paper. UNICEF Innocenti Research Centre IWP-2009-21.

UNICEF (2010) *The State of the World's Children*. Special Edition: Celebrating 20 Years of the Convention on the Rights of the Child. New York: UNICEF.

UNICEF (2013) *The State of the World's Children: Children with Disabilities*. New York: UNICEF.

UNICEF Office of Research (2013) *Child Well-being in Rich Countries: A Comparative Overview*. Innocenti Report Card 11. Florence: UNICEF Office of Research.

United Nations (1989) *Convention on the Rights of the Child (UNCRC)*. New York: United Nations. Available at: www.ohchr.org/en/professionalinterest/pages/crc.aspx (accessed 4 March 2013).

United Nations Committee on the Rights of the Child (2006) Implementing Child Rights in Early Childhood. General Comment No. 7 (2005)/Rev 1. Available at: www2.ohchr.org/english/bodies/crc/comments.htm (accessed 28 October 2013).

United Nations Committee on the Rights of the Child (2009) The Right of the Child to Be Heard. General Comment 12. Available at: www2.ohchr.org/english/bodies/crc/comments.htm (accessed October 2013).

United Nations Committee on the Rights of the Child (2013) The Right of the Child to Rest, Leisure, Play, Recreational Activities, Cultural Life and the Arts (art. 31). General Comment No. 17. Available at: www2.ohchr.org/english/bodies/crc/comments.htm (accessed 4 April 2013).

Uprichard, E. (2008) 'Children as "being and becomings": children, childhood and temporality', *Children and Society*, 22: 303–13.

Urban, M. (2010) 'Rethinking Professionalism in Early Childhood: untested feasibilities and critical ecologies'. *Contemporary Issues in Early Childhood,* 11(1): 1–7.

Urban, M. (2012) 'Researching early childhood policy and practice: a critical ecology', *European Journal of Education*, 47 (4): 477–612.

Urban, M., Vandenbroeck, M., Van Laere, K., Lazzari, A. and Peeters, J. (2011) *Competence Requirements in Early Childhood Education and Care: Final Report*. London and Brussels: European Commission, Directorate General for Education and Culture.

Urban, M., Vandenbroeck, M., Van Laere, K., Lazarri, A. and Peeters, J. (2012) 'Towards competent systems in early childhood education and care: implications for policy and practice', *European Journal of Education*, 47 (4): 508–26.

Valentine, K., Katz, I. and Griffiths, M. (2007) *Early Childhood Services: Models of Integration and Collaboration*. Perth, Western Australia: Australian Research Alliance for Children and Youth.

Valentine, K. (2011) 'Accounting for Agency.' *Children and Society*, 25, 5: 347–358.

Van Beers, H., Invernizzi, A. and Milne, B. (2006) *Beyond Article 12: Essential Readings on Children's Participation*. Bangkok: Black and White Publications.

Vandenbroeck, M. and Bouverne-De Bie, M. (2006) 'Children's agency and educational norms: a tensed negotiation', *Childhood*, 13 (1): 127–43.

Vandenbroeck, M., Roets, G. and Snoek, A. (2009) 'Immigrant mothers crossing borders: nomadic identities and multiple belongings in early childhood education', *European Early Childhood Education Research Journal*, 17 (2): 203–16.

Vandewater, E. (2011) 'Infant word learning from commercially available video in the US', *Journal of Children and Media*, 3: 249–66.

Vandewater, E., Bickham, D. and Lee, J. (2006) '"Time well spent?" Relating television use to children's free time activities', *Pediatrics*, 117 (2): 181–191.

Van Laere, K., Lund, S.G. and Peeters, J. (2008) 'Young Children and Their Services: Developing a European Approach. Principle 8: Valuing the Work: A 0–6 Profession and Parity with School Teachers'. A Children in Europe Policy Paper.

Vincent, C. (ed.) (2003) *Social Justice, Education and Identity*. London: RoutledgeFalmer.

Vis, S.A., Holtan, A. and Thomas, N. (2012) 'Obstacles for child participation in care and protection cases: why Norwegian social workers find it difficult', *Child Abuse Review*, 21: 7–23.

Vizard, E. (2013) 'Practitioner review: the victims and juvenile perpetrators of child sexual abuse – assessment and intervention', *Journal of Child Psychology and Psychiatry*, doi: 10.1111/jcpp.12047.

Vygotsky, L.S. (1956) *Selected Psychological Investigations*. Moscow: IAPNSSR.

Vygotsky, L.S. (1978) *Mind in Society: The Development of Higher Psychological Processes*, eds and trans. M. Cole, V. John-Steiner, S. Scribner and E. Souberman. Cambridge, MA: Harvard University Press.

Vygotsky, L.S. (1986) *Thought and Language*. New York: MIT Press.

Walker, G. (2008) *Working Together for Children: A Critical Introduction to Multi-Agency Working*. London: Continuum International Publishing Group.

Walkerdine, V. (1993) 'Beyond developmentalism', *Theory and Psychology*, 3 (4): 451–69.

Walkerdine, V. (2004) 'Developmental psychology and the study of childhood', in M.J. Kehily (ed.), *An Introduction to Childhood Studies*. Maidenhead: Open University Press and McGraw-Hill Education.

Walkerdine, V. (2009) 'Developmental psychology and the study of childhood', in M.J. Kehily (ed.), *An Introduction to Childhood Studies*, 2nd edn. Maidenhead: Open University Press and McGraw-Hill Education.

Waller, T. (2005a) 'Outdoor learning and well being: recording and evaluating young children's perspectives'. Paper presented at the Fifth Warwick International Early Years Conference, University of Warwick, UK, 20–23 March.

Waller, T. (2005b) 'Outdoor learning and well-being: recording and evaluating children's perspectives'. Paper presented at the European Early Childhood Education Research Association Annual Conference (EECERA), University of Dublin, 31 August – 3 September.

Waller, T. (2005c) '"This is the way we go to the park"! Recording and evaluating young children's knowledge and perspectives of geography'. Paper presented at the British Educational Research Association [BERA] Annual Conference, University of Glamorgan, Wales, 15–17 September.

Waller, T. (2006) '"Be careful – don't come too close to my Octopus Tree": recording and evaluating young children's perspectives of outdoor learning', *Children, Youth and Environments*, 16 (2): 75–104.

Waller, T. (2007) '"The Trampoline Tree and the Swamp Monster with 18 heads": outdoor play in the Foundation Stage and Foundation Phase', *Education 3–13*, 35 (4): 395–409.

Waller T. (2010a) '"Let's throw that big stick in the river": an exploration of gender in the construction of shared narratives around outdoor spaces', *European Early Childhood Education Research Journal*, 18 (4): 527–42.

Waller, T. (2010b) 'Digital play in the classroom: a twenty-first century pedagogy?', in S. Rogers (ed.), *Rethinking Play and Pedagogy in Early Childhood Education: Concepts, Contexts and Cultures*. Abingdon: RoutledgeFalmer.

Waller, T. (2011) 'Adults are essential: the roles of adults outdoors', in J. White (ed.), *Outdoor Provision in the Early Years*. London: Sage.

Waller, T. and Bitou, A. (2011) 'Research with children: three challenges for participatory research in early childhood', *European Early Childhood Education Research Journal*, 19 (1): 5–20.

Waller, T., Murray, J. and Waller, J. (2004) 'Outdoor learning and well being: children's spaces and children's minds'. Paper presented at the EECERA Annual Conference, Malta, 1–4 September.

Walsh, F. (2012) 'The new normal: diversity and complexity in 21st-century families', in F. Walsh (ed.), *Normal Family Processes: Growing Diversity and Complexity*. New York: The Guildford Press. pp. 3–27.

Warnock, M. and Norwich, B. (2010) *Special Educational Needs: A New Look* (Key Debates in Educational Policy). London: Continuum.

Warren, L. and Boxall, K. (2009) 'Service users in and out of the academy: collusion in exclusion?', *Social Work Education: The International Journal*, 28 (3): 281–97.

Waters, J. and Begley, S. (2007) 'Supporting the development of risk-taking behaviours in the early years: an exploratory study', *Education 3–13*, 35 (4): 365–78.

Waters, J. and Maynard, T. (2010) 'What's so interesting about outside? A study of child-initiated interaction with teachers in the natural outdoor environment', *European Early Childhood Research Journal*, 18 (4): 473–83.

Waters, J., Clement, J. and Maynard, T. (2012) 'Early years practitioners' constructions of children's wellbeing in South Wales, UK: who, what, where?' Paper presented at the 20th European Early Childhood Education Research Association (EECERA) annual conference, 29 August – 1 September. Porto: Portugal.

Watson, D., Emery, C. and Bayliss, P. (2012) *Children's Social and Emotional Wellbeing in Schools: A Critical Perspective*. Bristol: The Policy Press.

Watson, J.B. and Rayner, R. (1920) 'Conditioned emotional responses', *Journal of Experimental Psychology*, 3: 1–14.

Wave Trust (2013) *Conception to Age 2 – The Age of Opportunity*, 2nd edn. Croydon: Wave Trust.

Wedell, K. (2005) 'Dilemmas in the quest for inclusion', *British Journal of Special Education*, 32 (1): 3–11.

Weinstein, J., Whittington, C. and Leiba, T. (2003) *Collaboration in Social Work Practice*. London: Jessica Kingsley.

Welsh Assembly Government (WAG) (2003) *Iaith Pawb: A National Action Plan for a Bilingual Wales*. Cardiff: WAG.

Welsh Assembly Government (WAG) (2007) *All Wales Child Protection Procedures*. Cardiff: All Wales Child Protection Procedures Review Group.

Welsh Government (2012) *Adoptions, Outcomes and Placements for Children Looked After by Local Authorities, Wales, 2011–12*. Cardiff: Knowledge and Analytic Services.

Welsh Government (2013a) Flying Start. Available at: www.wales.gov.uk/topics/childrenyoung-people/parenting/help/flyingstart/?lang=en (accessed 4 January 2013).

Welsh Government (2013b) *Building a Brighter Future: Early Years and Childcare Plan*. Cardiff: Welsh Government.

Wenger, E. (1998) *Communities of Practice: Learning, Meaning and Identity*. Cambridge: Cambridge University Press.

Werner, E.E. and Smith, R. (1982) *Vulnerable but Invincible: A Longitudinal Study of Resilient Children and Youth*. New York: McGraw-Hill.

Whalley, M. (2001) 'Working as a team', in G. Pugh (ed.), *Contemporary Issues in the Early Years: Working Collaboratively with Children*, 3rd edn. London: Sage.

Whalley, M. (2006) 'Leadership in integrated centres and services for children and families – a community development approach: engaging with the struggle', *Childrenz Issues: Journal of the Children's Issues Centre*, 10 (2): 8–13.

Whalley, M.E. (2011) *Leading Practice in Early Years Settings*. Exeter: Learning Matters.

Whitaker, J. and Bushman, B. (2009) 'Online dangers: keeping children and adolescents safe', *Washington and Lee Law Review*, 66 (3): article 6.

White, J. (ed.) (2011) *Outdoor Provision in the Early Years*. London: Sage.

Whitmarsh, J. (2011) 'Othered voices: asylum seeking mothers and early years education', *European Early Childhood Education Research Journal*, 14 (4): 535–51.

Whittington, C. (2003) 'Collaboration and partnership in context', in J. Weinstein, C. Whittington and T. Leiba (eds), *Collaboration in Social Work Practice*. London: Jessica Kingsley.

Willan, J., Parker-Rees, R. and Savage, J. (2004) *Early Childhood Studies*. Exeter: Learning Matters.

Willow, C., Marchant, R., Kirby, P. and Neale, B. (2004) *Young Children's Citizenship*. York: Joseph Rowntree Foundation.

Wilson, G. (2001) 'Conceptual frameworks and emancipatory research in social gerontology', *Ageing and Society*, 21 (4): 471–87.

Wilson, H. (2002) 'Brain science, early intervention and "at risk" families: implications for parents, professionals and social policy', *Social Policy and Society*, 1: 191–202.

Winter, K. (2006) 'Widening our knowledge concerning young looked after children: the case for research using sociological models of childhood', *Child and Family Social Work*, 11: 55–64.

Wolfe, I., Cass, H. and Thompson, M. (2011) 'Improving childhealth services in the UK', *BMJ*, 342: d1277.

Wolfendale, S. (2000) 'Special needs in the early years: prospects for policy and practice', *Support for Learning*, 15 (4): 147–151.

Wolfendale, S. and Robinson, M. (2006) 'Meeting special needs in the early years: an inclusive stance', in G. Pugh and B. Duffy (eds), *Contemporary Issues in the Early Years*. London: Sage.

Woodhead, M. and Faulkner, D. (2008) 'Subjects, objects or participants: dilemmas of psychological research with children', in P. Christensen and A. James (eds), *Researching with Children*. London: Routledge. pp. 10–39.

Woodhead, M. and Montgomery, H. (2003) *Understanding Childhood: An Interdisciplinary Approach*. Chichester: John Wiley & Sons.

Woodhouse, B.B. (2009) 'The courage of innocence: children as heroes in the struggle for justice', *University of Illinois Law Review*, 5: 1567–90.

Workingtogetheronline (2012) Working Together to Safeguard Children Consultation. Available at: www.workingtogetheronline.co.uk/ (accessed 15 February 2013).

World Bank (2010) Private Participation in Infrastructure Projects Database: Glossary. Available at: http://ppi.worldbank.org/resources/ppi_glossary.aspx (accessed 15 July 2013).

World Health Organization (WHO) (1948) *Constitution of the World Health Organization*. Geneva: WHO.

World Health Organization (WHO) (2012) Population-based approaches to childhood obesity prevention. Available at: www.who.int/dietphysicalactivity/childhood/WHO_new_childhoodobesity_PREVENTION_27nov_HR_PRINT_OK.pdf (accessed 27 February 2013).

Wyness, M.G. (1999) 'Childhood, agency and education reform', *Childhood*, 6 (3): 353–68.

Wyness, M.G. (2000) *Contesting Childhood*. London and New York: Falmer Press.

Wyness, M.G. (2012) *Childhood and Society*, 2nd edn. Basingstoke: Palgrave.

Wyn Siencyn, S. and Thomas, S. (2007) 'Wales', in M.M. Clark and T. Waller (eds), *Early Childhood Education and Care: Policy and Practice*. London: Sage.

Wyse, D. (2004) *Childhood Studies: An Introduction*. Oxford: Blackwell.

Yelland, N. (2006) *Shift to the Future: Rethinking Learning with New Technologies in Education*. New York: RoutledgeFalmer.

Yelland, N. J. (2011) 'Reconceptualising play and learning in the lives of children', *Australasian Journal of Early Childhood*, 36 (2): 4–12.

Yin, R.K. (2012) *Applications of Case Study Research*. London: Sage.

Young Minds (2003) *Tuning into Our Babies: The Importance of the Relationship Between Parents and Their Babies and Toddlers*. London: Young Minds.

Zelizer, V. (1985) *Pricing the Priceless Child*. New York: Basic Books.

Zeng, E.J. and Silverstein, L.B. (2011) 'China earthquake relief: participatory action work with children', *School Psychology International*, 32 (5): 498–511.

Zuckerman, M. (1993) 'History and developmental psychology: a dangerous liaison', in G. Elder, J. Modell and R. Parke (eds), *Children in Time and Space: Developmental and Historical Insights*. Hillsdale, NJ: Lawrence Erlbaum Associates.

Index